THE HISTORY

OF THE

PARISH OF LLANGURIG.

BY

EDWARD HAMER. Esq., AND H. W. LLOYD, Esq.

LONDON:

PRINTED BY T. RICHARDS, GREAT QUEEN STREET.

—

1875.

INTRODUCTION.

THE following Collection of Papers is taken partly from the *Montgomeryshire Collections*, printed by the Powysland Club, and partly from the *Archæologia Cambrensis*. Having appeared in those publications in the form of scattered notices, they are here, for the sake of convenience, gathered into a single volume. They all bear a more or less direct relation to the History of the Parish of Llangurig, with the exception of the descent during the three last centuries of the family of Lloyd of Berth and of Rhagatt, through Cuhelyn of Pentre Cuhelyn, from Tudor Trevor. This having been given in a cursory and imperfect shape in one of the notes elucidating the pedigree of families descended from Tudor Trevor, it has been deemed desirable to complete it to the present time from the date to which it had

been brought by the "Pennant Pedigrees". The
"Legend of St. Curig" has been added towards
the close of the volume, the previous historical
papers having left the origin and history of the
Devotion of the Parish to its Patron Saint in a
more or less mythical state of uncertainty.

CONTENTS.

CHAPTER I.

PHYSICAL FEATURES AND DESCRIPTION.

CHAPTER II.

ARCHÆOLOGICAL.

CHAPTER III.

ECCLESIASTICAL.

CHAPTER IV.

LORDS OF LLANGURIG AND THE CLOCHFAEN FAMILY.

CHAPTER V.

AN ACCOUNT OF THE PLAS MADOG FAMILY.

CHAPTER VI.

GENEALOGICAL.

CHAPTER VII.

BIOGRAPHICAL.

CHAPTER VIII.

FOLK LORE.

CHAPTER IX.

MISCELLANEOUS.

CHAPTER X.

WELSH POETRY ILLUSTRATIVE OF THE HISTORY OF LLANGURIG.

HISTORY OF LLANGURIG.—PART II.

A PAROCHIAL ACCOUNT OF LLANGURIG.

BY

EDWARD HAMER.

PAROCHIAL ACCOUNT OF LLANGURIG.

BY

EDWARD HAMER.

CHAPTER I.

PHYSICAL FEATURES AND DESCRIPTION.

1. *Name.* The name *Llan-gurig* is a compound word, formed of the common Welsh prefix *Llan*, an inclosure, a church, and *Curig*, the name of its founder and patron ; so that the name may be rendered into its English equivalent—the Church of St. Curig.

2. *Position and Boundaries.* The greater portion of this extensive parish formed a portion of the ancient *Cwmmwd* (commot) of *Uwch-Coed* (above the wood) in the Cantref of Arwystli, which formerly belonged to the lords of the district stretching between the Rivers Wye and Severn, was subsequently conquered by the Princes of the house of Cyfeiliog, and now constitutes the south-western portion of the County of Montgomery.

It is bounded on the south by the parishes of St. Harmon, and Cwm-dau-ddwr (ravine of the two waters), both in Radnorshire ; on the south-west and west, by the parishes of Gwnws and Llanfihangel-y-Creuddyn, (St. Michael's Church in Creuddyn), both in Cardiganshire ; on the north and north-east, by the parish of Llanidloes, and on the east by the parish of Llandinam, both in Montgomeryshire.

The boundary line which separates it from the two parishes of Radnorshire forms part of the line of separation between that county and Montgomeryshire, while the line which divides it from the two Cardiganshire parishes constitutes part of the line of demarcation between the counties of Montgomery and Cardigan. The Severn from its source to the point at which it receives the waters of the Dulas (a distance of some ten miles) forms the most considerable portion of the line which separates it from the parish of Llanidloes, while the rest of the line which limits its bounds on the east is for the most part artificial, and not defined by any well-marked natural features.

3. *Extent.* The parish stretches from *Eisteddfa-Curig*[1] (Curig's seat) on the west, to its most easterly point on the confines of Llandinam parish, for a distance of eleven miles; the length of a line drawn nearly at right angles to this from *Cwm-Ricket* on the north to the banks of the River *Elan* on the south measures about eight miles. The whole extent within the above indicated limits amounts, according to the Tithe Commutation Survey, in round numbers to 50,000 acres, thus divided:

Arable land . . .	3,125 acres.
Meadow or pasture . .	9,375 ,,
Common land . . .	37,000 ,,
Wood land . . .	100 ,,
Glebe land . . .	4 ,,
Total	49,604 ,,

These figures plainly indicate the nature of the land in this extensive parish—one of the largest in Wales—only about a fifteenth of it being under cultivation, while only 100 acres of it are covered with timber.

---

[1] According to an old Welsh englyn which is still preserved (*Camb. Quart.*, iii, 403,) Eisteddfa Curig formerly marked the south-western limit of Powys-land.

> "O Gevn yr Ais, dur-ais a drig, O Gaer
> I Eisteddva Gurig
> O Garn Gynnull ar Conwy
> Hyd y Rhyd Helig ar Wy."

"From Cefn-yr-Ais and from Chester to Eisteddfa-Curig And from Carn Cynnull on the R. Conway to Rhyd Helig on the R. Wye."

Since the time of the survey, however, large quantities of the common land have been enclosed and cultivated, especially at two periods when *Waen Twrch* and *Bryn Postig* were shared by a mutual arrangement agreed upon by the surrounding freeholders. Some of the hills have also been planted within late years.

4. *Divisions.* In the Tithe Commutation Survey of this parish, the farms are not arranged under the respective townships in which they are situated, nor is the total acreage of each township given. The following particulars respecting its six townships are gleaned from the Rate Book :—

Townships.	Estimated Gross Rental			Rateable Value.		
	£	s.	d.	£	s.	d.
Glyn-Hafren	484	15	0	449	0	8
Glyn-Brochan	902	5	4	816	9	3
Glyn-Gynwydd	453	7	3	403	2	8
Cefn-yn-hafodan	711	19	9	742	8	9
Llan-y-fynu	1058	10	0	951	5	2
Llan-y-wared	971	15	0	855	16	7
	4,582	12	4	4,218	3	1

The townships of Llan-y-fynu and Llan-y-wared form a portion of the manor of *Clas*,[1] the remaining part of which is situated in the adjoining parish of St. Harmon, which was formerly included in the old commot of Gwrthrynion. This commot, which comprised the parishes of Nant-mel, Llanfihangel - fach, Llanfair - yn - Rhos, Rhaiadr, and St. Harmon, in the time of its early lords

[1] Clas as a tract of land became appropriated chiefly to church or abbey land ; *clas-dir*, glebe land. The English generally used the derivative *glas*, instead of *clas ;* hence so many names of places in England : Glassie, Glasson, Glansworth, etc. A bard in the thirteenth century has these words: "Woe be to him that infringes upon the *clas*," the cloistered or enclosed land of the church. In Wales we have *Clas* ar Wy, or Glasbury in Radnorshire, *Clas* Garmon, the patrimony of St. Germanus, [the St. Harmon Clas] a lordship belonging to the Bishop of St. David's.—*Gwaith Gwalter Mechain*, iii, 474. This derivation of the term supports the old tradition which asserts that a considerable portion of the parish once belonged to Strata Florida.

constituted a moiety of the lordship of Arwystli. In the list of manors in the county of Radnor the manor is styled Clas Garmon, proprietor the Bishop of St. David's, and the lessee Percival Lewis, Esq.[1] The Arwystli Clas is distinct from that of St. Harmon, and is the property of Sir Watkin Williams-Wynn, Bart., and its court leet is held at Llangurig. The other four townships form part of the manor of Arwystli Uwchcoed, the court leet of which is held at Llanidloes. This manor is also the property of Sir W. W. Wynn, whose ancestor is said to have purchased it from the Crown in the reign of George III.

5. *Surface.* With the exception of the level tracts along the banks of the Wye and the Severn, and the narrow picturesque valleys through which their tributaries flow, the whole parish is either mountainous or hilly. It may indeed be fairly termed mountainous, being almost covered by some of the numerous offshoots of the mountain mass of Plinlimmon, the skirts of which extend within its north-western limit. These spurs form a number of high moorland tracts, which are intersected by numerous nants, or narrow ravines, down which flow the mountain torrents. The slopes, and in some instances the summits, of these elevated tracts, are dotted with numbers of small farms, whose occupants maintain a laborious but cheerful struggle to extort a subsistence from Dame Nature, by the cultivation of the soil, or more commonly by attending to extensive sheep walks. The most important of the mountain spurs is that which occupies the country between the Severn and the Wye, and which only terminates at the junction of the Dulas with the Severn. Its crest forms the line of watershed between the two principal Welsh streams, and is known locally by various names, the most important being *Esgair-y-Maesnant, Bryn-garreg-wen, Gias, Drim-Maen, Allt-y-derw,* and *Pen-Cin-Coed.*

Another similar, but higher and more barren, tract of elevated ground stretches from the banks of the Wye on the north-east to the banks of the Ystwith and its tribu-

[1] Williams's *Hist. of Radnorshire* in *Arch. Cam.* for 1857, 242.

taries on the west. It is known in its northern part by the name *Esgair Ychion*, and by that of *Esgair Cloch-faen* in its southern part.

Among the other hills of the parish may be mentioned the following :—

Foel goch, a short distance to the east of the village. *Bryn Mawr*, in the township of Cefn-fodau, about two and a half miles to south-west of Llanidloes, from which place it is plainly seen. The view from its summit is very fine and extensive. On its southern slope, near the small farm of *Nant-y-gwernog*, is a small square enclosure, known as the "Quaker's Garden," or burial ground. The site was granted to the Friends by an indenture bearing the date of 25th March, 1708, for the term of 2000 years, for the annual rent of a peppercorn. The sect formerly flourished at Llanidloes.

Creigiau Tylwch (Rocks of Tylwch), in the eastern part of the parish, rise abruptly from the banks of the river of the same name, and present a bare, rugged, and precipitous front. They are a favourite haunt of hawks. There are two legends attached to the name Tylwch, which should perhaps be noticed here. The first states that it received its name from one of the victorious leaders in one of the numerous skirmishes which occurred between the followers of the last Llewelyn and Edward I, crying out *Attaliwch* (hold), or *Tawelwch* (peace)—the name being a corruption of one of these words ; the second tradition makes Oliver Cromwell its hero, who, after a victory gained in the vicinity, performed the feat of riding his horse over the rocks, his charger leaving the impress of his hoofs upon the hard rock. These old traditions and legends should not be looked upon as inventions ; they generally turn out upon examination to be founded upon facts. The wonder is, that when we take into consideration the length of time during which they have filtered orally through the rude society of the past centuries, we are at all able to discover any clue to the circumstances in which they originated. The germ of the first may be discovered in the fact that an engagement between the English and Welsh took place in the vicinity, the *attaliwch* or *tawelwch*, was a subsequent addition of the story teller, by way of ornament, and obviously suggested by the name itself which must have been in existence for centuries previously.   The historian of Radnorshire, in his account of the parish of St. Harmon,[1] has the following statement:

"On the moor which divides the parishes of St. Harmon and Llangurig, or that separates the county of Montgomery from that of Radnor, was slain in one of those bloody and violent commotions which too often agitated the ancient inhabitants of Wales, and contributed to ruin the country and destroy its independence, Gwynne, the brave son of Llewelyn ab Iorwerth Prince of North Wales."

The writer does not give his authority for the above statement, and I have failed to discover an allusion to the action in any other work, but, as if to confirm the truthfulness of the account which doubtless gave rise to the legend, there is a small farm near the spot indicated, about two miles from the hamlet Tylwch, called to this day *Lluest Llewelyn* (Llewelyn's Camp), where the followers of that prince are supposed to have encamped, and at a short distance from it one of the ravines on the eastern side of the same moor goes by the name of *Cwm Saeson* (the Englishmen's Glen).

The second, and later tradition, connects the locality with a victory obtained by Cromwell and his followers over the Royalists.   We may at once discard the account of the wonderful feats performed by his charger as the innocent romancing of the story teller, which doubtless originated in the strong anti-Cromwellian spirit which existed in the vicinity of Llanidloes during the period of the Civil War, and try to discover the incident upon which the tradition was founded.   The foundation very probably exists in the facts recorded in the following extract from the *Penbedw MSS.* printed in the first vol. of the *Cambrian Quarterly Magazine*, p. 72 :—

"About the middle of August, Harry Lingen, Knight, of

---

[1] *Arch. Camb.*, for 1858, p. 547.

Herefordshire, came with horse and foot, and advanced towards North Wales, intending to join with the Anglesey men, but being narrowly watched by the troops of the counties adjacent, who gave General Horton (Parliamentarian) intelligence of Lingen's design. Whilst they followed him, Horton came from Pembrokeshire crosswise, and met Lingen's men near Llanidloes, took Sir Harry, sore hurt, and ———— prisoners. The rest fled, whereof about thirty horse and some foot came to Malloyd."

The tradition assists in identifying the site of this action as being in the neighbourhood of Tylwch;[1] and the victory gained by one of the Parliamentary generals was, without greatly transgressing the license of oral tradition, easily transferred to Cromwell himself. Should these conjectures prove correct, they furnish an instance of the valuable hints to be obtained from these old stories which have been handed down from parent to child for so many generations.

6. *Geology.* The general character of the soil in the hilly and mountainous portions of the parish is that of a light turbary varied by one of a ferny nature. This soil accumulates very rapidly on the substratum of slate rock which is frequently crossed by dykes of trap and grau wacke. Some of the hilly knolls are covered by a gravelly soil known locally as *roche.* Peat was formerly extensively raised, and formed not only the principal article of fuel, but was carted off for sale to Llanidloes in large quantities. The construction of the canal to Newtown struck the first blow to this traffic, and the introduction of railways into Mid-Wales has caused a Llangurig peat cart to become a rarity in the streets of Llanidloes. Some of the upper nants are studded with boulders of trap and conglomerate.

The valleys are covered with an alluvial deposit, the farmers of the low grounds being in general prosperous and the land well cultivated.

Several mineral veins cross the parish, and yield abundant supplies of lead, together with copper in smaller quantities. It is supposed that lead ore was first ex-

---

[1] For the derivation of the word, consult the glossary.

tracted from the Llangurig hills shortly after the enter-
prising Sir Hugh Middleton infused fresh energy into
the mining operations of the adjoining Cardiganshire
parishes in the earlier half of the seventeenth century.
"Miners" are among the earliest trades mentioned in the
parish registers.   The principal mines are—

1. *Nant Iago*—on the stream of that name, a tributary of the Wye—yields lead and blend.

2. *Nant-yr-eira*, or *Snow Brook*, which has been abandoned lately.

3. *Siglen-las*, near the source of the Bidno, yields
lead.

4. *Cwm Ricket*, on the right bank of the Severn, about
six miles west by north from Llanidloes, is a very promising mine which has been lately discovered, yields lead
and copper.

5. *Pant Mawr*, on the left bank of the Wye, four
miles north-west of the village of Llangurig, was till
within late years a very productive mine.

6. *Gias*, at the foot of the mountain of the same name,
on the right bank of the Severn.

7. *Brynpostig* lead mine is situated two miles to the
south of Llanidloes.   This mine was worked several
years ago and abandoned, then re-started, and afterwards thrown into Chancery.   In 1865 a fresh lease for
twenty-one years was obtained by the present company,
whose prospects of success are very good ; yields at present about fifty tons of ore per month.

8. *Cwmfron* mine is one mile to the south-west of the
latter.   It yields lead, and though it has not been long
worked it promises to be productive.

It is the opinion of competent mineralogists that this
parish is rich in lead ore, and only needs capital and proper working to prove highly remunerative.   Mining
operations have, within the last few years, received a
fresh impetus which promises to develope rapidly the
mineral wealth of the locality.

The parish contains several good stone quarries, among
which may be mentioned the one formerly worked at

Coed-cae, and that on the grounds of *Tyn-y-fron*, which furnished large quantities of stone for the erection of the Public Rooms, National School, and Short Bridge at Llanidloes; those on the grounds of *Ystradolwyn Fach*, *Delfarch*, and *Crugnant*, all of which yield excellent stone for building purposes.

A celebrated chalybeate spring exists on the grounds of a small tenement called *Rhos-y-wrach*, half a mile to the north of the village. The small brook which discharges its waters into the Wye, flows by the vicarage, and is known by the name of *Nant Shân* (Jane's Brook). In former times this spring was much frequented by invalids, who came to enjoy the benefits to be derived from what in those days was regarded as the almost miraculous properties of its waters. Tradition asserts that numbers unable to visit it without the assistance of crutches, were healed, and could dispense with them in returning home. The spring is a very valuable one, and if the people who reside in its vicinity had half as much faith in its merits as their ancestors, it would perhaps save them something in the shape of doctor's bills. On the grounds of *Bryn Mawr* are situated in close proximity to each other two springs totally differing in the nature of their waters; the one is an ordinary spring of clear fresh water, the other a saline, bearing a strong resemblance to the celebrated one at Llandrindod. Another chalybeate spring exists between the road and the brook, near the third mile stone from Llanidloes.

7. *Drainage.* With the exception of a very limited area on its western borders, the rivers Severn and Wye receive the drainage of the whole parish. It will be necessary to notice here only the right hand affluents of the former, reserving a fuller description for the parochial account of Llanidloes.

The Severn. The first considerable streamlet which joins the infant Severn on its right bank, within the limits of the parish is—

a. Afon Hore, which rises near the boundary line between the counties of Montgomery and Cardigan, and

flowing at first south, then in an easterly direction
passes the Hore Farm, joins the Hafren (Severn) after a
course of three miles.

b. The *Colwyn* flows from *Ffosydd-Llwydion* in an
easterly direction, and after a course of about two miles
discharges its waters into the Hafren, a short distance
above Glyn-Hafren.

c. Nant-Bron-felen has its source within a quarter of
a mile of that of the Bidno (a tributary of the Wye,)
and runs in a north-easterly direction, joining the main
stream opposite the Old Hall.   Length, two and a half
miles.

d. The *Dulas*, which drains the eastern portion of the
parish, is formed by the junction of *Afon Tylwch* and
Nant Cwm-Belan.   The former, which is the longer and
principal branch, rises in the neighbourhood of Lluest
Llewelyn, and flows in an easterly direction through the
parish of St. Harmon to *Rhyd-Myherin*, where its waters
are augmented on its right bank by a small stream
which, through its course of about two miles, forms a
portion of the boundary line between the counties of
Montgomery and Radnorshire.   From this junction it
flows in a direction north-west by north, and for two
miles of its course forms the line of separation between
the counties mentioned above.   Near the small hamlet
of Tylwch its waters are further increased by several
small streams.   From this place it flows through a deep
narrow picturesque glen, round the base of Creigiau-
Tylwch to *Pen-bont-pren*, a little below which it is
joined by

Nant Cwm-Belan.   This stream rises in the same turbary as the Tylwch, but flows in a less circuitous route
by Bwlch-y-gar-eg and the hamlet of Cwm-Belan, and
after a course of about four miles mingles its waters with
those of the longer branch.   The united stream, now
called the *Dulas*, flows due north for a distance of rather
more than a mile through a pleasant and fertile valley,
and is joined on its left bank by the

Brochan, which rises about a mile to the north of the

village of Llangurig, and flows in a northerly direction for a mile and a half, when it is joined by the small stream which drains '*Marsh's Pool.*' Near Rhyd-yr-onen it is joined by the waters of *Nant-yr-Oerfa*, and thence flowing in an easterly direction through the delightful little vale to which it imparts its name, after a course of about four miles joins the Dulas. The latter then flows north for a few hundred yards and becomes lost in the Severn. Its length by the Tylwch branch is rather more than nine miles.

The Wye—

" Plinlimmon's fairest child
The peerless Wye!"

has its source within the limits of the parish, in a marshy slope on the eastern side of *Plinlimmon Fawr*, half a mile to the west of Carn Tarenig, and rather more than two miles south-west by south from the source of the Severn. At first it flows in a south-easterly direction through a wild and desolate mountain tract for a distance of five miles before it is joined on its right bank at Pont-y-rhyd-galed by the

Afon Tarenig, a stream which is rather more than a mile longer than the Wye. It rises at the foot of the highest summit of Plinlimmon, within the limits of Cardiganshire, three quarters of a mile to the west of the source of the Wye, and flows first to the south, then to the south-east past Eisteddfa-Gurig into the Wye. It forms the boundary line between Montgomeryshire and Cardiganshire for more than two miles of its course.

From Pont-y-rhyd-galed the Wye runs in a south-easterly direction by Pant Mawr, its valley expanding as it advances. On its right bank it receives in succession several small streams, such as *Nant-du-bach, Nant Aber-Trinant*, and *Nant Troed-yr-Esgair*, all of which flow down the slopes of Esgair-Ychion. At Aber-Bidno it is joined on the left bank by the

Bidno, which flows from Waun-goch by Lluest-Bidno and Mynachlog[1] (the history of both these places is lost),

[1] Probably a cell attached to Strata Florida once existed here.

in a south-easterly course till it is absorbed in the Wye. Its length is about six miles.

From Aber-Bidno the Wye meanders gently through a wide and open valley to the village of Llangurig, which is situated on its left bank. Here it changes its direction to the south, and receives successively on its right bank *Nant Clochfaen* and the *Dernol*. The latter rises near Carn-y-groes and flows south-east through a narrow valley for a distance of two and a half miles. For the greater part of its course it separates Montgomeryshire from Radnorshire. This stream is mentioned as a boundary line as early as 1184 in the grants to the Abbey of Strata Florida.[1]

Below the efflux of the Dernol the Wye enters Radnorshire. Its length from its source to this point, including its principal windings, is about fourteen miles; the village of Llangurig is situated about ten miles from the source along the course of the stream.

The western boundary line of the parish is for a distance of four and a half miles formed by the

Afon Dilliw, a tributary of the Ystwith, which rises on the northern end of Esgair-Ychion, and runs in a south-easterly course, receiving the waters of the numerous nants which drain the western slope of the Esgairs. Near Craig-y-lluest it is joined on its left bank by the *Ystwith-faes*.

The *Elan*, for about a mile of its course, separates the parish on the south-west from Cardiganshire, and receives on its left bank the waters of *Nant Mytalog*.

Lakes. The pools of the parish are hardly large enough to be dignified with the name of lakes. The most important is a beautiful artificial sheet of water covering about seventeen acres, situated a mile and a quarter to the north-east of the village, and three miles to the south-west of Llanidloes. It was constructed and stocked with fish by the late T. E. Marsh, Esq., in the year 1852, and has been called by his name, '*Marsh's Pool.*' Since that gentleman's death the pool has been

Arch. Camb., 1848, p. 196.

greatly neglected. Formerly it was a favourite resort of numerous pleasure parties in the summer time. About midway between the Pool and the town is *Cefn-bwlch* Hill, from which may be enjoyed a most pleasing view of the Vale of Llanidloes.

There are two other large pools situated on the hills about a mile and a half to the north-east of 'Steddfa, marked on the Ordnance map, and called *Trippau Steddfa*.

Productions. The (*a*) minerals have been already noticed *supra*.

(*b*) *Vegetables*. The principal cereals raised are wheat (in the low grounds), barley, oats, and rye; the latter being the more common. The rye is mixed with wheat and forms what is locally known as *muncorn*, from which a pleasant, healthy bread is made. Of roots the principal raised are potatoes, turnips, and on some farms mangel wurzel.

The parish is not well wooded, though of late years plantations of fir are becoming more common on the hill sides. The principal trees are oak, ash, alder, birch, black willow, mountain ash, sycamore, and the holly. Very large sycamores and holly are to be found round some of the farm houses. Near the Clochfaen there is a holly-tree of immense size; the trunk having become very much decayed, was earthed round about forty years ago, which caused fresh branches of great size to shoot forth, giving it the appearance of a cluster of trunks. It has a girth of 28 ft. 6 in., and is supposed to be more than five hundred years old.[1]

On the hills various species of peat and club mosses are common—*corn-carw*, or stag's horn, being plentiful. Of ferns the principal varieties are the common brake or bracken, which covers considerable portions of the hills,

---

[1] Though the spurs of Plinlimmon are now wholly destitute of trees, there exists some slight evidence to indicate that their sides were formerly covered with timber. Near the junction of the Horé and the Severn, at a place called Nant-y-tanlliw (fire coloured ravine) the remains of several large fir trees have been discovered.

the male fern, various species of maiden hair, and the hart's tongue.   Golden furze, three or four varieties of heath, and the cotton grass (*sidan-y-waun*) are also abundant.   Rushes, which are also plentiful, are largely used for various purposes, chiefly as litter for cattle, for thatching hay and corn-ricks, outhouses, etc., and the best of them are peeled and dipped into grease and used as rush-lights.   Formerly large quantities of these peeled rushes (*pabwyr*) were carried to the town of Llanidloes, and sold to the inhabitants.

(c) *Animals.*   The mountainous and hilly districts afford pasture to an immense number of sheep of a small hardy kind, which, during the winter months, are removed from the higher and more exposed hills to the farms in the valleys and low grounds.   Hill ponies are also reared.

The only wild animals are the hare, rabbit, polecat, hedgehog, weasel, and an occasional fox. . The principal birds are the red grouse, partridge, woodcock, snipe, wild duck ; buzzard, kestrel, sparrow hawk, owl, kite ; the crane is a frequent visitor of the Wye, curlew, lapwing or pee-wit, the grey and golden plover ; the mountain or missel thrush, fieldfare, ring ousel, thrush, blackbird, starling, cuckoo ; sandpiper, kingfisher, and the ' white-breast dowker' or water ousel, wheatear and whin-chat, goat sucker *(deryn-y-corff)*, etc., etc.

The Wye is one of the most celebrated salmon streams in the kingdom ; this fish has been killed even in the small river Tarenig.   The other fish found in the streams are trout, samlet, minnows, and the silver eel.

Inhabitants.   Industrial pursuits. The census returns give the population in the various decades as follows :—

Year	1801.	1811.	1821.	1831.	1841.	1851.	1861.
Pop.	1426.	1559.	1784.	1847.	1957.	1802.	1641.

Showing a trifling but steady increase in the forty years between 1801 and 1841 of 531, followed by a

decline during the next twenty years of 316. Taking
the area of the parish in round numbers at 50,000 acres,
we find that in 1801 there was one individual to every
35 acres, in 1840 one to every 25 acres, and in 1861 one
to every 30 acres, or a percentage of ·03 persons per
acre. Additional particulars may be gleaned from the
subjoined table :—

| Year. | Number of Houses. | | | Males. | Females. |
	Inhabited.	Uninhabited.	Building.		
1841	332	20	3		
1851	300	10	1	917	885
1861	285	8	1	824	817

The decrease in the population is attributable to various causes, the principal of which are, the depression
which formerly existed in the mining operations,
emigration, and in some degree to the fact that several
of the small tenements have been incorporated into small
farms. The returns of the next census, however, are
likely to exhibit a considerable increase in the population, now that the mines are once more in full vigour.
A further increase would probably be the result of the
opening of the line of railway connecting the village with
Llanidloes, which has been constructed by the Manchester and Milford Railway Company.

Nearly the whole population is devoted to agricultural and pastoral pursuits. The mines give employment to a considerable number, and there exist three
flannel factories with their accompanying fulling mills
within the limits of the parish—viz., at Cwmbelan, on
the Nant Belan ; in Glyn Brochan, on the banks of the
Brochan ; and at Cae-yn-y-coed, on the banks of the
Hafren. Factories also existed formerly on the banks
of the Bidno and Tylwch.

D

CHAPTER II.

ARCHÆOLOGICAL.

Ancient Roadways. A writer in the *Cambrian Quarterly Magazine* attempted to trace the route of an ancient British roadway—in his opinion existing anterior to the invasion of the country by the Romans— leading from the Isle of Wight to Anglesey. The writer supposes it to have followed the upper valley of the Wye—"from Rhaiadr Gwy, the *Wye-fords* in Radnorshire, to its source at the hill of Plinlimmon in Montgomeryshire, probably a place of worship of the Môn Druids. This being a great mining county, the road seems to be divided here into several branches, as over *Sarn Halen*, or the Salt-causeway, at Llanbadarn Odyn, in Cardiganshire." The evidence brought forward by the author of this paper in support of his theory is the frequent use of the term *ford*, which he interprets to be the Anglicised form of the ancient Celtic and modern Welsh *ffordd*, so that Hereford becomes *Hir* or *Hên-ffordd*, the long or old road, and Rhaiadr Gwy, supposed to mean the waterfall or cataract of Wye, is manipulated into *Wye-fords*.[1]

The learned and careful author of *Salopia Antiqua* has examined this theory, but the mass of evidence he has accumulated goes to prove that the term *ford* indicates traces of a[2] *Roman* thoroughfare. "From finding this word so continually on Roman roads, there is no doubt that it is allusive to the position of the places where it occurs, and that the modern acceptation of the term is only employed in its secondary and lowest sense." On the Watling Street he enumerates eighteen places into the construction of which the term *ford*

---

[1] Vol. iv, 373.   [2] *Salopia Antiqua*, p. 238.

enters; on the line of Ermine Street he has discovered eleven such places; on Icknield Street nineteen; on Akeman Street eleven; on Hayden Way five,[1] etc.

No vestiges, either monumental or traditional, of this supposed roadway have been found within the limits of the parish, but the remains of an ancient paved roadway running in another direction, were discovered by the late Rev. D. Davis on the summit of Esgair-Ychion, near the *Cistfaen*. Local tradition ascribes its construction to the monks of Strata Florida, who served the church of Llangurig until the time of the dissolution of the monastery. That they used it in their journeys between Llangurig and the Abbey is more than probable, but there is no evidence to show that they were its constructors.

Carneddau, or Carns. Rather more than three miles to the west of the village, on the summit of Esgair-Ychion, are the remains of a carnedd, denominated on the Ordnance map *Caerau*. Subsequent to the appearance of the paper on *Ancient Arwystli*,[2] the writer was informed that this carn was not wholly demolished. Upon visiting the spot in the summer of 1868, he found that three-fourths of the stones, which constituted the upper portion of the carnedd, were removed for the purpose of building a rude shed—with a view to afford shelter—only a few yards distant from the venerable relic, which supplied the materials for its walls. Probably the farmers who undertook this partial work of destruction never for a moment thought that they were desecrating a grave, and would shudder at the very thought of entering a churchyard for a supply of stones for a similar purpose. The inhabitants, to all appearances, did not proceed far enough with the work of demolition to reveal the remains concealed for so many centuries. The base of the carn is forty yards in circumference.

---

[1] *Ibid.*, 262, 265, and *Words and Places*, p. 254 (ed. 1865.)
[2] *Montgomeryshire Collections*, i, 229.

Another carnedd, known as *Carn-Bwlch-y-Cloddiau*, lies half a mile to the south by west from the first. It is a circular heap of stones about thirty-five yards in circumference, the stones in the centre of the mass being piled up to the height of about six feet, while those which form its base are partially overgrown with grass. It is situated upon one of the summits of the Esgair, and commands a magnificent, extensive, and varied prospect.

Cist faen. A mile and a quarter to the south-east of the second carn, and about three miles and a half to the south-west of the village occupying the crest of one of the most western elevations of the Esgair, is a high ridge several hundred yards long and between thirty and forty broad, lying in the direction of north and south. It appears to be the outcropping of a vein of the mountain stone, which, through exposure to the effects of the atmosphere, has become disintegrated, and covers the ridge with thousands of blocks of various sizes. These blocks are in part overgrown with grass ; some of them projecting out at the edges of the ridge look very much like an artificial barrier of stones placed edgewise, but which, no doubt, owe their position to natural causes. Upon the crest of this ridge are two carns, the larger one, not far from its southern extremity, is about eighteen feet high, and about fifty-seven yards in circumference at its base. Some of its stones have lately been displaced, but not in sufficient quantities to bring any remains to view. This displacement is evidently the doings of individuals who did not understand their work, and fortunately were tired with a couple of hours' labour. Eighteen yards to the north of this is the smaller carn, which is about five feet high and thirty-seven yards in circumference at its base. Some of its stones have also been displaced. A little further north are a great number of loose stones of various sizes, which to all appearances are the remains of a third carn. Perhaps its removal led to the discovery of the *Cist-faen*, which gave its name to these remains. From the ridge are seen the Cardiganshire hills to the south-west, Plinlimmon to the north-west, Llandinam hills and the vale of the Severn to the east. Rather more than a mile to the south-east like a landmark appears

Carn-y-groes, situated on an eminence overlooking the ravine of the Dernol. The greater part of the carn is low and covered with grass, but the stones in the centre form a heap seven feet high, and about six yards in circumference. All the before-mentioned carns, as well as Plinlimmon, Cader Idris, and the Llandinam hills, are visible from the spot. A probable derivation of the name is suggested in the following extract:—

" That the early Christians did actually perform divine worship in the bardic circles is pretty evident from the fact that some of these still retain in their names and other circumstances, clear marks of their having been used for evangelical purposes. Such is Carn-Moesen or the Carnedd of Moses in Glamorganshire. *Carn-y-Groes* in the same county, *where a very ancient cross stands;* and Ty-Illtud in Breconshire and many others."

If a cross was ever raised upon this carn, the raised stone work, which still remains, is at once explained.

Domen-y-Giw. Rather more than a mile to the north of the village, on the crest of a high tract of moorland, which here forms the line of watershed between the tributaries of the Wye and Severn, is a tumulus known locally as *Domen-y-Giw*. It is a low flat mound, about sixty yards in circumference and about three yards in elevation. From the vast extent of country which it commands it was most probably used as a beacon station. The view from it embraces the Plinlimmon Carneddau, with Cader Idris in the dim distance on the north-west ; to the north may be seen the Arran ; the horizon on the east being bounded by a belt of mountain masses stretching from the Arran to the Breidden Hill and Long Mynd ; while the Kerry hills and Rhydd-Howell limit

---

[1] *Ecclesiastical Antiquities of the Cymry,* p. 71.

the view on the south-east.   In front the town of
Llanidloes, nestling at the foot of Pen-rhiw, with the
sinuous Severn winding through the valley, forms a
pleasant picture.   To the south-west are the Esgairs with
their carns, and the beautiful Wye meandering plea-
santly through the cultivated valley at their feet.

The Earthwork on Rhyd-yr-onen.   This interesting
and well preserved earthwork is situated on the grounds
of a small farm called *Rhyd-yr-onen*, about two miles to
the north-east of the village, and three miles to the
south-west of the town of Llanidloes, in the upper part
of " Cwm-glyn-Brochan."   It occupies a small triangular
plateau elevated some sixty feet above two deep rapid
brooks, which flank it upon either side, and which unite
their waters at its apex.   These brooks form a natural
moat on two of its sides, and if dammed up near their
junction would materially aid in the defence of the position.   The third is defended by a deep, broad outer
ditch and a very strong rampart of earth, which stretches
from one edge of the plateau, in the direction of the opposite brook, for a distance of about 240 feet.   The rampart a short time ago was covered with oak trees, which
however, were marked for sale.   At a distance of 150
feet from the outer ditch is another deep, broad fosse
which surrounds a large circular mound, which measures
520 feet in circumference at its base, and is between
forty and fifty feet higher than the ditch.   On its top is a
flat space which covers about 200 square yards.   The space
situated between the mound and the junction of the
brooks is occupied by two platforms separated from each
other by a deep, broad fosse; the platform nearest the
mound being some three or four feet higher than the
other.   That portion of the work lying between the
outer agger and the mound, and marked D on the accompanying plan, is cultivated.   An entrance (A)—to
all appearance modern—broad enough for carts to pass
through, has been made at this end of the work.

Local tradition states that the mound is a great barrow, but the conductors of the Ordnance survey held

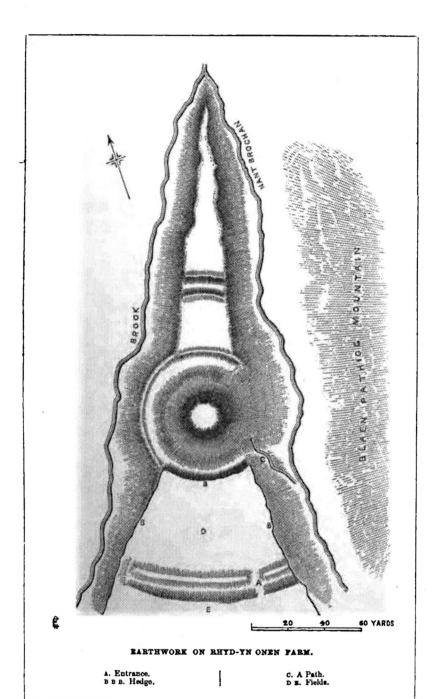

NANT BROCHAN

BROOK

BLAEN PATHOG MOUNTAIN

20   40   60 YARDS

EARTHWORK ON RHYD-YN ONEN FARM.

A. Entrance.

B B B. Hedge.

C. A Path.

D E. Fields.

another opinion, and in all probability the correct one, when they pronounced it to be a moat. It appears to be the site of one of those wooden castles, which were erected on mounds of this description, and which figure so prominently in the early history of the Principality. There is much in its form and position similar to the remains of Owen Cyfeiliog's Castle at Tafolwern, in the parish of Llanbrynmair.

The farm was purchased a short time ago by Mr. Edwards, of Brecknockshire, from the North and South Wales Bank.

Names implying military occupation. The situation of the parish on the south-western confines of the principality of Powys, with Cardiganshire on one hand, and Radnorshire, in possession of the South Wales princes— who erected a stronghold at Rhayader—on the other, caused it in some degree to be a high way between North and South Wales. Yet few well-marked traces of its being a fighting or camping ground have been preserved to add to those described in the preceding pages. The following names probably indicate traces of a period " when every man's house was in a literal sense his own castle also." The term *Castell* is perhaps of greater antiquity than that of *lluest*, the former originating probably during or immediately after the Roman occupation being derived from the Latin *Castellum*.

1. *Castell*, the name of a small farm on the right bank of the Severn, two and a half miles west by south from Llanidloes.

2. *Castell Greido* (Greido's Castle), a farm two and a half miles north-west of the village of Llangurig, and four and a half miles south-west by south from Llanidloes.

3. *Rhos-y-Castell* (Castle-moor), a small tenement situated a mile and a half north-west by north from the village.

1. *Lluest-y-Bidno* (encampment on the Bidno), a small farm on the left bank of that stream, a mile and three-quarters to the north-west of the village.

2. *Lluest - dôl - gwial* (encampment on the Mead of Twigs), on the left bank of Afon Dilliw, four and a half miles to the south-west of the village.

3. *Graig-y-lluest* (rock of the encampment), in the valley of the same stream, a mile to the south-east of the latter.

4. *Lluest Llewelyn* (Llewelyn's encampment); for the probable history connected with this name, see *supra*.

Coins. Numbers of coins have been discovered at various times in the fields in the neighbourhood of the village, but none of them have been preserved. Lewis Morris, the celebrated antiquary, writing about the year 1755, states that " thirty-eight silver coins or shillings of Henry I [1099-1135] were found in a grave in this churchyard (Llangurig) two years ago."[1] In 1826 a rose noble of Edward III was dug up.[2] Numbers of the same coins have been discovered in the neighbouring town of Llanidloes.

Two other antiquarian relics are preserved at the Clochfaen. The first is the family *Hirlas* or drinking horn, which has been handed down as an heirloom from "time immemorial." It is made of a beautifully-polished white horn, richly mounted with chased silver. It is represented in the following cut, engraved from a photograph taken by Mr. Owen, of Newtown:—

The length of the horn 15½ inches, diameter of the opening at the mouth 2¾ inches. The Hirlas (long, blue) is thus described in the spirited poem which very appropriately bears its name, and which was written to commemorate the deeds of the chieftains who took part in the action of Crogen:—

[1] *Camb. Reg.*, vol. ii, p. 491.
[2] Lewis *Top. Dic.*, art. Llangurig.

LLANGURIG CHURCH.

> " This hour we dedicate to joy,
>   Then fill the Hirlas horn, my boy,
>   That shineth like the sea ;
>   Whose azure handle, tipped with gold,
>   Invites the grasp of Britons bold,
>   The sons of liberty."[1]

Mrs. Hemans has also written a beautiful song to the Hirlas, which is too long to quote at length; we must content ourselves with the last stanza, which contains an allusion to the poem of the Prince of Cyfeiliog:—

> " Fill higher the Hirlas ! forgetting not those
>   Who shared its bright draught in the days which are fled ;
> Tho' cold on the mountains the valiant repose,
>   Their lot shall be lovely, renown to the dead !
> While harps in the hall of the feast shall be strung,
>   While regal Eryri with snow shall be crowned,
> So long by the bards shall their battles be sung,
>   And the heart of the hero shall burn at the sound ;
> The free winds of Cambria shall swell with their name,
>   And Owain's rich Hirlas be fill'd to their fame !"

The second is a dressed stone in the form of an inverted coffee cup with its top hollowed out. It is nine and a quarter inches high, eleven and a half inches in diameter at its base, and seven and a half inches across its top. It has a hole through it, and appears to be a rude imitation of an ancient bell. This old relic is called " *Y Cloch-faen*," the stone bell, and the old people of the neighbourhood confidently assert that from it the farm derives its name.

CHAPTER III.

ECCLESIASTICAL.

1. *Saint.* The church was founded by *St. Curig*, or as he is styled by the mediæval bards, Curig *Lwyd*, or the blessed, an appellation given him either on account of his peculiar holiness or for the purpose of distinguishing him from another saint of the same name, with

---

[1] *Lit. of the Kymry*, p. 40.

E

whom he is sometimes confused.   Professor Rees ranks
him among the Welsh saints who flourished between
A.D. 664 and 700, and one of the *Iolo MSS.* (p. 550)
gives his parentage as "St. Curig, the son of Urien
[Rheged] the son of Cynfarch. (In another copy, the
son of Arawn, the son of Cynfarch)."   We are told by
Lewis Morris that he was a foreigner who landed at
Aberystwith, and that it was on the summit of the hill
called after him *Eisteddfa Curig* (Curig's Seat, or resting place), that he rested on his first journey inland, and
beheld the fine vale of the Wye before him, in which he
determined to build a church in a sheltered spot.[2] Llangurig was the site selected for rearing the humble structure covered with reeds and straw, which we are told
was the kind of building adopted by the primitive
Welsh Christians.[3]

His missionary labours were ultimately rewarded
with a bishop's see, probably the adjacent one of Llanbadarn[1]—founded by St. Padarn in the previous century,—which is supposed to have included within its
limits a considerable portion of Montgomeryshire.[4] Lewis
Morris, in his compilation of *Bonedd y Saint*, has the
following notice of him :—

"Kurig St., Eglwys yn Arwystli a elwir Llangurig. Un a
ddwg-Gurig lwyd dan gwrr ei glog. LLANGURIG Arwystli.
Eglwys Ilid a Churig, Morganwg.   Eglwys Porth Gurig, Morg.
Capel Curig a'i fam Julita yn Arvon."[5]

The compiler draws no distinction between the two
saints, but Professor Rees states that "Llanilid a Churig,
Glamorganshire, and Capel Curig a'i fam Julita, Carnarvonshire" are dedicated to Juliet and Cyrique, but
that it is uncertain to which of the persons named Curig
the churches of Porth Curig, Glamorganshire, and
Eglwys Fair a Curig, Carmarthenshire, are dedicated.[6]
As regards "Porth Cirig," it is stated in the list of those
who founded churches and choirs in Glamorganshire,

---

[1] *Welsh Saints*, p. 307.
[2] *Camb. Reg.*, ii, 491, *Enwogion Cymru*, art. Curig.
[3] *Welsh Saints*, p. 59.   [4] *Ibid.* p. 216.
[5] *Myf. Arch.*, p. 522 (Gee's Reprint.)   [6] *Welsh Saints*, 307.

that " St. Cirig founded Porth Cirig for the benefit of
the sailors' souls, and a port for them."[1] But Taliessin
Williams argues that neither of these saints founded the
port, but that it was the residence of a Silurian prince
of the name of *Ceri*, its true name being *Porth-Ceri*.[2]
Thus we find that the bishop can only lay undisputed
claim to be patron of one church—that of Llangurig.[3]

He has always been held in the highest estimation by
his countrymen. Giraldus tells us that—

> " In this same province of Warthrenion, and in the church
> of St. Germanus (St. Harmon) there is a staff of Saint Curig,
> covered on all sides with gold and silver, and resembling in its
> upper part the form of a cross. Its efficacy has been proved
> in many cases, but particularly in the removal of glandular and
> strumous swellings, insomuch that all persons afflicted with
> these complaints, on a devout application to the staff, with the
> oblation of one penny, are restored to health. But it happened
> in these our days that a strumous patient, on presenting one
> halfpenny, the humour subsided only in the middle; but when
> the oblation was completed by the other halfpenny, an entire
> cure was accomplished. Another person also coming to the
> staff with the promise of a penny, was cured; but not ful-
> filling his engagement on the day appointed, he relapsed into
> his former disorder. In order, however, to obtain pardon for
> his offence, he tripled the offering by presenting threepence,
> and thus obtained a complete cure."[4]

The historian of Radnorshire informs us that this venerable staff was committed to the flames at the time of
the Reformation.[5]

Two centuries later than the time of Giraldus we find,
from the works of Lewis Glyn Cothi, that he was still
a popular saint, for the poet, in ridiculing the custom
then prevalent among the mendicant friars of vending
the images of favourite saints as charms, etc., receiving
in exchange cheese, bacon, wool, corn, etc.—

---

[1] *Iolo MSS.*, 636.   [2] *Ibid.*, 345.
[3] The Hymns given in the *Cambro-British Saints*, pp. 609-611, are
those ascribed to the martyr Cyrique.
[4] *Hoare's Giraldus*, i, 5.
[5] *Arch. Camb.*, 1858, p. 548.

"Un a arwàin, yn oriog,
    Gurig lwyd dan gwr ei glog ;
Gwas arall a ddwg Seiriol
    A naw o caws yn ei gôl ;"[1]

"One bore by turns the blessed Curig under the skirts
of his cloak, another youth carried Seiriol, and nine
cheeses in his bosom." Traditions respecting Curig's
miraculous powers of healing are still prevalent among
several of the old people of the parish. His festival is
observed on the 17th of June.

2. *Mother Church.* There is one subject connected
with the establishment of the parish churches of Arwystli
that requires a few words, and this is perhaps the proper place to make the observations. A belief has long
been prevalent in the neighbourhood that Llangurig is the
"mother church" of the other six churches of the deanery.
When and whence this notion originated cannot now be
determined. The earliest notice of it appears to be in
a letter of Lewis Morris, preserved in the Cambrian
Register, and, as the work is rather scarce, we take the
liberty of quoting the humorous description of his visit
to Llangurig rather more than a century ago :—

"I also crossed on my road, near Llan-Gurig, the river Gwy
(Wye) which takes its rise in Pumlymmon Hill, or as pronounced in that country, Plymhummon. Query whether it be
derived from Pen Luman, or Lummon, the hill of the banner ?
In this mountain are the sources of the Severn, Wye, and
Rheidiol. The small rivers Bidno and Elain fall into the Gwy
(Wye), and their junction is called Aber, as Aber Bidno, Aber
Elain ; so that word signifies not only the fall of a river into
the sea, but also that of a small river into a larger. The vicar
of the parish (Llan Gurig) who is a tolerably ingénious man,
(as he excels most mountain clergymen) could not inform me
what the word Curig meant ; he said some derived it from the
Scotch kirk, *as Llan-Gurig was a mother church, and might
have been so called by way of eminence.* But I told him there
was a Welsh poem. (Mr. Morris here quotes the extract from
Lewis Glyn Cothi, given above.) The vicar was extremely
pleased to find that he had a saint to his church, as well as
his neighbours, and a grey one.[2] (Lwyd) too ; he, therefore

---

[1] *Gwaith Lewis Glyn Cothi*, 280.

[2] Mr. Morris gives *grey* as the equivalent of *Lwyd* ; but the old
bards would not use the epithet in that sense when applied to the
Almighty, as they frequently do.

spent his threepence for ale, and after some discourse about
tithes we went to rest.   We lodged at the sexton's, a fat, jolly
fellow, more like a parson than his master; he is a relation of
Bennet's of Bangor, and like him. This Llan-Gurig is in Montgomeryshire.   I could find here a remarkable distinction for
the better between their Welsh and the inhabitants of Aberteivi
(Cardiganshire)   .   .   I forgot to tell you that there is a good
proverb at Llan-Gurig.   ' Pan fwrio gwr ei gywilydd, nid gor-
chest iddo i fyw'; *i.e.,* When a man is past shame, or has bid
adieu to modesty, what difficulty can he have to live, or do
well."[1]

To return to the subject.   Malkin next helps to perpetu-
ate the dogma that has become one of the articles of the
creed of the inhabitants, for which they are prepared to
do battle manfully.   Apparently the only grounds
brought forward by them in its support are the facts,
that Curig Lwyd was a bishop, and that the vicar still
continues to receive the tithes of one of the townships
of Llanidloes parish, and about £18 per annum from the
parish of Trefeglwys.   If tested by the criterion of the
payment of tithes we shall find that Llandinam has far
better claims than Llangurig for appropriating to itself
the title of mother church, for it was formerly endowed
with the tithes of a district embracing the modern
parishes of Carno, Llanwnog, Llandinam, and consider-
ble portions of the parishes of Llanidloes and Trefeglwys.
The tithes of this district were retained up to the year
1685, when by an Act of Parliament they were divided
between the Dean and Chapter of Bangor and the several vicars of the different parishes.   This sufficiently
proves the claim of Llandinam to be the first or oldest
foundation within the limits of the district defined
above.   Again, if we appeal to chronology, and taking
Professor Rees as our guide, we find—

(*a*) That *Llonio*, the founder of Llandinam, and
Gwrhai, the founder of Penstrywed, flourished between
the years 500 and 542 A.D.[2]

(*b*) *Gwynno* or *Gwynnog*, the founder of Llanwnog,

---

[1] *Camb. Reg.*, ii, 491.   [2] *Welsh Saints*, pp. 221, 231.

himself a bishop like Curig, flourished about a hundred years before the latter ;[1] and

(c) *Idloes*, the founder of Llanidloes, belonged to the generation preceding that in which the founder of Llangurig flourished.[2] If it be granted that the Professor is correct in his dates, then no other conclusion can be arrived at than that Llangurig could not have been the mother church of those four, which were evidently founded before it.

3. *The Church* consists of a nave, chancel, and a small narrow, north aisle. The nave measures internally 62 feet by 24 feet, and is separated from the chancel (which measures 27 feet by 24) by a high chamfered pointed arch; the aisle is separated from the nave by three low, plain, stone pillars supporting pointed arches, all of which are built of ordinary rubble stone.   On the north side of the chancel are to be seen traces of a narrow winding stone staircase which formerly led to the rood loft, which existed in the church previous to the year 1836. Remains of " an elaborately-carved screen and rood loft are still preserved," is the statement made in Lewis's *Topographical Dictionary*,[4] published in 1833.   Three years later, when the church was repaired, the screen and loft were taken down, and the churchwardens, who must have been ignorant of its value, allowed anyone who expressed a desire to become possessed of samples of the tracery, to carry away specimens, so that literally bit by bit it disappeared, and not a vestige of it was left when Mr. Evans, the present vicar, was appointed to the living in 1852.   It was undoubtedly the principal object of interest in the church, and its fate is a sad example of the shameful neglect and utter indifference through which so many similar relics have disappeared from the churches of the neighbourhood.   Fortunately the late Rev. John Parker, of Llanyblodwel, visited the church in the summer of 1828, and his artistic and accurate

---

[1] *Welsh Saints*, 257. [2] *Ibid.*, 233.
[3] *Top. Dict.*, art. Llangurig. [4] Sub voce Llangurig.

REFERENCE:

A Traces of Stone Staircase.
B Vestry.   C Communion Table.
D Pulpit.   E Modern Wall.

GROUND PLAN OF LLANGURIG CHURCH

E. POWELL, DEL.

DETAILS OF ROOD SCREEN.

FROM A DRAWING BY REV. JOHN PARKER, MADE IN 1828.

pencil has preserved for us admirable drawings of the screen, which, through the kindness of Sir Baldwin Leighton, one of our members, we are able to reproduce.

The present contracted north aisle, which only disfigures the building, was formerly several feet broader, so that the church in its original form was similar in its plan to that of Llanidloes, but the old north wall having fallen down about the year 1780, the present narrow aisle was built. The vestry, situated to the north of the chancel, appears to have formed part of the old aisle.

Only two of the windows—that at the east end and the one which lights the vestry (see illustration)—have any architectural pretensions. The former is divided into three cinque-foliated lights with its head filled in with tracery, the second is divided into three trefoliated lights, and both are constructed of red sandstone. This material must have been transported thither from a considerable distance, or which perhaps is quite as probable, the windows may have formerly belonged to one of the adjacent abbeys of Strata Florida, or that of Cwmhir. The church had direct claims upon the former.

The font consists of an octagonal basin, measuring 1 foot 11 inches in diameter inside the bowl, and about a foot in depth, resting upon a short shaft which connects it with its base. Its total height is 3 feet 9 inches. The head of each compartment is filled with tracery (see Mr. Parker's sketch in the view of the interior). Some ambitious Vandal has scratched his initials and the date 1661 upon it.

The most ancient part of the building seems to be the massy square tower at the west end, with strong angular buttresses at its corners. It is surmounted by a small octagonal spire 16 feet high, including the vane. The height of the tower is 48 feet; its summit, together with the spire, is constructed of wood work covered with sheet lead ; a fact which explains a passage in the works of Lewys Glyn Cothi, to whom the structure must have been familiar. He has hit off its appearance in the following line :—

"Gloew sgwar val Eglwys Gurig."[1]
[Bright and square like the church of Curig.]

The epithet "bright" is apt to puzzle a stranger; but anyone who has viewed the church (as the old bard most probably did in the course of his wanderings in Arwystli) from one of the many heights surrounding the village, with the sun shining upon the spire, cannot fail to perceive the accuracy of the old poet's description.

The ascent to the belfry is by a narrow spiral stone staircase; it contains three bells, the second of which has the date 1700, with the names of John Owen and Adam Hatfield, the churchwardens for that year.

The church is built of common rubble stone of the neighbourhood, and is a rude specimen of early English architecture. The belfry doorway is surmounted by an elliptical arch, the ellipse being formed by two large stones (see illustration.) Tradition points out the spot whence the building materials were obtained upon the summit of the adjacent *esgair*, at a spot which still bears the name, *Cerrig waun-y-llan*.

At the principal entrance to the churchyard stands a lich-gate, upon the wood-work of which may be seen the following initials and date:—C.D., S.H., 1740. D.C., I.O. Formerly there existed a remarkably large yew-tree, which was greatly admired, but latterly it had become so decayed that it was necessary to have it removed. The following two epitaphs are copied from monuments in the churchyard:—

"O earth, O earth, observe this well—
That earth to earth shall come to dwell;
Then earth to earth shall close remain
Till earth from earth shall rise again."

———

"From earth my body first arose;
But here to earth again it goes.
I never desire to have it more,
To plague me as it did before."

4. *Living and Tithes.* The living is a vicarage, and was up to the year 1861 in the patronage of the Bishop

[1] *Gwaith Lewis Glyn Cothi*, 21.

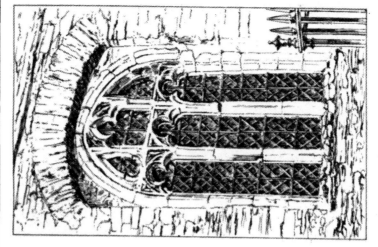

NORTH WINDOW,
FORMERLY IN THE EAST END OF NORTH AISLE.

BELFRY DOOR.

LLANGURIG CHURCH.

EAST WINDOW.

of Bangor, but by an Order in Council, bearing the date of the 25th of July that year, it was transferred to the Bishop of Llandaff, from whom it subsequently passed to the patronage of the Crown.

As Llangurig was the only part of Arwystli which belonged to the Abbey of Strata Florida, the following entry in the Taxation of 1291, under the head, "*In Decanat. Arostly,*" refers to the value of the rectory at that date:—

"Beneficia Abb'is de Strata Florida . . . £16 0 0"

While the abbey existed the church of Llangurig was served by its members. Shortly after its dissolution we find that the rectorial tithes were in possession of Lady Dorothy Devereux, daughter (by Anne his wife, daughter of Henry Stafford, Duke of Buckingham) of George Hastings, Earl of Huntingdon, and relict of Sir Richard Devereux, Knt., eldest son of Walter, Lord Viscount Hereford, K.G., who died in 1558. Sir Richard died in the lifetime of his father, leaving issue a son and heir, Walter, Lord Viscount Hereford, who was created Earl of Essex and Ewe. Subsequently the great tithes passed into the hands of the family of Steadman (who had likewise possession of the Abbey of Strata Florida), and thence to the Powells of Nanteos, who held them as late as the year 1722. But before the year 1762 they were sold by the late Dr. Powell, of Nanteos, to Sir W. W. Wynn, Bart., and are now held by the Baronet of Wynnstay.

From the *Valor Ecclesiasticus* of Henry VIII, we learn that the vicarage was then rated at £9 9s. 10d., the sources of revenue, etc., being as follows:—

Tithes of corn and hay, per ann.	£1	6	8					
,, wool and lambs		4	0	0				
Oblations (four in the year)		4	13	4				
Value of glebe land, per ann.			2	0				
					10	2	0	
Thence in reprisals :—								
Yearly Procuration to the Bishop			10	0				
,, at visitation			2	2				
						12	2	

F

Clear yearly value					9	9	10
Thence a tenth						19	0

At present the vicarial tithes are—

From Llangurig	£177	0	0	£177	0	0
„ Llanidloes	106	0	0			
„ Trefeglwys	18	0	0			
	301	0	0			
Rectorial tithes	420	0	0	420	0	0
Total				597	0	0

5. *Registers and List of Vicars.* At present only two volumes of registers are in existence. A third volume, which existed thirty years ago, was accidentally destroyed through the wilful carelessness of the parish clerk. The entries in the older volume begin with the year 1742 and close with the year 1813, when the entries in the second commence. The entries in these volumes call for no special remark.

A complete list of the vicars can now only be compiled from documents preserved in the diocesan registry at Bangor, no list of incumbents of the different livings similar to those given in Edwards' edition of Browne Willis' St. Asaph having been printed. It is greatly to be regretted that no one has undertaken for the diocese of Bangor that which Mr. Edwards carried out in his edition of the older antiquary's account of the diocese, and which the Rev. D. R. Thomas is about to bring down to the present time.

In the absence of a full and correct list the following names may prove acceptable:—

From a return made by Bishop Meyrick we learn that in 1561 "Thomas Lloyd Priest" was vicar, that he was resident, kept house, and was licensed to preach.[1] His successor probably was

David Lewis, who is mentioned in the *Add. MSS.* 9865.[2] He was the son of Lewis of Llangurig (ab Thomas ab Gwilym, a descendant of Cadivor ab Gwaethfod), and Tangwystl, daughter of Jenkyn ab David. He

---

[1] Browne Willis' *Bangor*, 267, 269.   [2] *Infra.*

married Margaret, daughter of Howell ab Philip, and had a son, Jenkin, who was alive in 1599.

It is very probable that the living was sequestered during the domination of the Puritan party, for we find that the adjacent living of St. Harmon, in possession of the Parliamentary commissioners in 1649,[1] and in the neighbouring parish of Llanidloes, there are no entries in the registers from the years 1649 to 1660, a proof that the ministers' duties were suspended during those years. That Llangurig was not exempted may be gathered from the following extract from a pamphlet entitled, "The Parliament explained to Wales," quoted in Rees' *History of Nonconformity*, p. 81:—

"In some places in Wales, the gospel doth already kindle; and that—which our counties can never too gratefully acknowledge—by the worthy and godly endeavour of Mr. Cradock; and especially which is worth our notice, it begins to shine in a place heretofore noted for untowardness, called Llangyrug in Montgomeryshire, a place formerly of very sorry fame, but now pointed at as the Puritans and Roundheads of Wales; and all this through the godly pains of some persecuted ministers resorting thither through manifold discouragements and dangers."

At the close of the seventeenth century Thomas Ingram, LL.B., was vicar. He was educated at Jesus College, Oxford, and in 1703 he was made a Canon of Bangor. He died about the year 1711.[2]

William Jones, B.A., was collated to the vicarage, April 29th, 1698.

Thomas Pritchard, B.A., was collated to the vicarage, July 26th, 1712.

Edmund Price was collated to the vicarage, April 27th, 1765.

Thomas Lewis, B.A., was collated to the vicarage, October 23rd, 1788.

Maurice Anwyl, B.A., was collated to the vicarage, May 27th, 1805.[3]

[1] *Hist. of Radnorshire*, in *Arch. Camb.*, 1858, p. 548.
[2] Browne Willis' *Bangor*, p. 172.
[3] The names of these five vicars, with the dates of their appointments, were supplied by the Ven. Archdeacon Evans, M.A., of Llanllechid.

The first signature which occurs in the older of the two volumes of the Registers is that of

John Jones, curate, who appears to have been curate in charge for the year 1742 to 1780, as his name appears last in that year.   Thomas Lewis' signature occurs from 1788 to 1805, and that of Maurice Anwyl from 1807 to 1832.   Mr. Anwyl was alive after that date, but the duties of the parish were discharged by the curate, Evan James.

James James succeeded Mr. Anwyl as vicar.   This gentleman, who also held the curacy of Llanwnog, died in 1841, when

Evan James, who was curate from 1831, became vicar.   He died on 17th June, 1852, and was succeeded by the present vicar,

John Evans, who is in the commission of the peace for the county, and chairman of the Board of Guardians for the Llanidloes and Newtown Unions.   To this gentleman the writer is greatly indebted for much valuable information, and for free access to the Registers and other documents in his possession.

6. *Benefaction.* The Parliamentary returns of 1786 state that *David Vaughan* (date unknown) gave £10, the interest thereof to be given to the poor.

This sum is now in the hands of a private individual resident in the parish, who pays 10s. annually for the interest, and it is distributed by the churchwardens in small sums of money to the poor.

It was recommended that application should be made for the principal, and that when received it should be deposited in the savings' bank.[1]

The above suggestion does not appear to have been carried into effect, and the principal has been lost.

The church at present is in a dilapidated condition, and the worthy vicar is actively engaged in raising a fund for its reparation.

[1] Charity Commissioners' Report.

CHAPTER IV.

THE LORDS OF LLANGURIG AND THE CLOCHFAEN FAMILY.

LLANGURIG appears from the most ancient times to have been an integral portion of the lordship of Arwystli, and to have passed through the same vicissitudes which the rest of the Cantref suffered. When the country was portioned out into the five different principalities of Gwynedd, Powys, Morganwg, Fferllys, and Deheubarth, Arwystli was reckoned among the lordships of Elystan Glodrudd, prince of the country between the Severn and the Wye. It continued in the possession of the descendants of Elystan for several generations, the last of the family who appears to have been in actual possession of the territory was Howel (ab Ieuaf ab Cadwgan ab Elystan), who is described as lord of Arwystli[1] in 1157, who fought in its defence against Owen Cyfeiliog in 1161, and was buried in the abbey of Strata Florida in the year 1186. He bore *gules*, a lion rampant *argent*, crowned *or*.

Shortly after his death Arwystli passed into the possession of the princes of the house of Cyfeiliog. This

[1] *Montgomeryshire Collections*, i, p. 251.

transfer of the Cantref from its original lords, is generally asserted by the Welsh heralds and chroniclers to
have been the result of the marriage of Gruffydd (ab
Meredydd ab Bleddyn) with Gwerfyl,[1] daughter of Gwrgeneu ab Howel ab Ieuaf, the issue of the marriage
being Owen Cyfeiliog. It requires but a slight examination to prove this union to have been a fiction
created by the genealogists. Is it at all probable that
Gruffydd, who died in 1125 leaving two sons (who were
then minors), could have married the grandaughter of
a prince who died sixty years later (1186)? If this
usually received pedigree of the mother of Owen Cyfeiliog be correct, then would history present the singular spectacle of a great-grandfather (Howel ab Ieuaf)
invading the territory and burning the castle of his
great-grandchild (Owen Cyfeiliog), and of that great-
grandchild retaliating and defeating his great-grandfather in open battle at Llandinam in 1161, and of
those two relatives dying within a few years of each
other, both apparently in full years! Rejecting this
theory, the true one will be found in the weakness of
the descendants of Elystan, and in the restless and ambitious spirit of Gwenwynwyn, the young lord of Cyfeiliog, who appears to have assumed the reins of power
during the declining years of his father's life. Gwrgeneu,
the son of Howel, being unable to resist him, the Cantref was seized and kept merely by the right of the
strongest.

> " .   .   Gwenwynwyn, sanguinis hæres
> Ante obitum patris, totam subjecit Arustli."[2]

Shortly after his defeat at the battle of Crogen, King
Henry II, while passing through South Wales on his
way to Ireland in 1171,[3] granted Arwystli to Prince
Rhys, overlooking the rights of its true lord Howel ab
Ieuaf, then alive. Henry was doubtless prompted to

---

[1] *Wynne's ed. of Powell*, p. 182. *Burke's Landed Gentry*, article,
Morris of Hurst.

[2] *Pentarchia*, quoted in *Royal Tribes*, p. 71.

[3] *Wynne's ed. of Powell*, p. 198.

this step by the consideration that he was retaliating upon Owen Cyfeiliog for the important services which he rendered the Confederates at Crogen, by placing such a powerful prince as Rhys in possession of a lordship to which Owen himself had some claim as its conqueror. On the death of Rhys in 1197, Gwenwynwyn readily accepted the overtures of Maelgwyn to assist him against his brother Gruffydd (the successor of the deceased Rhys), who was surprised and slain by the Confederates at Aberystwith. On his return from this expedition the Powysian prince "having got together an army entered into Arwystli and brought it into his subjection."[1] It was probably at this time that Gwenwynwyn rewarded the services of his faithful follower, Madog Danwr,[2] by granting him the Lordships of Llangurig, which formed the south-western part of the newly conquered territory, reserving for himself the seignorial rights of the same. The greater part of this parish is still in possession of Madog's descendant J. Y. W. Lloyd, Esq., of Clochfaen.

From the various documents illustrating the papers on the Princes of Upper Powys and the Barons of Powys[3] it appears that the manorial rights or suzerainty of the parish of Llangurig were always possessed by the lords of Arwystli, though the descendants of Madog had possession of the land.

Arwystli was conquered by Llewelyn the last Prince of North Wales, and therefore does not appear among the lands of which Prince Gruffydd, son of Gwenwynwyn, died seized of in 1286. But on the death of Owen, son of the preceding Gruffydd, in 1293, " Langerik " is mentioned among the lands which he held *in capite* from the English king, the profits received therefrom amounting to £3 13s. 4d. per annum.

In 1310 a *post mortem* inquisition enumerates Llangurig among the lordships held by Gruffydd ab Owen,

[1] *Wynne*, p. 198.
[2] Burke's *Landed Gentry*, article, Owens of Glansevern.
[3] *Montgomeryshire Collections*, vol. i.

the last prince of the house of Cyfeiliog, who died a
minor in 1309.[1]

On the death of John de Cherleton—who had acquired Powys-land by his marriage with Hawys, sister
and heiress to the preceding Prince Gruffydd—in 1353
he was seized of Arwystli.[2] His son John in 1360,
died seized of the same cantref, and in 1374 we find
John de Cherleton, third baron, dying in possession of
it.[3] Among the lands which John, the son of the preceding baron, and fourth of the name, died seized of, is
the "lordship of Llangarick," and Edward his brother
and successor died in 1421 possessed of the same lordship.[4]

From the Cherletons the manorial rights of Arwystli
passed by the marriage of Joyce, second daughter and
co-heiress of Edward de Cherleton to Sir John Tiptoft,
whose son and successor, John, was created Earl of Worcester in 1449, and for his firm adherence to the cause
of Edward IV was beheaded in 1470. He died seized
of the "manors and advowsons of the churches of
Llanydlos, Arustile," &c.[5] Afterwards the Manor of
Arwystli passed into the possession of the Crown, and
it remained a Royal manor for a century, and subsequently, after several devolutions, it became and still
remains part of the possessions of the House of Wynnstay.

THE CLOCHFAEN FAMILY.[6]

This family traces its descent from *Gwrtheyrn Gur-
theneu* or *Vortigern*, lord of Erging, Ewias, and Gloucester, who, upon the assassination of Constans, was

---

[1] *Montgomeryshire Collections*, vol. i, p, 148.   [2] *Ibid.*, p. 277.
[3] *Ibid.*, pp. 279, 280.   [4] *Ib.*, pp. 283, 301.
[5] *Ibid.*, 358.
[6] The pedigree of the Clochfaen family was drawn up in the first
instance by the late Mr. Joseph Morris of Shrewsbury. It was subsequently collated by J. Y. W. Lloyd, Esq., with the Heraldic
Visitations preserved in the British Museum, more especially the
Harl. MSS., 4181, 1973, 2288, and *Add. MSS.*, 9864, 9865. To
the information thus brought together, and to family papers, the
writer has been greatly indebted in the compilation of this chapter.

elected King of Britain, A.D. 425.[1] In the year 448 he
was compelled by Aurelius Ambrosius to take refuge in
his fortress of Caer Gwartheyrn, whither he was accompanied by St. Germanus, who is said to have remained
with him to the last, imploring him to repent and make
his peace with God. Seeing that remonstrance was in
vain the Saint left the king and retired to Italy, where
he died at Ravenna, 25th July, in the same year.
Other accounts state that Vortigern did not perish in
this citadel, but that he escaped and died in obscurity
at Llanhaiarn in Carnarvonshire, where a tomb, in
which the bones of a man of large stature were found,
and which has always been designated as "Bedd Gwrtheyrn," the grave of Vortigern.

He was the son of Gwydodol, son of Gwydolin, son
of Glouiw Gwladlydan, the founder of the city of Caer-
louiw or Gloucester. From the inscription on the
monumental cross erected by King Cyngen II to the
memory of his great-grandfather, King Eliseg, who died
A.D. 773, and was contemporary with Offa, King of
Mercia, we find that Vortigern married Seveira,[2]
daughter of Maximus Magnus, Emperor of Rome, who
slew the Emperor Gratian. Maximus, who was put to
death by Theodosius near Aquileia, A.D. 388, married

[1] This is the date adopted in Haigh's *Conquest of Britain by the
Saxons*.

[2] The following is that part of the inscription which bears on the
text. It differs from that given by Llwyd—the additions are from
Mr. Haigh's *Conquest of Britain by the Saxons*, p. 230.

.. IL . E . . . . . . MONARCHIAM
. AIL MAXIMUS BRITANNIÆ
. NN . PASCEN . . MAVI . ANNAN
. BRI [G]UA[R]T[IMER] FILIUS GUARTHI[GERNI]*
. QUE BENED GERMANUS QUE
. . PEPERIT EI SE[E]IRA FILIA MAXIMI
[RE] GIS QUI OCCIDIT REGEM ROMANO
RUM + CONMARCH PINXIT HOC

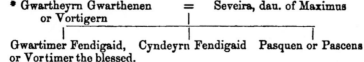

* Gwartheyrn Gwarthenen   =   Seveira, dau. of Maximus
    or Vortigern

Gwartimer Fendigaid, Cyndeyrn Fendigaid Pasquen or Pascens
or Vortimer the blessed.

Helen Lluyddawg, only child of Eudaf or Octavius, Duke of Cornwall, who was made governor of Venedotia (Gwynedd) by the Emperor Constantine the Great. Eudaf kept his Court at Segontium, where he died A.D. 385. At this place his daughter Helen Lluyddawg was born; and there is still in the neighbourhood of Car-narvon a place called Coed Helen, now the residence of the ancient family of Thomas, also the possessors of Trevor Hall.

Cyndeyrn Fendigaid, or *Catigern*, the second son of Vortigern, was the father of *Rhuddfedel Frych*, the father of *Rhydwf*, the father of *Pasgen*, the father of

Cadell Deyrnllwg. He was Prince of Teyrnllwg, a territory consisting of the Vale Royal and part of Powys-land. By his wife Gwawrddyd, daughter of Brychan, he was the father of a numerous family.[1] He was succeeded by his son Cyngan, the father of Brochwel Ysgythrog (slain in the battle of Chester, 613), whose descendants continued to be princes of Powys for many generations.[2] The third son of Cadell was Tegid Foel, lord of Penllyn, in Edeirnion, formerly a portion of Powys-land,[3] the grandfather of Gwynllw Filwr, who was the father of St. Cadoc and grandfather of St. Beuno.[4]

Ninth in descent from *Gwinfiw Frych*, a younger son of Cadell's, was

Ynyr, lord of Chirk, Whittington, Oswestry, Maelor Gymraeg and Maelor Saesnaeg in Powys-land, being the son of Cadfarch ab Gwrgeneu ab Gwarddgar ab Bywyn ab Iorddwyfyn ab Gwriawn ab Gwylawg ab Gwynan ab Gwinfiw Frych. In the year 870 Ynyr built the Castle of Whittington, which continued for many generations to be the chief residence of his descendants.[5] By his wife Rhiengar, daughter and heiress of Lluddocaf ab Caradoc Freichfras, lord of Hereford, Gloucester, Erging and Ewyas (who bore *azure*, a lion

[1] *Welsh Saints*, p. 161, where a table of the descendants of the two eldest sons will be found.

[2] *Enwogion Cymru*.　　　[3] *Ibid*.

[4] *Welsh Saints*, p. 170, and p. 268.

[5] Burke's *Landed Gentry*, art. Owen of Woodhouse.

rampant, party per fess, *or*, and *argent* in a border of the third charged with eight annulets *sable*), Ynyr had issue two sons,—Tudor Trefor, his successor, and Ynyr Frych, Abbot of Abbey d'Or, in the Golden Vale, in Herefordshire.

Tudor Trefor (so called because he was born or nursed at Trefor), Lord of Hereford, Gloucester, Erging, Ewyas, Chirk, Whittington, Oswestry, and both Maelors, was founder of the noble tribe of the Marches of Powysland.   In A.D. 907[1] he married Angharad, daughter of Howel Dda, King of Wales.   He bore party per bend sinister, *ermine* and *ermines*, a lion rampant *or*, and died A.D. 948, being the father of three sons :—(1) Goronwy, who died in his father's lifetime, married Tangwystl,[2] daughter of Dyfnwal ab Alan ab Alsar ab Tudwall Gloff, son of Rhodri Mawr, King of Wales, by whom he had issue an only daughter and heiress, Rhiengar, who succeeded to her grandfather's lands in Hereford, Gloucester, Erging and Ewyas.   She married Cyhelin ab Ifor ab Severus ab Cadifor ab Wenwynwyn, lord of Buallt, Radnor, Kerry, Maelienydd, Elfael and Cydewain, who bore *azure* three open crowns in pale *or*. By Cyhelin she was mother of Elystan Glodrudd, Prince of Fferllys and founder of the fifth Royal tribe of Wales. He was born in the Castle of Hereford in 927, and was named after Athelstan, King of England, who was his godfather.   He was living in 1010, but was slain in a civil broil at Cefn Digoll, in Montgomeryshire.   (2) Lluddocaf was Lord of Chirk, Whittington, Oswestry and Maelor Saesnaeg, died in 1037, leaving by his wife Angharad (daughter of Iago ab Idwal, Prince of North Wales) a son, Llywarch, who by Lucy his wife, daughter of Gwrstan ab Gwaethvod, lord of Cibwyr in Gwent (who bore *vert* a lion rampant *argent*, head, paws, and tail imbrued *gules*), had a son and heir, Ednyfed, who married Janet, daughter and co-heiress of Rhiwallon ab

[1] For a history of Whittington Castle in connexion with this family, the reader is referred to an interesting paper by the late Joseph Morris, Esq., in the *Arch. Camb.*, for 1852, p. 282, etc.

[2] Eyton Pedigree.

Cynfyn, Prince of Powys (who bore *or* a lion rampant *gules* on a canton *azure* a dexter hand couped *argent*), and was the father of Rhys Sais, lord of Chirk, Whittington, Oswestry and Maelor. Lluddocaf was also the ancestor of the families of the Mostyns, of Mostyn, Talacre, and Segroid ; the Trefors of Bryncynallt, Plas-Teg and Trefalyn; the Wynns of Eyarth; Lloyds of Leaton Knolls ; the Youngs of Bryn-Yorkyn ; the Edwards of Sansaw Hall; the Trefors of Trefor Hall, now represented by Trefor Lloyd, late of Plas Llanasaph, Esq., and the family of Thomas of Coed-helen, the possessors of Trefor Hall and Valle Crucis Abbey ; the Lloyds of Plas Madog, and of Berth, now of Rhagatt ; the Eytons of Park Eyton ; the Vaughans of Burlton Hall ; the Pennants of Downing and Penrhyn Castle and the Dymoks of Penley Hall.

The third son of Tudor Trefor was *Dingad*, lord of Maelor Gymraeg or Blomfield. He married Cecilia, daughter of Severus ab Cadifor ab Wenwynwyn, lord of Buallt, and had issue—

Rhiwallon, lord of Maelor Gymraeg, who died in 1040, and left by his wife Letitia, daughter of Cadwalladr ab Peredr Goch of Môn, a son

Cynwrig ab Rhiwallon, who succeeded his father as

lord of Maelor Gymraeg. He was slain in 1074 during an incursion of the Danes into Maelor, and was buried in Wrexham Church. The stone lid of the coffin, on which he was represented in armour, recumbent, with a lion rampant sculptured on his shield, and with the inscription HIC IACET CYNVRIG AB RHIWALLON round the verge of the stone, was seen by John Erddig, of Erddig, Esq., affixed to the wall of the churchyard, in 1660. He bore *ermine*, a lion rampant *sable*, armed and langued *gules*. From him the township of Christionydd Cynwrig takes its name. By his first wife Judith, daughter of Ifor Hên lord of Rhôs (who bore *argent*, a rose *gules*), he had five sons :—(1) Niniaf, the eldest, was ancestor of the Jones-Parrys of Madryn Park, and Llwyn-Onn ; the present head of this family, Thomas Love Duncombe Jones-Parry, of Madryn, Esq., is Chief of the descendants of Cynwrig ab Rhiwallon. When the old church at Wrexham was destroyed by fire in 1457 and the Pope gave instructions to have it rebuilt as it now stands, the Llwyn-Onn family were the first to respond to the injunctions of the Holy Father ; their teams carried the first loads of stone for the restoration of the present beautiful edifice, and it is a very curious fact that this family alone, of all the once numerous descendants of Cynwrig ab Rhiwallon possess their lands by an unbroken male descent from Cadell Deyrnllwg,—"They who honour me I will honour," saith the Lord. The other families who descend from Niniaf are the Lloyds of Llwyn-y-Cnotiau ; the Robertses of Hafod-y-Bwch ; the Joneses of Croes-Foel, Edward Jones of Plas-Cadwgan, who was attainted and executed in 1586 ; Edwards of Sealyham, and Lord Kensington ; Erddig of Erddig ; Traffords of Esclusham ; Goronwy ab Hwfa of Hafod-y-Wern, now represented by Philip Davies Cooke of Hafod-y-Wern and Owston, Esq. ; Madog yr Athraw ab Hwfa, of Plas Madog and Erbistog ; the Bershams of Bersham ; the Wynns of Gerwynfawr ; the Eytons of Eyton-Uchaf, and the Sontleys, of Sontley. Anne, daughter and heiress of Robert Sontley, of Sontley Hall, Burton Hall in Gresford, and Plas Uchaf in Rhiwabon, was the second wife of John Hill, of Rowley's Mansion in Shrewsbury, Esq., by whom she had a son and heir, Thomas Hill, of Sontley, Esq., who by Matilda his wife, daughter of Charles Elstob, D.D., Dean of Canterbury, had issue two sons, John and Charles. John died unmarried in 1755, and Charles died unmarried in 1780. The estates of Sontley, Burton, and Plas-Uchaf, then reverted to their mother, at whose death the Sontley estates were all sold. The Badies of Rhiwabon, now extinct, likewise descended from Niniaf. Awr ab Ieuaf ab Niniaf was the ancestor of the Jefferies of Acton, and also of the Lloyds of Plas Madog, who are now represented by J. Youde William Lloyd, Esq., of Clochfaen. Some heralds, however, say that this Awr was the son of Ieuaf ab Cyhelyn of Trefor, which is also affirmed by Mr. Joseph Morris.

Ednyfed, the second son of Cynwrig, who bore *ermine* a lion statant guardant *gules*, was ancestor of the Broughtons of Broughton and Marchwiail; the Powells of Alrhey and the Ellises of Alrhey and Wyddial Hall, in Hertfordshire. Cynwrig's third son was Gruffydd, the fourth Bleddyn, and the fifth Hoedliw of Christionydd.

Cynwrig ab Rhiwallon married secondly, Agnes, or Annesta, daughter of Idnerth Benfras, lord of Maesbrug or Maesbrook (who bore *argent* a cross flory engrailed *sable*, inter four Cornish choughs, ppr., on a chief *azure*, a boar's head, couped *argent*), by whom he had issue a sixth son, *David* of Maelor, of whose descendants we shall speak presently; (7th) Hwfa; (8th) Llewelyn, who was ancestor of David Burd Hên, Esq., who married Efa, daughter and heiress of Gruffydd ab Llewelyn Fychan ab Llewelyn ab Goronwy, of Pentre Madog, in Duddlestone, Esq., fourth son of Sir Roger de Powys, Knight, Lord of Whittington (who bore *vert.* a boar, *or*), by whom he had issue Philip Bride or Burd of Pentre Madog, Esq., who by Alice, his wife (daughter of John ab Richard ab Madog of Halchdyn in the parish of Hanmer) had an elder daughter and heir, Margaret, who married James Eyton ab John Eyton (youngest son of William Eyton, of Eyton, in the parish of Bangor-Iscoed) ancestor of the Eytons of Pentre Madog.[1] (9th) Einion, (10th) Iorwerth, (11th) Ieuaf and (12th) Bledrws together with a daughter Jane, third wife of Madog ab Cadwgan, lord of Nannau, by whom she had issue Rhiwallon, ancestor of the Gwynns of Llanidloes; the Joneses of Trewython in the parish of Llandinam, and several other Montgomeryshire families now extinct.

David the sixth son of Cynwrig ab Rhiwallon was the father of *Meredydd*, the father of *Madog*, whose son *Ieuan* was the father of

Madog Danwr ("Ignifer"), or, as he is called in some MSS., Madog Danwy Trefor, lord of Llangurig. He was a brave soldier and a faithful servant of Gwenwynwyn. In a pedigree drawn up by the late Rev. Walter Davies,[2] who was assisted by the late Joseph Morris, Esq., of Shrewsbury, we are told respecting Madog that "the Prince of Powys knew his value in that age of perpetual warfare, and accordingly stationed him as a guardian of his frontier, on the border of South Wales, by granting him the parish of Llangurig on the skirts of Plinlimmon. Here he settled and became the

progenitor of many families in the hundred of Arwystli and its vicinity. The same prince, as an honorary

---

[1] For a further account of this family, see Lewis Dwnn, i, 324.
[2] Ex. inf. A. J. Johnes, Esq., of Garthmyl.

reward for his faithful services, gave Madog the privilege of bearing a new shield of arms in augmentation of his paternal coat."[1] These new arms were a border *gules* charged with eight mullets *argent*.[2] He married a daughter of Idnerth ab Meredydd Hên, lord of Buallt (who bore *gules*, a lion rampant regardant, *or*), by whom he had three sons, Meredydd, his successor, Idnerth, and Gruffydd, of Cefn-yr-Hafodau. Madog was the first member of the family who settled at the Clochfaen, and in allusion to his being the founder of so many families in the district, an old bard of the neighbouring parish of Trefeglwys has the following lines :—

> " Danwr hael yn dwyn rheolaeth
> Hen ben haeddol boneddig
> Ai brig ar Gurig i gyd."

> [Danwr the generous, the bearer of rule
> The noble, meritorious, ancient stock
> Whose branches are spread over the whole of Llangurig.]

Meredydd, of Llangurig, lord of Aberhafesp and Dolfachwen, married Arddun, daughter of Einion ab Llewelyn ab Meilir Grug, lord of Tregynon and Westbury, descended from Brochwel Ysgythrog, King of Powys (quarterly, first and fourth *sable*, three horses' heads, erased *argent*, Brochwel Ysgythrog; second and third, party per pale, *or* and *gules*, two lions rampant, addorsed countercharged for Brochwel ab Aeddan of Llanerchbrochwel, lord of Cegidfa (Guilsfield), Broniarth and Deuddwr); by whom he had issue four sons :—(1) Iorwerth, (2) Llewelyn of Clochfaen; (3) Gruffydd and (4) Philip. Iorwerth was ancestor of David Lloyd, of Berthlloyd, in the parish of Llanidloes (who bore *ermine*, a lion rampant, *sable* in a border *gules*, charged with eight bezants), whose only daughter and heir, Gwenhwyfar, married to Philip ab Ieuan Bwl ab Ieuan ab Meredydd ab Madog ab Ieuan ab Gwyon ab Trahaiarn ab Iorwerth, lord of Garthmul (who bore *argent*, three lions passant in *pale gules*), by whom she had a son,

---

[1] Burke's *Landed Gentry*, article Owen of Glansevern. *Supra.*
[2] *Her. Vis.*, by Holmes and Chaloner, *Harl. MSS.*, 1973.

Ieuan, ancestor of the Lloyds, of Berthlloyd. Iorwerth was likewise the ancestor of Gwenllian, daughter and and heir of Ieuan ab Gruffydd Goch, and wife of Ieuan ab Gruffydd, of Clochfaen.

Llewelyn, the second son of Meredydd, was of Clochfaen in this parish, and was the father of

Howel Lloyd, of Clochfaen, whose son

Gruffydd of Clochfaen; married Alice, daughter of Rhys ab Meredydd ab Owain, lord of Towyn in Cardiganshire (who bore *gules* a chev. inter two fleurs-de-lys in chief, and a lion rampant in base, *or*). He left issue two sons, Ieuan and Rhys Ddû, of Pont-y-rhydgaled, ancestor of the Richardses of Llangurig.

Ieuan ab Gruffydd succeeded his father at Clochfaen, and married first, Gwenllian, daughter and co-heir of Ieuan ab Gruffydd Goch ab Philip ab Iorwerth ab Meredydd ab Madog Danwr, by whom he had issue two sons, Jenkyn Goch, his successor, and Llewelyn, of Llangurig. Ieuan married, secondly, Gwenllian, daughter of Rhys ab David ab Ieuan ab Rhys ab Llewelyn, by whom he had one daughter, Goleubryd, wife of David ab Rhys ab Adda ab Howel, of Henfaes, in Kerry, descended from Einion ab Cynfelyn (*azure*, a lion passant *argent*.)

Jenkyn Goch, of Clochfaen, bore *ermine*, a lion rampant *sable*, in a border *gules* charged with eight annulets

or. He married Catherine, daughter and heir of

H

Maurice Fychan ab Maurice ab Madog ab Einion, of
Kerry and Mochdref, second son of Tudor ab Einion[1]
Fychan, lord of Cefnllys, descended from Ifor, eldest
son of Idnerth ab Cadwgan[2] ab Elystan Glodrudd. By
this lady he had issue a son, Maurice, who succeeded
him, and four daughters :—(1) Catherine, the wife of
Ieuan Wynn ab Jenkyn, of Cefn-yr-Hafodau, descended
from Cadifor[3] ab Dyfnwal, lord of Castle Howell and
Gilfachwen, Cardiganshire; (2) Angharad, wife of
Llewelyn Lloyd, of Llanidloes, Esq., descended from
Einion ab Cynfelyn, lord of Manafon, ancestor of the
Gwynns of Llanidloes; (3) Deilu, who married Ieuan
Goch ab Maurice ab Rhys ab Cadwgan ab Llewelyn ab
y-Moelwyn Mawr, lord of Buallt, by whom she had an
only daughter and heiress, Deilu, who became the wife
of Thomas, of Aber-Magwr, in the parish of Llanfihangel-
y-Creuddyn, younger son of Maurice Vaughan, of Traws-
coed, county of Cardigan, Esq.; (4) Annie, the wife of
Morgan ab Ieuan ab Dio ab David, of Creuddyn, de-

[1] This Einion ab Howel of Mochdref married Agnes or Annesta,
daughter and heir of Adda ab Meurig ab Adda ab Madog, Lord of
Kerry, who was one of the hostages for Llewelyn ab Iorwerth put
to death by King John, 1213. This unfortunate chief was the son
of Maelgwyn, lord of Maelienydd and Kerry, son of Cadwallon, the
second founder of Abbey Cwm Hir, in the year 1143, which he intended for the accommodation of sixty monks. He was slain in
1179, and was buried in the church of the abbey. Cadwallon was
the son of Madog, lord of Malienydd and Kerry (who died 1139)
second son of Idnerth ab Cadwgan.—*Lewis Dwnn.*

[2] Prince Cadwgan was the first founder of the Cistercian monastery of Abbey Cwm Hir, and also the founder of three churches
which he dedicated to St. Michael; one in Kerry, one at Cefnllys,
and the other on Bryn Ty Ieuan, near Newbridge on Wye, which
was restored and re-opened in 1868.

[3] "The arms of Cadivor ab Dyfnwal are: *sable,* a spearhead
argent embrued between three scaling ladders of the second, two
and one; on a chief gules a tower triple-towered, ppr. These are
the true arms not the absurd ones given in Clarke. The legend is,
Cadivor was deprived of his castle by Fitz Stephen, a Norman.
Collecting his retainers he divided them into three parties, and
having surprised the castle by night, stormed it and retook it with
great slaughter, killing Fitz-Stephen himself with his spear." *Notes
and Queries,* 4th series, ii, 541.

scended from Llowddyn, lord of Uwch-Aeron, who bore *gules*, a griffin segreant, *or*.

Maurice, of Clochfaen, married Margaret, daughter of Llewelyn ab Rhys Lloyd, of Creuddyn, ab Gruffydd ab Ieuan ab Llewelyn ab Rhys ab Gruffydd ab Rhys ab Iorwerth ab Cadifor ab Gwaethfod, lord of Cardigan, who bore *or*, a lion rampant regardant *sable*. Maurice left issue, (1) Evan, of Crugnant, of whom presently; (2) Owain, who married Tangwystl, daughter of Morgan (ab Maurice ab Thomas) by Catherine his wife, daughter of David ab Ieuan ab Maurice, of Llwyn Newidion, in the parish of Llanfihangel-y-Creuddyn, county of Cardigan; (3) Jenkyn, who succeeded at Clochfaen; and (4)[1] William, who died unmarried; and four daughters:—(1) Elen, wife of Llewelyn ab Maurice ab Rhys, of Llangurig, descended from Einion ab Cynfelyn; (2) Goleubryd; (3) Margaret, second wife of Thomas ab David Dêg, of Carno, descended from Einion ab Seisyllt, lord of Mathafarn; and (4) Tangwystl.

Jenkyn, of Clochfaen, who succeeded his father Maurice, married Catherine, daughter of Morgan (ab Rhys ab Howel, of Llangurig, ab David ab Howel Fychan, of Gilfachwen, county of Cardigan, Esq., descended from Cadifor ab Dyfnwal, lord of Castle Howel, Gilfachwen and Pant Streimon), by whom he had issue two sons, David Lloyd, his successor, and Evan, of Clochfaen Issaf, who married and had one son, Edward ab Ieuan, of Clochfaen Issaf, together with a daughter, Catherine, the wife of Owain Gwynn ab Morgan Gwynn, of Llanidloes, Esq.

David Lloyd Jenkyn, of Clochfaen, married Catherine, daughter of Evan ab David ab Ieuan ab Gutto ab Gruffydd, of Creuddyn, ab Meredydd ab Rhys ab Ieuan

---

[1] Huw Cae Llwyd, an old bard, who flourished from 1450 to 1480, has left behind in MS. an ode to these four brothers, the sons of Maurice, which will be given *in extenso* in the appendix to this paper. The poet speaks highly of them as warriors, and describes them as—

" Four comrades are they who one and all
Have been found mighty to oppose deeds of wrong."

ab Rhys ab Llowddyn, lord of Uwch-Aeron, who bore *gules*, a griffin segreant, *or*. Her mother was Tangwystl, daughter of Evan Wynn, of Dolbachog, Esq., descended from Cadifor ab Dyfnwal. By this marriage David Lloyd had issue, Evan, his successor, and Jenkyn, who married Elizabeth, daughter of Owain Blaeney, of Ystyngwen, Esq., descended from Ieuan Blaeney, of Gregynog, and one daughter, Elen, wife of Jenkyn ab Maurice ab Rhys, of Llangurig, descended from Madog Danwr.

Evan ab David, of Clochfaen, whose name is on the list of jurymen summoned for the Assize held at Llanidloes in 1606, married Elizabeth (or according to other authorities Mallt), daughter of David Lloyd Blaeney, of Gregynog, in the lordship of Cydewain, Esq., and Mary his second wife, daughter of Richard ab Maurice, of Rhiwsaeson, in Llanbrynmair, Esquire. The Blaeney family is now represented by Cadwaladr Davies, twelfth baron of Castle Blaeney, descended from Edward, second son of David Lloyd Blaeney, who accompanied the Earl of Essex to Ireland in 1598, and was elevated to the peerage of Ireland, 29th July, 1621. The arms of the Blaeney family were quarterly, first and fourth *sable*, three horses' heads erased *argent*; second and third per pale two lions rampant addorsed countercharged. By his marriage Evan had issue :—(1) Rhys, his successor ; (2) David Lloyd, together with a daughter, Gwenhwyfar, the wife of John, second son of Morgan Glynn, of Glyndywedog, in the parish of Llanidloes, Esq., descended from Aleth, King of Dyfed, who bore *azure* three cocks *argent* crested and wattled, *or*.

Rhys Lloyd, of Clochfaen, the successor of Evan ab David, was a staunch royalist, and was obliged to compound for his estate with the Parliament by a payment of " £011 000s.10d." as appears from a book[1] in the

[1] See also *Montgomeryshire Collections*, i, 474. Some idea of the unsettled state of the county at this time may be gathered from a perusal of two papers—the one printed in the *Camb. Quart.*, i, pp. 60, 74, the other in the *Arch. Camb.*, i, pp. 33, 42.

library of the College of St. Beuno at Tremeirchion,
which contains a list of the nobility and gentry who
had to compound with the rebels for their estates. He
married (1626) Margaret, daughter of Jenkyn Lloyd, of
Berthlloyd, Esq., high sheriff of Montgomeryshire, in
1588 and 1606, and seneschal or steward under James I
and Charles I, of the lordship of Arwystli, and Dorothy,
his first wife, daughter of Edmund Walter, of Ludlow,
Esq., Chief Justice of South Wales. In Ludlow Church
there is a handsome altar tomb of white marble, display-
ing the recumbent effigies of the chief justice and his
lady ; on the front are figures representing their issue.
The following is the inscription :—

"Heere lye the bodies of Edmond Walter, Esqvier, chieffe
justice of three shiers in Sovth Wales, and one of His Majes-
tie's Councill in the Marches of Wales ; and of Mary, his wife,
davghter of Thomas Hacklvit, of Eyton, Esqvier, who had
issve three sons named James, John, and Edward, and two
davghters named Mary and Dorothy. He was bvried the 29th
day of January, anno domini 1592."[1]

Arms, *sable* a fesse indented inter three eagles displayed
argent membered *gules* ; impaling *argent* on a bend
collised *gules* three fleurs-de-lys *or* ; of the children
mentioned in the inscription the second son was Sir
John Walter, of Sarsden, county Oxon, Knight, Lord
Chief Baron of the Exchequer ; Mary, the eldest
daughter, married Sir Edward Littleton, of Henley,
county of Salop, Knight (chief justice of North Wales,
who died 1621 and was buried at Llanfair, in Denbighshire), by whom she had issue seven sons, two of whom
were Fellows of All Souls College, Oxford ; but all died
without issue, with the exception of the eldest, Sir
Edward Littleton, Knight, Lord Keeper of the Great
Seal of England, who was created Lord Littleton of
Mounslow, by Charles I, 1635, and was married to
Sydney, daughter of Sir William Jones, of Castell
March, in Lleyn, Knight. Dorothy, the second daughter
of the chief justice, married Jenkyn Lloyd, of Berthlloyd, Esq., who died 1627, and was the mother of Mar-

[1] Wright's *History of Ludlow*, p. 468.

·garet, the wife of Rhys Lloyd, of Clochfaen, whose eldest son Edward died without issue. The second son was

Jenkyn Lloyd, who succeeded his father at the Cloch-- faen, and married Mallt, daughter of Morgan ab David, of Llanbrynmair (ab Ieuan ab David Gethyn ab Gruf- fydd ab David ab Madog, second son of Llewelyn, ab Iorwerth, of Abergwidol, in the parish of Darowen, ab David ab Howel, of Darowen, ab Philip ab Uchdryd ab Edwyn Goronwy, Prince of Tegaingl who bore *argent* a cross flory engrailed *sable* inter four Cornish choughs, ppr., chief of one of the sixteen noble tribes of North Wales and Powys) by whom he had issue eight sons :— (1) Rhys, his successor; (2) Morgan, who married Bridget, daughter of Richard Morgan, of Caelan, in Llanbrynmair, descended from Ednowain ab Peredur lord of Dolgellau (*gules* three snakes ennowed in triangle *argent*), by whom he had issue one son, Littelton Lloyd, of Caelan, a clergyman of the Established Church, who died without issue ; and one daughter, Sarah, the wife of Edward Pritchard, of Ceniarth, Esq., descended from Y Llyr Craff, of Meifod. Morgan Lloyd's will bears the date of the 13th November, 1702 ; by it he bequeathed a " tenement in the parish of Trefeglwys, called *Cefn-y Cloddiau*[1] to the poor of the parish of Llanbrynmair, the rents, issues and profit thereof to be distributed at the discretion of the vicar and overseers of the poor of the said parish."[2] Part of the rent is applied to the maintenance of the parish school. An old local bard named David Manuel, whose residence was in the neigh- bourhood of Cefn-y-Cloddiau, wrote an elegy on the death of Mr. Lloyd, which is given in the appendix. His wife Sarah seems to have died before him, for the same poet composed some lines upon her death, which bear the date of 1696 ; (3) John, of the parish of St. Harmon ; (4) David, of Darowen ; (5) Jenkyn ; (6) Evan ; (7) Kyffin ; and (8) Richard. Of the daughters,

[1] *Montgomeryshire Collections*, i, p. 222.
[2] Charity Commissioners Report for Montgomeryshire, p. 279

Mabel was the wife of Humphery Williams, of Pentre Cynddelw, in the parish of Llanbrynmair, descended from Elystan Glodrudd.

Rhys Lloyd succeeded his father at the Clochfaen. He married Mary, daughter of John Thomas, of Belan Dêg, in the parish of Manafon, and of Llanllodian in the parish of Llanfair Caereinion, high sheriff of Montgomeryshire in 1681. Mr. Thomas became possessed of the estate in Llanfair in right of his wife Margaret, daughter and heir of John Owen, of Llanllodian, Esq. Arms, first and fourth *sable*, three horses' heads, erased *argent*; second and third Brochwell ab Aeddan. Rhys Lloyd was buried at Llangurig, 11th December, 1699, and was succeeded by his eldest son,

Jenkyn Lloyd, of Clochfaen, who was born in 1681, married at Llangurig, 21st February, 1698, was mayor of Llanidloes, 1705, and high sheriff for Montgomeryshire in 1713. His wife was Rachel, sister and co-heir of Edward Fowler, of Abbey Cwmhir, in the county of Radnor, high sheriff for that county in 1715, and daughter of John Fowler, of Abbey Cwmhir and Brondrefawr, Esq., high sheriff for Radnorshire in 1690. He was younger son by Margaret his wife (daughter of Richard, Lord Newport, of High Ercall, and Rachel his wife, daughter of John Levison, of Haling, in Kent), of Richard Fowler, of Harnage Grange, in the county of Salop, Esq., high sheriff for Radnorshire in 1655, eldest son of William Fowler, eldest son of Richard Fowler, of Harnage Grange, in the county of Salop, Esq., high sheriff of Radnorshire in 1600[1] by Mary, eldest daughter of Sir Edward Littleton, of Pillaton Hall, county of Stafford, Knight, and Margaret his wife, daughter and co-heir of Sir William Devereux, Knight, youngest son of Walter, Lord Viscount Hereford, K.G., who died 1558. John Fowler, who inherited Abbey Cwmhir from his father, made an immense fortune as a merchant, and purchased several other large estates.

[1] The dates of the sheriffs are taken from Williams' *History of Radnorshire.*

He died in 1697, and was buried at Llanbister. By his will, which was proved the following year at Doctor's Commons, he left all his lordships, manors, estates, and hereditaments in the several counties of Radnor, Hereford, Salop and Montgomery, to his three children, Edward, Rachel, and Jane. Edward died unmarried in 1722, and was buried at Llanbister. He entailed the Abbey Cwmhir estate upon his sisters and their heirs, appointing his cousin, Sir Richard Fowler, of Harnage Grange, Bart., to be trustee. In the Llanbister parish registers the names of John Fowler and Edward Fowler have been nearly erased and those of Sir Richard Fowler and Sir William Fowler written over them upon the erasure. Jane, the second daughter of John Fowler, married George Robinson, of Brithdir, in the county of Montgomery, Esq., of the family of Nicholas Robinson, Bishop of Bangor, and died without issue. The arms of the Fowler family are : 1. *Azure*, on a chev. inter three lions passant gardant, *or*, three crosses moline *sable* ; 2, barry of six *gules* and *argent*, on a chief *or*, a lion passant *azure* (Englefield, of Rycote and Lanynton Gernon, county of Oxford) ; 3, *Azure* two bars *argent* over all a bend compony *or* and *gules* (Leigh, of Morpeth).[1]

[1] The Fowler family was one of great antiquity before the reign of Richard I, when the then representative of the family, Sir Richard Fowler of Foxley co. of Bucks, Knt., accompanied that warlike monarch to the Holy Land with a body of archers raised among his own tenantry. At the siege of St. Jean d'Acre, 1190, an attack of the Saracens upon the Christian camp by night was frustrated by a white owl, which, being disturbed by their approach, flew into the tent of Sir Richard Fowler and awoke him. He soon became acquainted with the threatened danger, and hastily arousing his men, immediately engaged and defeated the enemy. King Richard rewarded his fidelity by knighting him upon the scene of the engagement, and changed his crest, which was the hawk and lure, to the vigilant owl. Subsequently in the reign of Henry IV, his descendant Sir William Fowler of Foxley, Kt, became possessed of Rycote co. Oxon, by his marriage with Cecilia daughter and heiress of Nicholas Englefield of Rycote and Lanynton Gernon co. of Oxford, Esq., who died 1414, as we learn from his epitaph.

"Here lieth Nicholas Englefield, Esq., some time Comptroller of

Jenkyn Lloyd died in 1722, and was buried at Llangurig, December 11th : his wife Rachel survived him, and dying in 1749, was also buried at Llangurig, leaving issue three sons and three daughters :—(1) Rhys, of Clochfaen ; (2) John, born 1702, and who died *s.p.* in 1766, leaving his estate of Llwyngwyn to his sister Jane ; (3) Edward, who died *s.p.* ; (1) Anne, born in 1701, became the wife of Charles Richards, of Penglas, county of Cardigan, Esq., whose family is now represented by George Griffiths Williams, of Rhoscellan, county of Cardigan, Esq. ; (2) Jane, born in 1702, became the wife of the Rev. Richard Ingram, rector of Cemaes in 1747 (*ermine*, on a fesse *gules* three escallops *or*), by whom she had an only daughter, Mary Ingram, heiress of Llwyngwyn, who married David Owen, of Glyngynwydd, who persuaded his son, Evan Owen, when he came of age to cut the deed of entail, and the estate passed by mortgage to their relative Sir Arthur Owen, of Glansevern, county of Montgomery, Knight. The third daughter Mary, was born in 1707, and married first to Lingaine Owen, of Bettws Hall, in the county of Montgomery, Esq. (*argent* a lion rampant and canton *sable*) ; secondly to John Gethyn, of Vaynor, Esq. (*or*, a cross moline pierced inter four lozenges *azure*), which family is now represented by Robert Devereux Harrison, Esq., coroner of Montgomeryshire, eldest son of Sarah, who was only surviving daughter of Robert Griffiths, of Welshpool, Esq., and relict of the late George Devereux Harrison, Esq., brother of Major Harrison, of Caer Howel and Llandysilio Hall. Mrs. Gethyn died in 1797, leaving issue by her first

the House to King Richard II, who died 1st of April in the year of grace M.CCC.XIV., whose soul IESU pardon Amen, Amen, Amen."

He was the third son of Sir Philip de Englefield, Lord of Englefield, the head of an ancient family, which, according to Camden, takes its name from the town of Englefield in Berkshire, of which place they were stated to have been the proprietors in the second year of Egbert's reign, 803. (For a full account of the Fowler and Englefield families, see Wotton and Kimber's *Baronetage*, and Burke's *Extinct Peerage*.)

I

husband one son, Pryce Owen, of Bettws, Esq., and four daughters ; Elizabeth, married to William Jones, Esq., of Newtown ; Mary, who became the wife of the Rev. Mr. Morgan ; Rachel, married to Roger Pryse, of Cae Howel, Esq., and Jane.

Rhys Lloyd, of Clochfaen, was baptized at Llangurig, March 10th, 1699, and was married the 20th December, 1723, to Sarah, daughter and heir of William Platt, of Rhydyronen, in Llanynys, county of Denbigh, by Mary his wife, eldest daughter and co-heir of Thomas Hughes, of Pen-y-nant, in the parish of Rhiwabon, descended from Robyn ab Gruffydd Goch, lord of Rhôs (*azure* on a chevron inter three escallops *argent*, three leopards faces *gules*, Platt ; 2nd *or*, a griffin segreant *gules*, Hughes).   The Abbey Cwmhir estates were the property of Mr. Lloyd's mother, who in her old age became imbecile, affording an excuse for the trustee, Sir Richard Fowler's, retaining the management of the property, and he at his death, in 1737, transmitted it to his son Sir William Fowler.   Rhys Lloyd was high sheriff of Montgomeryshire in 1743, and dying in 1748, was buried at Llangurig the 15th of July, in that year. His wife, who was born in 1696, survived him and was buried at Llangurig, 10th of January, 1781 ; the issue of the marriage was three daughters :—Mary, who died *s.p.* ; Rachel, appointed Maid of Honour to Caroline, wife of Frederick, Prince of Wales (mother of George III), and afterwards housekeeper of Kensington Palace, who died in 1793, and was buried at Llangurig ; Sarah, born in 1728, wife of John Jones, of Dôl-y-Myneich, county of Radnor ; and one son,

Jenkyn Lloyd, who succeeded his father at the Clochfaen in 1748.   He was born in 1724, and married April 30th, 1743, at Erbistog, to Elizabeth, daughter and heir of Edward Lloyd, of Plâs Madog, in the county of Denbigh, Esq., lineally descended from Tudor Trefor, and by heirs female from Margaret, eldest daughter and co-heir of David, fifth son of Gruffydd ab Gwenwynwyn.   Mr. Lloyd was appointed high sheriff of

Montgomeryshire in 1755, and shortly after the death of his grandmother, Rachel Fowler, which took place at Llangurig in 1749, he commenced a law-suit for recovering the Abbey Cwmhir estates, which were then retained by Sir William Fowler. To meet the expenses Mr. Lloyd had to sell a considerable portion of the Clochfaen estates. The suit was progressing favourably up to the Christmas of 1765, at which time, Mr. Lloyd not feeling very well, proceeded to Shrewsbury to consult his medical adviser. At Shrewsbury he had an interview with Sir William Fowler, and in a few days afterwards (January 6th, 1766) he died suddenly from the effects of poison which is supposed to have been administered to him in his medicine. He was buried at Rhiwabon, February 5th, 1766.

Acting upon the advice of his friends, Sir William very shortly afterwards left England in a ship bound for Calcutta, which foundered at sea, and all on board perished. His son and successor, Sir William Fowler, made a summary attempt to bring the litigation respecting the Cwmhir estates to an end, by trying to carry off the young heiress of Plâs-Madog and Clochfaen from a boarding school at Chester. But, owing to the vigilance of her friends, he failed in carrying out his design, and for this and some other misdeeds he was compelled to quit the country, never to return. He died unmarried at the Hague, leaving three married sisters, who had children then living, none of whom, however, claimed the abbey, which was allowed to remain without an owner until Sir Hans Fowler, uncle of the preceding Sir William, who had been serving in the army of Frederick the Great, returned to England and succeeded to the title and estates. To pay the expenses of the heavy lawsuits in which he was engaged before obtaining possession, he sold large portions of the estate, and reduced it to the comparatively small property now belonging to the abbey. He died without issue in 1771, and, although he left three married nieces, daughters of his elder brother, Sir William, he was succeeded at

Abbey Cwmhir by his sister Sarah, who had married Thomas Hodges, a colonel of the guards, by whom she had issue a son, and a daughter, Sarah. Sarah, in 1769, became the wife of Lieut.-Col. George Hastings, of Lutterworth, in the county of Leicester, by whom she had issue four sons, the youngest of whom, Hans Francis, eventually became eleventh Earl of Huntingdon, in 1819. His son, the present Earl, lays claim to Abbey Cwmhir. The son, Thomas Hodges Fowler, succeeded his mother at the Abbey, and dying in 1820, left issue by Lucy, his wife, daughter and co-heiress of Thomas Hill, of Court-Hill in the county of Salop, Esq., an only daughter and heiress, Sarah Georgina, wife of the Rev. Durant Baker, of Christ's College, Cambridge, son of Thomas Baker, Esq., of Ashurst Lodge in Kent. On Mr. Fowler's death, however, the Abbey became the property of the late Mr. Fauntleroy, who was hung for forgery. His agent, Mr. Wilson, was the next possessor. He went to Botany Bay, where he died, and his creditors, in 1837, sold the estate to Mr. Phillips of Manchester, whose son is the present possessor. Leaving this digression, giving the details of the sad history of the Fowler family, we return to

Sarah, the heiress of Clochfaen and Plâs-Madog, who was born February 19th, 1746. In her person the line of Gwenwynwyn again came into possession of the greater part of the parish of Llangurig. In 1768, she married her first husband, John Edwards of Crogen Iddon (in Glyn Ceiriog), Gallt-y-Celyn and Plâs Iolyn (in Yspytty-Ieuan,) Esquire, lord of the manor of Yspytty-Ieuan, and descended from Edwyn Prince of Tegeingl. By this gentleman, who died in 1771, she had no issue. She married secondly, in 1773, the Rev. Thomas Youde, B.C.L., of Brasenose College, Oxford, eldest son of Thomas Youde, of Ruthin, son of Francis Heude (or Youde) a French gentleman, who was sent by the court at St. Germains on a political errand to Sir Gruffydd Jefferies, of Acton, near Wrexham, in 1711. Here he became acquainted with Mary, eldest daughter and co-heiress of John Hill, Esq., of Rowley's Mansion in Shrewsbury, by his first wife, Priscilla, daughter and heiress of Seth Rowley, of Rowley's Mansion (*argent* on a bend *sa.* inter two Cornish choughs, ppr, three escallops of the field.) John Hill was on the 17th March, 1684-5, appointed to be an alderman of Shrewsbury by James II, but on account of his favouring the cause of the Prince of Orange, was deposed 1st Jan., 1687-8. In 1689, he was elected Mayor of Shrewsbury, was Justice of the Peace for the county, and High Sheriff of Denbighshire, in 1697. He refused to give his consent to his daughter's marriage with Mr. Youde, on account of the latter's political opinions, and hoping to prevent the union, removed her from Acton, the residence of Sir Gruffyd Jefferies, to his own house in Shrewsbury. Miss Hill, however, contrived to escape her father's vigilance, and was married to Mr. Youde. Her father, who never forgave her, died on March 29th, 1731, and was buried with his second wife, the heiress of Sontley, (who died in 1693) in the churchyard of old St. Chad's, Shrewsbury. Mr. and Mrs. Youde, hoping to avert the effect of his anger, did open penance in white sheets in that church.[1]

The mother of the Rev. Thomas Youde (who was buried at Rhiwabon in 1806, at the age of 78) was Dorothy, daughter of John Jones, of Calchog, near Ruthin (who had considerable property in the parishes of Evenechtyd, Cyfeiliog, Clocaenog, Llanrhudd, Llanfwrog, and Llanfair-dyffryn-Clwyd) and Mary, his wife, sister of Eubule Thelwall, of Jesus College, Oxford, and daughter and heiress of Edward Thelwall, of Ruthin, son of Thomas Thelwall, son of Edward Thelwall, second son of John Wynn Thelwall, of Bathafarn Park, Esq. The arms of the Youde family are (1) *argent*, a lion rampant *az.*, charged on the shoulder with a fleur-de-lys *or* ; (2) ermine on a fess *sa.*, a castle *arg.* Hill ; (3) *Vert* a stag trippant *arg.* attired *or.* Jones of Calchog ; (4) *gules* on a fess *or* between three boars' heads couped *arg.* three trefoils *sable* Thelwall. The pro-

---

[1] Owen and Blakeway's *History of Shrewsbury.*

perty acquired from his mother was sold by Mr. Youde's trustees.[1]

Mrs. Sarah Youde died December 20th, 1837, and was buried at Rhiwabon. By her second husband she had issue : 1, Thomas Watkin, born 1775, who succeeded to the Clochfaen and Plâs Madog estates, on the death of his father in 1806. He served the office of high sheriff of Montgomeryshire in 1816, died unmarried, at Cheltenham, and was buried at Rhiwabon in 1821. 2, Edward Youde, born in 1781, who succeeded to the property at the death of his mother, sold Rowley's Mansion, and dying at Ostend, was buried at the village of Ghistalles, near that town, in 1846. He married Mary, sister and heiress of Charles Greenaway of Barrington, co. of Oxon., Esq., and late M.P. for Leominster, by whom he had one daughter, Mary Jane Youde, now of Burford Priory. 3. Charles Madog, who died unmarried in 1797.

Mrs. Youde had also three daughters ; 1, Sarah, who died unmarried in her eighteenth year, and was buried at Rhiwabon, 1798 ; 2. Julia Elizabeth, who was born 29th May, 1793, succeeded to the Clochfaen and Plâs-Madog estates, on the death of her brother Edward, and dying unmarried 19th September, 1857, was buried at Llangurig ; 3. *Harriet*, who was born 30th March, 1787, in 1815 became the wife of the late Jacob William Hinde, Esq., formerly of the 15th Hussars, deputy-lieutenant for Middlesex, and son of Charles Hinde, Esq., of Langham Hall, county of Essex, and Deputy-Lieutenant for the counties of Essex and Middlesex. Mr. Hinde died at Heffleton House in the county of Dorset, 24th October, 1856, and was buried at Llangurig. Her husband died July 1st, 1868, and was the father of three sons :

1. *Jacob Youde William*, who was born in 1816, on the 12th December, 1868, received Her Majesty's license and authority to assume the name of Lloyd of Cloch-

---

[1] Judge Lloyd, of Berth, and Mr. Wynne of Plâs Newydd, now Plâs Heaton in Henllan parish.

AD · TE · DOMINE · SPERAVI.

Arms of J.ᵈ Youde W.ᵐ Lloyd, of Clochfaen,
Coy of Montgomery, and late of
Plas Madoc, Coy of Denbigh, Esq.ʳ

faen, in lieu of that of Hinde, and also to bear the arms of Lloyd. By this act, the name and memory of the oldest family in the parish will enter upon a new lease of existence. The Plas Madog estates, with the tithes of the townships of Christionydd-Cynwrig, and Bodylltyn in the parish of Rhiwabon, which once belonged to the Cistercian monastery of Valle Crucis, passed in 1857 into the hands of G. H. Whalley, Esq., M.P. for Peterborough, who had a mortgage upon the property. Mr. Lloyd is a private in the Pontifical Zouaves.

The second son, Charles Thomas Edward, born at Plâs-Madog in 1820, entered the service of the East India Company in 1840. In 1853, he volunteered his services to Omar Pasha, commanding the Turkish army on the Danube, and was appointed a lieutenant-colonel under the name of Beyzad Bey. Shortly afterwards he acted as adjutant-general to the force under General Cannon (Bairam Pasha) which was dispatched from Shumla for the relief of Silistria. He took part in the defence of the latter town, and was lying side by side in an embrasure at Redoubt Kale with the late Captain O. Butler, at the time he received his death-wound. In July of 1854, he took an active part in the passage of the Danube and the battle of Guirgevo. He accompanied the army of the Danube to Bucharest, thence to Eupatoria, and was present at various skirmishes before Sebastopol in the years 1855-56. From the Crimea he accompanied the force of Omar Pasha to Mingrelia, and was present at the passage and battle of the Ingur. For these various services he received the English Crimean medal, the Turkish medals for Silistria, Danube, and the Order of Medijee, together with his brevet majority, and honorary lieutenant-colonelcy. He returned to India in 1857, and was at once appointed to a command in the state of Rewah, where he raised and organised a force of 800 men, and at their head in January 1858, opened the grand Deccan road by capturing six forts with forty guns and two mortars from the mutineers, for which service he received the thanks of the Governor-General in Council. Twice more during the mutiny he received the thanks of the Governor-General of India in Council. He was promoted to the rank of colonel in 1867. By his wife Harriette Georgina, only daughter, of the late Captain Souter, he has issue an only daughter Harriet Julia Morforwyn, married in 1866 to George Hope Verney, Esq., of the Rifle Brigade, second son of Sir Harry Verney, Bart., of Claydon, in the county of Bucks.

The third son Edward died in his infancy. Of the three daughters, the eldest, Harriet Esther Julia, married Daniel Todd, Esq., of Buncrana Castle, county of Donegal, J.P., and deputy-lieutenant for that county; she died without issue, 16th December, and was buried at Torquay, where her husband had been previously buried. 2. Julia Sarah, died at Aberystwith, 11th August, 1843, and was buried at Llangurig. 3. Mary Charlotte.

CHAPTER V.

THE PLAS-MADOG FAMILY.

HAVING in the previous chapter given an account of the Clochfaen branch of the family, we will now proceed to give a sketch of the descent and history of that branch of the house of Tudor Trefor, which settled at Plas-Madog in the parish of Rhiwabon. The Plas-Madog family claims for its ancestor

Rhys ab Ednyfed ab Llywarch ab Lluddoccaf ab Tudor Trefor, more commonly known as Rhys Sais,[1] because he had acquired a knowledge of the English language. He succeeded his father in possession of Chirk, Whittington, Oswestry, and Maelor Saesnaeg, and by his wife Efa, daughter and heiress of Gruffydd Hir, a descendant of Tudor Mawr, Prince of South Wales, he had issue three sons and one daughter; 1, Tudor, his successor; 2, Elidir, lord of Eyton, Erlisham, and

---

[1] *Supra.*

Borasham, (bore *ermine* a lion rampant*az.*) married Agnes
or Annesta, daughter of Lles ab Idnerth Benfras, and
was the father of Meilyr Eyton, ancestor of the once
distinguished family of the Eytons of Eyton; 3, Iddon,
lord of Duddleston, in the lordship of Chirk (bore *arg.*
a chev. inter three boar's heads, couped *gu.*), ancestor
of the Vaughans of Burlton Hall, and the Heylins of
Pentre-Heylin; Generys married Ednowain ab Ithel,
lord of Bryn in Powys-land, who bore *arg.* three greyhounds courant in pale *sa.* Rhys Sais apparently came to
a friendly arrangement with the Norman conquerors of
the Marches, for in 1170 he divided his possessions
among his sons.[1]

Tudyr or *Tudor*, the eldest son of Rhys, succeeded to
his father's lands in Whittington and Maelor, which he
appears to have held under Roger de Montgomery, to
whom he paid a chief-rent of four pounds, five shillings, according to the entry in the Domesday Book,
under "Wilitone." He married Janet, daughter of
Rhys Fychan ab Gruffydd ab Rhys ab Tudor Mawr, by
whom he had issue four sons; 1, Bleddyn, who, at his
father's death, became lord of Chirk and Maelor Saesnaeg, was by his wife, Agnes or Annesta, daughter of
Llewelyn ab Idnerth ab Meredith Hên, lord of Buallt,
descended from Elystan Glodrudd, ancestor of the
Joneses of Brynkynallt; Wynns of Eyarth; Lloyds of
Leaton Knolls and Domgay; Lloyds of Talorne and
Halchdyn; Lloyds of the Bryn, now represented by
Lord Kenyon and J. Y. W. Lloyd, Esq., of Clochfaen; the
Youngs of Brynyorkyn, in the parish of Hope,[2] the

[1] The late Joseph Morris, Esq., *Arch. Camb.*, 1852, p. 284.

[2] A younger branch of the Youngs, of Brynyorkyn, eventually
settled at West Ram, in the county of Lincoln, shortly after the
Reformation. On the death of John Young, Esq., in the year 1707,
the parish register of West Ram curiously records that the incum-
bent testified to his death and burial upon oath before a magistrate.
His successor, John Young, of West Ram, died in 1719, and shortly
after his burial a flight of bees descended and settled upon his
grave. The simple villagers regarded this as a good omen, prog-
nosticating the future prosperity and exaltation of the family of the
deceased gentleman. By his wife, Elizabeth, daughter of — Thorn-

K

eldest branch of which is now represented by William
Shipley Conway of Bodrhyddan and Brynyorkyn, Esq. ;
the Mostyns of Talacre and Segrwyd; the Edwardses of
Chirk; Trefors of Brynkynallt, Plas-têg and Trefalyn ;
Pennants of Downing, and of Penrhyn Castle, and the
Dymokes of Penley Hall. 2. Goronwy, or as he is sometimes called Goronwy *Pefr* (*i.e.*, Ranulphus the Smart,
or handsome) married Maud, daughter of Ingelric, a
noble Saxon (who had previously borne a son, William,
of whom the Conqueror was the father) and by her was
the father of three sons, Hamon, William, and Payne.[1]
By another wife, Goronwy had Roger, known afterwards as Sir Roger de Powys, (so-called from his estate
being in Powys-land) Sir William de Powys and Jonas
of Llanerch Banna. 3. Cyhelin, of whom presently.
4. Meurig, ancestor of David, abbot of Valle Crucis,
bishop of St. Asaph from 1500 to 1503.

Cyhelin, the third son of Tudor, had lands in the
parishes of Llangollen and Chirk. Pentre Cyhelin
takes its name from him.   He was the father of

Ieuaf, who married Mallt, daughter of Llywarch ab
Trahaiarn, lord of Cydewain, and was the father of

Awr of Trefor (*i.e.*, Tref-awr) in the parish of Llangollen.   He had two sons; 1, Adda of Trefor, who
married Tangwystyl, daughter of Iorwerth (ab Ednyfed
ab Meilyr Eyton, lord of Eyton) by whom he had a
son Ieuaf, who, by his wife, Myfanwy (descended from
Hoedliw, fifth son of Cynwrig ab Rhiwallon) was ancestor of Robert Trefor,[2] of Trefor Hall, and Valle

burgh, Esq., of Kendal, he left issue two sons, 1, John, who married Jane, daughter of Dr. Vavasour, brother of one of the baronets
of Hazlewood Castle, county of York; 2, David Young, Esq., of
Nomanby-le-wold, county Lincoln, who had issue one son and five
daughters, one of whom, Elizabeth, became the wife of John Williams, Esq., father of the Rev. Edward Williams, of St. Beuno's
College, Tremeirchion, Flintshire.

[1] Miletta, sister and heiress to this Payne *Pefr*, or Peverell, became the wife of Fulk Fitz-Warine, by which marriage the Warines
claimed Whittington, etc.—*Arch. Camb.*, 1852, p. 284.

[2] Mary, only daughter and heiress of Robert Trefor, married
Thomas Lloyd, of Glanhafon, in the county of Montgomery, high

Crucis Abbey, which was purchased by his ancestor, John Trevor, Esq. Ieuaf and his wife were buried in

sheriff for that county in 1716, and was the mother of two daughters, co-heiresses, Mary and Margaret. Margaret, the younger, married (1) Edward Lloyd, of Plâs-Madog, Esq., who died s. p. 1734, and (2) Arthur Meares, of Plâs Benion. The eldest daughter, Mary, became the wife of Edward Lloyd of Pentrehobyn, county of Flint, Esq., descended from Goronwy, Prince of Tegeingl, and was the mother of five sons, Robert, Thomas, John, Edward, and Trevor Lloyd, (all of whom died without issue) and two daughters, Mary and Margaret, co-heirs of their brother Trevor, who was high-sheriff of Montgomeryshire in 1787. Mary, the eldest, married Thomas Mather, of Ancoats, Esq., by whom she had issue an elder son, Samuel Lloyd Mather, who was the father of an only son, Thomas, (who died a midshipman) and one daughter, Mary Palmer, the wife of Robert Baldwin Lloyd, of Plâs-Llanassa, by whom she had issue one son, Trefor Lloyd, Esq., and two daughters, Margaret Baldwin and Mary. Margaret, the second sister, and co-heiress of Trefor Lloyd, Esq., married Rice Thomas, Esq., of Coedhelen, in the county of Caernarvon, and left issue five daughters; 1, Margaret, the wife of Thomas Trevor Mather, Esq., of Pentrehobin; 2, Jane; 3, Anne, who married John Browning Edwards, Esq., of Nanhoran; 4, Trevor; 5, Pennant, who in 1808 married William Ironmonger, Esq., of Wherwell Priory, county of Hants, who became owner of Trefor Hall, Valle Crucis Abbey, and the other estates (Burke's *Landed Gentry*, art. Ironmonger; *Arch. Camb.*, vol. i, p. 21.) The Lloyds of Rhagatt likewise descended from Adda ab Awr. David Lloyd, the first of the family who assumed the surname of Lloyd, settled at Berth, near Ruthin, about the year 1600. He was the son of Thomas ab Tudor ab Robert ab Meredydd ab Gruffydd ab Adda ab Llewelyn ab Ieuaf ab Adda ab Awr, of Trefor. His descendant, the late Edward Lloyd, Esq., of Rhagatt, in the county of Meirionydd, who died October 1859, had issue by his wife Frances Lloyd, daughter of John Madocks, of Fron Iw, county of Denbigh, Esq. 1, John Lloyd, married, 1847, Gertrude, daughter of the late Philip Lake Godsal, Esq., of Iscoed, in the county of Flint; 2, Edward, married, 1855, Mary Eliza, daughter of the late John Madocks, Esq., of Glanywern, county of Denbigh; 3, Howel William, married in 1850 to Eliza Anne, daughter of the late George Wilson, Esq., of Nutley, county of Sussex; 4. Charles Owen, Ensign in 8th N.I., E.I.C.S., who was killed at the age of nineteen in the battle before Moultan, 12th September, 1848, by a Sikh, whose life he had saved a few moments before; of the daughters, Frances, the eldest, married, in 1835, the late Sir Robert Williames-Vaughan, of Nannau, who succeeded his father, Sir Robert, the second baronet, in 1843, died 28th April, 1859; Charlotte became the wife of the late Richard John Price, Esq., son and heir of the late Richard Watkin Price, Esq., of Rhiwlas, co. of Meirionydd; Jane Margaret, wife of

the nave of the church of the Abbey of Valle Crucis.
The lids of the stone coffins in which their bodies are
deposited, with the inscriptions upon them, are still to
be seen.   Adda bore party per bend sinister ermine
and ermines in a border *gules*.   2. The second son was

Iorwerth ab Awr.   He married Margaret, daughter
of Ednyfed ab Iorwerth ab Meilyr Eyton, by whom he
had issue,

Iorwerth Fychan (junior) of Trefor, who was living
in 1332, and married first Agnes or Annesta, daughter
of Hwfa ab Iorwerth ab Gruffyd ab Ieuaf ab Niniaf
ab Cynwrig ab Rhiwallon (*gules* two lions passant arg.)
by whom he had issue, Howel of Trefor, whose only
daughter and heiress, Gwenllian, married Llewelyn ab
Ieuaf ab Adda, of Trefor.   Iorwerth married secondly,
Margaret, daughter of Madog[1] ab Llewelyn ab Gruffyd,
lord of Eyton, Erlisham, and Borasham) by whom he
had issue one daughter, Lucy, third wife of Madog
Llwyd, lord of Iscoed, descended from Tudor Trefor,
and one son,

Ednyfed Llwyd, Esq., who married the sister and
heiress of Ednyfed ab Iorwerth ab Madog, of Horslli in
the parish of Gresford, Esq.,[2] descended from Sanddef
Hardd, who bore 1st, *vert. seme* of Bromoslips, a lion
rampant *or* ;   2nd, *or*, a lion rampant *az.*;   3rd, *vert*, three
eagles displayed in fess *or*.   By this lady, Ednyfed had
issue, Llewelyn (his successor) Gruffyd, and a daughter,
Elen, who became the wife of Llewelyn Fychan, of
Pentre-Madog in Duddleston, Esq., son of Llewelyn ab
Goronwy ab Sir Roger de Powys (*supra.*)

Llewelyn ab Ednyfed married Angharad, daughter
of Adda, second son of Llewelyn ab Ieuaf ab Adda ab

the Ven. Archdeacon Ffoulkes, of Llandyssul; Eliza Blackburne
married Meredith Vibart, Esq., late captain in E.I.C.S., and adjutant of the Edinburgh Artillery Volunteers; Mary Charlotte,
of Hengwrt, Harriet Frances Julia Ann, died at the age of twelve
years; besides seven other children, who died in infancy.

[1] Madog died 1331, and was buried upon the Feast of St. Matthias, in the north aisle of Gresford Church, with his wife's family.
His tomb still remains in the church.

[2] Ab David Hēn ab Goronwy Hen of Burton ab Iorwerth ab
Howel ab Moreiddig ab Sanddef Hardd.

Awr of Trefor, and niece of John Trefor, bishop of St.
Asaph, by whom he had issue, 1. David, his successor.
2. Gruffyd. 3. Madog. 4. Iorwerth Goch of Christionydd-Cynwrig, who was killed in the year 1490.

David ab Llewelyn, who was living in 1497, became,
jure uxoris, of Plas-Madog, having married Margaret,
daughter and sole heiress of David ab Hwfa, of Plas-
Madog. But before proceeding further with the account
of the issue by this marriage, it will be necessary here
to deduce the descent of the heiress of Plas-Madog
from the Princes of Upper Powys.

Owen Cyfeiliog, on his death in 1197, was succeeded
by his son *Gwenwynwyn*, after whom Upper Powys was
thenceforward known as Powys-Gwenwynwyn. Allusion has already been made to his conquest of the cantref of Arwystli, a considerable portion of which he
bestowed on his follower, Madog Danwr,[1] another moiety,
with his accustomed liberality to the religious houses in
his territories, was granted to the neighbouring Cistercian monastery of Abbey Cwmhir;[2] he also confirmed the
grant of lands to the church of St. Michael at Trefeglwys and the Abbey of Haghmon in Shropshire.[3]
Dying about the year 1218, he left by his wife Margaret, a son Gruffydd (who ultimately succeeded to all
his father's lands), together with a natural son, Madog.
The latter received the lordships of Mowddy and Caereinion, which at his death reverted to his brother
Gruffydd, Madog having left no male issue. His
daughter Efa, married first Iorwerth ab Owen Brogyntyn, and secondly Owen ab Bleddyn, lord of Chirk.
Gruffyd, the son of Gwenwynwyn, who was a minor at
his father's death, in 1242, married Hawys, daughter of
Sir John le Strange of Ness, and by her had issue
six sons and one daughter, Mabel, who became the
wife of Fulke Fitz-Warine, lord of Whittington. The
sons were, 1. Owen, who, by the terms of his father's
will, received for his share of the territories, Arwystli,
Cyfeiliog, Ystrad Marchell (with the exception of the

---

[1] *Supra.*   [2] Rees' *Account of Abbey-Cwmhir*, p. 30.
[3] *Arch. Camb.*, 1860, p. 331.

township of Hirgyngrog, which was settled upon his mother for the term of her life.)   2, Llewelyn, who received Tal-y-bont, Olerton-de-Hope, and Dau-ddwr. 3, John, who was a secular priest, received for the term of his natural life the township of Blaen-y-coed-talog, Llyswenan, and Llangadfan. 4, William, had Mowddy (with the exception of Llandybo, which was settled upon his mother).   5, *David*, from whom the heiress of Plas-Madog traces her descent, received Pentyrch, Cellicaswallon, Penarth, and Rhiwhirarth.   6, Gruffyd Fychan, the youngest son, had Mochnant.

In his valuable paper on the Princes of Upper Powys, (*Montgomeryshire Collections*, i, 59, 75) and in the pedigree prefixed to the same article, Mr. Bridgeman has asserted that David was a priest.   He admits it is true that he was not in holy orders at the time of his father's death, for the terms of the latter's will do not support him in his inference.   Prince Gruffyd in that document grants a portion of his estate to his son John, (the Rector of Pool) " *to have and to hold for the whole time of his life.*"[1]   A plain indication that he had no lawful male issue, but in speaking of the lands bequeathed to his son David, the father plainly declares " *which we have assigned to our son David and the heirs of his body lawfully begotten,*" in precisely the same terms as are employed in the bequest to his sons Llewelyn and William, who are admitted to have had lawful male issue.   Had David been trained for the priesthood, the father could never have spoken of him in these terms, but, on the contrary, from the phraseology of the will it can fairly be inferred that if no heirs had been born to David at the time it was drawn up, there was then in existence no lawful impediment to his being the father of such.   Llewelyn, William, and Gruffyd had sons, yet the father wills in their case, as in that of David, that their portions in the event of their dying " without issue lawfully begotten," should revert to their elder brother, Owen.   So

---

[1] *Montgomeryshire Collections*, i, 41.

that in the will itself there is no distinction in the conditions upon which these four brothers were to enjoy the lands which they inherited at the death of their father.

Neither is there aught in the terms of the documents[1] which record the family compact between David and his elder brother, Prince Owen, which justifies the inference that the former was an ordained priest at the time of the final concord in 1290. But these documents are in accordance with the statements of all the manuscripts which assert that David was married, but left no male issue. And as his two daughters could not inherit by gavel kind, but would have a claim according to the English law, which was beginning at this time to gain ground in Powys, the elder and stronger brother, to secure the reversion of the lands to the head of the family, induced the younger to relinquish all claims to it on the part of his children. As David had no son to succeed him, he would the more readily agree to the conditions imposed upon him, which limited him to a life interest in the lands. Here we see enacted over again what occurred at the death of Madog, the natural son of Gwenwynwyn, who was not a priest. The strained inference of Mr. Bridgeman is thus proved to be weak in itself, and can have no weight at all, as it is contrary to the direct evidence afforded by the oldest and most authentic pedigrees,[2] which expressly state that David was married, and left two daughters. An unsupported inference of this description, particularly when the circumstances from which it arises can be explained quite satisfactorily on other grounds, should not be drawn, more especially in this case, as it has a tendency to cast dishonour upon the priestly character, and to discredit pedigrees which have every appearance of authenticity.

Whatever value the " old tradition" relating to the contention between Hawys, the niece of David, and

[1] *Montgomeryshire Collections*, i, 132-4.
[2] *Harl. MSS.*, 4181, 2299, 173. *Add. MSS.*, 9864, 9865.

her uncles, and the imprisonment of the latter in Harlech Castle, may possess, and, whoever its author may
have been, Dr. Powel was not its originator,[1] for it is
to be found in an old MS. in the British Museum, (a
transcript of which appeared in the *Brython*, iii, 124-127)
which was compiled, or copied, in the year 1498,[2] eighty-
six years before the appearance of the first edition of
the History of Wales.

Prince David married Elina, daughter and heiress of
Howel, third son of Madog ab Gruffydd Maelor, lord
of Castell Dinas-Bran, and Prince of Powys Fadog,
founder of the Abbey of Valle Crucis, by whom he had
issue two daughters, co-heiresses: 1, *Margaret*, who was
married to Howel Grach, of Bodylltyn, in the parish of
Rhiwabon, third son by Gwenllian, his second wife,
(daughter of Owen ab Trahaiarn ab Rotpert, lord of
Cydewain) of Llewelyn ab Gruffyd ab Cadwgan, lord of
Eyton, descended from Tudor Trefor.   By this marriage
she had issue an only daughter, *Angharad*, who married Madog yr Athraw, of Erbistock, and, in right of his
wife, possessor of lands in Bodylltyn, where he built
the house which was called in honour of him Plas-
Madog.   2, Mary, the second daughter, married Caradog ab Collwyn ab y Llyr Crach, of Meifod, ab Meredydd ab Cynan, a younger son of Owen Gwynedd,
Prince of North Wales.   This Meredydd was driven
from his territories by his uncle David ab Owen, Prince
of North Wales in 1173, and took refuge with Owen
Cyfeiliog, who gave him the lordships of Rhiwhiraeth,
Neuadd Wen, Llyssin, and Coed-Talog.   He bore *gu.*
and *arg.* four lions passant guardant counterchanged.
The last heir male of this line, Ieuan ab Owen ab
Meredydd, of Neuadd Wen, had an only daughter and
heiress, Margaret, who married, first Howel ab Gruffydd
ab Jenkyn, of Llwydiarth, descended from Celynyn, (of
Llwydiarth, who killed the Mayor of Carmarthen) who

[1] *Montgomeryshire Collections*, i, 58.
[2] This date seems too late for Gutyn Owen.   The number and
class of MSS., from which the transcript is made, are not given in the
Brython.

bore *sa.*, a he-goat *arg.*, armed, etc., *or*, and was descended from Aleth, King of Dyfed. Mary married, secondly, Rhys ab David Lloyd of Newtown Hall, Esquire of the body to Edward IV, who fell at Banbury, 1469, and was descended from Elystan Glodrudd. By Rhys she had issue an eldest son and heir, Thomas Pryse, of Newtown Hall, ancestor of the baronet family of that place. The representative of Mary is the right heir of the late Sir Edward Manley Pryse, the seventh baronet, who died without legitimate issue in 1791. Margaret married, thirdly, Gruffydd ab Howel ab David.

Madog yr Athraw was the youngest son by Efa, his second wife (daughter of Llewelyn ab Ynyr of Iâl) of Hwfa ab Iorwerth, of Hafod-y-Wern (who bore *sa.* three lions pass. in pale *arg.*) ab Ieuaf ab Niniaf ab Cynwrig ab Rhiwallon. By Angharad, his wife, Madog was the father of a son and heir,

Hwfa, who succeeded him at Plâs-Madog. He married Agnes, daughter of Madoch Goch, of Lloran Uchaf (descended from Einion Efell, Lord of Cynllaith, who bore party per fess *sa.* and *arg.*, a lion rampant counterchanged), and was the father of

Ieuaf, of Plâs-Madog, who by his wife Agnes, daughter of Gruffydd ab Cynwrig (ab Ieuaf ab Caswallon ab Hwfa ab Ithel Felyn, Lord of Iâl, who bore *sa.* on a chev. inter three goat's heads erased, *or*, three trefoils of the field), was the father of

Hwfa, of Plâs-Madog. This gentleman married Gwenllian, daughter of Ieuan Llwyd, and was the father of

David, the father of *Margaret*, the heiress of Plas-Madog, who became the wife of David ab Llewellyn, who was living in 1497 (*supra*). The issue of this marriage was four sons, John, Gruffydd, David Fychan, and Iorwerth, together with one daughter, Gwenllian.

John ab David married Margaret, (daughter by Philippa, his first wife daughter of Sir Randle Brereton, of Malpas, Knight), of Howel ab Ieuan ab Gruffydd, of Bersham, descended in the male line from Ednyfed,

L

second son of Cynwrig ab Rhiwallon, and by heirs
female from Llewelyn, the second son of Gruffydd ab
Gwenwynwyn, Prince of Upper Powys.   Arms—1,
ermine, a lion statant guardant *gu*. Ednyfed ab Cynwrig—2, *arg*. on a chief *gu*., three fleurs-de-lys, *or*.
Madog of Hendwr—3, *or*, a lion rampant, *gules*.   By
his wife, John had issue one daughter, Angharad, wife
of Madog ab David, descended from Cynwrig ab Rhiwallon, and one son,

Randle ab John, of Plâs-Madog, who by Angharad,
his wife, daughter of John ab Ieuan ab David ab Dio,
of Llanerchrugog, had a son,

John Lloyd, of Plâs-Madog, who was living July
5th, 1563.   He married Janet, daughter of Geoffrey
Bromfield, of Bryn-y-Wiwair, in the parish of Rhiwabon, descended through Iorwerth Benfras, Lord of
Maesbrook (arms, *supra*), from Edwin ab Goronwy, Lord
of Tegeingl, founder of one of the sixteen noble tribes
of North Wales and Powys.[1]   John was succeeded at
Plâs-Madog by his son,

William Lloyd, who married Catherine, daughter of
Owen Brereton,[2] of Borasham, Esq. (high sheriff of

[1] The Bromfields of Bryn-y-Wiwair became extinct in the male
line at the death of Edward Bromfield, Esq., whose only daughter
and heiress, Elizabeth, was married to Sir Gerard Eyton, of Eyton,
in the parish of Bangor-is-y-Coed, Knight.

[2] The Breretons of Borasham deduced their descent from William, second son of Sir Randle Brereton, of Malpas, Knight, by his
wife, Alicia, lady of Ipstans, only daughter and heiress of William
Ipstans, lord of Ipstans, son and heir of Sir John Ipstans, Knight,
lord of Ipstans, in the county palatine of Chester, who died A.D.
1394, and Elizabeth, his wife, daughter and sole heiress of Thomas
Corbet, of Moreton Corbet and Wattlesborough (*Harl. MS.*, 1396.)
Sir Randle Brereton was fifth in descent from Sir Randolphus de
Brereton, Knight, lord of Brereton, in Cheshire, and the lady Ada,
his wife, relict of Henry de Hastings (who in her right was one of
the claimants of the crown of Scotland), and fourth daughter and
co-heiress by Maud, his wife, daughter of Hugh Cyfeiliog, Count
Palatine of Chester, of David, Earl of Huntingdon, brother of
Malcolm, and William the Lion, kings of Scotland, and third son
of Henry, crown prince of Scotland, who died in the lifetime of his
father King David I.   Margaret, the eldest daughter and co-heiress
of David, Earl of Huntingdon, was grandmother of John Baliol,

Denbighshire in the years 1581 and 1588), and Elizabeth, his wife, only sister of the unfortunate Thomas
Salusbury, of Llyweny, who was executed in 1586 for
his connection with Babington's conspiracy. By his wife
Catherine, Mr. Lloyd had issue five sons and two
daughters—1, Edward (his successor). 2, Owen, who
married Jane, relict of John Ffachmallt, of Ffachmallt,
in the county of Flint, Esq., second daughter and coheiress (by Margaret, relict of Robert Empson, of London, and daughter of Hugh Wynn, of Wigfair, in
Meiriadog, Esq.) of John Brereton,[1] of Esclusham, Esq.,
who died 24th of January, 1622, and was buried at
Wrexham ; (arms—1 *arg.*, two bars *sa.*—Brereton, 2
arg., a chev. inter three crescents, *gules.*—Ipstans, 3
or, two ravens, ppr.—Corbet of Wattlesborough, 4, an
escarbuncle of eight rays, *or.* Tirret.) By this lady,
Owen Lloyd had issue one son, Thomas, a merchant,
who died without issue at Hamburg, and one daughter,
Elizabeth, wife of Edward Lloyd, of Plas-Madog.) 3,
Richard. 4, John. 5, Roger. Catherine, the eldest
daughter, married Hugh (ab John Wynn ab John ab
Robert of Rhiwabon,) and Mary, the second daughter,
became the wife of Humphrey Lloyd, of Llwyn Ynn,
Esq., descended from Edwyn ab Goronwy, Prince of
Tegeingl.[2]

Edward Lloyd, of Plâs-Madog, who was living in
1620, married Anne, daughter of John Eyton, of Lees-
wood, in the county of Flint, and Jane, his wife,
daughter of John Lloyd, of Bodidris, in Iâl, Esq., and
had issue—1, Edward, who succeeded his father; 2,
Piers, of London ; 3, Thomas ; 4, John ; 5, Owen ;

King of Scotland, and John the Red Comyn, lord of Badenoch,
who was killed in the convent of the Minor Friars, 1306, by Robert
Bruce, grandson of Isabel, the second daughter and co-heiress
of Earl David. (For an account of the Brereton family, who were
lords of Brereton in Cheshire, consult Ormerod's *History of Cheshire*,
and Lewis Dwnn's *Visitations*.)

[1] John Brereton, of Esclusham, was the second son of Owen
Brereton, Esq., and Elizabeth, his first wife.

[2] *Harl. MSS.*, 1969.

6, Matthew; together with two daughters, the eldest
of whom, Jane, married Owen Bady, the son of Roger
Bady, Esq., of Rhiwabon, descended from Cynwrig ab
Rhiwallon, while Elizabeth, the second daughter, be-
came the wife of John Lloyd, the son of John Lloyd of
Coed Christionydd (who was living in 1620) ab Richard
Lloyd ab Ellis Lloyd of Llwyn Ynn.

Edward Lloyd, of Eglwysegl, M.A., died, in his
father's life-time, in Cambridgeshire, leaving by Rebecca, his wife, daughter of the Rev. Mostyn Piers, of
Cambridge, two young children—Catherine, who was
subsequently married to John Powell, of Rhuddallt,
eldest son of Daniel Powell, son of David Powell, D.D.,
Vicar of Rhiwabon, the celebrated Welsh historian, a
lineal descendant of Llewelyn Aurdorchog, and one
son,

Edward Lloyd, who succeeded his grandfather at
Plâs-Madog. He married Elizabeth, only daughter
and heiress of Owen Lloyd ab William Lloyd,[1] by
whom he had issue—1, John, of Plâs-Madog, a captain
in the royal army, who in 1660 was one of the seven
Denbighshire gentlemen deemed fit and qualified to be
made a Knight of the Royal Oak. At that date his
estate was valued at £800.[2] He was living in 1667, but
was killed in London with Sir Evan Lloyd, of Bodidris. 2, William, who died without issue. 3, Samuel,
who succeeded at Plâs-Madog; and one daughter,
Anne, married to William Lloyd, of Plâs-Benion and
Tref-y-Nant, in the parish of Rhiwabon, descended
from Edwin ab Goronwy.

Samuel Lloyd, of Plâs-Madog, married Sarah, second
daughter and co-heiress of Luke Lloyd, Esq., of the
Bryn, in the parish of Hanmer, descended from Tudor
Trefor, by whom he had issue, beside a younger son
Luke who died without issue, an elder son,

Edward Lloyd, of Plâs-Madog, who died August,
8th, 1760, having married Anne, second daughter and

---

[1] See preceding page.
[2] *Gwaith Gwalter Mechain*, ii, 192.

co-heiress of William Lloyd, of Plâs-Benion and Tref-y-Nant, second son of Joseph Lloyd, of Castle Lyons, in Ireland, second son of John Lloyd, of Coed Christionydd, descended from Edwin ab Goronwy. Mrs. Lloyd died September 23rd, 1745, leaving issue one son and five daughters—

Edward Lloyd, who married Margaret, second daughter and co-heiress of Thomas Lloyd,[1] of Trevor Hall, and Glanhafon, high-sheriff for Montgomeryshire in 1716, and Mary, his wife, but died without issue in 1734, aged eighteen.

1. Elizabeth was the first daughter. The eldest daughter, *Elizabeth*, who was born April 31st, 1718, was married at Erbistog, April 30th, 1743, to *Jenkyn*[2] *Lloyd*, Esq.,of Clochfaen, in the parish of Llangurig (*supra*).

2, Mary married Edward Williams, who assumed the name of Lloyd upon his succeeding to the estate of Pen-y-lan,[3] in the parish of Rhiwabon, and had issue an only daughter, Mary Lloyd, heiress of Pen-y-lan, who married Roger Kenyon, Esq., of Cefn, brother of Lloyd, first Lord Kenyon, and son of Lloyd Kenyon, Esq., by whom she had issue Edward Lloyd, who succeeded at Pen-y-lan, George, Thomas, Jane, and Anna Maria.

3, Anne, who received for her share of the property Plâs-Benion and Tref-y-Nant, married John Rowland, Esq.

4, Margaret became the wife of Robert Ingram, Esq., of Neuadd Glyn-Hafren, in the parish of Llanidloes,

---

[1] Thomas Lloyd, the high sheriff in 1716, was the eldest son of Oliver Lloyd, Esq., by Mary, daughter and co-heiress of Robert Lloyd, Esq., of Glanhafon, high sheriff for Montgomeryshire in 1685 (see note, *supra*, p. 289.)

[2] *Supra*, p. 280.

[3] The Lloyds of Pen-y-lan, in the parish of Rhiwabon, were a younger branch of the Lloyds of Ceiswyn, in the parish of Tal-y-Llyn, in the county of Merionydd, who were descended from Gwaethfoed, lord of Cardigan, who bore *or*, a lion rampant regardant *sable*.

(grandson of Richard Ingram, Esq., of the same place, high-sheriff for Montgomeryshire, 1680) and had issue Edward, the father of the late Robert Ingram, a distinguished captain in the Royal Navy, who sold the old family residence; Robert and Mary: arms, *ermine* on a fess *gules*, three escallops *or*.

5, Bennette, married to Lewis Lewis, of Rhuddalt.

A PAROCHIAL ACCOUNT OF LLANGURIG.

Continued from vol. ii, p. 300.

THE following verbal blazon of the arms of J. Y. W. Lloyd, Esq. (see Engraving opposite p. 62, etc.), was unintentionally omitted from chap. v.

1. Quarterly: 1st and 4th, party per pale, erminois and ermine, a lion ramp. *sa.*, between two flanches *gu.*, charged with three annulets *or ;* 2nd and 3rd party per bend sinister ermine and ermines, a lion ramp. *or.* Lloyd of Clochfaen.

2. *As.*, a lion ramp. party per fess *or* and *arg.*, in a border of the third charged with eight annulets *sa.* Lluddocaf ab Caradoc, Earl of Hereford.

3. Quarterly : 1st and 4th *gu.*, a lion ramp. regard. *or ;* 2nd and 3rd *arg.*, three boars' heads couped *sa.*, tusked *or.* Maurice Vychan, of Kerry and Mochdref.

4. *Sa.*, three greyhounds courant in pale *arg.*, in a border indented *or.* Angharad, wife of Howel, second son of Tudor ab Einion Fychan (lord of Cefn-y-llys), and d. and h. of Llewelyn ab Madog ab Ranulph of Mochdref.

5. As 3. For Annesta, wife of Einion ab Howel ab Tudor of Mochdref, and d. and h. of Adda ab Meirig ab Adda of Kerry.

6. *Az.*, on a chevron *arg.*, between three lions passant guardant *or*, three crosses moline *sa.* Fowler, of Abbey Cwmhir.

7. Barry of six pieces *gu.* and *arg.*, on a chief *or*, a lion passant *as.* Englefield, of Rycote, Oxfordshire.

8. *As.*, two bars *arg.*, over all a bend compony *or* and *gu.* Lee, of Morpeth.

9. Per bend sinister ermine and ermines, a lion rampant *or.* Lloyd, of Plâs Madog.

10. Lluddocaf ab Caradoc. (See 2.)

11. *Vert*, semó of broomslips, a lion rampant *or.* Sandde Hardd, lord of Morton.

12. *Or*, a lion rampant *as.* Cadwgan, lord of Nannau.

13. *Vert*, three eagles displayed in fess *or.* David ab Owen, Prince of North Wales.

14. *Sa.*, three lions passant in pale *arg.* Madoc yr Athraw, of Plâs Madog.

15. Ermine, a lion rampant *as.* Howel Grach ab Llewelyn of Bodylltyn.

16. *Or*, a lion rampant *gu.* David ab Gruffydd ab Gwenwynwyn, lord of Caereinion.

17. Lloyd, of Plâs Madog. (See 9.)

18. *Arg.*, two bars *sa.* Brereton, of Borasham.

19. *Arg.*, a chevron inter three crescents *gu.* Ipstans, of Ipstans.

20. *Or*, two ravens proper. Corbet, of Wattlesborough.

Crests.

1. On a wreath *or* and *sa.* a lion ramp. *sa.*, a fleur-de-lys issuing out of his mouth, and supporting an antique shield *gu.*, charged with three annulets interlaced *or.* Lloyd, of Clochfaen.

2. On a wreath *or* and *gu.* a lion ramp. regardant *or.* Maurice Fychan.

3. On a wreath *or* and *az.* an owl *arg.* crowned *or.* Fowler.

4. On a wreath *arg.* and *sa.* a demi lion rampant *sa.* holding a wreath of laurel proper. Lloyd, of Plâs Madog.

M

CHAP. VI.—GENEALOGICAL.

CEFN-YR-HAFODAU, GLANSEVERN, AND UPPER GLANDULAS.

CADIFOR (ab Dyfnwal ab Gwynn ab Aelaw ab Alser ab Tudwal Gloff, lord ╪ Catherine, d. of of Dyfed, fifth son of Rhodri Mawr), lord of Castle Howel, who lived during │ Rhys, Prince of the reign of Henry II. *Sa.*, a spear-head *arg.*, embrued between three │ South Wales. scaling-ladders of the second two and one ; on a chief *gu.* a tower triple towered ppr.

Rhydderch, lord of Castle Howel ╪ Jennett, d. of Sir Rhys ab Bledri, Knight of the Holy
 │ Sepulchre.

Rhys = ...d. of Sir Elidyr Ddu, Knight of St. John of Jerusalem.

Rhys Foel of Gilfachwen, cir. 1290 ╪

Howel of Gilfachwen ╪

Howel Fychan ╪ Gwerfyl, d. of Rhydderch ab Ieuan Lloyd of Glyn Aeron.

Dafydd ab Howel Fychan of Gilfachwen ╪

Rhys ab Dafydd ╪ ...... d. of Llewelyn ab Howel ab Gwion.

Howel ab Rhys ╪ Jane, d. and c.-h. of Dafydd Fwya, derived from Aleth, king of Dyfed.   Ieuan.

Llewelyn ab Howel ╪ Angharad, d. of Llewelyn ab Philip (descended from Madog Danwr), heiress of Cefn-yr-Hafodau.   Rhys (p. 84.)

Jenkyn of Cefn-yr-Hafodau = Catherine (2nd wife), d. of Jenkyn ab David ab Rhys ab Ieuan.
 │
 a

¹ This portion of the pedigree differs materially from that given in the Add. MS. 98i:4.

a

Thomas = Margaret, d. Owen ab Ieuan, from Bleddyn ab Cynfyn.

Dafydd = Catherine, d. of Jenkyn ab Dafydd ab Rhys ab Ieuan ab Howel ab Rhys ab David ab Howel Fychan.

Owen = Margaret, d. and heir of Gruffydd Gwyn of Dôl-llys (living 1599).

¹ Jenkyn Owen, of Cefn-yr-Hafodau = ...   ¹ Edward Owen, of Dôl-llys.

Owen Owen, of Cefn-yr-Hafodau = Mary.

Owen Owen, of Cefn-yr-Hafodau = Matilda, relict of Samuel Lloyd, of Bwlch-y-garreg; ob. 1736.   Morgan, living 1685 = Patience.

David Owen; b. 1700, = Frances, d. of John Rogers, of Cefn-y-   Dorothy.   John;   Elizabeth,   Rev. R. Owen,   Thos. Owen,
ob. 1777.   Bernin, in Kerry; ob. 1754, aged 66.   ob. 1733.   ob. 1740.   of Iford.   of London.

Owen Owen; b. 1723, = Anne, d. and h. of   Richard Owen, of = Miss Stevens.   Edw. Owen, M.A.;   Capt. Wm. Owen, ob. 1778,
High Sheriff 1766, ob.   Charles Davies,   Upper Glan-   ob. s. p. 1807.   father of Adml. Sir Ed. Owen
1789.   Esq. of Llivior.   Dules.   and Vice-Adml. W. F. Owen.

William Owen, of Upper   Richard Owen, of New- = Miss Baxter,   Francis; ob. 1849.   Jane.
Glandulas; ob. 1833,   town, solicitor; ob. 1826   of the Book.   They succeeded their elder brother, but
aged 70, s. p.   dying unm. left Glandulas to their neph.

Rich. Owen, of Glan-   J. B. Owen suc. his bro- = Anne Evans.   Wil-   Edward.   David.   Henry.   Char-
dulas; ob. s. p.   ther; living 1870.   liam.   lotte.

J. B. Owen = Elizabeth, d. of J. Brown, Esq.   Frances = David Kinsey.

Sir A. D. Owen, Knt., of   David   William Owen, of = Anne Warburton Owen, only child of Capt.   Mary, ux. Thomas Jones, Esq.,
Glansevern; High She   Owen,   Glansevern, K.C.;   Slaughter, and relict of the Rev. Thomas   of Garthmyl, and mother of A.
riff 1814, ob. s. p. 1816.   M.A.   ob. 1837.   Coupland, of the Priory, Chester.   J. Johnes, Esq.

The authority for the early part of this pedigree is Dwnn (i, 143), and the late Rev. Walter Davies, who compiled the article on the Owens of Glansevern, in Burke's *Landed Gentry*. Mr. Davies's article does not agree with Dwnn, i, 309.

M 2

CEFN-YR-HAFODAU.

Harl. MSS, 1973, 1969; Add. MS, 9864.

LLEWELYN ab Ho-wel ab Rhys ab David ab Howel Fychan of Gilfach-wen, co. Cardigan. = Angharad, d. and h. of Llewelyn ab Philip of Cefn-yr-Hafodau ab Llewelyn ab Philip ab Iorwerth ab Gruffydd ab Madog Danwr. = Rhys ab Llewelyn ab David Chwith of Cyn-wyl-Gaio ab Rhys ab Iorwerth, to Cadifor ab Selyf (p. 91).

Angharad, heiress, ux. Evan ab Rhys ab Adda, ancestor of the 2nd son.

2nd wife.

Ieuan, of Nenadd Glyn-Hafren, ancestor of the Wynns of Dol-bachog (Lewis Dwnn, i, 302).

Angharad, d. of Gruffydd Goch ab Mere-dydd ab David ab Gruffydd ab Mere-dydd Ddu. *Az., a lion passant arg.* = Jenkyn, of Cefn-yr-Hafodau. = Catherine, d. of Jenkyn ab David ab Rhys ab Ieuan.

1st wife.

2nd wife.

Ieuan Wynn, of Cefn-yr-Hafodau. = Catherine, d. of Jenkyn Goch, of Clochfaen.

Thomas =

Llewelyn Lloyd = ux. Gruffydd ab Gwy-lym ab Gruffydd ab Gruf-fyd Durwas.

Malli, ux. Mere-dydd ab Howel ab Maurice.

Gwenllian, ux. Howel ab Owen ab Y Bedo of Llanidloes.

David = Cadwallader =

Owen, 1599. Owen, 1599.

David of Glascrug, in = Margaret, d. of David ab Llewelyn ab Ieuan Goch.

Thomas = Gwenllian, d. of Jenkyn ab Ieuan of Llangurig ab Y Bedo ab Cadwgan.

Lewis = Mallt, d. of Llewelyn ab Mau-rice ab Llewelyn ab David ab Meredydd ab Madog.

John. Jen- David. kyn.

Ieuan = Lowry, d. of David ab Llewelyn ab Y Bedo ab Gruffyd ab Llewelyn Goch.

Lowry. Catherine.

James. Margaret. Maude. Jane. Catherine.

Lewis = Margaret, d. of David ab Mor-gan ab Ieuan ab David ap Gruffydd.

Morgan = Annesta, d. of Jenkyn ab David ab Rhys ab David ab Howel ab Adda.

Owen = Margaret, d. of Ieuan Gwynn ab Gwilym ab Rhys.

Rhys = Lowry, d. of David ab Rhys ab Gutto ab Meredydd.

John = Goleu, d. of Evan ab Maurice ab Jen-kyn of Crugnant. (p. 89).

| a

| b

| a

Elen, ux. Maurice ab Owen ab John Goch ab Maurice Goch ab David ab Gruffydd Lloyd ab David ab Howel Ddu to Aleth, king of Dyfed.

| b

Catherine, ux. Rhys ab Ieuan ab John ab David.

The Cefn-yr-Hafodau estate became the property of the Lloyds of Clochfaen by purchase, and was sold in 1781. The farms of Cefn-yr-Hafodau and Glascrug were purchased by the late Thomas Evans, Esq., of Maenol, near Llanidloes, and were by him bequeathed to his grandniece, Mrs. Phillips, of the Vicarage, Aberystwith, the present owner.

1 For the arms of Llewelyn, and his descent from Cadifor, see preceding pedigree.

CWM-YR-ONN : TOWNSHIP OF CEFN-YR-HAFODAU.

THIS farm, which is generally called Cwm-fron, is situated about two miles south of Llanidloes, on the roadside to Tylwch, and is now the property of Mrs. Mears.

SKISYLLT, lord of Mathafarn ⊤ Nesta, d. of Goronwy ap Einion, Prince of Tegeingl.

Einion, lord of Mathafarn. *Arg.*, a lion ⊤ Agnes, or Annesta, d. of Madog ap Cadwgan, pass. inter 3 fleurs-de-lys *gu.* | lord of Nannau. *Or*, a lion raunp. *az.*

Goronwy, lord of Mathafarn ⊤ Methefys, d. of Owen Cyfeiliog, Prince of Powys. *Or*, a | lion rampant *gu.*

Tudor, lord of Mathafarn ⊤ Gwenllian, d. and heiress of Meredydd ab Uchdryd ab Edwyn | ab Goronwy, Prince of Tegeingl.

Llewelyn, lord of Mathafarn ⊤ Gwenllian, d. and heiress of Llewelyn ab Howel ab Madog | to Elystan Glodrudd.

Ieuan Llwyd, lord of Mathafarn ⊤ Mabli, d. of Philip Fongam ab Meredydd Benwyn, of | Arwystli, descended from Brochwel Ysgythrog.

David, 3rd son ⊤ 1. Gruffydd, lord of Mathafarn ⊤ 2. Llewelyn Gogof, Esq.

| a

Llewelyn=Elen, d. of Howel ab Ieuan Blaeney, of Ystymgwen, Esq. *Sa.*, three horses' heads erased *arg.*
1st wife.

....d. of Howel ab ¹Gruffydd Derwas, of Cemaes=Gruffydd Mowddwy=Efa, d. of Meredydd ab Rhys ab Ieuan ab David Goch,
ap Meurig Lloyd, Lord of Nannau. (Her mother   2nd wife.   of Caelan, in Llanbrynmair. *Gu.*, three snakes en-
was Elen, d. of David Lloyd, of Newtown Hall.)   nowed.

Janet, d. of Gwilym ab ¹Gruffydd Derwas, of Cemaes, Esquire=Howel Mowddwy.=Gwenllian, d. of Rhys ab Ieuan ab Rhys ab
of the body to Henry VI, and son of Meurig Llwyd, lord of   ab David ab Howel Fychan, of Gilfachwen,
Nannau.   descended from Tudur Mawr, according to some
                                                                             MSS., but, according to others, descended from
                                                                             Cadifor ab Dyfnwal, p. 80.

Machallt, ux. Maurice ab Llewelyn, second son of Ieuan ab Gruffyd, of Clochfaen ; secondly, Llewelyn ab Ieuan Ddu, of Esgair-graig (see that pedigree).

Lewis of Cwm-yr-Onn=Elen, d. of Ieuan ab David ab Llewelyn Goch.

Rhys of Cwm-yr-onn=   David.

Dyddgu, ux. David ab John ab David of Llanidloes, descended from Meredydd Benwyn.

¹ "Meuric Lloyd had also Howel Sele, Griffith Derwas, Rees, and (as some say) Llewelyn Goch, who married an heir at
Darowen, in the county of Montgomery....... Griffith Derwas, Esq. of the body of King Henry VI, became tutor and guardian
to Meuric Vaughan, sonne to his brother, Howel Sele, and was chiefest man in command in our country all his tyme. He had
two sonnes, Howel the eldest, and Gwillim, the 2 sonne, whose mother was an heretrix of Kemes, in the county of Montgomery,
where his posteritie are very flourishing at this day. Gr. Derwas had many daughters, whom he preferred to great houses, as Cwchwillan, Ynys-maengwyn, Plas-du, Madryn, and Penllech, &c."—Robert Vaughan, of Hengwrt, 1649 (*Arch. Camb.*, 1868, pp. 131-133).

LLANGURIG.

Rhys ab Howel ab Rhys ab David of Gilfachwen. (*Vide* Cefn-yr-Hafodau pedigree.)=

Morgan of Llangurig=   Goleubryd, d., ux. Jenkyn ab Llewelyn ab Ieuan ab Gruffyd of Clochfaen (p. 90).

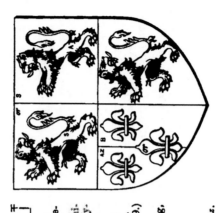

Rhys of Llangurig ╤

     a | b |
Catherine, ux. Jenkyn ab Maurice of Clochfaen. (*Add. MS.* 9865.)

Ieuan of Llangurig ╤ Gwenllian, d. of Lewis ab Lewis of Abermayde, co. Cardigan. *Gu.*, a griffin segreant or.   Angharad, ux. Maurice Herbert, son of William Herbert, of Park, ab Sir Richard Herbert, Knt. Party per pale *az.* and *gu.*, three lions ramp. or.

Jenkyn of Llangurig ╤ ......   Elen, ux. Thomas ab Rhys ab Maurice ab Llewelyn ab Ieuan ab Gruffydd of Llangurig (p. 80).

Evan of Llangurig, 1593 = Elen, d. of Morgan Herbert, of Hafod Uchdryd, co. Cardigan, Esq.

LLANGURIG (Lewis Dwnn).

Rhys Lloyd, of Creuddyn, co. of Cardigan, ab Gruffyd ab Jeuan ab Llewelyn ab Rhys ╤ ab Gruffyd ab Rhys ab Iorwerth ab Cadifor ab Gwaethfod, lord of Cardigan

Llewel = Efa, d. of Gruffydd ab Llewelyn of Creuddyn.   Jenkyn of Llangurig ╤ ...

David ╤ of Llangurig.

Rhys ╤ of Llangurig.

Margaret, ux. Rhys ab Maurice ab Llewelyn, 2nd son of Ieuan ab Gruffydd of Clochfaen.

Goleubryd, ux. David ab Llewelyn ab Ieuan Blaeney ab Philip ab Ieuan Fychan ab Ieuan ab Rhys ab Llowdden, lord of Uwch-Aeron. (*Harl. MS.*, 1969.)

Llewel = Efa, d. of Gruffydd ab Llewelyn of Creuddyn, descended from Collwyn ab Tango, lord of Eifionydd and Ardudwy. *Sa.*, a chev. inter 3 fleurs-de-lys *arg.* (*Harl. MS.*, 1973.)

John of Llangurig, living in 1543.

Margaret, ux. Maurice ab Jenkyn Goch, of Clochfaen. (*Harl. MS.*, 1973.)   Jenkyn of Llangurig ╤ ... (*Add. MS.* 9865.)

Florence, ux. Llewelyn Fychan ab Llewelyn ab David Esgairgraig (p. 89).

Arms. — 1. *Or*, a lion ramp. regard. *sa.*   2. *Sa.*, a lion ramp. *arg.*   3. Party per pale *az.* and *sa.*, three fleurs-de-lys or.   4. As the first.

LLANGURIG.

Harl. MS. 1973; Add. MS. 9865.

Rhys ab Adda ab Howel, of Henfaes, in Kerry, Esq., ab Adda Ddu ab Gruffydd, of⹋Isabel, d. of David Lloyd ab David ab Maesmawr, ab Meredydd ab Einion ab Cynfelin ab Dolphyn ab Rhiwallon ab Madog | Howel Ddu, of Arwystli. *Az.*, three cocks ab Cadwgan, lord of Nannau. | *arg.*, crested and wattled or.

Evan, ancestor   Maurice of⹋Gwenllian, d. and heiress of Maurice ab David Tabarn ab   David of⹋Golenbryd, d. of Ieuan ab of the Gwrynns   Llangurig. | David Lloyd ab Llewelyn ab Gruffydd Ddu ab Gruffydd of   Llangu- | Gruffydd, of Clochfaen. of Llanidloes. | Maesmawr.   *Az.*, a lion pass. *arg.*   rig.

Golenbryd, d. of Thomas ab Rhys Ddu, ⹋ Llewelyn of Llangurig ⹋ Elen, d. of Maurice ab Jenkyn Goch,   Jenkyn. of Pont-y-Rhyd-galed. | of Clochfaen.

[1] Jenkyn Man-⹋Mary, d. of William Herbert,   [2] John Fychan⹍Mary, d.   Gwenllian, ux. John   [2] David   [2] Morgan, living 1548, rice, of Llan- | of Park, Esq.   Party per   of John   ab Thomas ab Rhys   Lloyd.   and was High Consta- gurig. | pale *az.* and *gu.*, three lions   ab Mau-   ab David Lloyd.   ble of the Hundred of | ramp. *arg.*   rice.   Llanidloes 8th Eliz.

Richard Maurice, of⹋Catherine, d. of Edward Maurice ab   Jane, ux. Richard Williams,   Elizabeth, ux Jenkyn, son of David Llangurig, 1599. | John ab Evan Gwynn.   of Llwynrhyddod.   Lewis, vicar of Llangurig.

Edward Maurice.   Jane Maurice.   Ursula Maurice.   Margaret Maurice.

Arms.—1. *Az.*, a lion passant *arg.*, for Einion ap Cynfelin, Esq., lord of Manafon. 2. *Or*, a lion ramp. *az.*, for Cadwgan, lord of Nannau. 3. *Or*, a lion ramp. *gu.*   Bleddyn ab Cynfyn, Prince of Powys. 4. As the first.

[1] Name appears on Grand Jury List, 10th Eliz.
[2] Their names are mentioned on the Gaol File, 35th Henry VIII.   (*Mont. Coll.*, ii, 376.)

LLANGURIG.   (*Add. MS. 9865*).

Thomas ab Gwilym ab Ieuan ab Philip ab Rhydderch ab Ieuan Llwyd of Glyn Aeron ab Ieuan ab⹋Gwerfyl, d. of David ab Gruffyd Foel ab Ifor ab Cadifor ab Gwaethfod, lord of Cardigan.   *Or*, a lion ramp. regard. *sa.* | Philip ab Jenkyn.

¹ᵃ
Lewis ⊤ Tangwystl, d. of Jenkyn ab David ab Ieuan Fychan ab Ieuan ab Rhys ab Philip ab Rhydderch ab Ieuan Llwyd, of Glyn
| Aeron.

Evan ⊤ Anne, d. of Morgan ab Ieuan ab Gwilym   David Lewis, ⊤ Marg., d. of Howel   Thomas of ⊤ Gwenllian, d. of Maurice
| ab Ieuan ab Philip ab Rhydderch ab   vicar of Llan- | ab Philip ab Rhys   Nantgwnlle | ab David ab Owen.
| Ieuan Llwyd.   gurig. | ab David.

Thomas Evans, = Tangwystl, d. of Ieuan ab David ab Deio ab Gruffydd   Jenkyn, = Elizabeth, d. of Jenkyn Maurice   Richard,
1599.   ab Meredydd ab Rhys ab Ieuan ab Rhys ab Llowdden,   1599.   ab Llewelyn ab Maurice ab   1599.
lord of Uwch-Aeron.   Rhys (p. 86).

LLANGURIG. (Harl MS. 4181.)

IORWERTH ab Meredydd ⊤ .... d. of Ieuan Goch ab Goronwy ab Meilir of Geneu'r Glyn ab Gwallog ab Gwrgenen Fychan ab
ab Madog Danwr. | Gwrgeneu ab Hoedliw ab Cadwgan ab Elystan Glodrudd. Gu., a lion ramp. regard. or.
(Lewis Dunn.)

Madog ⊤   Einion ⊤   Philip ⊤   Margaret, ux. Meredydd ap Ieuan Glyn of Glyn Clywedog.

Meredydd ⊤   Gruffydd ⊤   Gruffydd Goch ⊤ Alice, d. of Rhys ab Meredydd ab Owen, lord of the Towyn, co. Cardigan.
| (Add. MS. 9865.)

Ieuan ⊤   Rhys Ddu ⊤ David Lloyd, of Berthlloyd ⊤   Ieuan ⊤ Angharad, d. of Adda ab Howel ab Adda Ddu, of Henfaes, in Kerry

Ieuan ⊤ Gwenllian, d. of Llewelyn   Gwenhwyfar, heiress of Berth-   Gwenllian, ux. Jeuan   Tangwystl, ux. Meredydd ab
Bwl. | ab Ieuan Goch.   lloyd, ux. Philip ab Ieuan Bwl.   ab Gruf. of Clochfaen.   Rhys Fychan ab Rhys Ddu.

Philip, jure ux. ⊤ Llewelyn ± Margaret, d. of Ieuan ab David ab Ieuan ab Gutto of Crenddyn ab Gruffydd ab Meredydd ab Rhys
of Berthlloyd | ab Ieuan ab Rhys ab Llowdden. Gu. a griffin segreant or.

Ieuan of Berthlloyd ⊤

Jenkin.   David ⊤ Gwenllian, d. of David ab Llewelyn Lloyd.
David.

LLANGURIG.   (*Harl. MSS.* 1969, 2299, 1949.)

PHILIP ab Gruffydd ab Meredydd ab Madog Danwr ᵮ

Ieuan ᵮ Myfanwy, eldest d. and c.-h. of David Fychan of Manafon,   Philip Fychan ᵮ Myfanwy, d. of Hugh ab Madog   Iorwerth.
fourth in descent from Cynfelin, lord of Manafon. | Fychan of Muellenydd.

Lucy, ux. Ednyfed ab Gruffydd ab Jorwerth ab Einion   Tangwystl, ux.   ......ux. Meilir ab   Lucy, ux. Adda ab Howel ab Adda
Goch, of Sonlli, ancestor of the Sontleys of Sontley.   Llewelyn, 'Vaer   Llewelyn   Ddu, of Henfaes, in Kerry, ancestor
Erm., a lion ramp. sa.   (Lewis Dwnn.)   of Llanidloes.   Fychan.   of the Gwynns of Llanidloes.

¹ This Llewelyn, "Mayor of Llanidloes", was living cir. 1350. His daughter Margaret was married to Gruffydd of Pen-rhudd-
lan. (Lewis Dwnn, ii, 23.)

ESGAIRGRAIG : TOWNSHIP OF LLANYWARED.

Harl. MSS. 4181, 2299.

THE estate of Esgairgraig became a part of the Clochfaen property; but, in 1781, on the death of Sarah, widow of
Rhys Lloyd, Esq., it passed by mortgage into the hands of Mr. Evans, of Neuadd, in Radnorshire; and the Sheepwalk of Esgair-
graig became the property of Mr. Prys of Pant-drain.

IEUAN ab Gruffydd ab Meredydd ab Madog Danwr. ᵀ Annesta, d. of Meredydd ab Ieuan ab Madog of Manafon.

Philip = ...

Ieuan Dwn = ...d. of David Lloyd ab Howel ab Adda.

Ieuan Ddu = Jessie, d. of Ieuan ap Meredydd ab Howel of Kerry.

David ᵀ Deilu, d. of Rhys ab Adda ab David ab Meredydd.   *Gu.*, a lion ramp. regard. *or*.

Llewelyn = Mallt, d. of Howel Mowddwy, Esq.   *Arg.*, a lion pass. *sa.*, inter 3 fleurs-de-lys *gu.* (p. 84).

a

Jenkyn of=Margaret, d. of David ab Morgan Esgair-graig, ab Ieuan, descended from Llow-ddon, lord of Uwch-Aeron. *Gu.*, 1588. a grif. segreant or.

b

Llewelyn=Florence, d. of Jenkyn ab David ab Jenkyn Fychan. of Llangurig, descended from Gwaithfoed, lord of Cardigan. *Or*, a lion ramp. reg. *sa.*

c

Gwenhwyfar, ux. Jenkyn ab Llewelyn ab Maurice of Llangurig (post).

Elizabeth.

Jenkyn ab=...... d. of Thomas ab Jenkyn Bedo ab Philip of Rhaiadr-gwy.

David=Anne, d. of Rhys ab James of Pontyrhydgaled.

John.

Deilu, ux. Rhys ab Thomas ab Y Bedo of Trefeglwys.

Dyddgu, ux. David ab Meredydd ab Lewis of Trefeglwys.

Gwenllian, ux. Evan ab Lewis ab Evan ab Llewelyn Goch of Gwrthrynion.[1]

[1] Formerly part of the lordship of Arwystli.

CRUGNANT : TOWNSHIP OF LLAN-Y-WARED.

CRUGNANT is now a farm on the left bank of the Wye, rather more than a mile to the south of the village, and was formerly the residence of the Rev. Morris Anwyl, vicar of the parish. It was purchased by Edward Fowler, of Abbey Cwmhir, Esq., and at his death in 1722 he left it to his niece Anne, daughter of Jenkyn Lloyd, of Clochfaen, and wife of Charles Richards, of Penglais, co. of Cardigan, Esq., from whom it was bought by Rhys Lloyd, of Clochfaen, and subsequently, with Cilgwrgan Fawr, passed by mortgage to Mr. Pryse, of Pant-drain, whose family originally came from Radnorshire.

Add. MS. 9865.

IEUAN OF CLOCHFAEN, eldest son of Maurice ab Jenkyn of Clochfaen. His=Elen, d. of Thomas Lloyd, third son of Rhys Lloyd name appears as one of the two coroners for the co., 8th Eliz. *Erm.*, a lion | ab Thomas Lloyd of Rhôs Fferrig, co. of Radnor, ramp., *sa.* in a border *gu.*, charged with eight annulets or. Esq. *Gu.*, a lion ramp. regardant or.

Thomas Lloyd, of Crugnant,=Elizabeth, d. of David ab Rhys ab Man- living in 1588. | rice ab Llewelyn of Llangurig (p. 90).

Jenkyn=...... Evan.

Goleubryd ux. John ab David ab Ieuan Gwynn of Glasgrûg (p. 82).

[1]Rhys ab Thomas Lloyd,=Catherine, d. of Evan ab Maurice ab Evan ab of Crugnant. | David of Llanwnog, descended from Einion ab Seisyllt.

Evan=Jane, d. of Rhys ab Thomas ab Y Bedo.

Florence, ux. David ab Evan ab David ab Owen.

Thomas. Edward. Anne.

Evan ab Rhys, of Crugnant.

[1] Rhys ab Thomas Lloyd's name appears on the jury list at the Assize held in Llanidloes 1606.

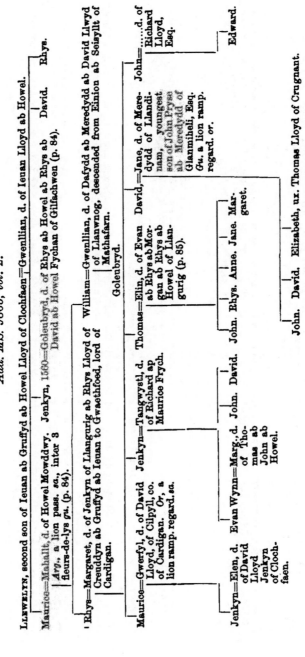

LLANGURIG.

Add. MS. 9865, vol. 2.

LLEWELYN, second son of Ieuan ab Gruffyd ab Howel Lloyd of Clochfaen=Gwenllian, d. of Ieuan Lloyd ab Howel.

Maurice=Mahallt, d. of Howel Mowddwy. Arg., a lion pass. sa., inter 3 fleurs-de-lys gu. (p. 84). — Jenkyn, 1560=Golenbryd, d. of Rhys ab Howel ab Rhys ab David ab Howel Fychan of Gilfachwen (p. 84). — David. — Rhys.

¹Rhys=Margaret, d. of Jenkyn of Llangurig ab Rhys Lloyd of Crenddyn ab Gruffyd ab Ieuan to Gwaethfoed, lord of Cardigan.

William=Gwenllian, d. of Dafydd ab Meredydd ab David Llwyd of Llanwnog, descended from Einion ab Seisyllt of Mathafarn. Golenbryd.

Maurice=Gwerfyl, d. of David Lloyd, of Cilpyll, co. of Cardigan. Or, a lion ramp. regard. sa.

Jenkyn=Tangwystl, d. of Richard ap Maurice Frych.

Thomas=Elin, d. of Evan ab Rhys ab Morgan ab Rhys ab Howel of Llangurig (p. 85).

David,=Jane, d. of Meredydd of Llandinam, youngest son of John Prys ab Meredydd of Glanmiheli, Esq. Gu. a lion ramp. regard. or.

John=.....d. of Richard Lloyd, Esq.

Edward.

Jenkyn=Elen, d. of David Lloyd Jenkyn of Clochfaen.

Evan Wynn=Marg., d. of Thomas ab John ab Howel.

John. David. John. Rhys. Anne. Jane. Margaret.

John. David. Elizabeth, ux. Thomas Lloyd of Crugnant.

¹ Probably "Ricus Mores, gen", on the grand jury list 10th Eliz.

LLWYNRHYDDOD: TOWNSHIP OF LLANIFYNI.

Lewis Dwnn. Add. MSS. 9865.

SELYF, King of Dyfed ⊤ Elsa, d. and c.-h. of Gruffydd ab Morda Fryoh, lord of Cil-y-Cwm.
Erm., a chev. or, on a chief arg., a lion passant gu.

Cadifor ab Selyf, lord of Cil-y-cwm. ⊤ Lucy Fechan, d. of Einion ab Seisyllt, lord of
Arms: those of his mother. | Meirionydd.

Gruffydd, lord of Cil-y-Cwm ⊤ Janet, d. of Madog ab Howel, descended from Elystan
| Glodrudd.

Meurig Goch, lord ⊤ Lucy, d. and c.-h. of Gruffydd ab Rhys ab Rhydderch ab Cadifor ab
of Cil-y-Cwm. | Dyfnwal, lord of Castle Howel.

David, lord of Cil-y Cwm ⊤ Lucy, d. of Sir Gruffydd Lloyd, of Tregarnedd, Knt. *Gu.*, a
| chev. on a chief *arg.*, three ermine spots.

David Fongam, lord of Cil-y-Cwm ⊤ Gwenllian, d. of Gruffydd ab Cadwgan of Esgair Gaib,
(*Lewys Dwnn*, vol. i, p. 100). | Esq., descended from Eidio Wyllt, lord of Lliwel.

Gruffydd of Cynwil Gaio (*Lewys Dwnn*, vol. i, p. 226) ⊤

Meurig of Cynwil Gaio ⊤   Iorwerth of Cynwil Gaio (*Add. MS.* 15,017) ⊤

Gruffydd of Cynwil Gaio ⊤   Rhys of Cynwil Gaio (*Add. MS.* 15,017; *Lewys Dwnn*, vol. i, p. 226) ⊤

Meurig ⊤   David Chwith of Cynwil Gaio (*Add. MS.* 15,017) ⊤

David ⊤   Llewelyn of Cynwil Gaio ⊤

Gruffydd ⊤   Rhys of Cynwil Gaio (*Add. MS.* 15,017 ⊤ Angharad, d. and h. of Llewelyn ab Philip ab Llewelyn of Cefn-yr-Hafodau.

Gwilym ⊤   Llewelyn, ob. s. p.   Bedo, ob. s. p.   Angharad, ux. Ieuan ab Rhys, of Henfaes, Esq.

Jenkyn ⊨

William of Cynwyl Gaio ⊤ Elen, d. of Jenkyn ab Rhys David ab Thomas ab David of Blaen-cnn, in the parish of Pencareg, co.
| Carmarthen. (*Lewys Dwnn*, vol. i, p. 239.)

Jenkyn Williams of Llanidloes ⊤ Margaret, d. of Owen Gwynn of Llanidloes.   William ⊤ Margaret, d. of William ab Jenkyn.
Lewys Dwnn, vol. i, p. 240.)

[a]
Richard Williams,=Jane, d. of Jenkyn ab Llewelyn ab Maurice ab Rhys   Rhys. [b] He had a daughter, Catherine, wife of Morgan
of Llwynrhyddod. | ab Adda. *As.*, a lion pass. *arg.* (p. 86).   ab Thomas.

Lewis Williams, of Llwynrhyddod=Margaret, d. of Morgan Herbert, of Hafod Uchdryd, co. Cardigan, Esq.

Richard Williams,=Elen, d. of Cadwalladr Owen, of Llanbrynmair,   Jenkyn=Mary, d. of Hugh Lewis,   Matthew Williams, m.
of Llwynrhyddod. | Esq. *Gu.*, a lion ramp. regard. or.   Williams. of Ciliau, in Cardigansh.   Margaret, d. of Edw....

Lewis Williams, of Llwynrhyddod=Jane, d. of Edward Morgan, of Glan-hafren.

Jenkyn Williams, of Llwynrhyddod=Jane, d. of Rees Evans, of Cardiganshire.

The farm of Llwyn-rhyddod is situated on the left bank of the Wye, about two and a half miles above the village. It is now the property of Mr. Hugh Lloyd.

PONT-Y-RHYD-GALED: TOWNSHIP OF LLAN-Y-FYNU.

PONT-Y-RHYD-GALED, situated near the junction of the Rivers Tarenig and the Wye is now divided into two farms. The upper one belongs to Sir Watkin Williams-Wynn, Bart.; and the lower one to the widow of the late Mr. Richard Lewis, of Pont-dulas, in the parish of Llangurig.

Add. MS. 9865.

Rhys Ddu of Pont-y-rhyd-galed, second son of Gruffydd ab Howel=Margaret, d. of Ieuan ab Rhys Gethin of Creuddyn ab
Lloyd. *Erm.*, a lion ramp. *sa.*, in a border *gu.*, charged with eight | Ieuan ab Rhys ab Llowddyn, lord of Uwch-Aeron. *Gu.*, a
mullets *arg.*   griffin segreant or.

Thomas of Pont-y-rhyd-galed=Margaret, d. of Ieuan ab Gwilym ab Goronwy Gethin.

Ieuan of Pont-y-rhyd-galed=Dyddyn, d. of Ieuan ab Dio ab   Gwenllian, ux. Ieuan Wynn of   Goleubryd, ux. Llewelyn ab Mau-
Gruffydd ab Ieuan.   Dolbachog.   rice ab Rhys of Llangurig (p. 86).

James of Pont-y-rhyd-galed=Goleubryd, d. of Morgan ab Llewelyn ab David ab Richard.

Richard=Gwerfyl, d. of Evan ab Richard of   Rhys=Elen, d. of Gruffydd ab Llewelyn ab Maurice   William.   Owen.
| Cyfeiliog.   ab Ieuan ab Llewelyn.

[1] Evan Richards=........   Jenkyn.   John.   David.   Anne, ux. David ab Jenkyn ab Llewelyn of Llangurig (p. 89).

[1] The present representative of this family is Mr. William Richards, who is now tenant of Clochfaen. The Richards family have been tenants of Tan-yr-allt on the Clochfaen estate for the last two hundred and fifty years.

PEDIGREE OF THE FOWLERS, OF ABBEY CWMHIR, CO. RADNOR.

Heraldic Visitation of Shropshire. Harl. MS. 1570. Kimber's Baronetage.

Sir John Fowler, of Foxley, co. of Bucks, Knt., lineal descendant of Sir ..... d. and h. of — Loveday. This name occurs in the Richard Fowler, of Foxley, a crusader, *temp.* Rich. I. ┤ Roll of Battle Abbey.

Sir Henry Fowler, of Foxley, Knt. = —— sister and heiress of John Barton.

Sir William Fowler, of Bycote, co. Oxon, Knt. = Cecilia, d. and h. of Nicholas Englefield, of Bycote and Lanynton Gernon, co. Oxon.

Sir Richard Fowler, of Bycote, Knt. = Jane, d. of Sir John Danvers, of Colthorpe, co. Oxon, Knt.

Sir Richard Fowler, of Bycote, Knt. Thomas Fowler, Esq., of the = Margaret, d. of — Colville. *Or, ten billets gu.,* 4, 3, 2, 1.
body to Edw. IV.

Edward Fowler, of Twickenham = Alice (1) = Edith (2) = Margaret (3).

Roger Fowler, of Broomhill, co. of Stafford. = Isabella, d. and h. of William Lee, of Morpeth, Esq., Treasurer of Berwick, and
(3rd son.) sister to Bowland Lee, Bishop of Lichfield and Coventry, Lord President of the
Marches of Wales.

William Fowler, of Harnage Grange, co. of Salop. and of Middle Temple, *ob.* 1597 = Maria, d. of John Blythe, M.D.

Richard Fowler, of Harnage Grange, High Sheriff for Radnorshire, = Mary, eldest d. of Sir Ed. Littleton, of Pillaton Hall, co. of
1601, 1615, and 1626. Stafford, Knt.

William, Fowler, of Harnage Grange, Esq. = Anne, d. of Thomas Parks, of Willingworth, co. of Stafford.

Richard Fowler, of Harnage Grange, Esq., b. 1618, = Margaret, d. of Richard Lord Newport, of High Ercall, co. of Salop, and
Sheriff for Radnorshire, 1655. Rachel his wife, sister of Sir Richard Levison, of Trentham, Knt.

a

Francis Levison ⫽ Anne, d. of Peter Venables, Baron of Kinderton.
Fowler, Esq.

Frances, sole heiress ⫽ Thomas Needham, Lord Viscount Kilmorey.
⫽ Theophilus Hastings, Earl of Huntingdon.
⫽ The Chevalier de Ligonday, of the House of Auvergne, one of the French prisoners taken with Count Tallard at the battle of Hochstedt.

b

Sir William Fowler, ⫽ Mary, d. of of Harnage Grange, Sir Richd. created a Bart. 1704. Cotton, of Sheriff of Radnor- Comber- shire 1696; ob. 1717. mere Abbey, Bart.

c

John Fowler of Brondre fawr and Abbey Cwmhir, Sheriff of Radnorshire 1696; ob. 1696.

Edwd. Fowler, of Abbey Cwmhir, Sheriff 1715; ob. 1722.

Rachel, w. of Jenkyn Lloyd, co-heir.

d

Jane, w. of Geo. Robinson ob. s. p.

Col. Hodges ⫽ Sarah, ejected from Abbey Cwmhir by her brother.

Col. Geo. Hastings of Lat- ⫽ Sarah terworth, co. of Leicester. | Hodges

Hans Francis, eleventh Earl of Huntingdon, who claimed the Abbey.

Sir Richard Fowler, of Harnage ⫽ Sarah, d. and h. of William Grange, M.P. for Radnorshire, Sloane, brother of Sir Hans 1711-1722; ob. 1737. Sloane, Bart.

Sir William Fowler, of ⫽ Harriet, d. of Brig.-Gen. Harnage Grange; Newton; ob. 1738-9. drowned 1766.

Sir Hans Fowler, of Abbey ⫽ Miss Dilk. Cwmhir, Bart.; ob. 1771, s.p.

Thos. Hodges Fowler ⫽ Lucy, d. and c. h. of Abbey Cwmhir, | of Thom. Hill. ob. 1830.

Sarah Georgina, of Abbey ⫽ Rev. J. Du- Cwmhir, ejected by Mr. rant Baker, Fauntleroy, the forger. of Christ Ch. Cambridge.

Sir William Fow- | Lucy, Lætitia, Harriet. These ler died unmar- ladies married, and their de- ried at the scendants are still living, but Hague. none of them ever claimed Abbey Cwmhir.

ARMS.

1. Az., on a chev. arg., inter three lions passant gardant or, three crosses moline sa.   Fowler.
2. Party per pale arg., and sa., an eagle displayed with two necks counterchanged, gorged with a ducal coronet or.   Loveday.
3. Ermine, on a canton gu., an owl arg., crowned or.   Barton.
4. Barry of six gu. and arg., on a chief or, a lion passant az.   Englefield.
5. Arg., a chev. inter three rooks sa.   Clarke, of Bycote and Lanynton Gernon.
6. Arg., three wolves' heads erased gu., in a border az., charged with eight turrets or.   Bycote of Bycote.
7. Vaire, arg. and az.   Gernon, of Lanynton Gernon.
8. Az., two bars arg., over all a bend compony or and gu.   Lee, of Morpeth.
9. Vert, three goats rampant arg., attired or.   Trollope.

CHAP. VII.—BIOGRAPHICAL.

DAVIES, REV. DAVID was the son of Mr. Davies of Clochfaen Issa in this parish, where he was born in the year 1823.   He received the elements of his education in the village school of Llangurig, then conducted by Mr. Edward Rees, the parish clerk, and was subsequently placed in the office of the late Mr. T. E. Marsh, solicitor at Llanidloes.   His strict integrity, industry, and careful business habits commended him to the notice of his employer, who in a short time made him his head clerk.   His parents were anxious that he should adopt the law as his future profession, but a more intimate acquaintance with his employment, however, only created in him a distaste for it, and he felt a strong inclination to enter the church.   The late Rev. Evan Pugh, B.A., then Vicar of Llanidloes, encouraged him in his predilection, and gave him some excellent advice regarding his studies and preparation for his future calling.   His parents reluctantly consented to his entering St. David's College, Lampeter, through which he passed with credit, having gained Hannah Moore's scholarship.

In 1848 he was ordained deacon, and appointed to the curacy of Llanwnog by the Bishop of Bangor.   The vicar, Mr. James, who was previously connected with Llangurig, was advanced in years, so that the burden of the parochial work fell upon the young curate, who found plenty of employment to call forth the whole of his energies.   He laboured zealously to improve his parishioners both morally and intellectually; was the means of establishing the present excellent National school, having previous to its opening maintained a night school.   The neighbouring hamlet of Caersws seems to have inspired him with a strong love for archæology, and having turned his attention to the study, he employed his leisure in investigating the antiquities of the district.   His name

N

first appears on the list of the members of the Cambrian Archæological Association in 1853, when he was appointed one of the local secretaries for Montgomeryshire. At the general meeting of the society held at Ruthin in September 1854, Mr. Davies read a paper on "the Roman remains discovered at Caersws," and also exhibited some fragments of pottery discovered there, which were deposited in the temporary museum. He subsequently rendered further valuable service to the cause of Welsh archæology by conducting to their completion the excavations at Caersws: a detailed account of them has already been submitted to the members of the club. While at Llanwnog he was appointed diocesan inspector of schools for the deanery of Arwystli, was a contributor to the English *Journal of Education*, and was also a frequent writer to the Welsh newspapers and periodicals.

Mr. Davies in 1856 was collated by the Bishop of St. Asaph to the incumbency of the newly-formed ecclesiastical district of Dylife, worth about £200 a year. A handsome commodious church had been erected in this flourishing mountain mining village, at the cost principally of the lord of the manor, and the proprietors of the mines. No sooner was Mr. Davies appointed than he turned his attention to providing means for educating the children of Dylife. He was enabled in a short time to have a substantial National school erected. A comfortable parsonage was the next desideratum which claimed his energies, and this also he managed to get built. But he very imprudently took up his residence in his new house before it was thoroughly dried and well aired. The natural consequence was that he caught a severe cold, which brought a painful lingering illness which terminated fatally. He died at the Trewythan Arms Hotel, Llanidloes, on his way to the Clochfaen, February 12th, 1865. His remains were interred in Llangurig churchyard.

DAVIES, OWEN, a well known character in this and the neighbouring parish of Llanidloes, affords a striking example of perseverance and industry triumphing over difficulties in realising an ample fortune. His parents were in very humble circumstances; he was born in 1777, and passed his youth as a farm servant at the Beili, before he entered service at Llanidloes in the capacity of a labourer, at the New Inn. Here he manifested a very strong inclination for mechanics, especially clock and watch work, which seemed to possess a peculiar fascination for him. After some practice, he procured an old watch, which, after his day's work was done, he was in the habit of taking with him to the hay-loft, and there take it to pieces and rebuild it. By these means he thoroughly familiarised himself with the mechanism of a watch, and obtained a good insight into clock-work. Like most self-taught mechanics, he evinced more than ordinary skill in constructing tools out of the most unpromising materials; for he was not in a position at first to buy even the simplest appliances needed. When his skill became known to his neighbours, he was allowed to clean their clocks, the money thus gained being carefully expended upon the most useful tools. He was soon enabled to quit his calling of labourer for the more congenial one of clock-cleaner, eking out his time by glazing. By means of the most rigid economy he raised himself to the position of an employer of labour, and opened a fresh business as an ironmonger, and soon became known far and wide by his superior goods, especially in the cutlery department. Unfortunately the love of money proved stronger than the love for mechanics, and the latter part of his life was devoted wholly and solely to its acquisition. Even when he was a large landed proprietor, and the possessor of thousands, he lived in the same simple unpretending style, never indulging in the slightest luxury of food or dress, would not even pay for the services of servant or housekeeper to keep his house clean and cook his food, so that his eccentric manners passed into a proverb among those that knew him. He died October 17th 1862, in the eighty-sixth year of his age, and was buried in Llangurig churchyard. The bulk of his property he left among his poorer relatives; he was never married.

HOWEL, WILLIAM *(Gwilym Hywel)*, was a native of this parish, but spent the greater portion of his life at Llanidloes. He was born in the year 1705. We have no record of his early life or of his education, but we have ample proof that the latter was not neglected, and that it was supplemented by extensive reading and careful study up to the very last year of Mr. Howel's life. He held the post of steward upon the Berthlloyd estate in the neighbourhood of Llanidloes, and was chosen by his fellow-townsmen to be mayor of the borough.

He was not only a poet himself (several of his productions being published in his almanacks) but was a loving and industrious collector of the works of the old bards, and of those of his contemporary poets. One of his especial favourites was *Eos Ceiroig* (Huw Morris). Iolo Morganwg states that Mr. Howel had collected about three hundred of the productions of that prolific writer, doubtlessly with a view to publication. The late Rev. Walter Davies (Gwallter Mechain) made a more extensive collection, and published it in two volumes in 1828, and there is reason to believe that he availed himself of Mr. Howel's labours.

His fame, however, rests chiefly upon his astronomical abilities, and as the publisher of a series of Welsh almanacks, which in their day enjoyed great popularity. The old Welsh almanacks of the seventeenth and eighteenth centuries may be regarded as the precursors of the monthly magazines and other periodicals now so plentiful in the Welsh language, and were a kind of medium for the literary intercommunication of those days, being conducted and compiled by men of considerable literary pretensions. The series of annuals were kept up by a succession of different editors from the appearance of the first in 1680 up to the year 1780. But in the year 1770 the first Welsh magazine, the *Eurgrawn Cymraeg*, appeared, and deprived the old almanacks of some of their prominent characteristics. The first almanack compiled and published by Mr. Howel was issued in the year 1766 from the press of Eddowes of Shrewsbury, where the whole series—ten in number—were printed. Some notion of their contents may be formed from the following translation of the title page of that for the year 1770 :

"The Intelligencer of the Heavens or the Seasons, or a New Almanack for the Year of the World 5719, Year of Our Lord 1770, the 18th year of the New Style, the 10th year of the reign of George III, the 5th year of publication, and the 2nd year after leap year. Containing a correct calender for the twelve months of the year, showing the time of sunrise and sunset, phases of the moon, appointed feasts, aspects of the planets, etc. . . . . . Chronicles, lists of the M.Ps. and Sheriffs, fairs and markets of Wales, an[1] excellent elegy composed in the twenty-four metres, carols, new stanzas, etc. Collected by Gwilim Howel." Then follows an extract from the Bible, Eccles. xviii, 7, 8, and a list of the towns

---

[1] Among the principal poems published in the series may be mentioned—In No. 2. A pastoral poem, (*Bugeilgerdd*,) by Edward Richards of Ystrad-meirig, written in 1766 ; a Christmas carol by Sion Powel of Llansannan. In No. 3. An elegy on the death of the celebrated antiquary, Lewis Morris, written by Evan Evans in 1765, with valuable explanatory notes appended in English. In No. 4. An elegy written by Evan Evans on the death of another Welsh antiquary, Robert Davies of Llanerch ; a carol by Sion Powel ; stanzas on the new bridge at Pont-y-pridd, written by Lewis Hopcyn. In No. 5. Goronwy Owen's celebrated elegy on the death of Lewis Morris, written in the 24 metres, 1767 ; a carol by David Jones of Trefriw. In No. 6. Another elegy on Lewis Morris from the pen of Huw Hughes (*Bardd Coch*), and a carol by John Edwards clerk of Manafon. In No. 7. The *Bard's Confession*, by William Cynwal, 1580, and various poems by Dafydd Evan, Huw Hughes, and Rice Jones. No. 8 contains poems by Ieuan Brydydd Hir (the elder), Huw Hughes, John Rhys, Ioan Siencin, etc., and an account of the Eisteddfod at Llanidloes. No. 9. An ode in praise of Richard ab Sion (*Rhisiart Sion Greulon*), by Sion Tudor, 1580, with English explanatory notes by Mr. Howel. It was this poem that suggested to the Dean of St. Asaph the idea which he worked out in his *Legend of Captain Jones*. In No. 10. An elegy on the death of William Morris, by Evan Evans, 1764 ; carol by David Jones of Trefriw.

(embracing the most important in the principality) where the work might be obtained. " Printed and sold by J. Eddowes near the market-house, Shrewsbury, price 8*d*."

The instruments necessary for carrying on the study of astronomy were very costly, and in those days difficult to be procured in the centre of the principality. This difficulty Mr. Howel overcame to a considerable extent by turning his mechanical ingenuity (which was of no mean order) to the best account in constructing the more simple of the instruments which he needed in taking his observations. Some of these were for several years preserved at the Green, Llanidloes. In 1772 he succeeded in establishing annual local Eisteddfods, the first being held at the Red Lion Inn, Llanidloes. He died in 1775, and lies buried under the branches of the yew-tree at the entrance of the Llanidloes churchyard. An *englyn* (stanza) of his composition, which appeared in the last of his almanacks, has been engraved upon his tombstone.

OWENS of Cefn-yr-hafodau. In a parochial account of Llangurig it would not be just to the distinguished members of this family to pass them over without a fuller notice (however brief and imperfect) than that which is conveyed in the pedigree of the family, given previously. To the last, the representatives of the elder branch of the family asserted their connexion with the parish by styling themselves " of Glyngynwydd."

I. *David Owen*, who died in 1777, by his wife, Frances, was the father of a remarkable family of four sons. The eldest,

Owen Owen, who was born in the year 1723, in 1745 married Anne Davies, daughter, and eventually heiress, of Charles Davies, Esq., of Llivior, in the parish of Berriew (Aber-rhiw). Mrs. Owen's mother was Sarah Evans, daughter and heir of Edward Evans, Esq., the last male representative of the family of Evans of Rhyd-y-Carw, in the parish of Trefeglwys, who were descended from Llewelyn Aurdorchog. By his marriage

Mr. Owen acquired the estates of Rhyd-y-carw, Glan-rhiw, and Ty'n-y-coed.   He removed to the last about the year 1760.   In the year 1766 he served the office of high sheriff of Montgomeryshire, and died in 1789, leaving a family of three sons and two daughters.

2. *Richard Owen*, the second son, upon his marriage in 1757 to Elizabeth, the youngest daughter of Maurice Stephen, Esq., of Neuadd-Llwyd, in the parish of Llandinam, and grand-daughter of Athelustan Hughes, Esq., took up his residence at Upper Glandulas, which was settled upon him by his father, and became the founder of the family settled there for the last hundred years.   Glandulas was formerly part of the Clochfaen estate, but early in the last century was in possession of the Rev. Richard Owen of Iford, who had sold it in or before 1740 to his cousin, David Owen, for in that year the latter gentleman received a grant of a pew in Llanidloes Church from the Bishop of Bangor, as owner of Glandulas.   Richard Owen left a numerous family, whose names appear in the pedigree.   The present representative of the family is J. B. Owen, of Upper Glandulas.

3. *Edward Owen*, M.A.   The following notice of this gentleman is taken from Mr. Marsh's sketch of the *History of Warrington in the Eighteenth Century*: " In connexion with the literary history of Warrington, it is impossible to omit the name of the Rev. Edward Owen, who became master of the school (Botcher's Free Grammar School) in 1757, and subsequently rector of the parish, each of which offices he retained till his death in the year 1807.   His principal claim to a niche in our temple is as the translator into English verse of the *Satires of Juvenal and Persius.*   The work has had a fair share of reputation, and was published in two vols., 12mo., 1785.   This, and a Latin Grammar, published in 1770, and the sermon I shall notice presently, and a controversial tract, which I alluded to in my notice of Samuel Fothergill, are the only productions

of Mr. Owen's pen with the existence of which I am now acquainted. On the personal character of Mr. Owen I need not dwell. As a schoolmaster, he secured the respect of his pupils, who in after life were accustomed to speak with almost enthusiasm of his classical taste, and the delight with which he regarded any indication of a similar taste having been communicated to his scholars. As an author I need only quote the character given to him by so competent a judge as Mr. Wakefield, who says that "for propriety, perspicuity and elegance of expression, Mr. Owen had not many equals at a time when good writing had become so general." As a townsman he was not regardless of the literary interests of the community among which he was placed, and in promoting objects of this nature he was forgetful of those religious and political prejudices which too often obstruct the progress of useful institutions. He was the president of the Warrington Library, in the management of which he was associated with so many of the eminent men whom we have already had occasion to mention. Indeed, he seems to have lived on terms of agreeable intercourse with the circle to which I allude, and is noticed with much respect by Mr. Gilbert Wakefield, who speaks of him as his "respected friend Mr. Owen, a man of most elegant learning, unspeakable suavity, and peculiar benevolence of heart."

He spent a large sum of money in improving the school house and premises, and by his will, dated the 8th February, 1806, he left £600 for the use of the organist of Warrington parish church. He died in the year 1807, and was buried in Warrington church, where a white diamond shaped marble slab formerly marked his grave. This unfortunately was destroyed during one of the many alterations which the church has undergone since the time of his interment. Fortunately the inscription had been previously copied, and through the kindness of Mr. Beaumont, of Warrington, a copy is here given.

Quis
Hic sepultus est
Fortasse
Cito obliviscentur superstites
Flocci facient posteri ;
Quantum vero omnibus
Quibuscunque poterat
Studuerat vivus inservire
Judicet Christus.

Interea (postquam hujus ecclesiæ ann' xl Rector
et l scholæ magister commoratus fuerat)
Ut sua placide quiescant ossa,
Locum quo obtecta jacent,
Hoc marmore parvulo designari
Voluit, moriens

Anno ætatis suæ lxxix
Annoque Christi mdcccvii.
EDWARDUS OWEN, A.M.,
Cambro-
Britannus.[1]

4. *William Owen.* He entered the Royal Navy
when very young, and in the year 1760, when he was
a midshipman, greatly distinguished himself at the
taking of Pondicherry from the French, losing his right

[1]   (*Translation by Mr. Beamont.*)
Who
Here lies buried
mayhap
the survivors will soon forget
and posterity count at nought.
But how, to the extent of his utmost power,
he had in life tried to serve all,
let Christ be the Judge.
Meanwhile (after he had been rector of this church xl years,
and master of the school l years),
that his bones might rest in peace,
he wished this place where they lie
to be covered with this marble.
Dying
in the lxxixth year of his age,
and in the year of Christ, mdcccvii.
EDWARD OWEN, A.M.,
A Cambro-
Briton.

arm in the action. He was a lieutenant in 1769, and
was shortly afterwards promoted to the command of
H.M.S. *Cormorant*, in which he again distinguished
himself. Captain Owen was bringing home dispatches
when he lost his life by an accident at Madras in 1778.
He was the father of two distinguished sons, *Admiral
W. F. Owen*, and

Sir Edward William Campbell Richard Owen,
G.C.B., G.C.H. The latter gentleman died October
8th, 1849, at his residence, Windlesham House, Surrey,
at the advanced age of 78. We are indebted to the
Gentleman's Magazine for the following summary of the
principal incidents in the life of this gallant sailor. He
entered the Royal Navy August 11, 1775, became a
lieutenant November 6th, 1793, and post captain November 30th, 1798. After the peace of Amiens he
was stationed, with several sloops and smaller vessels
under his orders, on the coast of France, and by his
activity and zeal kept the enemy in a constant state of
alarm, at one time driving their ships on shore, and at
another bombarding the towns of Dieppe and St.
Valery. Subsequently, in 1806, Commodore Owen
(having then hoisted a broad pendant) superintended
a very successful attack on Boulogne, and in 1809
accompanied the expedition to Walcheren, where he
gained warm commendation for the ability and energy
he displayed in the arduous duties imposed upon him.
In 1815 he was honoured with the insignia of a Knight
Commander of the Bath ; in 1821 appointed a colonel
of Marines; and in 1825 advanced to flag rank. From
1828 to 1832 he held the chief command on the East
India station, and from 1841 to 1845 that in the
Mediterranean. He was made a Grand Cross of the
Hanoverian Guelphic Order in 1832, and of the Bath
in 1845. Sir Edward was member of Parliament for
Sandwich from 1826 to 1829; became Surveyor-General
of Ordnance in 1827; was a member of the Council of
H.R.H. the Duke of Clarence when Lord High Admiral, and held office again in 1834-5, as Clerk of the

Ordinance. He married in 1829 Selina, daughter of the late Captain J. B. Hay, R.N.

Vice-Admiral William Fitzwilliam Owen, born in 1773 at Manchester, was the younger brother of Sir Edward Owen, and was educated with him at the celebrated Hanway School, Chelsea. The following notice of him is taken from the nineteenth volume of the *Monthly Articles of the Royal Astronomical Society*. After attaining the first rank at that seminary, he entered the Royal Navy in the summer of 1788, on board the *Culloden*, of 74 guns, commanded by his relation, Sir Thomas Rich. By this officer he was from time to time placed in several ships, of different rates, for the purpose of acquiring knowledge in his profession; but he rejoined the *Culloden* so as to be present at the great battle fought on the 1st June, 1794. Shortly after that glorious conflict Mr. Owen sailed in the *Ruby*, 64, for the Cape of Good Hope, where he witnessed the capture of a Dutch squadron of three sail of the line and six frigates and sloops in Saldana Bay, in August 1796. Returning to England after this exploit he joined the *London*, 98, bearing the flag of Admiral Colpays, with whom he quitted that ship during the alarming mutiny at Spithead in May, 1797; for his firm conduct on that trying occasion he was promoted in the following month to the rank of lieutenant, and at the same time placed in command of the *Flamer* gunbrig. In this and other vessels he experienced much active and harassing channel service till the close of the first French revolutionary war. At the commencement of hostilities Owen was among the foremost to tender his services, in consequence of which, in July, 1803, he was appointed to command the *Sea Flower*, a brig of 14 guns, and very shortly afterwards sailed for the East Indies, on which station he was employed upon various missions by the Commander-in-chief. In 1806 he captured *Le Charle*, a mischievous French ketch, and explored several of the channels between the eastern islands, to the great improvement of the charts. To-

wards the close of that year he piloted Sir Edward
Pellew's squadron through an intricate navigation into
Batavia Roads. Here his bravery and skill were
conspicuous in the command of a division of armed
boats at a successful attack on a Dutch frigate, seven
men-of-war brigs and about twenty armed vessels, for
which he obtained a very honourable mention in the
Gazette. In the following year he contributed to the
capture and destruction of the dockyard and stores of
Griessik in Java, together with all the men-of-war remaining to Holland in India, consisting of the *Revolu-
tion*, *Pluto*, and *Kortenaar*, of 70 guns each, with the
Rustoff frigate, and a flotilla of gunboats. In 1808
Lieutenant Owen had the misfortune of being forced to
surrender the useful little *Sea Flower* to a couple of
French frigates in the Bay of Bengal. The brig was
soon retaken, and commissioned by Lieutenant George
Stewart; but Owen was carried prisoner to the Isle of
France, where he was detained till June, 1810, when he
was exchanged. While preparing to depart, he playfully told the French Governor that perhaps they might
soon meet again; at which General de Caen laughed—
albeit not often in that mood—and hoped that he
would be brought to Port Louis in a vessel more
worthy of capture than his last was. The *badinage*
proved to be rather predictive of coming events.

Meanwhile Owen had been made a commander, by a
commission dated in May, 1809, and on his return to
India was occupied in assisting the authorities at
Madras with his opinions, and in superintending the
transports for the expedition against the Isle of France,
which fell in December, 1810. Our officer's next appointment was to the *Barracouta*, an eighteen-gun
ship-of-war, which he joined in time for aiding at the
blockade of Batavia, previous to the invasion of Java.
On the arrival of the forces under General Sir Samuel
Auchmuty and Commodore Broughton, he assisted in
the debarkation of the troops at Chillingching, and continued attached to the army until after the surrender

of Batavia, in August, 1811. He had been advanced
to post-rank in May of the same year, and after acting
in command of the *Piedmontaise* a short time, he was
appointed a captain of the *Cornelia*, of thirty-two guns.
In this frigate he sailed from Batavia Roads in March,
1812, with a small squadron, consisting of the *Phœnix*,
Bucephalus, and other vessels under his orders, to take
possession of the commissariat depôt at the mouth of the
Palembang river, at the eastern end of Sumatra. Having
achieved this object he returned to England, in charge
of a valuable convoy from China, in June, 1813.

After paying unceasing attention to the hydrography
of the East during his cruises, Captain Owen had rendered very material assistance to his friend, the late
Captain Horsburgh, in the compilation of his well-
known *Oriental Navigator*; and he moreover employed
his half-pay leisure in correcting charts, and in making
a translation of Franzini's *Sailing Directions* from the
Portuguese. At length, in March 1815, he was appointed to the surveying service on the Lakes of Canada,
where he opened the line of operations which has since
been so ably completed by his *élève*, the present Rear-
Admiral Bayfield. In August, 1821, he was appointed
to the *Leven*, twenty-four, in which corvette, with the
Barracouta, he was for upwards of four years employed
in an examination of the west and east coasts of Africa—
an arduous duty carried on in the face of malignant
fever and deadly casualties. In the Ashantee war he
was able to render an effective co-operation to General
Turner, as was acknowledged by the latter in the
London Gazette.

On his return from this mission, Captain Owen's re-
presentations were so strong that the Island of Fer-
dinando Po, in the Bight of Benin, would not only prove
more healthy than Sierra Leone, but would also afford
greater facilities for the suppression of the slave trade,
that he was commissioned in February 1827 to the
Eden, of twenty-six guns, for the purpose of forming a
settlement there and to complete his surveys. On this

duty he was occupied till the close of 1831, when he retired to half-pay, but not to idleness, for his charts, remark books, and attention to improving the means of maritime surveying, fully occupied his time.   In this society he worked on our council; and he presented us with two specimens of his professional ingenuity in a double reflecting circle, and quadruple reflecting sextant.

The island of Campo Bello, in Passamaquoddy Bay, New Brunswick, belongs to the Owen family, and had descended to the subject of our notice and his brother: and as William evinced a desire to settle there, Sir Edward surrendered his portion to him.   Here he had full occupation for a time in getting it in order, and in establishing his family, consisting of a wife and two daughters. Soon after his arrival he was elected member for that locality in the House of Assembly at Fredericton, where he brought to light various abuses, and involved himself in the cares of a staunch reformer. As he was still zealous in the cause of hydrography, Sir Francis Beaufort procured an appointment for him in a fine steam-vessel, the *Columbia*, of 100-horse power, to survey the Bay of Fundy, and the coast of Nova Scotia. Being superseded on his promotion to flag rank in December 1847, he continued the rest of his life on half-pay.

In conduct and bearing our excellent admiral was at once firm and kind, shrewdly sensible and unostentatious, with a manner bordering on the eccentric ; on service he was authoritative without being at all tyrannical, a man of steady resources and unremitting zeal, In speech he was fluent and blunt. When a ministerial peer made him a proposal which he considered as not quite proper, he replied : " My lord, I may be poor, but still I am proud."   On the Admiralty forwarding him a complaint which they had received from the Marquis Palmella, relative to some differences at Mozambique, he closed his explanations with, he "trusted that the word of a captain in the British navy was as good as that of a Portuguese marquis." He built a church at Campo Bello, which he endowed, and after considerable trouble prevailed on the provincial bishop to appoint a clergyman of the Church of England to it. This gentleman regularly officiated until one Sunday the admiral gave him notice that he wished to occupy the pulpit himself that day! So singular and abrupt a hint led to an altercation, and as Owen declared that he would take possession, if necessary, by force, the clergyman resigned the living, and the Admiral for a time regularly performed the clerical duties—the congregation attending even more regularly than before.

Vice-Admiral Owen, whose faculties had been declining for some time, died at St. John's, New Brunswick, on the 3rd of November, 1857, at the advanced age of eighty-four years. He had been very long a Fellow of the Society, which he regularly attended while in town.

The three sons of Owen Owen, the high sheriff of 1766, were

1. *Sir Arthur Davies Owen*, knight, of Glyngynwydd (in the parish of Llangurig) and Glansevern. Was a lawyer by profession, one of the deputy-lieutenants for the county, an active magistrate, and for many years chairman of the Quarter Sessions. In 1814 he was appointed high sheriff of the county, and, from the formation of the troop to the time of his death in 1816, was second in command of the Montgomeryshire Yeomanry Cavalry. He was buried in Berriew Church.

2. *David Owen*, M.A. He entered Trinity College, Cambridge, and was senior wrangler of that university in the year 1777. He became fellow of his college, and subsequently was ordained priest. He died unmarried in 1829, at Campo Bello, in New Brunswick, and, in accordance with his own request, his remains were conveyed across the Atlantic, and deposited in the family vault in the church of Berriew.

3. *William Owen*, K.C., was born in the year 1758, educated at the Free Grammar School at Warrington under his uncle, and thence proceeded to Cambridge.

In the year 1782 he took his degree of B.A. at Trinity College, and was fifth wrangler. Among the members of his own college who graduated at the same time were Professors Porson and Hailstone, Drs. Raine and Wingfield. Mr. Owen and these four gentlemen were afterwards chosen fellows of Trinity College. He subsequently became a member of Lincoln's Inn, and eventually a bencher of that society. After attending the Oxford and Cheshire circuits for several years, he confined his practice chiefly to the Courts of Chancery and Exchequer. He was a Commissioner of Bankrupts until he was advanced to the rank of King's Counsel. About the year 1821 he quitted his profession, and retired into the country, where he acted as magistrate and deputy-lieutenant, taking an active part in all the public business of the county, and generally presiding as chairman of the Quarter Sessions. Mr. Owen was instrumental in abolishing the system of Welsh judicature, and took a leading part in the parliamentary reform agitation previous to the passing of the Reform Bill of 1832, the county of Montgomery being the first to petition in support of it. In 1823 he married Anne Warburton, only child of Captain Sloughter, and relict of the Rev. Thomas Coupland, of the Priory, Chester, and died without issue 10th of November, 1837, aged 79. He was buried in Berriw Church, where a handsome marble monument was erected in his memory by his widow, who still survives.

CHAP. VIII.—FOLK LORE.

As many of the old customs, superstitious beliefs, legendary lore, etc., which fall under the title placed at the head of this chapter are common to most of the Arwystli parishes, a fuller notice of them is reserved for the parochial account of Llanidloes. Llangurig has, however,

from time immemorial been locally famed for its conjurors" (*gwyr-hysbys*), its manner of keeping the wakes,
and for retaining the old custom of *Arian-y-rhaw*, and
therefore deserves a passing notice here.

The parish, from its very situation, in the centre of
the mountain fastnesses of the principality, far distant
from the great centres of civilisation and progress, with
a sparse scattered agricultural population, few of whom,
until of late years, enjoyed any advantages of a good
education, or intercourse with the outer world, seems
to have been admirably adapted by its physical and
social isolation for keeping alive the smouldering fire of
the old superstitions which in times past prevailed in
every valley of Wales. Sufficient vestiges of this wide-
spread and firmly-rooted species of mythology still exist
to enable the curious to trace its characteristic features,
and to form a conception of the influence it obtained
over the minds of the majority, and the important part
it played in almost every action of their daily lives. It
recognised the existence of a number of noxious spirits,
who were the supernatural authors of the greater part
of the "ills which human flesh is heir to," whose
earthly devotees and agents were pre-eminently the
witches. Some of these were supposed to have sold
themselves body and soul, like *Sion-y-Cent* (the Welsh
Faust), to the devil, to obtain his aid the more effectually
to carry out their purposes. There were, however,
various grades of guilt and power of working mischief
among them. To counterbalance this principle of *evil*,
and, as it were, to make their mythological creed dually
perfect, the existence of beneficent spirits, who had the
well being of humanity at heart, was acknowledged.
The fairies, or, as they are called among the Welsh
hills, *Tylwydd Teg* (fair family), were generally classed
among the *good* spirits; but this principle in human
form manifested itself in those very important person-
ages whose calling was hardly dignified enough to en-
title them to be styled astrologers, but who were well
known as *Conjurors*. Low and sordid as their motives

o

were, their special province was to do battle with the
spirit of evil in its most common form—that of witchcraft—or by granting spells, charms, and foretelling the
future, to avert the ill which would otherwise have befallen those who placed implicit reliance upon them.
Some of the lower class of these " cunning-men " were,
it is true, believed to have been the familiars of the
spirits of darkness, but the better sort were known to
be men who, in addition to a " gift " for their special
calling, qualified themselves by a study more or less
thorough of the works of Michael Scott, Lily, and other
expounders of the mysterious craft, and professed to be
able to hold the devil himself in subjection.   Add a
profound belief in ghosts, corpse-candles, *deryn-y-corph*
(the corpse bird), jack o' the lanterns, etc., and some
notion may be formed of the secular creed prevalent in
the parish in the " good old days " which are past.

The key-stone of the whole undoubtedly was the belief in witchcraft, which held its ground till within a
late period, and cannot even yet be said to be wholly
eradicated.   Formerly its existence was regarded as a
necessary deduction of the truthfulness of Holy Writ.

" Had his Majesty King George II read the *History of
Witchcraft*, and known as much as we do in some parts of
Wales, he would not have called upon his Parliament to deter-
mine that there are no such things as witches, and his Parliament would hardly have complimented him therein.   If they
say there never was (*sic*) such things as witches in the world,
the Scripture is against them, both the Old and the New
Testament, for there were witches in the days of Saul and in
the days of Paul."[1]

This is the quaint language of a nonconformist minister
of the last century, and it may fairly be taken as the
typical stock argument used upon all occasions by the
believers in witchcraft when a doubt was expressed as
to the power of witches.   The following extract from the
same author of " ghostly memory " illustrates another
phase of superstition prevalent in the parish in the last
century :

[1] *Apparitions, etc., in Wales*, by the Rev. Edmund Jones, p. 25.

"Edward Lloyd, in the parish of Llangurig, being very ill, those that were with him heard the voice of some person very near them; they looked about the house, but could see no person; the voice seemed to be in the room where they were. Soon after they heard these words, by some thing (*sic*) un- seen, 'Y mae nenbren y ty yn craccio' ('the uppermost beam of the house cracketh'); soon after, 'Fe dorr yn y man' ('there it breaks'); he died that moment, which much affected the company."[1]

To the same industrious writer in this peculiar branch of literature we are indebted for a short notice of the first recorded conjuror who resided in the vicinity. One Sir David Llwyd, who lived not far from Yspytty Yst- with, in the adjoining Cardiganshire parish, appears to have been a "curate likely of that church, and a phy- sician, but being known to deal in the magic art, he was turned out of the curacy, and obliged to live by practising physic. It is thought that he learnt the magic art privately in Oxford in the profane time of Charles the Second, when many vices greatly pre- vailed." "Sir" David was in the habit of regularly visiting the neighbouring market towns of Llanidloes and Rhayader, passing through Llangurig on his way to and from the former. Our author relates several instances of his extraordinary skill. On one occasion his Satanic majesty was in the habit of visiting a drunken tailor, wishing to have a suit of clothes made. The terrified tailor appealed to Sir David, who soon sent the unwelcome visitor about his business.

"Another time, being at Llanidloes town, in Montgomery- shire, twelve miles from home, and as he was going home very late in the evening, seeing a boy there of his neighbour- hood, offered him to ride behind him if he was for going home, which the boy accepted, and they came home in about two hours. The boy had lost one of his garters in the journey, but, seeing something hang on an ash tree near the church, climbed up to see what it was, and, to his great surprise, he found it was his garter which he had lost; which shows they rode home in the air."[2]

[1] *Apparitions, etc., in Wales*, p. 56.   [2] *Ibid.*, pp. 66-7.

Unfortunately for the history of Welsh folk lore, the mantle of old Jones does not appear to have fallen upon anyone.   To judge from the tales related by the old people of the parish, there is every reason to believe that the line of conjurors from Sir David's time to the present has been unbroken.   One of the best known of his class in the latter part of the last century, and in the early part of the present, was Edward Savage, who was born in the year 1759.   He resided at Felin Fawr, and subsequently at Troed-y-lon.   During his long life he was consulted "far and wide" upon the mysteries of the magic art.   He was a small farmer, a herb doctor, and gun-smith, but derived his chief source of income from his more superstitious fellow-mortals, who made pilgrimages to Llangurig from the neighbouring counties, that they might have the benefit of the great man's advice.

The following incident, related by a highly respectable and trustworthy person as a "remarkable coincidence which I cannot explain," will show the nature of the old conjuror's method of procedure, and the means by which he earned his money and his fame.   The father of the narrator had lost one valuable pig from disease, and a second was purchased in his place, which was suddenly taken ill, and for days would eat nothing. Some of the credulous neighbours at once suggested that human agency had something to do with the pig's illness, in fact, that it was "witched."   The young man resolved to secretly visit "Old Savage," and elicit his opinion, with no great faith in the result.   Carrying his resolution into effect, he arrived at the conjuror's house and stated his errand to the wise man, who at once consulted his books, wrote out a charm, and gave him some herbs to mingle with the pig's food.   He also gave him particular directions regarding the charm, and described its immediate effect upon the patient, and further stated that the cause of his sufferings resided between the young man's home and the north, and that she should not rest during the night if his advice was carefully attended to. Savage's directions were duly carried out, the paper upon which the charm was written was rubbed over the pig from head to tail the prescribed number of times, and then placed for his further protection in a crack in the wall of his cot. Some of his bristles were then taken, placed between two flat irons, and put on the top of the fire, where they remained all night. On the following morning, to the utter astonishment of the operator, a neighbour who lived only a few doors to the north came into the house as the family were at breakfast, and complained that she had not rested during the night, having suffered acutely from tooth-ache. The spell was broken, the pig recovered, and knew no more suffering till placed in the hands of the butcher.

The old man, like other great men, was no hero among his immediate neighbours. He prided himself upon his faculty for detecting thefts and tracing stolen goods. A humorous story is related of the means adopted by a number of young men for destroying the old man's prestige in this respect. Watching their opportunity, they entered his house one Sunday morning when no one was within, took down a dried ham that was hanging up, hid it very carefully, and then spread a report that it had been stolen. Of course the news created a sensation, and upon his return Savage at once missed the bacon, and shortly afterwards heard of the visit which had been paid to his house during his absence. He vowed to punish the thieves with the most terrible visitations his art could inflict upon them; horns should grow upon their heads, they should be smitten with blindness in one of their eyes, etc., if they did not immediately restore the pilfered bacon. His threats, however, were uttered in vain, his vaunted books were powerless, the thieves met him with taunts—"Savage, where's your ham?" "Who stole your bacon, Savage?" The conjuror had met with his equals in cunning, for they completely baffled his art for days. His wife was more successful, for in changing the straw beneath the paliasse of their bed she found the missing ham, and in a plaintive voice informed her husband of the discovery. The old man, who was consulting his books at the time, cried out exultingly, "Well done the old books, they never failed me yet!" After serving his generation in his own peculiar manner, he died in the year 1849, having attained the patriarchal age of ninety years; his wife, who lived to be eighty-five, survived him one year. Both lie buried in Llangurig churchyard, where a head-stone marks their graves.

One R—— J—— was a contemporary of old Savage. He resided nearer Llanidloes, was a freeholder, and considered a well read, enlightened man. Yet he could not resist the temptation of making a gain out of the credulity of his more superstitious brethren. He also pretended to be a doctor, and professed to be particularly skilful in counteracting the influence of witches, in laying the evil spirits who visited the earth in the form of ghosts, and in giving spells or charms for cocks. Before the brutal sport of cock-fighting was put down by the legislature some twenty years ago, it was often customary for the owners of game-cocks to pay a sum of money to a conjuror to obtain a spell, which was written upon a small strip of paper, to be securely fastened round the bird's leg with the view of rendering him invincible. One of these spells, which was preserved for a long time, was found to be taken from Ephesians vi, 16. J—— had, for a man of his position and education, a valuable library.

Another conjuror of extended fame was one William Pryse, of Pen-cin-coed, whose principal visitors were residents in Shropshire, Herefordshire, and Radnorshire, who must have had great faith in the man's abilities before they undertook such distant pilgrimages, for this was long before railways were introduced into Mid-Wales. Pryse's reputation locally was not very high, for some one had stolen *his* watch, and he was never able to discover the thief, nor regain possession of the lost property.

The mantle of old Savage, with a double portion of

the old man's skill, shrewdness, and intelligence, has
fallen upon his grandson, who resides at the family residence, Troed-y-lon, and enjoys a comfortable income
from his various callings of herb-doctor, gunsmith, and
conjuror. He is no niggard in his manner of living,
being what is generally styled a " free jolly fellow," and
strongly addicted to the sports of coursing and shoot-
ing. Among his neighbours he is known as one who
is ever ready to assist in doctoring patients, whether
human or farm stock, and many are the cures with
which he is justly credited, for he possesses very considerable knowledge of herbs and their medicinal properties. The higher pretensions of his art are reserved
for more distant admirers, who call upon him regularly
at appointed places of meeting at Llanidloes, Newtown,
and Welshpool. One of the most ordinary manifesta-
tions of witchcraft is the inability of the "churner" to
convert the cream into butter, and is the frequent cause
of a visit to the wise man. Respectable farmers from
a great distance either go or send messengers to Llangurig in order to have the spell broken. Another subject which leads to frequent consultations is the illness
of farm stock, in which case the conjuror's knowledge
does him good service. One example out of many that
could be given will suffice to show the general *modus
operandi* in these cases. The following anecdote was
related to the writer by a thoroughly original character,
who had imbibed the belief in witchcraft with his
mother's milk, and who brought it forward with the
intention of making a convert. A well-to-do and respectable farmer in an adjoining parish, who was a
deacon of his chapel, was desirous that the Llangurig
conjuror should be consulted, as his calves were very
unwell. But the farmer was anxious not to appear in
the matter, so he asked a second person to employ the
individual who related the facts, who readily undertook
the necessary journey to visit the wise man. Arrived
at his house, his errand told, the conjuror at once retired to his sanctum to consult his books, while some

one remained in the kitchen to watch the clock, and give him the correct time when he required it. The ceremony gone through, the charm and simples were handed to the messenger, and the necessary directions given as to the use of the same. But they did no good. One of the calves died, and on the following week the same man was again sent to Llangurig, in the hope that the second journey would prove more beneficial to the surviving calves. When informed of the death of the calf the conjuror said that the failure was to be attributed to a mistake in giving him the correct time on the occasion of the first consultation. Once more the inner room was entered, and the same ceremony repeated, more herbs and another charm was handed to the messenger, and very careful directions as to their use were given. Arrived at the cow-house, the herbs were administered, and each calf was duly rubbed with the charm[1] from head to tail nine times, and the name of the Trinity invoked. This done the charm was placed in a hole in some of the timber-work of the ceiling of the " bay " to avert future misfortune. The calves, of course, recovered.

At a considerable distance in the profession—as fortune-teller—came one of the weaker sex, an old lady whose proper name was Mary Evans, but who from the habit of telling fortunes and making forecasts for the small charge of one penny, was familiarly known as Pal-y-geiniog (Penny Mary). Her mode of looking into futurity was very simple. It consisted in pouring tea-grounds into a cup, which were turned round rapidly and then allowed to settle in the bottom of the cup.

---

[1] My informant could not say what was written upon the paper which constituted the charm, but Mr. Baring Gould gives the following one which was used upon a similar occasion.
        " A charm for cattle—
Our Lord Jesus Christ went over the land,
With His staff in His hand,
The Holy Ghost in His mouth.
        In the name, etc.
And the sign of the cross is made nine times over the cattle."

From the disposition of the tea-leaves the old dame used to read her prognostications. She was also frequently consulted by persons who were about making trading ventures, purchases, or upon their undertaking long journeys. She resided in a small cottage on Rhos-y-wrach (Hag's Moor), and often upon a fine Sunday afternoon in the summer numbers of ladies, some of them upon horseback from a considerable distance, would visit the old woman to have their fortunes told. She was in the habit of charging the "upper-class" visitors half-a-crown. A short time before her death she abandoned the practice of fortune-telling, and became a member of the church.

The Wakes (Gwyl-mab-sant). This holiday originated in the religious ceremony observed upon the day commemorating the dedication of the church by Curig Lwyd to his patron saint, *St. Cyrique.* This day falls upon June 16th, and the wake generally began on the Sunday following the saint's day, the anniversary being regarded by the parishioners as the great feast and holiday of the year. In the time of the Stuarts there is evidence to show that in the neighbouring parish of Llanidloes the usual games and sports were carried on upon Sunday, in which respect Llangurig most probably was not behind its neighbour,—a custom which perhaps tended to obtain for it from the followers of Vavasour Powell the character of being "noted for untowardness." In the early part of the present century, Llangurig wakes possessed sufficient attraction to collect in the village the "choicest spirits" and athletes of the neighbouring parishes, who took an active part in the various games that were going on, in the fun and frolic which were the usual concomitants of the holiday, which, while it lasted, converted the small village into a fair. Unfortunately, the feasting, drinking, etc., were often prolonged for days in succession, the visitors and parishioners gradually returning to their homes as their pockets grew lighter, and the wakes were frequently brought to a close when the participators in the various pastimes had spent all their money in one of the two inns of the village. Sometimes drunkenness and party fights disgraced the proceedings. This caused right-minded persons to exert their influence in putting an end to such scenes. Their efforts were successful, and latterly the athletic games and out-door sports so prevalent in the parish in olden times gradually became neglected, and the wakes itself to be considered among the things of the past.

Arian-y-rhaw (Shovel-money). At all funerals which take place at Llangurig, when the coffin has been lowered into the grave, the parish clerk holds a shovel over the open grave, upon which he receives the contributions from the relatives and friends of the deceased. This custom is a relic of the times when the Roman Catholic religion prevailed in the principality, and it was customary to pay money to the priest for offering masses for the souls of the dead. The money placed upon the shovel is called *Arian-y-rhaw*, and is the clerk's fee. As it is regarded as a mark of respect and esteem towards the deceased to contribute, and as nothing but silver[1] or

---

[1] In connexion with the custom of contributing only silver or gold coins, the following incident was related to the writer. An eccentric character, who was a confirmed lover of his beer, named Richard James, a glazier at Llanidloes, on one occasion accompanied a funeral to Llangurig. Arrived at the village and examining his pockets he found himself the possessor of a solitary silver sixpence, his mite for *Arian-y-rhaw*. His five miles walk had not tended to allay his customary thirst, and the state of his funds provoked a mental debate. Should he have his beer, or should he practise self-denial? It was very difficult to carry out the latter suggestion; his mouth watered at the very thought of his favourite beverage: yet he was too proud to leave the churchyard without contributing, and too dignified to enter the inn moneyless. A happy thought occurred to him which he at once carried out. He entered the church in the funeral *cortège*, and when it came to his turn to place some piece of money upon the extended shovel, he gravely deposited six copper pennies upon it, for which he had exchanged his sixpenny-piece. Observing the act, old George Bennett who then officiated as clerk, quietly addressed him in Welsh.

"I am greatly obliged to you, Richard James, but no copper coins are received at this offering."

"I am very much obliged to you, my dear George," was the

gold is received, it frequently happens that the clerk collects a large sum. If in adding up the money an odd sixpence occurred, it was formerly deemed an omen that another funeral would take place shortly.

CHAP. IX.—MISCELLANEOUS.

1. *Nonconformity.*—When the parochial clergy were expelled from their livings, by virtue of the "Act for the better propagation and preaching of the Gospel in Wales," which was passed February 22nd, 1649, their successors appear to have made some progress in bringing over the people to their views, for Llangurig was held up as an example of their influence (*vide supra*, chap. iii, § 5). But their authority, as far as can be ascertained, appears to have terminated at, or very shortly after, the Restoration.

Early in the last century the influence of the great Welsh Methodist revival penetrated into this remote district; one Richard Tibbot, who in the year 1743 was appointed to report upon the "state of the Church" in Montgomeryshire to an association in South Wales, made the following statement :—

"*Society in Llangurig.*—The members resident here go to the Tyddyn and join that society."[1]

The Tyddyn farm house alluded to is in the adjoining parish of Llanidloes, seven miles distant from the village

ready response; "our good friend, Evan Davies" (landlord of the lower inn) "will gladly receive them." James picked up the money, and wended his way to *Ty Curig* (the inn).

The George Bennett referred to above died in the year 1817 at the age of 69. He was landlord of the Blue Bell, or upper inn, and was succeeded as clerk by his son, Samuel Bennett, who held the post for a great number of years. After his death it was filled by Edward Rees, who was also the village schoolmaster. His successor was Evan Jones, the present clerk.

[1] *Methodistiaeth Cymru*, i, 173.

of Llangurig, and was one of the earliest places in the neighbourhood which afforded shelter to the persecuted Methodist preachers of those days. The Rev. Peter Williams visited the district in 1746, and others of the great revivalists—Daniel Rowlands, of Llangeitho, and Howel Harris visited Llanidloes more than once in the following years, and the short distance between Llangurig and Llanidloes offered no obstacle to people who were in the habit of walking between forty and fifty miles to receive the communion at the hands of Daniel Rowlands.

The preachers were generally treated at first with ridicule, scorn, and persecution. Sometimes their lives were in danger. But they also occasionally met with gentlemen who made efforts to get the people to allow them to preach in peace. An example of this more humane disposition is quoted in *Methodistiaeth Cymru* (iv, 357). As the incident affords a glimpse at the state of society in the district in those days, a translation of it is here given.

" On one occasion a number of the leading men of the town (Llanidloes) and the neighbourhood were collected together in one of the inns at the time that the old Reformers (the Revivalists) began preaching in the vicinity. These strangers, who were going about the country agitating and disturbing the peace of their neighbours, became the subject of their discussion, and the greatest readiness was evinced, not only to treat them with ridicule by styling them Caradocs[1] and Roundheads, but to punish them if it could be done safely. There happened to be among them an elderly gentleman, who was highly respected, of the name of Jenkyn Lloyd, Esq. (of Clochfaen). This gentleman was a justice of the peace, and to him nearly the whole town and country resorted to seek advice upon matters relating to the law. After the other gentlemen present had delivered themselves of their strong opinions about the preachers, styling them unruly and hateful wanderers, Mr. Lloyd rose and addressed them to the following effect :—
' Well, gentlemen, you know very well the manner in which our clergymen discharge their duties—the vicar of Llangurig, so and so, the vicar of Llanidloes, —— Llandinam, —— Tref-

[1] The name was given them as followers of Walter Caradoc.

eglwys, —— Carno, —— Llanwnog, —— Penstrowed' —— —
depicting their irregular style of living and their utter indifference
for the spiritual welfare of their parishioners. 'And what
wonder,' he continued, 'if these strangers, who are anxious to
save men's souls, should come among us and tell us the naked
truth about our behaviour.' Having heard this address without
being able to gainsay it, they held their peace and let these
men alone."

For a long period the Nonconformists were neither
numerous enough nor in a position to erect suitable
edifices in which to conduct their services, but held
them from house to house, chiefly in some of the more
commodious farm-houses in the neighbourhood of the
village, and in other centres of population, such as
Cwm-belan, Glyn-Brochan, etc., where chapels were
subsequently built. Early in the present century each
of the great sects had established themselves in the
parish, and began building chapels in the more populous
districts. At present there are nine dissenting chapels
within the limits of the parish.

The *Calvinistic Methodists* have three, viz., 1, Dernol
Chapel, built about the year 1825; 2, Capel Ucha (Upper
Chapel); 3, a chapel in the village of Llangurig, enlarged
and re-opened in 1866.

The *Wesleyans* have three chapels, situated 1, in the
village; 2, in Cwm-belan; 3, on Pen-cin-coed.

The *Baptists* have one, called *Zion*, in Cwm-belan,
built in 1827, re-built 1837, and enlarged in 1860.

The *Independents* have two chapels, one in Glyn-
Brochan, the other in Glyn-Hafren, in the neighbourhood of the Old Hall.

2. *Education.*—As far as can be ascertained no
regular and well-conducted school appears to have
existed in the parish, although for the last forty years
a school has been kept for a considerable portion of the
year at the church, either in the vestry or the gallery.
It was first established by Mr. James, the vicar of the
parish, in 1832, and shortly after its opening numbered
some sixty scholars, forty-three of whom were paid for
by annual subscription, every subscriber of ten shillings

being allowed to send a child for one year, the rest being instructed at the expense of their parents.[1] This school was conducted for a number of years by the late Mr. Edward Rees, who also discharged the duties of parish clerk. He was a well-informed and intelligent man, and the school while under his care was above the average of country schools conducted by untrained teachers. Since his death the school has occasionally been carried on in the winter months by the letter carriers from Llanidloes.

It is greatly to be regretted that the inhabitants have not long ago bestirred themselves, and, following the example of the other Arwystli parishes, established a well conducted day school under the care of a competent teacher. Perhaps Llangurig, of all the Arwystli parishes, suffers most from the evils of absentee landowners. Taking the Rate-book of 1869 as our guide, we find the gross estimated rental of the parish given as £5,740; *four-sevenths* of this property is in the possession of half a dozen proprietors, *all of whom are absentees.* The backwardness of the parish in educational matters may to a great extent be attributed to this cause, but it is one that is likely to be remedied by the new educational bill.

Small private schools have at various periods been established in different parts of the parish, more especially in the hamlets of Cwm-belan, Glyn-Brochan, Glyn-Hafren, &c.

The number attending Sunday schools in the parish amounted to 376 in 1831, and the numbers at present attending have been estimated at from 300 to 350.

3. *Roads.*—This section was unintentionally omitted from the first chapter.

The old road formerly connecting the village with the town of Llanidloes went by *Pen-y-croesau, Rhos-y-wrach, Blaen-y-glyn* through *Glyn-Brochan,* and entered the town over the Short Bridge. Another old line of roadway connecting Llanidloes with Aberystwith led over

[1] Lewis's *Top. Dictionary,* art. Llangurig.

the mountains to the north of the village.   Both routes
appear to have fallen into disuse before the close of the
last century.

The road connecting the village with Rhayader was
constructed in 1830, and placed the village on the great
coach route between London and Aberystwith via
Hereford.   This route continued to be used by coaches
until the opening of the Cambrian system of railways.

The late Rev. Walter Davies writing to a friend in
the year 1813, respecting a journey through the village,
has the following passage in his letter :—

"May 26.—Went to Llangurig by six o'clock ; proceeded
through the desert of Pumlumon, through which Mr. Johnes
had the vanity to suppose that an iron railroad would cause
plenty to smile over the forlorn waste."[1]

The Manchester and Milford Company have constructed a line of "iron railroad" between Llanidloes
and Llangurig, but it has never been opened for traffic.

4. *Fairs.*—Two fairs are held annually in the village,
one in the month of April (first held April 23rd, 1869)
and the other in October.   The latter is called "Sheep
Fair."   From a paragraph in a local paper it appears
that upwards of two thousand sheep were penned in
the fair of 1868.

[1] *Gweithiau Gwalter Mechain*, iii, 383.

CHAP. X.—A TOPOGRAPHICAL GLOSSARY OF NAMES IN THE PARISH.[1]

ABBREVIATIONS.

f. farm.   t. tenement.   o. owner.   t.p. township.

ABER, defined by Llwyd as "the fall of a lesser water into a greater." According to E. Llwyd, *Arch. Brit.*, p. 50, Aber-= "Cymmer, Lat. confluvium, a place where two or more rivers meet." So Isaac Taylor in *Words and Places*, "a confluence of waters, either of two rivers or of a river with the sea, in which sense it = also the Gaelic 'Inver.' From the fact that 'Inver' (spelt Ynver) occurs in two poems ascribed to Taliessin, and that 'Aber' occurs in places in Ireland, as well as in Wales and parts of Scotland inhabited by the Picts, as well as by the Britons, Mr. Skene, (*Four Ancient Books of Wales*, i, 150-4,) concludes that both words were at one time common to the three languages, and that all three were formed from an old word 'ber', signifying water. To such a word there appears a resemblance in the Irish 'bir,' aqua, noted by E. Lluyd, *Arch. Brit.*, Til. ii, p. 3." H. W. LL.

Cymmer = conflux, confluence. In a cymmer both streams ought to lose their name. The term is never used of a river falling into the sea. D. S. E.

ABER-BIDNO, the confluence of the Bidno (with the Wye): a f. of 28 ac., t.p. Llanifynu, part of the Clochfaen estate.

ABER-GYNWYDD, the confluence of the Gynwydd (with Afon Tylwch): the united stream is afterwards known as the Dulas. In a deed of the year 1757, Aber-Gynwydd is the name by which the present Pen-pont-bren mill is described. This old deed gives us the original name of the stream now called Nant Cwm-Belan, and shows that the farm of *Glyn*-Gynwydd ought more properly be called *Glan*-Gynwydd; the township lying along the banks of the stream retains its proper appellation, *Glyn*-Gynwydd.

ABER-TRI-NANT, the confluence of the three ravines or brooks, name of a small t. in the t.p. of Llanifynu, o. Mr. John Morgan. C. f. *Aber-tri-dwfyr* in Glamorganshire and *Aber-dau-nant* in the parish of Llanidloes.

ABER-UCHA, the upper Aber (so called to distinguish it from Aber-Bidno), a f. of 35 ac. in the t.p. of Llanifynu.

AFON (Avon) the Welsh for a river. It is never used in Welsh as a proper name, but as a common name prefixed to the designations

---

[1] The compiler gratefully acknowledges the assistance which he has received from the following gentlemen :—the Revs. D. S. Evans and R. H. Jones, H. W. Lloyd, Esq., and J. C .Hughes, Esq., all of whom kindly perused the MS. before it was placed in the printer's hands. Some of their notes, with their initials attached, have been inserted.

of the various streams, and is more especially used when the distinctive proper name is also the appellation of some other object, as *Afon Horè*, *Afon Tylwch*, etc.

ALLT-Y-DERW, slope of the oaks, name of a hill three miles to the N.W. of the village. Its sides now are destitute of trees, but the name preserves the memory of the time when its sides were covered with timber.

BAILI or BEILI. Baili is defined by Dr. Pugh to be a court before a house, and synonymous with *buarth*, a fold. This is the general meaning of the term in South Wales. In Irish the term is equivalent to an abode, synonymous with the Welsh *tre* (*Words and Places*, p. 484). It is the name of a farm of 84 ac. in the t.p. of Glyn-Hafren, o. C. J. Elwell. There is a cluster of three fs. of this name in the adjoining parish of St. Harmon.

BELAN. Various conjectural meanings of this term have been given. The late Rev. Walter Davis has the following observations upon it:

"I once thought that the derivation was from *Bel-lan* (Llan-Bel), the enclosure of Bel, Belinus, Baal, etc. We have Belan-deg (fair Belan) in Manafon, Belan-ddu, Belan Wydd, Belan-las, Belan Argae in the parishes adjoining, but I never witnessed any remains, stone or earthen, which might favour the idea that they were places consecrated to any kind of worship. A *rounded hill*, a frustum of a cone might have been denominated Belan from its shape; but some of our Belans lie on flat ground.

"That a heathen deity was once idolized in Britain is proved by the inscription on the altar found in the country of the Brigantes, which exhibited in Roman characters, '*Deo Marti Bela tu Cadra*.' The last word is evidently Welsh—Bel y Duw Cadr; Bel the Potent God. The Romans persuaded the colonized Britons that the British *Bel* was identified in their *Mars*, hence *Deo Marti* of the inscription. In the British language *bela* and *rhyvela* is to wage war. *Belgæ*, warlike Gauls in Cæsar, etc., emigrated to Britain and Ireland; hence the *Fir-bolg* of the latter. Their fires on the eve of the first of May, still called *Beal-teine* (the fire of Baal), savours of a Phœnician origin."[1]

The author of *Words and Places*[2] sees in the word vestiges of an ancient cultus, showing some original connexion between the Syrian Baal and the Celtic Bel. Baal, according to Professor Nilsson,[3] has given his name to many Scandinavian localities, *e. g.* the Baltic, the Great and Little Belt, Belteberga, etc.

In Llwyd's *Arch. Brit.* tit. i, p. 33, is found the following:—
"A Berry or Barrow [a hillock], Beru; Twyn, bellan, brynkyn. As the modern 'll' is invariably written 'lh' by Llwyd, it is evident that his 'bellan' = the modern 'belan,' and that it meant a hillock, mound, tumulus, or barrow. H. W. LL.

[1] Collected Works of *Gwallter Mechain*, iii, 514.
[2] P. 325 (ed. 1865). See also *Arch. Camb.*, 1848, pp. 21, etc.
[3] Quoted in *Prehistoric Times*, p. 71, 2nd ed.

Mr. Silvan Evans thinks there can be no doubt about the term being descriptive, and most probably is a diminutive of *bâl*, a hill, a peak. Both the Llangurig Belans are situated on hills, and the ravine at the foot of one of these hills is known as Cwm-belan.

BOD TALOG, see Mytalog.

BOL-HAUL, rotundity facing the sun, the converse of *Cil-haul* (where the sun does not shine), a name given to the southern slope of Cefn-hir-brisg.

BLAEN, a generic term which enters largely into the composition of Welsh topographical names. It signifies literally a *point, end*, or *extremity*, and when applied to streams indicates their sources.

BLAEN-BYTHIGION, the source of the Bythigion, the name of a small f. of 14 ac. in the t.p. of Glyn-Hafren, o. John Morgan.

 Bythigion, the plural of *Bythig*, never failing streamlets. R. H. J.

BLAEN-Y-CWM, the end of the hollow, or dingle, the name of a f. of 42 ac. in the t.p. of Llaniwared, part of the Clochfaen estate.

BLAEN-Y-GLYN, end of the glen, a mountain f. of 126 ac., t.p. of Glyn-Brochan, o. Mr. Williams.

BLAEN-TWRCH, source of the Twrch. Twrch is a common name of Welsh streams.

BLUE-BELL INN, one of the two inns of the village, has a f. of 11 ac. attached, part of Clochfaen estate in 1771, now the property of Mrs. Jane Bennett.

BRITH-DIR, variegated land, a name which it probably received when the furze or heath was in full blossom; a small f. of 13 ac., t.p. of Llaniwared, o. Mr. Williams.

BROCHAN, noisy, foaming, a trib. of the Dulas (see p. 12).

BRON-FELEN, the yellow knoll, a f. of 92 ac., t.p. Glyn-Hafren, o. Mr. Williams.

BRON-HAUL, the sunny knoll, a f. in the t.p. Glyn-Brochan.

BRYN, hill.

BRYN-CYLLAU, pronounced *cylle*, probably derived from *cyllen* or *cyllan*, the diminutive of *cyll*, the plural of *collen*, the hazel-tree. If this derivation be accepted it means the hill of the hazel-tree. R.H.J.

 Dr. Pugh, s. v. *cyll*, plural *cyllau*, gives as the meaning a separation, what separates, so that it may mean the hill of separation. H.W.LL. It is the name of a f. of 39 ac., t.p. Llanifynn, part of the Clochfaen estate. One of its fields is called *Gwar-y-castell*.

BRYN-DAITH, the hill of flame, or the blazing hill, probably derived from the old custom of burning the furze, heath, etc., on the hill tops. By the laws of Howel Dda this operation was restricted under a penalty to the month of March.[1] Llywarch Hên alludes to the custom in his poem to Geraint Feib Erbin, stanza 14.

[1] *Myf Arch.*, p 1066 (Gee's Reprint).

"Twruf goteith ar diffeith mynit."[1]
A noise like that of the consuming fire on a wild mountain].[2]
"Drwy'r aweddwr, drwy'r oddaith."[3]
[Through the rapid stream, through the blazing heath].

This hill is situated between Nant Iago and Nant-y-Cawrdy.

BRYN-DU, black hill, elevated land on the eastern confines of the parish, also the names of several holdings on its slopes.

BRYN-DULAS, hill of the Dulas, a small f. of 17 ac. on a rising knoll on the right bank of the Dulas, t.p. Cefn-yr-hafodau, o. Mrs. Phillips, Aberystwith.

BRYN-MAWR, large hill, a high hill in the t.p. of Cefn-yr-hafodau, from the summit of which there is an extensive and pleasant view.

BRYN-Y-GARREG-WEN, hill of the white stone, situated to the south of Maes-nant.

BWLCH, a generic term signifying a hollow, gap, defile, or pass. There is a farm of this name in the township of Llanifynu, o. Mrs. Owen Glansevern.

BWLCH-HAFOD-Y-GOG, the hollow of the cuckoo's summer abode, a f. of 74 ac., t.p. Glyn-Gynwydd, o. Mrs. Phillips

BWLCH-Y-GARREG, the pass of the stone, a f. of 118 ac., t.p. Cefn-yr-hafodau, o. Mrs. Owen ; formerly part of the Clochfaen estate.

Mr. J. C. Symons, in a paper[4] on the *Permanence of Races*, quotes a letter from a correspondent, which mentions this farm as the residence of a descendant of the notorious *Gwilliaid Cochion* of Mawddwy. "I was fortunate enough to find out some descendants of the 'Gwilliaid' on the maternal side, and those in my native parish of Llangurig. When these Welsh Caffirs were sent from Mallwyd, they wandered here and there, and some of the females were pitied by the farmers and taken into their houses and taught to work. One of these was married to a person not far from this place, and their descendants live at Bwlch-y-garreg, Llangurig. I knew the old man quite well. There certainly was something peculiar about him; he was seventy when I was a boy of fifteen ; he had dark lank hair, a very ruddy skin, with teeth much projecting, and a receding brow. I never heard his honesty questioned, but mentally he was considered much below the average ; the children, also, are not considered quick in anything." Descendants of the 'Gwilliaid' are also to be found in Mawddwy to this day.

BWLCH-Y-PRIDD, hollow or pass of the loose earth, a f. in t.p. of Llanifynu, o. Mrs. Owen.

BWLCH-Y-SIGLEN-LAS, pass or defile of the green bog or quagmire, about 5 m. to the w. of Llanidloes.

[1] Skene's *Four Ancient Books of Wales*, ii. 38.
[2] *Ibid.*, i, 268; see also Owen's *Llywarch Hen*, p. 9. note a.
[3] Lewis Glyn Cothi's Works, p. 432, line 20.
[4] In the *Arch. Camb.* for 1854, p. 120.

CAE-CRWN, round field, a small f. of 9 ac., t.p. Glyn-Brochan.

CAE-MAWR, large field, a f. of 40 ac., t.p. Llanifynu, o. Mrs. Owen of Glansevern.

CAN'COED, a contraction of CAE-YN-Y-COED, field in the wood, a f. of 35 ac., t.p. Glyn-Brochan, o. Mr. Williams. Also the name of a small hamlet on the banks of the Hafren, 1½ mile w. of Llanidloes, consisting of a factory, fulling mill and several cottages.

CAN'FEDW (CAE-YN-Y-FEDW), field in the birch grove, a f. of 98 ac., t.p. Glyn-Brochan, o. Mrs. Marsh.

CARN-BWLCH Y-CLODDIAU, carn of the defile of the ditches (noticed p. 20).

CARN-Y-GROES, carn of the cross (p. 21).

CARREG-BWLA, ¹Bwla's stone, a f. of 18 ac., t.p. Llaniwared, o. Mr. Williams.

CASTELL, castle, a small t. with 6 ac. of land attached, t.p. Glyn-Brochan.

CASTELL-GREIDO, *Greido* or *Grido* (as it is pronounced) may be a proper name, but Mr. R. H. Jones thinks that it is Montgomeryshire corruption of the word *gwaredog*, if so the name would mean castle of refuge.   Fields belonging to the Old Hall farm are known by the names of Hafren *Grido* and *Y-Grido*.   Castell Greido' is a f. of 42 ac., t.p. Glyn-Hafren.

CASTELL-Y-DAIL, leafy castle, a f. of 32 ac., t.p. Glyn-Hafren, o. Mr. Williams.

CEFN literally means back, applied to a ridge in topography.   Apart from being a generic term it is also the name given to several farms in this and the adjoining parishes.

CEFN-BRWYN, the rushy ridge, a f. of 65 ac., t.p. Llanifynu, lately purchased by Sir W. W. Wynn.   A lead mine has lately been discovered upon this farm ; it is called *Dôl-miner.*

CEFN-BLWCH, a corruption of CEFN-BWLCH, ridge of the hollow, name of a hill (see p. 15) and a f. of 52 ac., formerly the property of the late T. E. Marsh, Esq.

CEFN-BEIDIOG, the ivy-ridge, a f. of 58 ac., t.p. Glyn-Brochan, part of Clochfaen estate.

CEFN-COWNEN, ridge of the reed grass, a small mountain of 18 ac., t.p. Llanifynu.

CEFN-HAFOD-WEN, ridge of the fair summer abodes, the hill situated to the north of the Beili.

CEFN-HIR-BRISG, ridge of the long copse, the hill situated to the N. of the village.

¹ *Bwla* may be a proper name, but Mr. D. S. Evans points out that it also is applied in South Wales to a gelt bull, and that " Gwellt-y-bwla" is a coarse mountain grass.

CEFN-FODÈ (CEFN-YR-HAFODAU), ridge of the summer abodes, the name of one of the townships, and of a f. of 121 ac., formerly part of the Clochfaen estate, and long the residence of one of the old Llangurig families, see pp. 80-82.

CERRIG-WAEN-Y-LLAN, stones of the church Moorland, the name of a large level tract on the summit of Esgair, Clochfaen; for the tradition connected with it see ii. p. 32.

CILGWRGAN, Gwrgan's retreat or hiding place, the names of two fs. in the t.p. of Llaniwared, the lesser has an area of 20 ac.; part of Clochfaen estate; the greater (fawr) 58 ac.; o. Mr. Pryse, Pant-drain.

CILGWYN, the white or fair nook or retreat, a f. of 50 ac., in the t.p. of Cefn-yr-hafodau, o. Mr. Williams.

CIN-COED, cin may be a corruption of Cefn, ce'n; in which case the word would mean the ridge of the wood. It is the name of a hill in the t.p. of Glyn-Brochan, and also of several small fs. and tenements on its slopes.

CLOCH-FAEN. This is the orthography of the word for the last three centuries, and it means literally a stone bell. As if to confirm this interpretation of the term, a stone relic called Y cloch-faen (the stone bell) is still preserved at the present farm which has been erected on the site of the old mansion. This old stone (see p. 25), which is here figured in two positions, appears to have been intended when finished for the upper stone of a quern, though it now presents no traces of its having been used for the purpose of grinding corn.

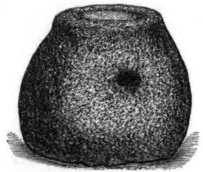

The author of the *Eccles. Antiq. of the Cymry* (p. 188) states "That the word *Cloch* would seem to imply that a hard slate or flat stone was originally used by the Cymry to answer the purpose of a bell."[1] Is this name a relic of the times when such stone bells were used? Maen-clochog, a parish in Pembrokeshire, according to Fenton (p. 348), obtained its name from "Maen-clochog, the

[1] "From the authors of those times it however appears that the *signum* was not a bell, and *clocca* was a wooden board having knockers affixed to it, as still used in the Eastern churches, where the use of bells was unknown till

Welsh for ringing stone, from two large stones that lay near the road side about a bowshot from the church to the south-west, possessing that property, now broken and removed."

Another theory as to the origin of the word is that it is derived from *Clochi*, to bubble, and *fan*, a place, the place of bubbling water. There are numerous springs of excellent water in immediate proximity to the farm. An old well formerly in the kitchen of the old mansion still exists, and its water is used by the present residents.

CNUWCH, a bush, or according to another explanation it is a corruption of *Cefn-ych* (ridge of the ox) : its pronunciation (as if written *cnuch*) favours the latter theory. It is the name of a f. 53 ac., t.p. Llaniwared.

COED-CAE, brushwood or wood for fencing, a detached portion of Lower Glan-Dulas farm, lately reclaimed ; formerly a favourite haunt of the lads of Llanidloes in the nutting season.

COED-COCHION, red wood (the name probably given in the autumn), a f. of 46 ac., t.p. Glyn-Gynwydd, o. Dr. Davies.

COED-YR-EIRESS may be either the wood of the heiress, or it may be a corruption of *eirias*, burning cinders, in which case it would mean the wood that was cut down to be converted into charcoal. A small holding of 7 ac., t.p. Glyn-hafren, o. C. J. Elwell.

COLWYN, a bantling, a whelp, a trib. of the Severn (see p. 12). Two other Montgomeryshire streams are known by this name, one flows into the Taranon in Llanwnog parish, the other in the Virnwy near Ystym-Colwyn.

CRAIG-LAS, blue rock, a f. of 22 ac., t.p. Glyn-Brochan, o. Mrs. Matthews.

CROES-TY, cross house, a f. of 23 ac., t.p. Llaniwared now joined to Tan-yr-allt ; part of Clochfaen estate.

CRUG-NANT, heathery ravine, a f. of 18 ac., t.p. Llaniwared, o. Mr. Pryse, Pant-drain.

CWM, Dr. Pugh (Dict. *sub voce*) defines it to be " a piece of ground between two hills when the sides come together in a concave form, whereas the sides of a glyn approach in a convex form."[1] Another

A.D. 865, when a belfry was first attached to St. Sophia according to Bona. In fact *clocca* is a *Celtic name* for the instrument with which the ancient Druids called the Irish to congregate together (O'Conor's *Bibl. Stowensis*, App., pp. 31-2). Thus, in process of time, according to the practice of the early Christians, the name of a Pagan instrument was transferred to its representative in the ceremonies of the Christian Church." *Arch. Camb.* for 1848, p. 307.

On the above Mr. Harries Jones remarks " Cloch—clock, Russian kolokol, is undoubtedly a Teutonic word and not Celtic. The Welsh verb *clochi*, to bubble, is formed from *cloch-dwfr*, a bubble or water-bell, and therefore proves nothing."

[1] A *glyn* has sides or slopes running parallel or nearly so, while a *cwm* has more of the resemblance of a milk-pan. When there is no outlet a lake will be found at its bottom.   D. S. E.

authority defines it as a hollow between two hills open at one end only. It is frequently used as the name of a farm, but it is more commonly employed as a generic term, and it enters largely into the composition of names throughout the principality. Sometimes it is used in conjunction with the term glyn, as *Cwm Glyn-Brochan* and *Cwm Glyn-Hafren*, etc., and in some instances we find it repeated, in the same appellation as in *Cwm-byr-gwm*, affording what the author of *Words and Places* (p. 211) calls the reduplication of synonyms.

It is the name of a f. of 76 ac., t.p. Cefn-yr-hafodau, o. Hugh Davies.

CwM-BELAN, the hollow of the Belan, the name of a hamlet on the road side which leads from Llanidloes to Llangurig, two miles from the former. It is situated at the foot of the hill on the summit of which is Belan farm, and contains a factory for the manufacture of flannel, two chapels, two inns, a smithy, and several cottages; t.p. Glyn-Gynwydd.

CwM-COCH, the red hollow, a small holding of 5 ac., t.p. Glyn-Brochan.

CwM-DULAS, hollow of the Dulas, a f. of 102 ac., t.p. Cyfn-yr-hafodau, o. Rev. Mr. Jacob.

CwM-FRON, a corruption of CwM-YR-ONN (ash hollow), which is the orthography of the old Herald's visitations (p. 83). A f. of 160 ac., t.p. Cefn-yr-hafodau, o. Mrs. Mears.

CwM-RICCET, Riccett's hollow, a f. of 36 ac., t.p. Glyn-hafren, o. Mrs. Marsh. Two mines, the one yielding copper, the other lead, have been discovered lately upon this property.

CwM-PEN-LLYDAN, the hollow with the open end, a mountain f. of 37 ac., t.p. Glyn-Brochan, o. Edward Powel.

CwM-YR-HENGRE. *Hengre* is either a corruption of *hendre*, the old habitation, or derived from *hen* and *gre*, a flock or herd, most probably the former. It is the name of a small f. of 7 ac., t.p. Glyn-Hafren, o. Mr. Williams.

DEL-FARCH. *March* seems to signify a deep dingle or glen, and Delfarch may possibly mean the leafy dingle (D. S. E.), or it may be a corruption of Dôl-fach, the little mead. The name of two fs., the lower 150 ac., o. James Hamer; the upper 79 ac.. o. Mr. Williams, both in t.p. of Llaniwared.

DERNOL, oaklands (?), a f. of 87 ac., t.p. Llaniwared, o. Mr. Williams.

DEILDREF, the leafy homestead, the name of two fs. in the t.p. of Llanifynn, formerly part of the Clochfaen estate.

DILIW, AFON, the colourless river (see p. 14).

DOL-GORS, mead of the bog, a small t., t.p. Cefn-yr-hafodau.

A *glyn*, generally speaking, is a long *narrow* defile, a *cwm* a more expansive hollow, but short.   R. H. J.

DRAIN-BYRRION, short thorns, a f. in the t.p. of Glyn Hafren, o. Rev. H. Herbert.

DRIM-MAEN, stony ridge.   Drum (Anglicised Drim) is a mutation of *Trum*, a ridge,—*trum-y-ty*, ridge of the house ; the name of a high hill between the Bidno and the Colwyn.   Drim is also the name of another hill above Cefn Brwyn.

DULAS, dark blue, a tributary of the Severn (see p. 12).

ESGAIR, literally a shank, a leg, but applied in topographical designations to a *long ridge*, a steep or precipitous slope, corresponding to the Cumberland Scaw, and the Lancashire Scar.   As a generic term it enters largely into the names of Welsh hills.   Among those of Llangurig may be mentioned *Esgair-Clochfaen* (the long ridge of the Clochfaen), *Esgair-llys* (berry bearing ridge), *Esgair-maes-nant* (ridge of the field of the ravine), *Esgair-rhugog* (the heathery ridge), *Esgair-wen* (the fair ridge), *Esgair-ychion* (ychion, probably a corruption of ychain, oxen).   *Esgair-hir* (the long esgair), a f. of 22 ac., t.p. Cefn-yr-hafodau, o. Mrs. Owen.

FARM, THE, a f. of 154 ac., t.p. Glyn-Brochan, part of the late T. E. Marsh's property.

FEDW-DDU, the dark birch grove, a f. of 40 ac., t.p. Cefn-yr-hafodau, o. Mrs. Owen.

FELIN-DRE, the generic term *tref* (mutated into *dre*), in this word and in *Pen-tre* is often interpreted to mean a town.   According to the laws of Howel Dda, the term *tref* was a portion of land equivalent to four *gavels* or holdings, *i. e.* containing 256 Welsh acres ; the size of a Welsh acre, according to Aneurin Owen being 4,320 English square yards.   The same authority gives *vill* as synonymous with tref when used in the sense of a territorial division (*Myf. Arch.* 1042, 1040, 1070, Gee's reprint).   Subsequently *tref* signified an abode or dwelling place, and when used in this sense it enters into the composition of the words *car-tref* (the abode that is dear to us— home), *hen-dre* (the old abode or permanent residence), and perhaps in the term *pen-tre* ; and latterly *tref* was applied to a collection of abodes as in *tref-lan* (a village with a church in it), and *tref*, a town.   The *tref* or *tre* in the name Felindre appears to refer to the territorial division, and the name to signify the "mill of the vill." Attached to the mill, whose motive power is supplied by the Severn, is a f. of 123 ac., t.p. Glyn-Brochan, o. Mr. Hunter.[1]

[2]FOEL, bald hill, calvary, the name of a high hill on the left bank of the Wye, half a mile to the N.E. of Cefn-brwyn.

[2]FOEL-GOCH, the red bald hill (chap. i, sec. 5).   On the western slope of this hill is a f. of 81 ac. called *Y-Foel*, part of the Clochfaen estate.

---

[1] There are *melindres* where no mill ever existed.   The term is derived from *milein-dref* = the dwelling of the *milain* or *villein* of feudal times.—— D. S. E.

[2] Foel is a mutation of Moel, Fron of Bron, and Fuches and Buches, and ought therefore to be preceded by Y (the), which has been omitted in the Glossary.

FRANKWELL. Part of the village goes by this name, which, according to Mr. Wright (*Arch. Cam.*, 1864, p. 171) is a corruption of *Frank-ville*. He says, "the feudal princes and the great barons of the Middle Ages soon learnt to appreciate the value to their treasuries of encouraging commerce on their domains. . . . Hence they tried to draw merchants to their lands by establishing little towns with freedom and privileges, either commercial or municipal, by which they might be attracted, and such places were usually denominated in France by the name of a *francheville* or free town. In England where the Anglo-Norman dialect and the English were oddly inter-mixed, the form which the name took was Frankville or Frankton." The name is common in Montgomeryshire, portions of Llanidloes, Llawr-y-glyn, and Newtown being so designated.

FRON-GOCH, the red slope, a f. of 61 ac., t.p. Glyn-Brochan.

FUCHES-MORGAN, Morgan's cattle-walk, the land where his cows grazed; the name of a small t. in Llanifynu.

GELLI-AUR, the golden grove, a f. of 41 ac., t.p. Cefn-yr-hafodau, o. Hugh Davies.

GELLI-FAWR, the large grove, two fs. in t.p. of Glyn-Glynwydd, the one of 45 ac., o. J. B. Owen, and the other of 78 ac., part of the Clochfaen estate.

GEU-FRON, the enclosed hill, a portion of this f. (67 ac.) situated on the right bank of the Hafren, is within the limits of the parish; t.p. Glyn-Hafren, o. David Davies.

GLAN-BIDNO, banks of the Bidno, the name of two fs. in the t.p. of Llanifynu; the upper has an area of 24 ac., the lower 23 ac.

GLAN-DULAS, banks of the Dulas, name of two fs.; the upper is 85 ac., partly situate in Glyn-Brochan and partly in Cefn-yr-hafodau, and formerly part of the Clochfaen estate, now the property of J. B. Owen. Some of the fields are known by the names of *Rhos-y-cwrw* (moor of the ale), Sugar field, Pickerin field, and *Dôl-ganu* (mead of song). Of the Lower Glandulas 175 ac. is in the t.p. of Glyn-Brochan, o. Col. Hunter.

GLAN-GWY, banks of the Wye, a f. of 55 ac., t.p. Llanifynu.

GLAN-RHYD, banks of the ford, a small f., t.p. Glyn-glynwydd.

GLAS-CWM, the verdant cwm, a f. of 75 ac., t.p. Laniwared.

GLYN-BROCHAN, glen of the Brochan (chap. i, sec. 6). This glen gives its name to one of the townships of the parish, and to two farms.

    1. *Upper Glyn-Brochan*, 97 ac.
    2. *Lower Glyn-Brochan*, 123 ac.

One of the fields on the former farm is known by the name of *Cae oddiar Cwm Gwyddel* (the field above the Gael's ravine). The readers of the *Vestiges of the Gael in Gwynedd* are acquainted with the theory first propounded by Llwyd relating to the early occupa-tion of Wales by the Gael. Archdeacon Jones' chief argument in support of the theory is founded upon the frequent occurrence of the name *Gwydell.* Dol Gwyddell in the parish of Trefeglwys appears in the Archdeacon's book and the remains in its neighbourhood have been already noticed, but this *Cwm Gwyddel* and another *Dol Gwyddel* in the immediate vicinity of Llanidloes were unknown to him. It is only just to mention that those who oppose the above theory give another interpretation to the term *Gwyddel,* viz., that it means "of, or belonging to woods, woody, and like the corresponding Silvester or Silvaticus, in a figurative sense, wild or savage." If this explanation be accepted then *Cwm Gwyddel* simply means the woody ravine.

GLYN-GYNWYDD, glen of the Gynwydd, which gives its name to a township and a f. of 173 ac., t.p. Cefn-yr-hafodau, o. Mrs. Owen, Glansevern. (See ABER-GYNWYDD.)

GLYN-HAFREN, glen of the Hafren (Severn), name of a township in this parish and that of another in Llanidloes, also the name of a f., 179 ac. of which are in Llangurig, o. C. J. Elwell.

GOOD-GROUND, a small f. of 15 ac., ó. Mrs. Owen.

GWERN, defined by the Rev. Walter Davies (Works, iii, 513) as "the aldery, or rough meadow or pasture, natural to the springing up of alders;" name of a small holding, t.p. Glyn-Gynwydd.

GWERN-TYFIN, the aldery of the tenement, a f. of 67 ac., t.p. Cefn-yr-hafodau, o. Mrs. Phillips.

GWY (Wye), water (described chap. i, sec. 7). This generic term occurs frequently in the names of Welsh streams, *e.g.* Virn-*wy,* Ban-*wy* (? Banw), Colun-*wy* (now Clun), Cyn-*wy* (Conway), Myn-*wy* (Munnow), Eb-*wy,* El-*wy,* Ol-*wy,* Trog-*wy,* Clwyd, etc., etc. Under its Latin name *Vaga*[1] it is frequently alluded to by the poets.

> "Meander, who is said so intricate to be,
> Has not so many turns and crankling nooks as she."
>> DRAYTON'S *Polyolbion.*

> "Pleased Vaga echoes through her winding bounds,
> And rapid Severn hoarse applause resounds."—POPE.

HAFOD is thus explained by Llwyd, "Hafod is doubtless so call'd quasi *Bod-haf,* which word is at present used, and I suppose was anciently appropriated to signify a summer hut up in ye mountains, made use of onely that time of the year, for makeing butter and cheese, as they doe at present not only about Snowdon and Cader-Idris, and elsewhere in Wales, but likewise in Switzerland and many other places amongst ye Alps." (*Arch. Camb.,* 1848, p. 244).

---

[1] Gwy has been Latinised etymologically into "Vaga," the Latin meaning of which subsequently drew attention to the meanderings, from which it was erroneously supposed by persons ignorant of Welsh to have derived its name. C. f. the somewhat similar transmutation of the names (1) Glastonbury (originally Ynys Wydryn, the Watery Isle, from *Gwy* :—Iolo MS., p. 344); (2) Abbey D'Or, in the original Welsh written *Dwr,* water, thence by the English *Dore,* explained by a confusion of meaning as D'Or, hence by translation of the latter the valley in which the Abbey was situated became the Golden Vale, which again, by re-translation into Welsh, became the *Dyffryn Aur. Lib. Landav.,* 319.   H. W. LL.

HAFOD-FEDDGAR, the Hafod favourable to the production of mead, as if the Hafod liked it or loved it; a common figure of speech (D. S. E.). A f. of 132 ac., t.p. Glyn-Hafren, o. Mrs. Marsh.

HAFOD-FRAITH, the variegated Hafod, a mountain f. of 92 ac., t.p. Glyngynwydd, o. Mrs. Owen.

HAFOD-WEN, the fair Hafod, a mountain f. of 92 ac. t.p. Glyn-Hafren, o. J. C. Elwell, Esq.

HEN-DRE, old or permanent habitation, as opposed to Hafod, the summer or temporary residence. A f. of 138 ac., t.p. Llanifynu, o. Mr. Williams.

HENDRE-AUR[1], the golden Hendre, a f. of 89 ac., t.p. Cefn-yr-hafodau, part of the Green estate.

HEN-DY, old house, a f. of 14 ac., t.p. Llanifynu, part of the Clochfaen estate.

HEN-FAES, old field, a f. of 100 ac., t.p. Llanifynu, o. Mr. J. Hughes

HIR-BRISG, the long copse or brushwood, a small f. of 17 ac., t.p. Glyn-Brochan, part of Clochfaen estate.

HIR-GOED, long wood, a small f. of 15 ac., t.p. Llanifynu, o. Sir W. W. Wynn.

HORE, the name of one of the minor elevations which form part of the mountain mass of Plinlimmon, the small river which flows round its base (chap. i, sec. 7), and of the mountain on its left bank. The farm has 38 ac. of enclosed land attached to it, which however only produces coarse hay, its value depending entirely upon its extensive sheep walk; o. Sir W. W. Wynn.

On the summit of the mountain there is a large erect stone, called by the people of the neighbourhood *Maen-gwyn* (white stone). Its position is given on the Ordnance Map, where it is styled *Carreg Wen*. Its dimensions are 7 ft. 2 in. high (above ground), 4 ft. 3 in. broad, and 2 ft. 2 in. thick.

Down one of the ravines of the mountain flows *Nant-yr-eira* (Snow-brook), a tributary of the Horé. On the banks of the former, quarter a mile above Horé house, are to be seen traces of Roman mining operations. The action of the mountain torrent appears to have revealed the lode, the course of which for a short distance is nearly identical with that of the stream. This the Roman miners followed for several hundred yards, carrying their operations to a great depth by means of a series of narrow parallel platforms. The old work was cleared out some years ago by Mr. Reynolds, a mining agent, when two or three small picks and wedges were discovered in a good state of preservation. They were sent to Sir Hugh Williams of Bodelwyddan, who presented them to the Duke of Northumberland. The modern mine has for some time past been abandoned.

Horé appears to be derived from *Hor-au*; all the plural termina-

[1] ? *Aer*, a battle, the Hendre of the battle-field.   R. H. J.

tions in *u* are in the Powysian dialect corrupted into *e*. *Hor* is a rotundity, a round hill; *hor-au* corrupted into hore as above are the round hills, *moel-ydd*." R. H. J.

If the *Horé* is a roaring or noisy stream, I would derive it from *rhawr*, a roar. The disappearance of the initial *r* may be accounted for *Y Rhorwy* (rhawrgwy), then by corruption *Yr Howry, Horwy, Hore*." D. S. E.

[1]LLAN-I-FYNU, the upland enclosure, name of one of the townships. It includes the highest and most sterile land in the parish.

[1]LLAN-I-WARED, the enclosed or cultivated lowland, name of another township ; these appear to have been named in contrast to each other. The church and village are situated in Llan-i-wared.

LLANERTH, a corruption of *Llanerch*, a glade or open piece of level ground.

LLANERCH-BROCHAN, glade of the Brochan, a f. of 99 ac., t.p. Glyn-Brochan, o. Mr. Matthews.

LLECHWEDD-HIR-GOED, slope or declivity of the long wood. ? *Ir-goed*, the greenwood slope (R. H. J.).   An elevation between the Wye and Tarenig.

LLUEST, encampment, a small t. in Llaniwared t.p.

LLUEST-BIDNO, encampment on the Bidno, a mountain farm of 203 ac. (chiefly pasture land), t.p. Lanifynu, formerly the property of Lord Mostyn, now of Mr. Morris, of Oxon, Shrewsbury.

LLUEST-DOL-GWIAIL, encampment of the mead of twigs, a f. 45 ac., t.p. Llanifynu, part of Clochfaen estate.

LLUEST-LAS, green or verdant encampment, a f. of 15 ac., t.p. Llanifynu, o. Mrs. Marsh.

LLUEST-LLEWELYN, Llewelyn's encampment (chap. i, sec. 5, and chap. ii, p. 24.)

LLWYN-GWYN, the white grove or copse, a f. of 185 ac., t.p. Llaniwared, o. Mrs. Owen.

LLWYN-IAR, hen's grove, or ? *aur*, golden, a f. of 26 ac., t.p. Lanifynu, o. Mr. Whalley, M.P.

LLWYN-YR-HYDDOD, stag's grove, a f. of 153 ac., t.p. Lanifynu, o. Mr. Hugh Lloyd (chap. vi).

MAES-HOCYN, Hokyn's field, a f. of 32 ac., t.p. Cefn-yr-hafodau, o. Mr. Hugh Davies.

MAES-Y-BRYNAR, field of the fallow, a f. of 48 ac., t.p. Glyn-Hafren,

---

[1] "It is a phonetic law between Latin and Celtic, that words beginning in the former with *pl* are in the latter *ll*. The word *planum* in Latin signifying any cultivated spot, in contradistinction from a desert spot, becomes in Celtic *Llan*" (*Four Ancient Books of Wales*, i, 159). Later it came to mean an inclosure only, without reference to the nature of the thing enclosed, until compounded with another word, as *cor-lan, ber-llan, corff-lan*, which latter gave rise, by the omission of the first syllable, to the use of the word in its tertiary sense of church. H. W. LL.

o. Mr. Charles.   The remains of an old hostelry, which was known as *Tavarn yr Hwch* (Sow Inn), still exists on the grounds of this farm.   When the old road connecting Llanidloes with Llangurig which passed over this mountain was used, the inn was greatly frequented.

MAES-Y-FFIN, field of the boundary, 8 ac of this f. are in the t.p. of Cefn-yr-hafodau.   The f. is situated on the boundary between the parishes of Langurig and St. Harmon.

MALGWYN, probably so called in honour of the man who built the f. house ; a f. of 117 ac., t.p. Glyn-Hafren, o. Mr. T. F. Roberts.

MYNACHLOG, monastery (chap. i. sec. 7), a f. of 40 ac., t.p. Glyn-Brochan, o. Mr. R. H. Morgan.

MYTALOG, a corruption of *Bod Talog*, Talog's abode, a mountain f. of 44 ac., t.p. Llaniwared, formerly part of the Clochfaen estate, now in the possession of Mr. H. Williams.

NANT, a generic term which enters very largely into the composition of Welsh names, denotes primarily the[1] ravine or hollow through which the stream flows ; secondarily, and more commonly, the stream itself.

NANT-ABER-TRI-NANT, a ravine or hollow which receives the waters of three other ravines (chap. i, sec. 7).

NANT-BESSY, Bessy's ravine or brook, gives its name to a small f. of 9 ac., t.p. Glyn-Brochan.

NANT-BRYN-GWANNON, ? from *gwynnon*, dry sticks, or from *gwaen-onn*, ash meadow.

NANT-CRUG, the heathery hollow or ravine.

NANT-DU, the dark ravine, or NANT-TY, the house in the ravine, a large mountain farm (chiefly pasture) of 323 ac., t.p. Lannifynu, o. Mrs. Owen.

NANT-GWERNOG, the hollow abounding in alders, a f. of 79 ac., in the t.p. of Cefn-yr-hafodau, part of Clochfaen estate.

NANT-GWYLLT, wild brook.

NANT IAGO, James's brook (chap. i, sec. 6).

NANT-LLED-CWM, ravine or brook of the wide hollow.

NANT MYTALOG, or *Bod-Talog* (see Mytalog).

NANT RHYS, Rhys' ravine, 401 ac. of this extensive sheep f. is in the t.p. of Llanifynu, formerly the property of the Duke of Newcastle, now of Mr. Chambers.

NANT TIDNERTH, Tiduerth's ravine or hollow, a f. of 31 ac., t.p. Llanifynu, o. Miss Lloyd.

NANT-YR-EIRA (see *Horê*).

NANT-Y-GEIFR, goat's ravine, a f. of 34 ac., t.p. Glyn-Brochan, o. Mr. Daniel Rowland.

---

[1] *Nant* is more extensive in its meaning than ravine.   Every ravine may be called a Nant ; but every Nant is not a ravine.   D. S. E.

NANT-YR-GORLAN, ravine of the sheep fold. Its waters flow into Afon Dilliw.

NANT-YR-HEBOG, hawk's ravine, a f. of 87 ac., t.p. Glyn-Brochan, o. Mr. Tiece.

NANT-YR-HENDY, ravine of the old house, a f. of 79 ac., t.p. Llaniwared, o. Mr. Thomas Lewis.

NANT-YR-OERFA, ? from *oer-fan*, cold-place, or from *aer-fa*, battle field. Its waters flow into the Brochan.

OLE-DDU, dark ravine, name of two small fs. in Cefn-yr-hafodau, called Upper and Lower Ole-ddu.

PANT-CLYD, the sheltered hollow, a small t., 5 ac., t.p. Llanifynu.

PANT-DRAIN, the thorny hollow, a f. of 127 ac., t.p. Laniwared, o. Mr. Pryse.

PANT-MAWR, great hollow, a f. of 84 ac. t.p. Llanifynu, o. Mrs. Owen Glansevern (chap. i, sec. 6).

PANT-Y-BENT (ord. sur.), PANT-Y-BENI, pronounced *Pant-y-benny* by the people of the neighbourhood. "This word appears to be a corruption of Pant-*dibyni* or *dibeni*, the hollow at the end or termination of a ridge" (J. C. H.), which is descriptive of the situation of the house. It is a small mountain of 31 ac., t.p. Llanifynu, o. Lewis Owen.

PANT-Y-LLIDIARDAU, hollow of the gates, a small f., t.p. Glyn-Brochan, o. Mr. Snead.

PANT-Y-RHEDYN, ferny hollow, a small f. of 21 ac., t.p. Llanifynu.

PANT-YR-ESGYR (esgair), hollow of the esgair, small t., t.p. Glyn-Hafren.

PEN-HYLE, corruption of *Pen-tyle*, top of the acclivity or ascent, name of two fs. in the t.p. of Glyn-Gynwydd, the larger is 61 ac., the smaller 31 ac. in extent.

PEN-ISSA'R-LLAN, lower end of the enclosure, a f. of 48 ac., t.p. Llaniwared, part of Clochfaen estate.

PEN-TRE, head or end of the vill, or the chief tref or abode (see Felindre), a f. of 25 ac., t.p. Cefn-yr-hafodau. It is also the name of a small hamlet on the side of the road leading from Llanidloes to Llangurig, a mile and a quarter from the former. Its name was probably taken from the farm.

PEN-BONT-PREN, end of the wooden bridge, or foot bridge, name of two fs., the larger in the t.p. Cefn-yr-hafodau, o. Mrs. Owen ; the other of 81 ac., t.p. Llanifynu, o. Mr. Bull.

PEN-PLANWYDD, top of the plantation, a f. of 45 ac., t.p. Cefn-yr-hafodau, o. Mrs. Owen.

PEN-Y-BANK, top of the hill, a f. of 105 ac., t.p. Cefn-yr-hafodau, o. Rev. Mr. Jacob.

PEN-Y-CINCOED, top of the branching wood (?), name of a hill and of several holdings on its slope and summit, situate in the t.p. of Glyn-Brochan.

PEN-Y-CLAP, top of the hill, a small t. in the t.p. of Glyn-Hafren.

PEN-Y-CRUGYN, top of the mound, a f. of 39 ac., t.p. Llanifynu, part of Cochfaen estate.

PEN-Y-CROESAU (probably derived from cross roads), name of a small t. in the t.p. of Llaniwared.

PEN-Y-GEULAN, top of the shelving bank, a f. of 91 ac., t.p. Lanifynu, o. Mr. Whalley, M.P.

PEN-Y-RHOS, end of the moor or plain, small t., t.p. Llanifynu.

PONT-BREN-LWYD, grey foot bridge, a f. of 34 ac., t.p. Llanifynu.

PONT-DULAS, Dulas bridge, a small f. of 13 ac., t.p Cefn-yr-hafodau.

PONT-RHYD-GALED, bridge of the ford with a hard or firm bed, name of two fs. in the t.p. of Lanifynu, one of 66 ac., o. Sir W. W. Wynn, the other of 103 ac., o. Mr. D. Hamer.

PRYS-SYLWIDD, from *Prys*, a covert of *sylwidd* of the watchman, the watchman's ambush, c. f. Llanfihangel-din-sylwidd (*din*, fortification of the watchman), close to Beaumaris.   R. H. J.

Another suggestion is that it is a corruption of *Preswylydd*, the abodes. It is the name of a farm of 80 ac., t.p. Glyn-Gynwydd, part of the Clochfaen estate.

PWLL-GWINE, ? the wine coloured pool, a small t., t.p. Glyn-Brochan.

RALLT, *Yr Allt*, the cliff or ascent, name of two small fs., t.p. Glyn-Hafren.

RHIW-FRON-GELLI, the slope or ascent of the grove hill, a f. of 134 ac., t.p. Glyn-Brochan, o. J. C. Rowley, formerly part of the Clochfaen estate.

RHIW-LAS, green ascent, a small f., t.p. Llanniwared, part of the Clochfaen estate.

RRYD-YR-ONEN, ashford, sometimes called *Rhyd-ar-Darwen* (the ford on the Darwen), a f. of 59 ac., t.p. Glyn-Brochan, o. Mr. Edwards. One of its fields is known as *Caer Castell*, probably that adjoining, or the one within the limits of the earthwork described on p. 22.

RHŌS, Welsh for a moor, or waste coarse upland, name of a small f. in the t.p. of Cefn-yr-hafodau, part of the Green estate.

RHŌS-GOCH, the red rhōs, a f. of 28 ac., t.p. Llanifynu.

RHŌS-WEN, the fair rhōs, a f. of 12 ac., t.p. Lanifynu.

RHŌS-Y-CASTELL, rhōs of the castle, a f. of 19 ac., t.p. Llanifynu.

RHŌS-Y-WRACH, the hag's rhōs, a small t., t.p. of Glyn-Brochan.

TAN-Y-BERTH, below the bush, a f. of 99 ac., t.p. Llaniwared, o. Mr. Williams, formerly part of Clochfaen estate.

TAN-Y-LLWYN, below the grove, a f. of 98 ac., t.p. Llaniwared, o. Mr. Hughes, formerly part of Clochfaen estate.

TARENIG, ? diminutive of Taranon. Mr. Silvan Evans suggests that

Trenig is the proper name, derived from *tren*, impetuous, furious. It is the name of a tributary of the Wye (chap. i, sec. 7).

TAN-YR-ALLT, below the allt, a f. of 41 ac., part of the Clochfaen estate, t.p. Llaniwared.

TROED-YR-ESGAIR, foot of the esgair, a f. of 37 ac., t.p. Lanifynu, o. Mr. Whalley, M.P., part of the Clochfaen estate up to 1857.

TY-CERRIG, stone house, a f. of 56 ac., t.p. Llaniwared, part of the Clochfaen estate.

TY-GWYN, white house, a f. of 42 ac., t.p. Glyn-Gywydd, part of the Clochfaen estate.

TY-LUCAS, Lucas' house, a f. of 13 ac., part of the Clochfaen estate.

TYLWCH. Since the appearance of the first portion of this paper, the writer has paid *Cwm-Saeson* (chap. i, sec. 5) and the vicinity a visit with the view of searching for evidence to confirm the tradition mentioned in connexion with the word Tylwch. It may, perhaps, be of interest to state very briefly the result. In the bottom of the vale, on the left bank of the little stream, which is known a little lower down as *Afon Tylwch*, is a low circular tumulus, about 25 yards in diameter, and about 6 feet high in its centre. The field on which it is situated was enclosed within the memory of living persons and was cultivated for years by the farmer who now lives on the adjacent farm, which rejoices in the name of Babylon. On one occasion when he was ploughing the field the ploughshare brought several small pieces of bones to sight, which so excited the farmer's curiosity that it caused him to dig deeper into the barrow, which he found to be " made soil," very stiff and difficult to remove. Having dug to the depth of a few feet without finding anything but an occasional small piece of bone, he desisted, and the mound has not been disturbed since, except by the ploughshare, which lowers it year after year.

In the next field, about 100 yards due north from the centre of the tumulus is a large erect stone, similar to the one on the *Ffinnant* field, near the Roman trackway, in the parish of Trefeglwys, but of larger dimensions and softer material. Its height above the ground is 7 ft. 6 in., its breadth 3 ft. 6 in., and its thickness 2 ft. 3 in. Letters are said, by the farmers of the neighbourhood, to have formerly existed upon the stone, but there are no traces of them at present. Its base was formerly surrounded by a circle of smaller stones placed in the ground edgewise, but as they interfered with the cultivation of the field they were, as a matter of course, removed. In past times the remains in this valley were regarded with a superstitious dread, to which no doubt we owe their preservation ; wonderful stories are related of fearful storms, accompanied by thunder and lightning, which caused various persons to abandon their search for treasures supposed to be hid under the stone and concealed in the mound. But the days of credulity of this description are passed away, and it needs the constraining hand of the landlord to preserve them for future generations.

Ninety yards N.W. by W. from the erect stone, in the adjacent field, are to be found remains, which look like a short alignment in the direction of E. and W., measuring thirty yards, and consisting of seven erect stones, some of which have been partially destroyed. The largest and best preserved is 6 ft. 9 in. above the ground, and 3 ft. 8 in. broad. In a field upon the opposite side of the brook the present tenant of the farm, while constructing a fence, discovered an old sword, which he presented to a neighbouring blacksmith. If not destroyed, the weapon would materially assist in determining the date of the skirmish or battle which appears to have been fought in the valley.

Higher up the stream, about 40 yards from its left bank, is another erect stone, 6 ft. 3 in. high, 7 ft. broad, with an average thickness of about 1 ft. 8 in.

All these remains are just within the limits of the parish of St. Harmon, which in the eleventh and twelfth centuries formed part of the cantref of Arwystli. None of them are marked on the Ordnance map.

Lewis Morris gives it as his opinion that *Tylwch* originally was *Du-llwch*, *llwch* or *lough* being the Irish word for lake (*Camb. Reg.* ii, 493). The word is pure but very old Welsh. *Llwch*, now obsolete, in the time of Taliessin, and even later, was synonymous with lake, and in this sense occurs in the *Four Ancient Books of Wales*, ii, p. 154, and again in the same book, p. 204, we have

> " Kein gyfedwch
> Y am *dewlwch*
> *Llwch* am pleit."

[A bright festivity, About the two lakes. The lake on my side.]

A striking instance of how entirely obsolete this old word has become is given by Mr. Wynn in the *Camb. Reg.*, ii, 154. " There is," he states, " a parish in Caermarthenshire called *Llan-llwch*. Llwch is a very old word for lake, which being now unintelligible, the very lake or llwch itself, from which the consecrated ground originally took its name, is now called from the church or village *Llyn Llan-llwch*." Again we have a similar reduplication in the name of a lake in Brecknockshire, *Llyn Cwm-y-llwch*. In *Tal-llychau* (the name of an abbey and parish in Caermarthenshire) is another instance of the old word *llychau* being the plural of *llwch*, and *Tal* (which suggests the original form of the *Tyl* in Tylwch) meaning the end or head (of the lakes) which is exactly descriptive of the situation of the old abbey. We may, therefore, pretty safely conclude that the modern *Tylwch* is a corruption of *Tal-llwch*,[1] being synonymous with Pen-y-llyn and Tal-y-llyn, head of the lake. But no lake exists at Tylwch now ; yet the word affords undoubted evidence that a lake once existed in the immediate vicinity, perhaps

[1] C. f. *Talachddu*, in Brecknockshire; *tal* (the head), *-llwch* (lake), *Ddu* (black); *Amlwch*, in Anglesea; *Maeslwch*, in Radnorshire; *Ynys-pen-lwch*, in Glamorganshire. See also *Words and Places*, pp. 219, 227.

Q

in the neighboorhood of the present factory, which is once more in full work. The prospects of the little hamlet look very encouraging at present, owing to the mines being in active operation.

Ty-MAWR, large house, a f. of 68 ac. t.p. Llanifynu, o. Mr. Williams.

Ty-NEWYDD, new house, a small f. of 9 ac., t.p. Glyn-Brochan, o. Col. Hunter.

Ty'N-Y-COED, house in the wood, two fs., one of 58 ac., t.p. Glyn-Brochan, another 65 ac., t.p. Cefn-yr-hafodau.

Ty'N-Y-CWM, house in the hollow, a f. of 40 ac., t.p. Llanifynu.

Ty'N-Y-DDOL, house in the mead, a f. of 171 ac., t.p. Llanifynu, part of the Clochfaen estate.

Ty'N-Y-FRON, house on the slope, a f. of 77 ac., t.p. Glyn-Glynwydd, o. Dr. Davies.

Ty'N-Y-MAES, house in the plain or field, a f. of 172 ac., t.p. Llaniwared, part of Clochfaen estate.

Ty'N-Y-RHŌS, house in the rhōs, (see Rhōs), a f. of 88 ac., t.p. Llanifynu, o. Mr. Hugh Lloyd.

Ty'N-YR-HENDRE, house in the old ville, a f. of 25 ac., t.p. Glyn-Brochan, formerly belonged to Lord Mostyn.

Tyn-YR-WTRA, house in the lane. Formerly there existed two small fs. of this name, but they are now united, and form a farm of 90 ac., t.p. Glyn-Hafren, o. C. J. Elwell, Esq.

Ystrad-Olwyn, various explanations of this name suggest themselves. If derived from *Strata*, we should have *Olwyn's Street*, but there are no traces of a street or paved roadway in the neighbourhood; neither are the farms situated in a valley, so that we have to fall back upon (1) *Ystrad-olwyn*, the circular plat, in the form of a wheel, or (2) *Ystrad-y-dôl-wen*, the plat of the fair mead, both of them descriptive of the situation. The latter is the suggestion of Mr. J. C. Hughes, and I am inclined to think it to be the true meaning. The two fs. which bear this name are in the t.p. of Glyn-Gynwydd—the larger *(fawr)* is 89 ac., o. Mrs. Owen ; the smaller *(fach)* is 55 ac. in extent, and forms part of the Clochfaen estate.

Warren-house, a f. of 20 ac., t.p. Llanifynu, o. Mrs. Owen.

Waen (a mutation of *Gwaen*) is defined as "a flat marshy tract" by the late Rev. W. Davies (Works iii, 537), and as "a meadow, a down, a plain," in the latest edition of Dr. Pugh's *Dictionary*. It is the name of a f. of 20 ac., t.p. Glyn-Brochan, o. Mrs. Owen. A large marshy tract in the t.p. of Cefn-yr-hafodau is known as *Waen-Cilgwyn*, deriving its name probably from the farms so called. *Waen goch* (the red down) forms part of Esgair Maesnant.

ADDITIONS AND CORRECTIONS.

Bedd Gwrtheyrn (p. 41). One of the names of the traditional burial places of Vortigern is thus preserved in stanza xl of the collection entitled the "Verses of the Graves," or the "Verses of the Warriors," in the *Black Book of Caermarthen*:—

> "Ebet yn ystyuacheu,
> Y mae paup yny amheu,[1]
> Bet gurtheyrn gurtheneu."
>
> *Four Ancient Books of Wales*, ii, 32.

> "The grave of Ystyvachau,
> Which everybody doubts.[1]
> The grave of Gwrtheyrn Gwrthenau."
>
> *Ibid.*, i, 314.

Pillar of Eliseg (p. 41). Below is a specimen of the inscription on this important monument—so valuable to the future investigator of the early history of the Principality of Powys—as given by Edward Llwyd in his *Arch. Brit.*, tit. vi, p. 229. This pillar, or monumental cross, was erected at a place formerly called *Maes-yr-ychen*, but subsequently *Pant-y-groes*, about a quarter of a mile distant from the abbey of *Valle Crucis*, by Cyngen, or Concenn, Prince of Powys, in or before the year 850 (for he was slain at Rome that year), in memory of his great grandfather, Eliseg. Cyngen was the son of Cadell (who died in the year 804), the son of Brochwel, the son of Prince Eliseg, sixth in descent from Brochwel Ysgythrog,

— BENED — GERMANUS QUE
— PEPERIT EI SE . . IRA FI-
LIA MAXIMI
REGIS QUI OCCIDIT REGEM
ROMANO
RUM ✠ CONMARCH PINXIT
HOC
CHIROGRAFU REGE SUO
POSCENTE
CONCENN ✠ ETC.

[1] or, The grave in Ystafachau,
Which everybody suspects to be,
The grave of Gwrtheyrn Gwrthenau.

Mr. Haigh (*Conquest of Britain by the Saxons*, p. 230) reads the first part of it thus : " Guarthimer whom Germanus blessed, the son of Guarthigern whom Severa bare to him, the daughter of King Maximus, who killed the king of the Romans." Nothing is known of the Cynfarch, or Conmarch, who carried out the design of King Cyngen.

Jenkyn Goch (see pp. 49-50) is stated to have married Catherine, *daughter and heir* of Maurice Fychan of Kerry. Some doubt has been cast upon the accuracy of this statement. The authorities for it are :

1. *Add. MS.* 9865, one of the vols. of that celebrated genealogist John Davies, of Rhiwlas, to whose labours the editor of Dwnn's *Visitations* is indebted (i *Intro.*, pp. xxix,-xxx, *Llyfryddiaeth*, 311). This MS., which contains a fully drawn out tabular pedigree of the descendants of Elystan Glodrudd, asserts that Catherine was heiress to Maurice Fychan.

2. *Harl MS.*, 1973, p. 96 (Heraldic Visitations, by Randle Holme) also states that Catherine was daughter and heir of Maurice Fychan.

Owen, son of Maurice of Clochfaen (p. 51), married Tangwystl, daughter of Morgan (ab Maurice, younger son of Thomas ab Maurice Fychan, of Aber-Magwr, in the parish of Llanfihangel-y-creuddyn, descended from Einion ab Collwyn ab Tangno, lord of Eifionydd and Ardudwy), by whom he had one daughter, Mallt. He died on the evening of January 7th, 1500, and his *Marwnad* (or elegy) has the name of Huw Arwystl attached to it. In it the writer describes him as a " soldier of the sea," and laments that the festival should have been saddened by his death.

Note to pp. 63-4.—*Colonel Hinde* died at Brussels on the 15th of May, 1870, and was buried at Ucle, near that city. The following is the inscription upon his tomb :—

CAROLUS THOMAS EDWARDUS HINDE
LEGIONIS BENGALIENSIS TRIBUNUS
OBIIT IDIBUS MAII MDCCCLXX ÆTATIS SUÆ AN L°
REQUIESCAT IN PACE.

Note to p. 66. In addition to the information previously given respecting the castle and lordship of Whittington, we take the following allusion to the matter from the *Add. MS.* 9865 :—

"The township of Trefor was divided between Cuhelyn and Meurig, the third and fourth sons of Tudor ab Rhys Sais. The second son of Tudor was Goronwy, surnamed Pefr, who was the Wrennoc of the early romances, and had the lordship of Whittington for his portion. By his first wife he had (1) Sir Roger, of whom presently; (2) Sir William de Powys, Knt. (*Llywth Gwydd y Derwen*); he had an only daughter, named Miletta, who became the wife of Sir Fulke Fitz-Warren, son and heir to Sir Warren de Weaux, a nobleman of Lorraine; (3) Jonas of Penley (*Llywth Llanerch Banna*), who bore *az.* three boars passant in pale *or.* The Penley estate passed by marriage into the family of Dymoke, who still possess it (p. 66).

"The eldest son, Sir Roger de Powys, lord of Whittington (Blancheville) was a knight of Rhodes, and bore *vert* a boar *or.* In a note at p. 13, vol. ii of Dwnn's *Heraldic Visitations* there is the following notice of him : 'In an Anglo-Norman life of Fulk Fitz-Warren Iorwerth (Drwyndwn) it is said 'dona a Rogier de Powys Blancheville e Maylour,' and, after his death, 'Morys le Fitz Rogier de Powys' became 'Seigneur de Blancheville e Maylour,' and when he died we are told that Llewelyn ab Iorwerth regretted his death, 'par ce que Morys fut son Cousyn.' Sir Roger married Cecilia, daughter of Hwfa ab Iorwerth ab Gruffydd ab Ieuaf ab Niniaf (*gules* two lions passant *arg.* for Iorwerth ab Gruffydd) by whom he had issue : 1. Sir Maurice or Meurig Llwyd, lord of Whittington, who was slain by Sir Fulk Fitz Warren, who took possession of the castle and lordship of Whittington, and had it confirmed to him by Henry III. 2. Sir Roger de Estwick, heir to Sir Meurig Llwyd, by an estate of settlement made by Llewelyn ab Iorworth, Prince of Wales, and confirmed by Henry III of England. He had issue a son Meredydd. 3. Roger Fychan, whose only daughter and heiress Gwerfyl, married to Sir Philip Kynaston, ancestor of the Kynastons of Hardwicke (Dwnn, i, 326). 4. Owain: he had an only daughter and heiress, Gwerfyl, married to Einion ab Gwilym, which Gwilym was an illegitimate son of Gruffydd ab Gwenwynwyn, Prince of Powys.

5. Goronwy, ancestor of the families of Pentre Madog in Duddleston and the Estwicks of Estwick."

Note to Edward Lloyd of Pen-y-lan (p. 77).

MARY LLOYD, heiress of Pen-y-lan, married Roger Kenyon, Esq., of Cefn, brother of Lloyd, first Lord Kenyon, and was mother of

EDWARD, born 1771, who assumed the name of Lloyd and subsequently that of Williams. He married Annabella (born 5th April, 1777), eldest daughter and coheiress of the Rev. Philip Puleston, D.D., and heiress to her uncle, Watkin Williams, Esq., of Penbedw (son of Richard Williams, Esq., youngest brother of the first Sir Watkin), M.P. for Montgomeryshire, and afterwards for the Flint Boroughs; the youngest daughter and coheiress, Elizabeth, married William Wynn, Esq., of Peniarth, and was mother of the present W. W. E. Wynne, Esq, of Peniarth. Mr. Edward Lloyd Williams died without issue, and his widow married secondly Major General Molyneaux, who assumed the additional name of Williams and is now living (1870).

Corrections:

On illustration facing p. 22 *for* "Rhyd-yn-onen," *read* "Rhyd-yr-onen."

On p. 42, line 15 from top, *for* "Gwawrddyd," *read* "Gwawrddyd*d*."

" p. 43, „ 4 „ bottom, *for* "Gwrstan ab Gwaethhvod," *read* "Gwrystan ab Gwaeth*foed*."

On p. 50, note 1, *instead of* "son of Maelgwyn, lord, etc.," *read* "*son of Meredydd ab* Maelgwyn, lord, etc."

On p. 50, line 1 from top, *for* "Einion of Kerry," *read* "Einion *ab Howel* of Kerry."

On p. 51, line 6 from top, *for* "Gwaethfod," *read* "Gwaeth*foed*."

" p. 52, „ 7 „ bottom, *for* "Glandywedog," *read* "Glan*cly*wedog."

On p. 53, line 17 from bottom, *for* "collised," *read* "co*tt*ised."

„ p. 54, „ 10 „ top, *for* "Edwyn Goronwy," *read* "Edwyn *ab* Goronwy."

On p. 59, line 15 from top, *after* 1766, *insert, leaving an only daughter and heiress, Sarah.*

On p. 61, line 12 from bottom, *for* "Cyfeiliog," *read* "Cyffylliog."

" p. 68, „ 9 „ „ *for* "bromoslips," *read* "*broom*slips."

„ p. 74, „ 7 „ „ *for* "Iowerth," *read* "*Idnerth*."

„ p. 74, note 2, line 11 from bottom, *for* "Corbet of Moreton Corbet," *read* "Corbet of Wattlesborough, son of Sir Robert Corbet of Moreton Corbet and Wattlesborough."

On p. 75, line 15 from top, *after* 4, *insert* "sable."

In the Glossary, *for* "*Nant Tidnerth*," *read* "*Nant Idnerth*," and was probably so called from Idnerth ap Madog Danwr.

WELSH POETRY, ILLUSTRATIVE OF THE HISTORY OF LLANGURIG.

By HOWEL W. LLOYD.

It was to be expected that the district of Arwystli, abounding no less in picturesque scenery, than in historical associations, lying in and about the majestic Plinlimmon, the cradle of Severn, Wye, and other illustrious streams, should have given birth to poets, whose genius, fired no less by the grandeur of their native scenery than by the love of country, always conspicuous in the breasts of mountaineers, should have left to posterity memorials worthy of such sources of inspiration. Accordingly we find several whose works, few of which have hitherto been committed to the press, are scattered among the manuscript collections in the principality, in the British Museum, and elsewhere. Research has brought to light some poems among them which are not a little interesting in connexion with the local history of Llangurig, whether regarded from a social, religious, or historical point of view. These it is now proposed to introduce to our readers, together with translations, accompanied by such preliminary matter as may be requisite for the purpose of elucidating the sense, which is not unfrequently obscure, and also their relation to the special subject of our history.

The first in chronological order, with the exception, perhaps, of the author of a poem or two of uncertain date, which will be referred to presently more fully, is Ieuan Tew, called Ieuan Tew Hên, or Hynaf, who was born at Llanidloes, and is known to have presided at a "Gorsedd," or session of bards, held at Glamorgan in

R

1420.[1] Twenty-four of his compositions are enumerated in the catalogue of the British Museum as extant in that collection, none of which, however, appear to relate to the subject of this paper. The next is Huw Cae Llwyd, said to have flourished from 1450 to 1480, and known to have presided at the Glamorgan Gorsedd in 1470,[2] eight at least of whose poems are preserved in the British Museum. The third is Huw Arwystli, whose poems are exceedingly numerous, and whose period, though not yet precisely settled, would appear to have extended from the latter part of the reign of Henry VIII to nearly the close of that of Elizabeth. And lastly, we have his contemporaries, Sion Ceri, and Sir Ieuan of Carno, who, though not apparently natives of Arwystli, were denizens of its neighbourhood, and maintained intimate relations with its inhabitants. Of these we have one poem by Sion Ceri, another by Huw Cae Llwyd, and several by Huw Arwystli, most of which however have unfortunately reached us in a mutilated state, in which is presented a life-like picture of some of the principal features of the social and religious life of Llangurig in the fifteenth and sixteenth centuries. Prior to any of these in order of time is the following by Ieuan Deulwyn, a poet who flourished from about 1460 to 1490, and is known to have presided at the Gorsedd of Glamorgan in 1480.[3] It is entitled "an Elegy on Dafydd Fychan of Curig's Land," and relates apparently to an incident of warfare, which, if the period ascribed to the author be correct, must have occurred considerably later than the battle of Mortimer's Cross, fought in February, 1461, when Sir Owen Tudor, grandfather of Henry VII, was slain, and his half-brother, Henry VI, lost his crown. Perhaps it is to be referred to the revolt of Clarence and Warwick, 1465-70, which ended in the battle of Barnet, and in the course of

---

[1] Williams's *Dictionary of Eminent Welshmen*, p. 241.
[2] If the poem of *The Four Brothers* is correctly ascribed to him, he must have been living as late as the reign of Henry VIII.
[3] Williams's *Dictionary of Eminent Welshmen*, p. 120.

which was fought the battle of Danesmore, near Banbury, at which the Sir Richard Herbert, whose elegy by our bard is also extant,[1] was taken prisoner, and beheaded by the Lancastrians, together with his brother, Sir William, who, after the surrender of Harlech Castle, had been created Earl of Pembroke by Edward IV. As the poem has already been printed in Welsh,[2] it is unnecessary to reproduce the original here. Davydd, with his brother Ieuan, are referred to as having fallen victims to an ambuscade on the Wye, and one of them is stated to have been buried in the churchyard of Llangurig.

Elegy on Davydd Vychan and Ieuan of Curig's Land.

In tears for whom is Powys found,
And all the south, the country round?
I mourn, when I would rouse the chase,
On bank of Wye, in glen of Euas;
Woe's me! a host is come and gone,
Where two youths came, now come not one.
From Maelor one, too well I wist;
From Curig's Land another missed!
Mine office brings me nought but pain,
On moor and glen I call in vain.
For two—our best—we stay forlorn;
They come not—we may wait and mourn.
As Mary mourn'd, so I their loss,
Her Son's fell wounds beneath the cross.
She from her eyes wept tears of blood,
May mine weep, too, a kindred flood!
I can no more than turn my gaze,
Wistful, on yonder upland haze;
Long tho' I wait, there comes not one,
From moor to dell—both, both are gone!
Sole remnant from the slaughter, I,
Since when Siac Llwyd doth yonder lie;
I call—nought boots me to complain—
For gen'rous Davydd Vychan's slain!
For both drear sorrow chills my bones,
Llewelyn also heaves my groans.

[1] Printed in Rice Jones's *Gorchestion y Beirdd*, p. 135, Edition 1773.

[2] *Ibid.*, p. 139. See also *Montgomeryshire Collections*, vol. i, p. 390.

R 2

For Davydd and for Ieuan vent
Two thousand hearts their one lament.
For these two tribes are sunk in grief,
For these two lands find no relief;
In Llinwent's[1] mansion sorrow reigns,
And all Saint Idloes' town complains.
I, too—whom Llinwent led—complain
For Llinwent's chief, by ambush slain.
Deep laid the plan—thro' foul deceit—
He gave his hand—his fate to meet.
So was he slain—O shameful deed!
As tho' 'twere Arthur's self to bleed.
His wont was never to appear,
When raged the combat, in the rear;
In battle he the first to meet
The foe, the hindmost in retreat.
The rear that he should cover, I
Lamented, on the bank of Wye.
To quit their post, to break their troth,
Were false of him and Ieuan both.
Twain brethren of devoted mind—
It stirred them sore to stay behind.
Two lands diverse are reft of joy,
For Ieuan's land hath sprung from Troy.
Fair Curig's church is wrapped in gloom,
There lies the lion in the tomb.
Fall'n is that ancient line full low,
Glides Howel's stream with weaken'd flow.
Like land of court and church bereft
Is Powys without Ieuan left.
Vengeance in flood burst forth of yore,
For greater now the need is sore;
My heart would never broken be,
Such deluge for such men to see.

We now revert to the poems already glanced at as of
uncertain date, and so far as our present knowledge will
carry us, also of nameless authorship. In the MS.
volume, indeed, from which they have been extracted,
the name of Huw Arwystli is subscribed to them, probably by a conjecture of the transcriber. The first poem
is an eulogium upon a person named Ieuan, the son of
Gruffydd, of Clochfaen, together with his wife Gwenllian,

[1] This is a mansion in the parish of Llanbister in Radnorshire.

and Jenkyn Goch, their son.[1] Huw Arwystli, whose life extended late into the sixteenth century, was a contemporary of the grandsons of this Jenkyn Goch, who is known to have been living in 1470. It cannot therefore be supposed that he could have been living early enough to celebrate the virtues of Jenkyn's parents during their lifetime, as this would imply that his own life was protracted for as much as fifty years beyond the ordinary span. It may be as well to premise that this, and most of the following poems, are taken from a MS. collection, called the "Llyfr Ceniarth," from the fact of its preservation at a place of that name in Montgomeryshire, to the kindness of whose owner, Mr. D. Gilbertson, we are indebted for the liberty to copy them. The original compiler of the collection has not been ascertained with certainty; but there is reason to believe that the poems in it relating to Clochfaen may have been transcribed from the original (which were preserved at that place until its destruction by fire in 1760) by Mr. Morgan Lloyd, son of Mr. Jenkyn Lloyd, of the Clochfaen, who settled at Llanbrynmair towards the close of the seventeenth century. The MS. may have come into the possession of the Ceniarth family through his daughter Sarah, who was married to E. Pritchard, Esq., of that place.[2] The style and orthography of the MS. are the same as were in vogue at the commencement of the eighteenth century. Several of the leaves have been lost, and the volume has otherwise suffered from exposure to damp; many of the compositions, therefore, have come down to us in a deplorably fragmentary state. From the violation of the rules of consonancy in several instances, inconceivable in the composition of bards of such high reputation among their contemporaries, it is to be inferred that the text has undergone additional mutilation from the carelessness of the transcriber, or his ignorance of the rules of "*cynghanedd*."[3] As none of these have

---

[1] *Montgomeryshire Collections*, vol. ii, p. 271.   [2] *Ibid.*, p. 276.
[3] *i. e.* Alliterative consonancy. The *Cywydd deuair*, in which

been hitherto printed, so far as is known, it has been
thought proper to insert them here in the original text,
as well as in the necessarily imperfect form of a prose
translation.

COWYDD I HENAFIAID Y CLOCHFAN.

Duw a'i roi gynt, nid ar gam,
Drwy Ebrwy Dir [i] Abram,
Dyfawd iddo'r blaid [uf] ydd
O'i gordd, cyn amled a 'r gwydd.
Rhoed [gan] Dduw i rwyd dwyrain,
I'w rhwysg deuddegllwyth y rhain.
I ddawn Abram ddoen' Ebryw,
A'i rodd a ddiolchodd ei Dduw.
Fy rodd innau, 'nghefn[1] yr haf,
I Dduw eilwaith a ddiolchaf:
Mae Duw 'n rhoi i ni dy'n rhydd,
Rhwng gwar min Gwy a'r mynydd;
Mab Gwilym Gam, ddinam, ddoeth,
A gae Ieuan i'w gyfoeth.
Myfi'r haf, mwy yw fy rhan,
Yw gwr y ty ar Gwrt Ieuan:
Mwyn, brud yr wyf mewn bord rydd,
Mawl a'i hyder mal hedydd,
Cywydd a wna ef, hedydd haf,
Yn fwrw' n ochr y fron uchaf;
Cerais, ar hynt cwrs yr hydd,
Felly i fwrw fy lleferydd.[2]
Gwych, trym, oedd iach i'w tramwy,
Clochfan Gwrt cylch afon Gwy
.   .   gynnes gwar mynydd
.   .   .   d iach frig dy dydd
Ba le bynag y bai 'r nod,
Byw yno y mae'n benod.
.   .   a geiff enwog wedd
Morys [ar] ol a mawredd.
Mab yw, ni bydd i'm dydd dig,
Mur ceraint[3] ymro Curig,

most of these poems is composed, consists of rhyming couplets,
each verse of which contains seven syllables, and is divided into
two clauses, in the last of which must be repeated consecutively
three of the consonants contained in the first.

[1] Cefn, pars superior, Dr. Davies's *Dict., s. v.*   [2] "E. lly ei" in MS.
[3] In MS. *Twr Coraint.* The metre requires a word beginning
with *m.*

Corff Rolant Siancyn ffriwlwyd
Goch hil llin gwych Howel Llwyd.
Câr Rhys Llwyd accw rhoes lun
Craig ruddaur Ceri Creuddyn.
Llawn ei bord Wenllian bydd,
Hwynte rywl [iant] mewn trefydd.
Ystyried îs y Daren
A wna hi wrth wan a hên.
Gras a rhoes gwir Iesu i'w rhan,
Syn i ran synwyr Ieuan.
Araf yw'r gwycha' o'r gwyr,
Araf yw hedfa'r eryr.
Ar genedl pan fo'r gynhen,
Oni bydd Pont, ni bydd Pen.
Rhain geidw gweilch hengoed gynt
Heb wanhâu neb o honynt:
Cad[ar]na'r cornor coed allt,
I'w ennyn ar war wen'r allt.
Ond da yw yntau Ieuan,[1]
[Gy] da' i' droed gadw 'i ran.[2]
[Tra fydd ei r] hwysg, llew'r trefydd
Arwystli fawr ar ei ol fydd.
[Nid] dyn fu[3] mwy yno
[Yn ei farn] Ieuan tra fo,
[Ni bydd] gwaed heb unben gwyr.

* * * * *

TRANSLATION.

God, of old time, granted not unjustly
To Abraham, thro' the Hebrew land,
The coming to him of the obedient people,
By his impulsion, numerous as the forest.
God gave the east to be taken as in a net,
By the onslaught of their twelve tribes.
To the endowment of Abraham came the Hebrews,
And for his gift he gave thanks to God.
For my gift, too, in the height of summer,
To God in my turn will I give thanks.
It is God who freely gives us a house,
Between the slope of Wye's bank and the mountain.
The son of Gwilym Gam, blameless and wise,

[1] The MS has "d da in gulan Ieuan." The reading, as amended, is conjectural only.
[2] The original has "waed," and "a'i ran" in the next line.
[3] Dynru in MS.

Possesses Ieuan for his weal.
I, myself, in the summer—the greater is my portion—
Am goodman of the house over Ieuan's court:
Courteous and free am I at the generous board,
In praise whose boldness is like the lark's.
A strain he utters —he, the lark of summer,
Throwing his breast askant in its ascent.
I have loved, in following the chase of the hart,
In like manner to pour forth my voice.
Gay, trim, and pleasant to frequent,
Is Clochfaen Court on the winding of the Wye.
. . Warm is the slope of the hill,
And wheresoever my lot be cast,
To live there is best of all.
Morys[1] shall gain distinguished rank
And greatness in the future.
A youth who will never be angry with me,
A wall of strength to his kindred in Curig's land
Is Jenkyn Goch, of pale complexion—a Roland[2] in stature—
Scion of the noble line of Howel Lloyd,
Kinsman of Rhys Lloyd[3] yonder, who gave him
The rock of Ceri, Creuddyn,[4] red as gold.
Full will the table of Gwenllian be,[5]
They also shall rule in towns.
Consideration beneath the oak
Will she entertain for the weak and old,
Grace verily hath Jesus given for her portion,
Marvel at the understanding allotted to Ieuan,
Deliberate is the noblest of men—
Deliberate is the flight of the eagle.
In the Tribe when strife hath arisen,
No Head will there be, except there be a Bridge.
These shall preserve the hawks of the ancient forest,
Not one of them shall be made weak,
In the strongest corner of the wooded upland
To incite them[6] on the crown of the smiling hill.
But Ieuan also is well able

---

[1] Perhaps the son and successor of Jenkyn Goch, and grandson of Ieuan, is the person alluded to. *Mont. Coll.*, vol. ii, p. 273.
[2] The hero of romance, and nephew of Charlemagne.
[3] Probably his uncle, Rhys Lloyd, of Pont y Rhyd Galed, ancestor of the Richardses of Llangurig.
[4] One of the three comots of Cantref Penwedig in Cardiganshire.
[5] An allusion to the words of the Psalm, "Thy children like the olive branches round about thy table."   [6] The MS. text has *swyr.*

With his foot to hold his ground.
So long as his lion's career shall last,
Shall the towns of Arwystli be great at his back.
There no man has been greater than he.
. . . . so long as Ieuan shall live,
Its men shall not want a chieftain of their blood.

The next poem, although in the MS. subscribed with
the words and date, " Huw Arwystli ai kant, 1503," has
been, but perhaps with less reason, referred to the
same category of doubtful date and authorship as the
last. The title runs thus; *Cowydd, neu Englynion
Marwnad Elen, gwraig Howel ab Morys Goch o Langurig yn Uwchgoed*, i. e. " A Poem, or Elegiac Stanzas
on Ellen, wife of Howel, son of Morys Goch of Llangurig, in Uwchgoed." No such connexion as " Howel"
is, however, to be found in any of the Llangurig families. The statement probably has arisen from a mistake of the transcriber, who, in his ignorance of the
descent of the Clochfaen family from an ancestor of
that name, concluded hastily that the " Howel" referred to in the third and fifth stanzas, could have
been no other than her husband. It is strange that he
should have overlooked the fact that the latter is more
fitly represented by " Llewelyn," who, in the sixth
stanza, is designated by the title of " Llyw Aelwyd," the " Lord of the Hearth," an expression apparently equivalent to the prosaic one of " Head of the
Family." It is in Llewelyn, therefore, that the husband of Ellen must be sought. Accordingly, we find
that a lady of that name, a daughter of Maurice ap
Jenkyn Goch, and great granddaughter of Ieuan, the
subject of the last poem, was married to Llewelyn ab
Morys ab Rhys of Llangurig.[1] She was a sister of the
" Four Brothers of Llangurig," whose fame has been
preserved in the curious poem by Huw Cae Llwyd,
which will be presented the next in succession to our
readers ; both poems, therefore, must be assigned to
the same period. The name of one of this lady's brothers, Evan of Crugnant, appears as sixth on the grand

---

[1] *Montgomeryshire Collections*, vol. ii, p. 273.

jury, A.D. 1546. We shall not be far wrong in as-
cribing to them, therefore, a somewhat earlier date,—
not too early, however, to have been actually composed
by the poet indicated in the MS. as its author.

ENGLYNION, SEF MARWNAD ELEN, GWRAIG LLEWELYN[1] AB MORYS
GOCH O LANGURIG YN UWCHGOED.

1.

Mair ! pond du ein arddelydd—bla
    Blin yw gwaith elorwydd :
Mair ! Mair ! ni chawn ddial lawnddydd ;
Mwy lle i minau maen mynydd.

2.

Oer fydd blaen mynydd, blin i 'm yw—mhla
    Am Elen dda ei wyth ryw :
Nid braendod ond bâr un Duw,
Ni henwyd fath hono 'n fyw !

3.

Difyw[2] brig bro Cirig o'r cerydd—hil[3] llon
    Howel Lloyd nis gorfydd :
Dodau'r dull dyn o'r dydd,
Du rew'n glwyd ar ein gwledydd.

4.

I'r gwledydd trist troes Duw faith—bla
    I'n blino nosulgwaith :
Hwyr fydd i 'n byw, Duw, o'r daith ;
I wan esgor y nosgwaith.

5.

Nôs glaf a fu'n anaf i fonedd—Howel
    Tynnu'n holl ymgeledd :
Nid â, a ni 'n byw dan nenn bedd
Wraig rywogach o'r gwragedd !

6.

Cai bedd pen gwragedd Creuddyn[4] pan gadd
    Pen gwaed Curig breuddyn ;
Alaeth oedd ar dylwyth hyn,
A Llyw aelwyd Llewelyn.

[1] The MS. has "Howel."   [2] The MS. has "Dewrw."
[3] "Bill" in MS.
[4] "Ai gryn" in MS. I have ventured to restore "Creuddyn,"
which satisfies both context and metre.

7.

[Aelwy]d bywyd torri bon—y pren
   Adfyd prudd ei dylodion ;
A rhoi anaf ar weinion,
Le ymlaen fu'r glân blant hon.

8.

Glan feibion gwychion'n rhoi gawr—'n dost
   Yn dwyn derwenllawr ;
Ni chwardd na thylawd na chrythawr,
Weled roi lled gwlad i'r llawr !

9.

Aeth wlad i ddwyn cwyr iwch canol—lle
   Lle 'r â 'r byd olynol ;
Ond rhoi gair da rhagorol,
Ei cho' yw hwn—serch i'w hol.

10.

Elen yn ol pen lle 'i poenwyd[1]—ni thân
   Ac ni thyrr yr anwyd ;
Llwyr o'r cwyn yn ei difwynwyd,
Lle bu ar ben llwybr roi bwyd.

11.

A ru o 'i bwyd a gladdwyd Llysgelyddon[2]—braf
   Lle bu briffordd tylodion ;
Mawr yw 'r anap ar weinicn,
Mair ! bydd hwyr marw bath hon !

ELEGY ON ELEN, WIFE OF LLEWELYN, SON OF MORRIS
GOCH OF LLANGURIG IN UWCHGOED.

1.

Mary ! how black is our gloom ; a grievous
Affliction is the work of the bier :
Mary ! Mary ! a day of full vengeance may I not have ;
For me were a stone on the mountain a fitter abiding-place.

---

[1] This line seems corrupt, nor can I do more than guess at its
meaning.

[2] Llys Gelyddon. I know not if this place is named in other
Welsh writings, or whether it is here referred to as Elen's burial-
place ; or, with greater probability perhaps, as connected in some
way with her beneficence to the poor.

2.

Cold is the mountain-peak, painful to me is my sorrow,
For Elen, noble thro' her eight descents :
God alone is the cause of dissolution !
Her living like hath ne'er received a name.

3.

Lifeless is the Upland of Curig because of the chastisement,
The gentle race of Howel Lloyd will not endure it :
Like the outspread of a black forest over our lands
Is the closing of the day to her mortal form.

4.

God on our sorrowing lands hath laid a lasting grief,
To afflict us with vigils :
Wearisome, O God ! will be the travel of our life,
Unto the faint outbreak of the dawn from the night.

5.

A night of sickness and of pain to the noble stock of Howel,
Calling for all our care :
While we live shall not one more amiable among women
Go under the roof of the grave.

6.

The grave hath gained possession of the first of Creuddyn's
    women ; when it was found
That the best blood of Curig could perish,
Then upon the family came mourning,
And upon Llewelyn, the Lord of the Hearth.

7.

The Hearth whose life—the trunk of the tree—has been cut
    off ;—
A sore calamity to its poor,
A wound also to the sick,
In the land where the foremost were her fair children.

8.

Her fair and gallant sons uttering a bitter cry,
As they bear the oaken bier ;
Neither poor nor crowder make merry,
To see half the land laid low.

9.

Gone is the land to make mourning[1] in your midst,
Where all that is human shall follow ;
But the best of names, and the love
That she leaves behind her—that is her Memorial !

10.

To Elen's sufferings there is an end,—now
Nor heat nor cold shall hurt her ;
The spot only mourns its bereavement of her,
Where she was wont to distribute food at the end of the path.

11.

She who gave of her food is buried ; a brave sight
Hath Llys Gelyddon been, with its highway thronged by poor ;
Great is the calamity to the sick !
Mary ! far off is the day ere her like shall die !

By the aid of the little glimmering of light shed upon it by the grand Jury list of 1546, we see no reason to doubt that this little poem was actually indited by the bard of Arwystli. If so, it is not improbably the earliest of his extant compositions ; notwithstanding that the supposition may appear somewhat rash, when it is considered how many of these have still to be disinterred from the volumes of decaying MSS., in which they lie mouldering away. To our mind there is evidence of youthful poetic aspiration in the simple, but genuine, pathos that peeps out in some of the lines through the difficulties and imperfections of the text. Some of these may be attributable to the practical inexperience of the bard in the art of weaving the metric lay, of which he since became recognised as a master. And it must be admitted that the life-like picture presented to us, in a few gentle touches, of the Lady of Creuddyn, borne to her grave by her own sobbing children, followed with the tears and lamentations of the whole country-side, to whom she had endeared herself by her humble and unostentatious charity to the sick and poor, carries with it a certain foreshadowing of his future pre-eminence.

[1] "Dwyn cwyr," to bear wax tapers in the funeral procession.

From this clegy on Elen, their sister, we are led on by a natural transition to the poem addressed to her brothers by Huw Cae Llwyd, a bard who, though partly his contemporary, belonged to the foregoing generation. It were to be wished that some more prosaic record would reveal to us fuller particulars respecting these gentlemen, for which our appetite is decidedly whetted by those derived from the poem. But unfortunately we have none, save their names, Ieuan, Owen, Jenkyn, and William, connected with the few facts recorded in their pedigrees, and enumerated in the second volume of this work ;[1] also that already adverted to respecting Ieuan, viz., that he sat sixth on a grand jury in the last year but one of Henry VIII ; and last, not least, the one which, but for their " *vates sacer*," would have been consigned to oblivion, that they were known and regarded with more than ordinary respect in their day, as having earned by their character and conduct, exhibited in distinctive traits, the title *par excellence* of " The Four Brothers of Llangurig."

CYWYDD Y PEDWAR BRODYR O LANGURIG.[2]

Pwy a rydd peunydd aur pwys ?
Piau holl iachau Powys ?
A'r soldau gorau a gaid ?
Pond wyrion penawduriaid ?
Piau 'r glod pwy ar gwledydd,
Pa frodyr yn filwyr fydd ?
Pedwar cymar, rhag camwedd,
Cedyrn iawn y caid yr un wedd.
Ieuan, tarian anturwyr,
Torri y'mlaen tair mil o wyr,
Owain ddewr, yn y ddwy ran,
Awdr yw ni edy ei ran :

---

[1] P. 273. See also *Arch. Camb.* for 1867, p. 26.

[2] From the MS. in the British Museum called " Y Melynhir," and numbered Additional MSS. $\frac{14,999}{1671}$. The last twenty lines are found also in the " Llyfr-Ceniarth," tacked on to the fragment of another poem, ascribed to Huw Cae Llwyd, containing part of the Legend of S. Curig.

Siancyn, roddwin wreiddwych,
A llew dinam, Wiliam wych :
Meibion Morys, fur awchys frig,
Llyna geirw Llangurig,
Ag wyrion enwog eryr ;
Siancin, a roe win i wyr,[1]
Gwych a gadarn y 'th farnwyd,
A hael yw llin Hywel Llwyd.
Gwaed Fadog, enwog o wr,
Gwaed Einion, ag o Danwr,[2]
Coed Rhys, yn cadw 'r oesoedd,
Cawr o wr, Llwyd, car Iarll oedd.
Caid o hil coed wehelyth,
Caterw fydd coetir fyth.
Caid anian yn cadw ynys,
Cawn roddion gorwyrion Rys.
Ond haelion, gwychion, yw'r gwyr ?
Ond tewrion, ac anturwyr ?
Ond tyfeilch yn eu tyfiad,
I rannu 'r tir, o 'r un tad ?
O dderwen fawr, o 'r ddar ffon,
Y cadeiriodd coed irion :
Ceingiau yn golofnau gwlad ;
Ceirw a 'u hofn a 'u cariad ;
Cyd tyfu y caid hefyd,
Cyd ffynnu a'u caru i gyd ;
Curig, o, fewn y curas,
A'u cryfed, cadwed rhag cas !
Cyd treulio y caid rheolwyr,
Cyd gildio, cyd gostio gwyr :
Cyd henaint y caid[3] eu heinioes,
Cyd rhannu hwnt,[4] cyd rhoi 'n eu hoes ;
Cyd garu[5] 'r Cymru y caid ;

---

[1] This wine must have been imported direct from France to the neighbouring port of Aberystwyth. This passage, and one in another poem, in which Llangurig is described as noted for the excellence of its wine, furnishes a curious proof of the existence of a trade with France in wine on the Welsh coast at that early period.

[2] Madoc Danwr, the immediate founder of the Clochfaen family. See his History, *Mont. Coll.*, vol. ii, p. 269.

[3] Y caid. The *Ll. Ceniarth* has "cadwo."

[4] Cyd rhannu hwnt. The *Ll. Cen.* has "Cydran himp."

[5] Cyd garu. This is the reading of *Ll. Cen.* The British Museum MS. has "ffynnu," probably repeated by mistake from the seventh line above.

Cyd gynnal, cadw gweiniaid ;
Cadw meirch ar frasgeirch fry,
Cadw gwyr, a 'u cyd garu,
Cadw eu gwlad mal eu tadau,
Cadwasant naw cant yniau.[1]
Os gwyr yn garwyr a gaid,
Oes gerddiant yn esgweiriaid.[2]
Tyfasant at twf asen,
Mal ar hyd y milwyr hen.
Tri wyr o 'r un bortreiad,
Tri maen, gwn, tryma 'n y gäad ;
Tri ag un a fydd unair.
Tri chapten, tri phen y ffair.
Teiroes oll i 'r tri sydd,
l'edeiroes i 'r pedwerydd.

　　　　　　　　Huw Cae Llwyd a 'i cânt.

THE FOUR BROTHERS OF LLANGURIG.

Who gives daily gold by weight ?
Who possesses all the descents of Powys ?
And the best soldiers that are found ?
Is it not the grandsons of chieftains ?
Who possess renown over all lands ?
What brothers are they who are warriors ?
Four comrades, who, against wrong,
Alike have been found mighty.
Ieuan, the shield of daring men,
Would rout three thousand men before him ;
Stout Owen, in the two divisions,
Will suffer none to quit his post.[3]
Jenkin, the noble wine-giver,
And gallant William, the spotless lion,
These are the sons of Morys, a bristling rampart,
These are the Stags of Llangurig,
And the grandsons of an Eagle of renown.[4]
Thou, Jenkin, who givest wine to thy men,
Art deemed to be a man noble and powerful ;

[1] Yniall. *Ll. Cen.* The British Museum MS. has "nosau," which
is nonsense.

[2] The British Museum MS. has "gerddiant ysgweireriaid."

[3] I doubt the soundness of the text in this line. The meaning,
anyhow, is far from clear.

[4] See the pedigree of Jenkyn Goch and of Catherine his wife.
Vol. ii, p. 272.

And generous is the Line of Howel Lloyd,
Of the blood of Madoc ;[1] a hero of renown.
From Einion, and from the Fire-bearer,
Comes a perpetual forest of scions of Rhys Lloyd,
A gigantic hero, and kinsman to an Earl.
From that line hath proceeded a forest of descendants :
Wide-spreading for ever will that forest-land be ;
In defending the Island hath its spirit been proved.
From the great grandsons of Rhys[2] shall we receive gifts ;
Are they not men generous and gallant ?
Are they not men resolute and daring ?
In their increase are they not proud,
As sons of one father, to share the land between them ?
From a vast oak, from the stock of a female oak,
Hath spread forth a flourishing wood,
Whose branches are pillars in the land.
Stags are they alike feared and beloved,
They have been found both to grow together,
And all to prosper together in love.
May Curig, beneath their cuirass,
Strengthen them, and keep them from hate !
As rulers have they been proved to spend together,
Together to raise, and to pay their men,
Together hath their life attained its prime,
Together do they share in their life, together bestow,
Together have they been found to love the Cymry,
Together to maintain and support the sick,
To keep their tall steeds on finest oats :
Together to maintain, and love their men,
And preserve their country, as their fathers
Preserved it, with nine hundred energies.[3]
As their men have been found to love them,
So have they led the life of esquires.
They have grown to the growth of a rib,[4]
Like the warriors of old in stature.
Three of the heroes are framed on one pattern,—

[1] The great-grandson of Madoc Danwr. Though no special exploits or characteristics are connected with his name, yet, from
the frequency of reference to it, it would seem to have been associated in the minds of the bards with somewhat more noteworthy
than the single quality of birth.

[2] Rhys Lloyd of Creuddyn was the great grandfather of these
brothers.

[3] *I. e.*, With courage and spirit inexhaustible.

[4] *I. e.*, to a nicety.

Three rocks, the heaviest I know to be found.
The three and one will hold one language.
Three captains, three presidents at the fair.
The three will have three lives ;
The fourth will have a fourth life.[1]

The extract, of which the following is a translation, is from a poem by Cadwaladr ab Rhys Trefnant, who is stated in *Enwogion* to have flourished about the middle of the sixteenth century. In it are celebrated the virtues of Llewelyn, the husband of Elen, the subject of the above elegy; and her own praises are sounded in the closing lines, although she is not actually named in them. The poem is entitled, " An Ode to solicit the loan of a Bull for the Lady of Peutyn,[2] from Llewelyn, son of Morris, son of Rhys, son of Adam, of Llangurig."

Who is the man of renown, of pure virtue,
Resolute and gallant, of a bearing free from vanity ?
It is the Lion of Battle called Llewelyn,
The falcon of the hill-country of fair Curig,
Of bright aspect, sign of a pure heart,
In steel mail, quick as Dervel with his staff.[3]
A gallant wine-giver is Jenkin,[4]
Morris[5] is noble for his humility of speech ;
A man to draw the yoke of Rhys
Lloyd, like to a tawny lion.
Thou art the angel of the blood of Howel
Lloyd, the soul of all goodness ;
A man the best offspring of Griffith,
The pure progeny of highest descents.
With noble increase from the blood of David
Tabarn, mayst thou grow to be an Earl ;
If thine eight sires be reckoned,
Thy pedigrees become numerous ;

[1] *I. e.*, The life of each brother will be quadrupled, as it were, by its perfect unison with that of each of the other three.
[2] A place in Radnorshire.
[3] The patron Saint of Llandderfel, in Edeyrnion. See his History in *Enwogion*.
[4] The third of the "Four Brothers," and Llewelyn's brother-in-law.
[5] The name of the fathers of both Elen and Llewelyn.

Uncorrupt are thy four lines of descent,
Of no vile or base extraction is thine ancestor.
If thine ancient blood be stirred up,
No better blood exists in distant lands,
Than that which a sweet significance
Bespeaks in thy delicate features.
The blood of Rhys is a rampart, with his vast forest[1] yonder,
To prosper together with the Blood of Llawdden.
A wide-spread forest is the Blood of Trevor.[2]
Pure are thy degrees of affinity wherever the language is
    spoken.[3]
Mighty Mathavarn, with its men,
Is a portion of the fruit of the ancient warriors.

     *   *   *   *   *

From Urien came a privileged line of descent,
Degengl, a scion of branches many and illustrious;
Gwaithvoed, a stag whose work is of excellent fashion,
Came—together with thy kindred that loved thee—
Came from Rhys. Good are thy roots:
The veins of Gethin's roots are one with theirs.
This does not touch
The sixth part there of what is yours;
On you, as on Ivor,[4] hath God bestowed
The greatest store of wealth;
How true is it that, with a brave heart,
By wealth is gained the world!
Who doth not love thee, thou Chief over the multitude,
Thou Falcon yonder, circling round the cultivated land?
Thy Spouse—worthy of praise is she—
Llewelin's Lily, bright as the moon,
A Gwenhwyvar, a second Avarwedd.
In many virtues is she perfected,
Savoury messes are in her pantries.
Rampart of thy Tribe! may Mary uphold it!
Thou art one to distribute—thy fame shall endure,
Like that of the hero Brân, in the Upland of Curig.

With this poem we do not yet lose sight of the *Four
Brothers*. The *Llyfr Ceniarth* contains others addressed

---

[1] A forest, in Welsh poetry, often means a host of kindred or
clansmen.
[2] Tudor Trevor.
[3] Literally, " throughout the language."
[4] Ivor Hael.

respectively to three of their number, as far as may be
gathered from internal evidence, for their titles in the
MS. speak only of their being written in honour of " the
Clochfaen Family;" a circumstance which, together with
the numerous gaps and corruptions or mutilations of the
text which occur in them, tends greatly to obscure their
meaning.   In the MS. they are all (one by Sion Keri
excepted) subscribed with the name of Huw Arwystli,
with the addition of dates, which, however, are either
too early or too late to be calculated to do otherwise
than mislead ; one being fixed at 1570, and the others
so far back as at, or about, 1500. As many of these
poems have, with more or less appearance of probability, been ascribed to Huw Arwystli, who is thus,
perhaps, more than any other, entitled to the appellation of " Bard of Llangurig," it may be fitting to introduce them with an epitome of the few scattered notices
which we have been able to collect of his career.

WELSH POETRY, ILLUSTRATIVE OF THE HISTORY OF LLANGURIG.

By HOWEL W. LLOYD.

PART II.[1]

SKETCH OF HUW ARWYSTLI.

THE latest oral tradition relative to Hugh Arwystli, still, perhaps, current in some districts of Wales, is that he was remembered as a very old man and a cripple, who had no fixed abode, but was to be seen now at one place, now at another, chiefly at the mansions of the gentry, with whom he was wont to ingratiate himself, and to requite their hospitality, after the manner of the ancient bards of his country, by the composition of poems addressed to some member of the family, generally its head, in which its praises were sounded in a somewhat high-flown strain of panegyric. Such poems were usually commenced by a reference to the antiquity of the family-stock, traced up to the ninth degree. This was followed by details connected with the pedigree, deduced in the male, and, if possible, also in the female line, from some British hero, the founder of a royal or noble tribe, or failing that, of one of its collateral branches; concluding with a special encomium on the character of its existing representative, in which bravery, generosity, noble bearing, and last, not least, hospitality, were ever the conspicuous features. To this were generally added allusions to the profusion of his banquets and the excellence of his cellar; the former presided over by the lady of the house, whose beauty,

T

grace and birth were surpassed only by the inexhaustible resources and economy of her *ménage*, as well as bounty to the poor. Occasion for such effusions was furnished by any current event of domestic importance, as a birth, a wedding, or a funeral—especially the latter—so far as may be inferred at least from the predominance among their extant compositions of poems bearing the title of *Marwnad*, or "Elegy on the Dead."

Respecting the birthplace of Huw Arwystli we possess, unfortunately, but little or no information. His surname, however, may be itself accepted as evidence that it was somewhere in the hundred of Arwystli; and this is confirmed by the circumstance that, in the heading of a poem assigned to him in the British Museum, he is called Huw Arwystli of Tref Eglwys, in that district, as well as by the familiar allusions to this village which occur in his poems.[1] Some evidence, moreover, is afforded by the compositions, now for the first time printed, that part of his early life was passed in the village, or at least within the parish of Llangurig. It would lie beyond the scope of this paper to examine the question minutely; but, as tending to such an inference, may be instanced his perfect acquaintance with, and affection for, the locality—its ancient church, its bright and lovely Wye, its sacred and warlike traditions; together with his intimate acquaintance with all its principal households, and the most intimate details of their several connexions and relationships; the heartfelt interest which he displays in even their most trivial concerns, particularly of Clochfaen, which he sets forth to us as the fountain-head of the rest of the same descent from Madoc Danwr, or the "Firebearer," and more remotely from Einion, and Tudor Trevor. His devotion to Curig, its patron saint, springs manifestly from some peculiar tie, which he feels to be binding on him personally. There is a passage in which he alludes mysteriously to his own residence within the parish at some prior, and seemingly very early period of his existence; and, in another, the strain rises sud-

---

[1] "Cywydd y Benglog," in *Add. MSS.*, 14,875, British Museum.

denly from its commonplace alliterative style to one simply and unaffectedly poetical, when adverting episodically on the one hand to the picturesque features, and on the other to the well-remembered faith and devotion of his own beloved " Bro Gurig."[1]

A traditional story, in which is depicted the manner in which the peasantry loved to believe that their countryman came by his "Awen," or poetical genius, is precious for the characteristic morsel embodied in it of the old Welsh folk-lore, the spirit of which is now to all appearance extinct. It tells how a poor despised cripple, Hugh Arwystli by name, was wont upon occasion when a wayfarer through Montgomeryshire, and in want of a night's lodging, to turn aside into the church of Llanddinam and there compose himself to sleep. It chanced one May eve that, in this sacred refuge, he fell into a deep slumber, when he beheld a vision as of one who approached him, and made a sign as it were of causing somewhat to enter into his brain. On the morrow he was awoke by the merry voices of a bevy of maidens who came tripping by with their laps full of fresh-gathered may. One of these tossed to him a branch through the window under which he had reposed, remarking playfully tò her companions, "I will bestow on this poor cripple some may, as none of you will give him any." Thereupon Huw, who had heretofore never composed, or learnt to compose, a single stanza, improvised a sonnet of thanksgiving to the maiden for her gift. From that day forward he was able to compose poetry, and attained to such excellence in the art, that he maintained himself in high favour with the Welsh gentry by means of it throughout the rest of his life. The last fact is abundantly certified by the number and diversity of the compositions ascribed to his pen, many of them addressed to persons of rank in almost every part of the Principality. The tale ends simply with the explanation that what he had seen entering his brain was the " Awen," in which, it is added, in proof

[1] Curig's Land.

of the estimation formed of him by his countrymen, not
one of his contemporaries surpassed him.   Of this no
slight corroboration is found in the *Visitations* of Lewis
Dwnn, the Welsh herald,[1] who places the names of
" Huw Arwystli and Morgan Elvael, chief musicians",
among those " of the generation which I saw aged and
grey-headed, who were perfect poets, duly authorised,
and all graduated."   And it is confirmed by the testimony of William Lleyn, the " Poet Laurel," as John
Rhydderch terms him, in Elizabeth's reign, who, reply-
ing to some stanzas sent by Hugh to felicitate him on
his escape from drowning at the hands of a man who
had thrown him into the Dovey at Penal, writes

> " Arwystli ! to thy poet Huw
>   Both Lore and Art belong ;
>   And Nature hath inspired him too,
>   To weave the sprightly song."[2]

It would scarcely, however, be fair, with our present
limited knowledge, to attempt a critical survey of his
poetical merits.   The remarkable fecundity of his muse
is testified by the number of his extant compositions.
Sixty-six of his poems are enumerated in the " Cymm-
rodorion Catalogue" in the British Museum, and fifty-
five more which appear to be in his handwriting (besides some in other MS. volumes), are bound up with
others in a single quarto volume of the Hengwrt
Library, now at Peniarth.   If to these be added thirty-
three, the first lines of which are given in the famous
" Repertorium" of Moses Williams,[3] omitting to reckon
three poems, which are found also in one of the above
lists, and one ascribed, in " Gorchestion y Beirdd," to
Howel ab Rheinallt, together with one in the collection of the late Rev. Walter Davies : the sum total of

[1] Vol. i, p. 8.
[2]   Dysg ag addysg go weddol—o gywydd
              Ag awen ysbrydol ;
            Odid un nad ydyw 'n ol
            Huw Arwystl naturiol.—*Add. MSS.*, 14,892.
[3] British Museum Catalogue, No. 872, l. 4.

his compositions will amount to no less than one hundred and fifty-five.   Of these, perhaps from twenty to thirty may be dispersed in different collections, and thus are more or less known to the poetical public of the Principality.   Into them a considerable number of errors have crept in the process of frequent transcription, increased doubtless also, in many instances, by the fact that his handwriting is extremely difficult to decipher.   It would be necessary, therefore, that his works should be carefully collected, and edited in a scholarlike manner, to enable the public to form a sound judgment on the question of their average merit. Still the remark may be hazarded, in arguing from the known to the unknown, that it is unlikely that many of these would be classed in the highest rank of classical Welsh compositions—at least in the condition in which they have reached us.   Not a few of the poems best known to us bear the appearance of having been indited with facility, indeed, and with a considerable admixture of humour, but hastily, on the spur of the occasion, and (with certain exceptions) with no great regard to the rules of metrical symmetry, or even of grammatical construction.   In regard to the former, indeed, so frequent are the instances of laxity as to suggest the idea that the author must have declined, on some preconceived principle, to suffer himself to be trammelled by the more stringent requirements of his art; unless it is rather to be supposed that they were loosely put together in the first instance with a view to revision and amendment at some future opportunity, which in fact never arrived.   Be the explanation what it may, it is a fact that, in the quarto volume at Peniarth already mentioned, the compositions, which are in Huw's handwriting, but unattested by his signature, are for the most part penned in so cramped and attenuated a character as to puzzle even a practised eye to decipher; and, in one of them, a copy of which has been kindly furnished to the writer by the owner, who was unwilling, however, to certify fully to the correctness of the transcript, these seemingly characteristic defects of composition appear largely to prevail. They cannot, therefore, be wholly accounted for on the hypothesis of carelessness or ignorance on the part of transcribers, or even by the seeming impracticability of determining, in every passage, the words which the author actually wrote. It is strange that the text of the copies of some of his works in the British Museum which, from the frequency of their transcription, would seem to have been most popular, should be in so defective a state as to lead naturally to the inference that their very transcribers must have failed to understand them, or at least to appreciate their beauties; whence it may, perhaps, further be inferred that we owe their preservation rather to the inherent passion in our nature for heaping together a collection, rather because it is a fashion, than because its contents will improve or benefit ourselves.

In a few, however, as, for instance, the " Cowyddau Mab y Ffalsder a Chywirdeb," there is a certain appearance of finish and elaboration which is lacking to many of his compositions ; whence it is natural to conclude that they were the favourite offspring of his fancy, upon which he bestowed an amount of labour and thought which he scarcely cared to expend upon lines that originated merely with some jovial occasion, or were jotted down at once in the very shape which they first assumed in his teeming imagination, excited after a merry-making with the desire to glorify some hospitable host, or glowing with the frankness and *abandon* of a satirical correspondence in verse, with an appreciative and kindred spirit, like Sir Ieuan, the jovial and rollicking minister of the village of Carno in Arwystli, who would be slow to mark trifling inaccuracies of composition while enjoying and reciprocating his humour, even when too freely lavished at his own expense.[1] This sense of

[1] There is a passage in one of Sir Ieuan's poems which tells in act the other way, in which, while deferring to his antagonist's

humour in his character was largely intermingled with practical good sense and knowledge of the world, such as peep out in the following lines, translated, or perhaps more correctly speaking paraphrased, from the remarkable poem addressed to Rhys ap Morys of Aberbechan.[1] These qualities would probably be far more often apparent in the works of Huw, and of other Welsh poets, if not lost in the obscurity of tacit allusions to social habits and modes of thought now become almost unintelligible because obsolete. It may be added that the poem in question would seem to have been composed on the occasion of the young man's attainment of his majority, or entry into public life, an event which must have occurred in the reign of Henry VIII. It is remarkable for a certain tacit assumption of the old bardic authority to inculcate instruction and instil counsels of wisdom into the minds of young men of rank and position. In the palmy days of the bards, such counsel was far from being resented by its recipients; and, even at this later period, the language of the poem in question is a sign that the old social landmarks had not as yet become wholly effaced. ' There are, however, expressions in it which go far to show that 'the privilege, though still to a certain extent claimed and accorded, had need to be cautiously exercised; and any offence which might naturally have been taken at such freedom in the person of one who, albeit a graduated bard, was, in point of social position, but a poor wandering minstrel, is ingeniously obviated by the delicate way in which words of warning are rather insinuated than outspoken by the poet, who contents himself, moreover, with glancing indirectly at certain defects of character in their object, the mischievous tendency of which to mar an otherwise promising career he plainly

marked superiority to himself as a poet, he complains that Huw is unmercifully hypercritical in his judgment of his own petty faults of composition.

[1] For the original, and a prose translation of the former part of the poem, see *Mont. Coll.*, vol. iii, pp. 395, 397.

foresees, unless subjected to the timely counteraction
of a powerful self-control.

" Thou dealest justice, lovest truth,
   Sewer[1] and Squire,[2] a gallant youth !
As grows thy favour, be discreet,
So shalt thou rise, yet keep thy seat.
The shoot that springs from deep plough'd land,
With earliest wheat shall fill thine hand ;
From rays that warm the spring-time shower,
Will sprout in tufts the primrose flower ;
And of the noon-day heat is born
The fructifying ear of corn.
So, with thine auburn locks, at length,
Thou'lt ripen to thy prime in strength.
Well shall it be with thee, if wise,
Thou suffer not thy wrath to rise.
Of men uncouth thou canst but deign
To slacken, as thy steed's, the rein.
Rhys ! be not proud.   Man's haughty ways
God will not speed to length of days.
Thou needst it not ; yet I bestow
On thee the Seer's full mind to know.
Thus also, Heir and Lord ! twofold,
Thy counsel shall to fools be told.
No double tongue should e'er presage
An office from thy patronage.
The double-faced will overreach ;
Unjust is he of double speech.
No ill-considered judgment give,
Confirm'd by learning's page, 'twill live.
Nor rail—thine ignorance to hide—
Ere judgment given on either side.

[1] By an error of the press the word "seuer" in the Welsh poem
has been translated "receiver," on page 394 of vol. iii, for "sewer,"
an office, the nature of which has been described in note 2 to the
Welsh original, page 398.   The name is derived from the old French
esculier, or the *scutellarius, i.e.*, the person who had to arrange the
dishes, in the same way as the *scutellery* (scullery) was properly the
place where the dishes were kept.   *Domestic Architecture*, v. 3, p. 80,
n., quoted in a note to *John Russell's Boke of Nurture*, p. 162, of
Manners and Meals in Olden Time, published for the Early English
Text Society, Trübner, 1868.

[2] Possibly an esquire of the body to the reigning sovereign.   See
the notice of Edward Herbert, vol. iii, p. 356.

Temper thy too impetuous fire,
Nor lose thyself thro' treacherous ire.
By sound discretion wind thy ball,
Discretion will unravel all.
Whate'er may hap, gaze upward still ;
When yokes of oxen climb the hill,
The sober, even-temper'd beast,
Will longest last, and suffer least.
In framing honest oath be nice,
Nor ever frown for prejudice.
Tho' folly thwart thee, do not strike,
And sleep upon no man's mislike.
Of kith and kin uphold the brood,
'Tis thine—why weaken, then, thy blood ?"

The poetical correspondence, if it may be so termed, between Huw Arwystli and Sir Ieuan of Carno, above alluded to, is suggestive of another quality inherent in the muse of our crippled bard, namely, a pungent vein of satire, which is readily discernible under its outer integument of a rich, but not always delicate, humour. The actual circumstances which occasioned it are probably lost to history ; they are partly traceable, however, through the medium of the somewhat obscure allusions to them in the course of the poems. The first of the series is a " cywydd" or ode,[1] in which a young lady is urged to exert upon the too susceptible Sir Ieuan the influence of her charms, yet not to the extent of incurring risk to herself, for the purpose of restraining him from following the bard into Pembrokeshire to " Castell Gwys,"[2] or Wiston Castle, the mansion of Sir

[1] Commencing thus :—

> " Y ddyn sad, wych, ddawnus, deg,
> Ag ael fain, a gloyw faneg."

In a copy taken from a MS. by the Rev. D. Ellis of Cricaeth, in Caernarvonshire, it is entitled " Cywydd i Ferch i ddymuno arni i ddenu Syr Ieuan rhag canlyn y Bardd i dy Mr. Wgon o Gastell Gwys yn Sir Benfro." There is another copy in the British Museum (*Add. MSS.*, 14,874).

[2]
> " Rhyfig praff sy'm i'w gaffael,
> Ym muriau cwrt marchog hael,
> Coffr da lle 'r ceiff Huw 'r dewis
> Cistiau lle 'r gwn Castell Gwys."

John Wogan, the then representative of the Wogan family.[1] To Huw the consequences of her failure would be serious; the wine and the gold that would form his proper guerdon would fall, in part at least, to the share of the rival bard; and so enamoured, in fact, would the "reverend prelate" become of Sir John Wogan's hospitable entertainment that, once enthralled by its allurements, he might never thereafter be prevailed upon to quit them.[2]

It is difficult to imagine how a poor wandering cripple could be serious in attributing to the beneficed clergyman the intention of rivalling him in minstrelsy for the favours of the great; and we should simply be left to imagine that, beneath the semblance of such a charge was veiled a real compliment to the excellence, qualifying him for success in the imaginary competition, of the ecclesiastic's poetical powers, did not the appeal to the power of feminine charms[3] over the impressible temperament of the supposed rival, lead to the suspicion that more is intended than actually meets the eye. To this poem, as there is no rejoinder from Sir Ieuan, so should we be left to the merest conjecture on the subject, were it not that Huw has twice again reverted to it, and that in a manner which leaves us ultimately little room to doubt of his ulterior meaning. To the object of attack, in fact, was conceded, in the first instance, no interval for reply; for this was at once followed up by another of a similar character,[4] though somewhat vary-

---

1   " Rhwystr i 'r llen, rhy ystor lanwych,
       Flâs gwîn Syr Sion Wgon wych."

2   " Nad â 'r Prelad parchadwy,
       Barfog, o dai 'r marchog mwy."

3   " Addaw 'n deg, e ddaw 'n d' ogylch,
       N' ad i 'th gael, nawdd Duw i 'th gylch,
     Dy lun, Gwen, delw neu ganwyll,
     Dy liw byth a' i deil o' i bwyll."

4 This appears, from the use of the word "ddoe" (yesterday), in the following lines of the " Ode to the Blackbird":—
       " O Dduw mawr! fu ddoe 'mwriad,
       I 'w rwystro i Benfro heb wad;
       Da fyddai na fedrai fo,
       I dai 'r Wgon i drigo."

ing in form. It is entitled "An Ode,[1] wherein a blackbird is sent to Rhys of Carno (Aberbechan) to induce him to withdraw his protection from Sir Ieuan of Carno, and send him away." After apostrophising the bird with some poetical compliments to his characteristic features, qualities, and plumage, he bids him speed with a letter to Rhys ab Morys,[2] on whose mansion, spacious and wealthy, he skilfully introduces an encomium, and requests him to cease entertaining this dignified (*urddawl*) clergyman at the wine-banquet, nor suffer him to remain at Carno, where, though of acknowledged learning and eloquence, unless Rhys were at hand, he would be fain to deprive his flock of both matins and even song, in his haste to seek him at Aberbechan; nay, on one occasion, he had left for that purpose as many as nine of his sick parishioners bereft of extreme unction.[3] The priest, moreover, would insist upon following Huw throughout the Principality, diverting to his own behests the presents that were his perquisites as bard, and had even possessed himself of the

[O great God! but yesterday I purposed
Undoubtedly to keep him away from Pembrokeshire;
Well would it be that he should be unable
To go and stay in Wogan's mansion.]

[1] Beginning :—
"Yr edn a' i big is gwig gwydd,
A fflam awch, a fflu muchydd."

[2] "Draw mae'n rhaid, was byrfras big,
Danfon llythyr dan fin llithrig;
Marcia di, ym mro Cydewen,
Orsedd barch wr sydd ben,
Clymais ddoe 'nghyd gwynfyd gof,
Cerdd at Rys, cerdda drosof."

[3] "Ni erys yng Ngarno dirion,
Oni cheir Rhys yn ochr hon;
A' i geisio, didro, deudroed,
Plygain i Gydewain dod,
Ni cheir Gosber, nid erys,
On 'd eir i 'w ol i dai Rhys.
Caiff, sy 'n dal clwyf o' i blwyfwyr
Gam, na chân' gymmun, och! wyr:
A meirw fydd, mwy rhyfeddir,
Heb Olew, naw o' i blwy 'n wir."

parlour appropriated to his use in Rhys's house.   For
such enormities the poem ends with a suggestion that
the only remedy was to send him wandering for the
remainder of his days, as an incorrigible vagrant, from
Carno, it might be, to Cornwall.

To these effusions a reply from Sir Ieuan is extant,[1]
in which he seems partly to affect to regard them in
the light of ironical compliments, parrying, at the same
time, in a sort of mock-serious tone, the seeming attacks
upon his conduct.   Calling the blackbird again into re-
quisition, in a strain in which Huw's previous description of him is elegantly paraphrased and amplified, he
desires him to return to Rhys ab Morys, and, with
encomiastic speech,[2] outvying even that of Huw, to
plead his cause before him.   Adroitly ignoring the
young lady, to whom Huw's first poem was addressed,
the priest limits his defence to the justification of his
visits to Wiston and Aberbechan, enlarging upon " the
Nightingale of Arwystli's" proneness to exaggerate, not
these faults only, but those of his poetical compositions.[3]
If a service or two had been missing in his church on a
Sunday, this had been simply owing to a necessity
for the administration of extreme unction to some of
his sick parishioners, an office, he significantly adds,
which he would never fail to perform for any one of
Rhys's line.   As for Huw's complaints, " chief bard"
(brifardd) as he is, they arise from an excessive appetite, which he would do well to restrain, for the good
things of this world ; and adds that, while himself entitled to share the liberality of the great, his advanced

---

[1] Commencing :—
    " Yr edn sy 'n dwyn, gwych, mwyngall,
       Tân o'r llwyn tew iawn, i 'r llall."
[2] See the translated extract from this poem in *Mont. Coll.*, vol. iii,
pp. 395, 396.
[3]   " Mae bai ar fardd gloywfardd glyd,
       (Awydd yw 'r bai ar dda 'r byd,)
       Ac ni chair un gair angerdd
       Fau, yn y gwaith o fewn y gerdd ;
       Na chai 'r ddwyran, mab anfodd,
       Eos Arwystl a sorodd."

age might have sufficed to secure him from the envy of
one so young.

From the tenor of Arwystli's rejoinder, we may gather
either that the poet felt himself piqued into acrimony,
or that, agreeably to his original plan, he was now to
unmask his battery, and commence in earnest a fire
more calculated to produce a serious effect than volleys
of mere playful irony on his opponent. Be that as it
may, the style of this, his last attack, seems bitter, even
to virulence; still, however, there is an overflow of
exaggeration and hyperbole about it, which seems to
prove that he by no means intends the charges introduced into it to be taken as literally true. The poem
is addressed to a certain " Philip Goch,[1] an appellation
to which that of " the Fowler" is added by Sir Ieuan in
his rejoinder. This Philip is clearly referred to as a
person of considerable wealth and influence, but in so
vague a manner as to furnish a very slight basis for
identification. His physical courage is compared to
that of " Syr Ffwg" (Fulk Fitzwarine,)[2] the hero of
Welsh Border romance, and the constant theme of the
Welsh bards. He is complimented, also, for the courage and pertinacity evinced by him in the extermina-
tion of vagrants,[3] and it is in this special capacity that
his aid is invoked by the poet.[4] Sir Ieuan, a reverend

---

[1] The opening lines are :—
        " Y dyn sy 'n dwyn, er 's enyd,
          Draw 'n i balf draian byd,
        Ffurf Syr Ffwg, fferf surian ffon,
        Ffilip, gyflymwip fflowmon ;
        Cur siolau beilch Caer Sialed,
          Y gwreng rhydd, gorau ynghred ;
        Dean, Arfon, Meirionydd,
          Dwy Went, a' u sel, danat sydd."
[2] *Vide* Lewis's *Glyn Cothi*, p. 216, note to line 55 ; also *Arch.
Camb.*, iii, new series, p. 282.
[3]   " Byrhâ 'r hwarau, briw 'r herwyr,
            Brinara gig bronnau gwyr."
[4]   " I'm rhan, fy Nghymro hoynwyf,
            Buost erioed, bostio 'r wyf ;

dignitary, a man of learning, whose praise is in pedigrees, follows Huw everywhere throughout the Principality, from Mona to Aeron, from Aeron to the two Gwents, playing (the harp?) as he goes, gaining fame as a second Ieuan Deulwyn, or Iolo Goch, and this partly by plagiarising the *verve* of Huw's own verses,[2] so that, like the celebrated eagle, though

> " Keen were his pangs, 'twere keener far to feel,
>   His own the pinion that impelled the steel."

Hence results a popular distaste for the poor crippled bard's poetry. He finds himself completely ' ' cut out," as it were, by an unauthorised intruder, and, as a natural consequence, his bardic guerdons of hound, hawk, and gold,[3]—nay, more, the smiles of the fair, henceforward are lost to him. "Thomas[4]" would maintain him ; but there again at his side, "like his shadow," is the reverend greyheaded gentleman. He concludes, therefore, with a humorous appeal to Philip to come to his rescue. The prelate must be brought to reason, or he will leave him no room in the land. He must be driven forth by threats, and (if these suffice not) by the actual application of staff and spear. Let his hair be torn out by the

> Y mae urddawl, a mawrddysg,
>   Yn iachau mawl, yn eich mysg,
> Mae i 'm cerdd casâd i 'th wlad lân,
>   Oes, o ryfig Syr Ieuan.
>
> .   .   .   .
>
> Lle 'i bo, cerdd ni chaf dafod,
>   Lle 'i bwyf, er hyn, e fyn fod ;
> Ni throediais, ni fedrais fan,
>   O Bowys, na bai Ieuan."

[1] Upper and Lower, called also Nether and Blaenau Gwent.—E.H.

[2]   " Dwyn f'eurnerth, barch, Duw 'n farnwr,
>   Am euro' i gerdd, y mae'r gwr."

[3]   " Ni chaf, ni cheisiaf na chi,
>   Yn Neheubarth, na hobi,
>   Na marcho gaeth meirch hirwen,
>   Nag aur, er llwnc y gwrllen.

[4] Perhaps Thomas Price, son of Rhys of Aberbechan, whose mother, Gwenllian, was daughter of " Tudor Rhydderch." Vol. iii, p. 393, n. 5.

roots, and his body belaboured with buffets, till nought be left of the old " crane " (sic) but his crown.[1]

In all these attacks there would seem to be too much of an assumed appearance of levity and of hyperbole to admit of the hypothesis that they were meant to be taken literally. Sir Ieuan, indeed, in his reply, consisting of a hundred and twenty verses, so affects to deal with them ; but he must inwardly have felt that a something was implied by the author, the expression of which in words he carefully studied to avoid. Their positions were essentially different. The poet, a poor wandering cripple, albeit a graduated bard, depended upon his talents for his bread. The ecclesiastic was comfortably established in the world, and basked in the sunshine of its favours. Putting a bold front on the matter, he begins by demanding, "Who is this that projects alliance with a gallant gentleman ? Let him not meddle with powder and fire. A tall man, the very prince of fencers, with his long lance, ready to disperse whole cart-loads of vagrants, is the noble Philip Goch the Fowler. Woe to the vagabonds if they await his eagle's swoop !"[2] Then launching into the midst of his

---

[1]   " Dithau, Ffilip, doeth, glau, goch,
          Trâs dwys, chwyrn, trustiais arnoch,
       Pâr reoli y Prelad,
          Ni âd le i 'm yn dy wlad.
       Bwriwch ef hynt o 'ch bro chwi,
          Bygythiwch bigo ei wythi,
       Ag, oni ffy gan y ffon,
          Trwy'r llen tro 'r gwaew llinon.
       Yng Ngwynedd ni gai awen,
          Ymlyn â 'r palf ymlew 'r pen,
       Ynghyd â 'r gnawd, dygnawd ddyn,
       Na ad garan ond ei goryn."

[2]   " Pwy 'n bwrw *aliwns* paun breulan ?
          Peidier â thi powdwr a thân !
       Gwr hir, â 'r ben gwara 'r byd,
          A gwaew anian hir genyd,
       Gyrr williaid, f'enaid, ar fêr,
          Gwych Ffylip Goch y Ffowler.
       Gwae 'nhwy i 'th aros, gnith eryr,
          Genyd â gwaew i gwnidio gwyr ;
       Gwnewch olwg, (gwae ni chiliai !)
          Gwiber gwyllt, ffoi gwibwyr rai.

subject, he complains that his poetical powers have
subjected him to the assaults of a malice not inferior to
that of Melwas, the ravisher of Gwenhwyvar, King
Arthur's celebrated Queen.   Praised though Philip
might be by any number of bards, Huw would imagine
himself superior to them all, from Tudur Aled to Iolo
Goch, not omitting Davydd ab Gwylim.[1]   He would
not, if he could, suffer bard, singer, or beggar to approach him but himself.   He proceeds to express his
amazement that Huw should desire to interdict him the
presence of Thomas,[2] who had honoured him with his
affection, as well as his gold.   Were Huw to be credited,
Sir Ieuan would leave him not a single steed, hawk,
hound, nor yet a pretty lass in South Wales ; but the
fact was that, when the latter received the horses, dogs,
and rich vestments, and the former glory and gold, the
profits were fairly divided.[3]   In sober earnest, however,
the land was not large enough to hold Arwystli.   He
would chase all the bards away from it.   He would un-
dertake to decide for Sir Ieuan what part of the globe
he was to live in.   Did he so much as cast a look towards
Powys, presto ! Huw's harp was on his shoulders to follow him thither.   Southwards did he cross the Dovey,
Huw was off straightway to Gwent.   Did he so much
as cast his eye towards the Herberts' border, this clerical
opponent must at once be got rid of, and, in default of

> Gwr wyt a gwg ar dy gâs,
>   A geidw 'r dwfr gydâ 'r deufras."

[1]
> " Eithyr mae yn athro mawr
> I'th foliannu fyth, flaenawr ;
> Euryd cerdd i'th wryd cai,
> A Huw Arwystli a' i haerai ;
> Od â 'r feirdd, awdwr yw fo,
> Wedi Aled i Iolo,
> Nid yw 'n yr iaith dano rym,
> Heb gael Dafydd ab Gwilym."

[2] See vol. iii, p. 396.
[3]
> " O chawn y meirch, a chwn mawr,
> A 'r trwsiad gwych ar trysawr,
> A gair mawr, ag aur melyn,
> Ynte eu cae—on 'd teg hyn ?"

other means, cudgelled to death. The poem concludes with a spirited appeal to Philip Goch to stay his hand, and with a warning that he who wrongfully slays another shall die "the death of a Jew."[1] Malice for the nonce may gain its end, but has brought thousands of those who practise it to their graves.

The subject of this correspondence has been dwelt upon at some length, as not only illustrating the personal character and genius of our poet, but also as furnishing a glimpse of the social habits, feelings, and modes of thought of our countrymen at the period of its occurrence. Probably, as has been already intimated, much is significantly referred to in the poems, which, dark and mysterious to us after the lapse of three centuries, would be readily intelligible to the parties immediately concerned, and to their respective sympathisers. The clue to this, so far as it can now be unravelled, must be sought in the religious and political circumstances of the time.

To ascertain, however, with precision, what these circumstances are, is a matter of no little difficulty. No reliable date, in the first place, has been assigned to the poems themselves. Still they contain certain notes of time whereby their composition may be fixed within a definite period of years.

1. They were written during the lifetime of Rhys ab Morys, for allusion is made to him throughout, and we know that Rhys died in or about the year 1568.[2]

2. Huw was then a young man, and Sir Ieuan an old one, for their ages are contrasted in the concluding lines of the latter's first poem.[3]

[1]
> " A laddo yn llywio yn llew,
> Efe a leddir fal Iuddew;
> Malais a bair bedd miloedd,
> Malais Huw am ei les oedd ;
> Malais i 'th ddwyn i 'r hoenyn :
> 'Mogel, Huw, y magl er hyn."

[2] *Supra*, vol. iii, p. 395.

[3]
> " Gâd na all, i gyd yn un,
> Wr ifanc i warafun,

U

3. Sir Ieuan was then vicar of Carno, a benefice of which Rhys was the patron, and probably also lay impropriator, having received a grant of the revenues of that parish, in the dissolution, in the year 1540, of the Knights Hospitallers, to whom they had previously belonged,[1] doubtless in consideration of the acknowledgment on his part of the title and authority of Supreme Head under God of the Church of England, assumed by King Henry VIII.

4. Rhys was at this time, probably, a man of advanced age, since he had apparently a son, or son-in-law, Thomas, who was of age to support a separate establishment, as a member of which, in Huw's opinion, he would be able to maintain Sir Ieuan.

5. The use of the words "*Plygain*" and "*Gosper*" for the morning and evening service, together with the complaint of neglect to administer the Catholic Sacrament of extreme unction to the sick parishioners, points to a time when, although the use of Protestant formularies had been enjoined on the clergy, that of the rites of the ancient Faith had not yet been discontinued.

The poetical altercation, then, could not have taken place so early as during the reign of Henry VIII, nor yet in that of Queen Mary, when the only public offices of religion were those of the Catholic Church. The only remaining periods that can be assigned to it are the short reign of Edward VI, and the first few years of Elizabeth, prior to the penal enforcement of the revived innovations on the public offices of religion. Of these two periods the probability lies, perhaps, in favour of the former, for reasons, the discussion of which would scarcely be warranted by the scope of this publication. It is sufficient to remark that the vigorous protestations of our bard against the interference of the vicar of Carno with his own bardic peregrinations and their customary

> Er hynny, gan wr hen oed,
> O chaffo ei ran, na chyffroed."

[1] See under "Commandery of Hawston," *Carnoo*, in Valor of Henry VIII, *supra*, vol. ii, p. 104. See also Collier's *Ecclesiastical Hist.*, vol. ii, p. 179.

emoluments, would not unnaturally have originated at either period in the troublous vicissitudes of the times. Either bard, both the clerical and the lay, may have weakly felt it expedient, as so many others are known to have done, to conform outwardly to changes against which their hearts revolted, consoling themselves fondly with the hope and belief that the new state of things would expire with the removal of the causes that had led to it. If the mind of Huw Arwystli were preoccupied by such feelings, it is easy to conceive that it would have been deeply scandalised by the conduct of an ecclesiastic, who degraded the character of his ministry, and exposed it to obloquy by the assumption of that of one of the wandering minstrels, or *clerwyr*, as they were called, who did not in all cases bear the best of reputations. We may readily believe, therefore, that he was far from desiring to impute literally to this "grave and learned ecclesiastic," as he terms him, the actions which he seems to insinuate ; nor, in their respective positions, could he venture to depreciate openly the employment by Sir Ieuan of his time in a manner unworthy alike of his sacred calling, and of the dangerous crisis to religion. He seems, accordingly, to have attempted to divert him from his perilous course by veiling his real intent under the semblance of personal antagonism, and conveying to him some timely warnings in the guise of irony and satire. It is true, indeed, that Sir Ieuan, in his replies, to all outward seeming, has dealt with these criticisms as though meant to be literally understood. But it must be remembered that we possess now no means of judging how far they may have affected his subsequent conduct ; nor would it be a fair argument against the goodness of their purpose if they proved eventually to have been thrown away upon their object.

This view would appear to derive not a little confirmation from a remarkable couplet in one of the antithetical poems[1] already referred to, entitled "Cywyddau

[1] The one commencing :—

o Achau Ffalsder a Chywirdeb" (The Pedigrees of the
Child of Truth and the Child of Falsehood).   In the
British Museum copy,[1] the date assigned to the latter,
A.D. 1550, agrees very nearly with that attributed above
to this poetical passage of arms.

After contrasting the virtues and excellencies of the
one with the vices and mischievous propensities of the
other, he suddenly bursts forth into an exclamation ex-
pressive of amazement and sorrow that truth should
have perished out of the land :—

> " Rhyfedd na welir hoywfab,
>   Mewn rhinweddau, parthau 'r Pab."

It is wonderful that no gallant youth is seen,
In [possession of] virtues, on the Pope's side.

The sentiment is one of protestation against the time-
serving spirit of the day, which preferred present worldly
gain and prosperity to the risk which might be incurred
by earnest and single-minded advocacy of the Faith
once delivered to the Saints, with the expression of his
own stedfast adherence to which he proceeds to the conclusion of the poem.[2]   Whether our bard remained true
to the end of his days to that Faith, to the feelings
animated by which in his earlier compositions he gives

> " Ffalsedd, fab anwiredd nerth,
>   Fab ffol udonol dinerth."

The other :—

> " Fab cywirdeb, fab hoywdeb hedd,
>   Fab gwâr iawn, fab gwirionedd."

[1] *Add. MSS.*, 814, 972.

[2]
> " Wychlan diogan digoll ;
>   A chwi o waed ucha' oll ;
>   Och ! anamled yw 'ch nawmlwydd,
>   Eich trasau, a 'r hyntau rhwydd ;
>   Rhyw annedd clod, rhinwedd clau,
>   Er hyn gara 'i hwn goran.
>   Cyn dyddgwyl cwyn diwedd cnawd,
>   Fy ngobaith fydd drwy Ffydd ffawd.
>   Na bydd gradd yn y bedd gro,
>   Un doeth, gwar, ond a 'th garo.
>   Na bo enwi neb aned,
>   Ond yn gâr i 'wch un dan grêd."

such simple and pathetic expression, would be an interesting subject of inquiry, but one for which the material is not now forthcoming. There is, however, nothing, so far as the writer has had opportunity of judging, in any of his compositions relating more immediately to religion, to warrant a different conclusion.

Although Huw Arwystli seems to have been far from aiming at the sublime, or indulging in lofty flights of fancy in his poetry, still there are ever and anon passages to be met with in his compositions which show that he was not only a true worshipper of nature, but that he possessed the faculty of expressing his devotion to her with vividness and pathos. Of this remark, the following lines ascribed to him in Dr. Owen Pughe's "Welsh Dictionary,"[1] but not hitherto found in any collection of his poems, may serve for an illustration:—

> "Llwydlas edn, call odliad,
>   Cofion serch cyfanerchai,
>   Cofl mab, dan frig cwfl Mai."

The grey bird, with skilful melody,
Would bring recollections of love with reciprocal greeting
To the bosom of the youth under the skirts of the veil of May.

And the following sweet little sonnet :—

> "Gwych natur dymur dymunaf—o 'r deuddeg
>   Yw dyddiau Orphenaf;
>   Gwisg 'r Awen ei gwisg oraf,
>   Dydd o hyd, hyd ddiwedd haf."

The conception in which is perhaps partially conveyed in the following paraphrase :—

> "Of all the twelve I love the most
>   The month of bright July ;
>   Then genius fires the poet's lay,
>   Then is no night, but one long day,
>   Till summer's self shall die."

Huw possessed also pre-eminently the faculty, characteristic of most Welsh poets, of expressing apophthegms in alliterative verse with terseness and elegance, as in the couplet :—

[1] s. v., "Cyfanercha."

"A fo 'n gam ni fyn y gwir,
  A fo 'n iawn ni fyn anwir."
Honest men love Truth with zest,
Who do not are not honest.

The period during which Huw Arwystli lived an
wrote has not hitherto been precisely determined. I
Enwogion he is stated to have "flourished betwee
1540 and 1570." Both Dr. Davies in his *Dictionary*,
and Edward Lhuyd in the *Archæologia Britannica*,
give the year 1550 as his *acme*. Yet, if the poems in
the *Llyfr Ceniarth*[1] have been truly assigned to him by
its compiler, at least one of them must have been composed in the early part of the reign of Henry VIII.
There is a note by Richard Morris, in one of the *Peniarth MSS.*, to the effect that he died in 1583. If,·
however, the elegy, still extant, on Richard ab Ieuar
Lloyd, of Nant y Myneich,[2] in the parish of Mallwyd,
be correctly ascribed to him, he must have been living
so late as the year 1594, as it is stated by Lewis Dwnn[3]
that he received the sum of five shillings from this
Richard ab Ieuan Lloyd on the 15th of July in that
year. That he attained to a great age is not only
attested by the local tradition above mentioned, but
appears also from a passage in one of his poems, in
which he laments the decay of the poetic fire within
him by reason of his age. According to a notice in a
MS. in the British Museum[4] he was buried in St.
Asaph ; whether in the cathedral or parish church is,
however, not stated.

Next to the poem addressed to "The Four Brothers" collectively, those will naturally follow which are
intended to honour them individually. The subject of
the first of these is manifestly Ieuan of Clochfaen, the

---

[1] The writer desires to express his acknowledgments to Mr. N.
Bennett, of Glan yr Afon, near Llanidloes, for his kind permission
to make use of his valuable transcripts from that MS. for the purposes of this paper.

[2] *Add. MSS.*, 14,989.

[3] *Visitation of Wales*, vol. ii, p. 244.

[4] Quoted in the "Brython" for 1860, vol. iii, p. 137-8.

eldest of the four, according to the pedigrees. We learn from it a fact on which they are silent,—that Ieuan was married to a lady named Gwenllian, whose origin is, however, left in obscurity. This, and the subsequent poems, are assigned in the *Ceniarth MSS.* to Huw Arwystli, with the addition of the suspiciously early date of the 12th of July, 1501, in the case of the two first. Though of no great intrinsic merit, they are valuable for the glimpse of light which they let in upon the social and domestic manners of the period. The scene of the first appears to be a fair, or a festival, perhaps the annual wake of Llangurig, held in honour of its patron saint, in which Ieuan is represented as maintaining order by means of his own personal prowess and that of his retainers, while his wife Gwenllian distributes alms and hospitality to the poor.

Cowydd i rai o Henafiaid y Clochfan o Langurig ym Mhowys.

" Pwy, yn lew trin ar fyddin fawr,
Pan fai lewnach, pwy 'n flaenawr
Pwy draw 'n cael y powdri .
Palfau cawr gwych . . .
Plad[1] a dyrr, plaid a dery
Post ar frig y Pwysdir[2] fry ?
Ifan, ffurf ei[3] ewin a' i ffon,
Yn square ac[4] yn seyrion
Milwr gwrdd, mal a gwyddynt,
A mawr wayw square Morys gynt,
Coed gwin o Siancyn sydd
Cyd genedl i goed . .
Rhoen' wyr 'r hen . . . .
O flaen y lleill . . .
Llwyn lle derw . . . .
Llewod hil Howel Llwyd hen.
Dwyn d' enau fawr dan dy fys
Dy wain y bioedd dwy Bowys,
Crwn i d[r]oi wyr Ceri 'n d' ol,
.   .   .   pawb olynol.

[1] Plat in MS.   [2] Qy. for Powysdir—Powys-land.
[3] i in MS.   [4] ai in MS.

Pedair llinell ar goll.

.   .   oded yn ddidaw
.   .   .   allan draw
.   .   .   .   câr ydwyd,
.   .   a gwych cefnog wyd ;
un cadarn yw ein ceidwad
.   .   .   wedi eich tad
.   .   .   dy gar wyf
.   .   .   ffwrdd ydwyf
.   .   .   .   barn i
.   .   .   .   haelioni
Pob rhai ddaw, pob rhyw ddyn,
At dy deir bort i 'w derbyn :
Dy wraig, Ifan, dragywydd
I 'r byd rhoddai bwydau 'n rhydd,
Ni bydd gwyl heb weddi 'r gwan
Nac yn llaw wag Wenllian :
Ni lanwai o lawenydd

.   .   .   .   .
Heb weini dewr o ben y dydd,
I' w dylawd hen, o deled hwyr,
Ifan addwyn weinyddwr ;
.   .   .   .   .   dewr
.   .   .   .   gweision
Dy ran a phwys dwrn a ffon
Hwn drwy havog[1] a rhyfel

Tair llinell ar goll.

Ni bu erioed[2] heb angau
Far Owain frod Einion frau :
Trwm o' i gedyrn train[3] gydiwyd
Du aros llew dewr Rys Llwyd.
Dy wenith pur down i'th [barth]
Ydyw hoiew barch Deheubarth.
Da yw 'r achau[4] glan [odduchod],
Dichwyn yw dy achau ynod,
Dy les yn dy lys ennyd
A gaen' y Beirdd, gwyn eu byd,
Da les oedd dy lys iddyn',
Saig y wraig a wisg siwgr gwyn ;
Gwell y doe gwellhad i 'r gwan
O ganllawiaeth Gwenllian :

[1] Angl., havock.
[2] Angl., train.
[3] Yriod in MS.
[4] Dowchar in MS.

Gair mawr hyd gwrr môr aeth,
Ag ei dyg eu gwaedogaeth ;
Fe roi' i 'r milwyr aur melyn,
Ifan ei thad a wnaeth hyn ;
Dyn wyd a fydd dyn difalch,
A dant ar bob dyn taerfalch,
Ei arwain i ben trwyn y bangc,
Nawdyn cryf a dynn a crafangc,
Nid ae dyn, o[n]d oedd annoeth,
Ae ran draw dyn chwyrn dewr doeth,
Ni bu ddewr hael ni bydd y rhawg

.   .   .   .
.   .   .   na ddyg o wynt
.   .   wr distaw diwynt
.   .   nid hwynt a fid hwy
.   .   .   edwyn 'r adwy
.   .   .   dyn olwyn oes
.   .   .   am dy einioes
.   .   draw bin . et tra balch
.   .   .   .
.   .   Ifan ni ddygid
Ronyn bach o ran neb yd,
Nid oes wr o[n]d ei sorri
Na chryno chais i 'ch ran chwi
O red ar y iad orig
Waed un neu ddau, od ei yn ddig,
Ac ni ddwg dim yn ddig di
Ond ai eithei 'n dywchwi.
Cwynion bod cynnen ni bydd
Uwch y lan, o chei lonydd.
Ni ddygi law 'n dy ddagarr,
Oni red y gwaed ar dy warr ;
Nid da aros hwynt orig
Dan dy ddwrn o ei 'n dy ddig ;
Chwyrn wr wyd, chwyrnia 'r adwen ;
Chwarddwn bawb eich rhoddi 'n ben."
         Hugh Arwystl ai cânt, Gorphena y 12ed., 1501.[1]

ODE TO IEUAN AND GWENLLIAN OF CLOCHFAEN.[2]

" Who is the valiant arrayer of the mighty host ?
   When its complement is full, who is its leader ?

[1] The date is doubtless as apocryphal in the case of this as of the
other poems to which dates have been affixed, probably from conjecture only, by the compiler of the *Ceniarth MS*.

[2] In the MS. this poem is entitled merely " An Ode to some of
the Ancestors of the Clochfaen of Llangurig, in Powys."

Who is it yonder holds the powder . . .
With the hands of a stately hero?
Who will shatter a plate [of armour], who will strike its side,
A pillar on the topmost height of Powys-land?
It is Ieuan—in frame, grasp, and staff,
Square-built and impetuous,
A vigorous soldier, as they well know,
With the huge square spear of old Morris.
From Jenkyn there comes a forestful of wine.[1]

Four imperfect lines.

Lions of the lineage of old Howel Lloyd.
Bring but thy potent lips beneath thy finger,
And the two Powyses are subject to thy scabbard,
To turn the men of round Ceri behind thee
    . . . . . all in succession

A gap of four missing, and four imperfect lines.

A mighty one is our guardian,

Five imperfect lines.

All—every sort of person will come
To thy three ports to be received;
Thy wife, Ieuan, for ever
Would be freely distributing meats to all the world.
No festival will there be without the prayer of the poor,
Nor will Gwenllian be empty-handed.
Ieuan, a courteous server,
Would not fill (his cup) for joy,
Without ministering constantly, from the close of day.
To his old and poor one, if he come late;

Two imperfect lines.

Thy portion with weight of fist and staff,
He, thro' havoc and war

Three imperfect lines.

Never at any time has Owen's[2] spear,
Fervent with Einion's onset been without death.
A heavy train of his strong men were joined together
To await the black bold lion, Rhys Lloyd,[3]
Thy pure wheat, if we come thy way,
Is the [object of] the lively respect of South Wales.

---

[1] Viz., the wine-giver; so named from his supplying his soldiers with Bordeaux wine, thence brought by sea direct to a Welsh port, probably Aberystwith. *Vide supra*, vol. iv, p. 70.

[2] The second of the "Four Brothers."

[3] Of Creuddyn, his grandfather.

Good are thy pure pedigrees from their source,
Faultless are thy pedigrees in thee,
Thy bounty in thy mansion for a while
Would the bards obtain, happy they!
A good profit to them was thy mansion,
The lady's dish was covered with white sugar;
Very soon would the sick begin to mend,
From the ministration of Gwenllian;
The great reputation hath reached the (extreme) corner of
    the sea,
That her illustrious blood hath brought her;
She bestows on the soldiers yellow gold,
Ieuan, her father, hath caused this;
Thou art one who will be a man free from pride,
With a fang on every man obstinate in his pride;
Nine strong men shall drag him in their grasp,
And shall lead him to the farthest end of the bench.
No man would go unless he were unwise,
When yonder man impetuous, resolute and wise bears his
    part,
There hath not been—there will not be hereafter one resolute
    and generous

A line wantiug.

Seven imperfect lines.

A line wanting.

. . . . By Ieuan hath not been taken
The least grain of any one's share of corn;
There is not a man but it would be worse for him
Who would not quake at an inquiry on thy part.[1]
If there flow upon the cheek but for a little while
The blood of one or two, thou wilt become angry;
And when thou art angry, no one will take anything in thy
    wrath,
But should he have decamped, will bring it back.
Complaints tho' there be, dissension there will be none
Over the hill, if thou hast thy way;
Thou wilt not lay hand on thy dagger,
Unless the blood run on thy neck;
They had better not remain an instant
Under thy fist, if thou get angry;
Thou art an energetic man, the most energetic that I know,
We shall all be merry, now that thou art made our head."

[1] (Or) an attempt upon thy share.

COWYDD I IEUAN AB MORYS AB SIANCIN GOCH O 'R CLOCHFAEN
YN LLANGURIG.[1]

" Da fuw Duw, a difai dyn !
 Ai at rediad y tri dyn,
 Ifan ; tri chant ar eich ol
 A ddaw yn geraint dyn gwrol ;
 Pen wyt heddyw pont iddyn',
 Palf cawr gwych, plwy' Curig wyn ;
 Doeth, iraidd, a da y 'th riwyd,
 Dewr a i wynt[2] erioed wyd ;
 . dwyn 'r ôd yna 'r ydych
 Dau fâr dwrn, Edn Forys wych.
 . mae 'r anian mawr ynoch,
 Eres lan gwr, wyr Siancin Goch.
 Coed da Ifan cyd tyfant
 At hên ryw gweilch Tanwr gynt.
 Hil o wydd Howel oeddych,
 Hael llew dewr Howel Lloyd wych.
 . . yw[3] elw dwy 'n ol di
 . . .   cawr fâr Cerri[4]
 . . fawr bar edn Forys,
 . . bawb dan un bys."[5]

ODE TO IEUAN, SON OF MORYS, SON OF JENKYN GOCH
OF CLOCHFAEN IN LLANGURIG.

" God has been good, and man blameless.
 Thou goest to the course[6] of the three men,
 Ieuan ; at thy back come three hundred
 As kinsmen of a valiant man:
 To-day thou art at the head of the bridge for them—
 The people of Blessed Curig—with thy gallant giant's palm.
 Wise, vigorous and well bred art thou,
 Resolute ever art thou . . .
 . . there thou bearest the palm,
 With a spear in thy two fists, thou chick of noble Morys !
 . . great is the nature within thee,
 Thou marvellous man, grandson of Jenkyn Goch !

[1] The title in the MS. is " Cowydd i 'r Clochfan" only.
[2] *Sic ;* the line seems corrupt.
[3] iw in MS.   [4] Corri in MS.   [5] bus in MS.
[6] Rhediad, literally, a running. Perhaps a foot-race is meant.

To Ieuan shall a noble forest of sons grow up together
To. the old breed of hawks of the "Tanwr"[3] of yore.
From the wood of Howel were ye sprung—
The generous, resolute, gallant lion, Howel Lloyd."
The next four lines are imperfect and untranslateable.
Cætera desunt.

The following "Cywydd" would appear to have
been written in the time of Ieuan of Clochfaen, with
whom, as well as with his wife Gwenllian, it shows the
author to have been on terms of intimacy.

COWYDD I BONT GWY.

" Amcenais,[2] yma ei cwynaf,
   Mewn dull dewr myn 'd lle nesaf.
Tristâu 'r wyf am lwybrau i lys
   Ifan, fawredd hen Forys :
Ymrydd[3] i 'w dy mawr ydoedd,
   Iachau da 'leni uwch dôl oedd,
Blysais fod lle bai loewsaig
   Ifan ireiddlan, a 'i wraig :
Tynu tros[4] Wy lle tramawdd
   At hwn i 'r Clochfaen nid hawdd :
D'rysdawdd i 'm llif dd'rysglawdd draw,
   (Rhwydd lef Gwenllian rhoddaw),
Ffurf daer lif rhydaw redeg
   Ffwrdd a darn o 'm ffordd deg ;
Bwriodd Gwy i lawr bruddgolwaith
   Ben trwyn y bont ar lyn waith ;
Y Bont-goed bu hwnt gadarn,
   A wnai ddöe ddwr yn ddau ddarn,
. . suo . bryn wasgfa.
        darn gan Wy ddaeth.
. . . lwyd wedi 'r wlaw
. . . am anreithiaw
. . . osod rhyfalch
. . . punt feddw hynt[5] falch

---

[1] *i. e.,* Madoc, surnamed "Tanwr," or Firebearer, the founder of
the. Clochfaen family.
   [2] Ymcenais in MS.
   [3] Third person future indicative of the verb ymroi used as a
noun ?   [4] Dros in MS.
   [5] Hunt in MS.

.   .   .   fwlith gauafloer
.   .   goleddu i 'm gwlaw oer
.   .   gynilwraig y nant
.   .   arglwydd o 'r cornant
.   .   yw harferodd fan
.   .   .   gwpl a gipian
Pont rhyfedd gwnai 'r dialedd dig
'Does garw yn ymyl drws Gurig.[1]
Cyfodwch hon, cyfion ei caid.
Coedio dwyn cardod enaid.
Er hyd aros, rhoi dirwy.
I mendio gwaith garw daith Gwy
Cåf gan Dduw hoyw ffordd loywlân
O 'r diwedd i dy Ifan,
O wnewch er fy mwyn achwynwr,[2]
Godi 'r darn aeth gydâ 'r dw'r.
Trwsiwch hi, am gael, trwy Jesu,
Well y bont ar Wy lle bu."

Huw Arwystli, ai cant, 1570.[3]

ODE TO THE BRIDGE OF THE WYE.

"I purposed,—here will I lament it—
In resolute guise to go the nearest way,
I am sad for (want of) paths to the court
Of Evan,[4] who possesses old Maurice's greatness.
There was a vast gathering to his house,
Good families this year were above the dale ;
I longed to be where was the rich broth of Evan and his wife:
To draw, across the Wye, where it is wide-spread,
Towards Clochfaen to him is not easy :
A tangled dyke impeded the flood before me,
(The free speech of Gwenllian urged the gift[5]).
In impetuous fashion the flood rushed on unheard,

[1] Eight syllables in this line.   Perhaps the second *y* in " ymyl" is not reckoned.   [2] Achwymyr in MS.

[3] This date, of course, like the preceding, is an anachronism, as Ieuan, the eldest of "The Four Brothers," is referred to in the poem. The compiler, doubtless, confounded him with Ieuan ap David of Clochfaen, the grandson of his brother Jenkyn. *Vide supra*, vol. iii, p. 274.

[4] Ieuan, eldest son of Maurice of Clochfaen.

[5] The meaning seems to be that Gwenllian was herself moved by an impulse of her will to give the dyke, or that she persuaded some one else, her husband, perhaps, to give it.

And carried away a piece of my fine road.
The Wye threw down the projecting earth-work,
The end of the bridge's nozzle, with its water-work.
Of the wooden bridge[1]—hitherto its wood was strong—
The water yesterday made two pieces.

Twelve imperfect lines.

The vengeance of wrath made a strange bridge.[2]
Is it not cruel, close to Curig's door ?
Raise it up again; to bring wood for it
Would be found just.   'Twould be alms for the soul,
Against long delay, to grant a rate
For mending the work of the rough onset of the Wye.
I shall obtain of God a brisk, clear, and clean road
At last to the house of Evan,
If, for the sake of me, the complainant,
Ye will replace the piece that is gone with the water.
Repair it, that so we may, through Jesus,
Have a better bridge where it has been over the Wye."

The poem to be now introduced to our readers contains several expressions which, together with certain obscure references to historical events, render it matter for regret that it has not reached us in a more complete form.   It commences with a panegyric upon Siancyn, the third of the "Four Brothers" of Llangurig, after which it would seem to launch out into an encomium on them all collectively, were it not that, in the twenty-third stanza, the reference to two only appears to signify that this was the number of the survivors at the time it was written.

ENGLYNION I GENEDLE CLOCHFAEN.[3]

1.

" Hir iechyd, sadfyd, i wr syth—cry'
    Crafanc hawl o 'r gwalnyth ;
    Hir garw hael o 'r gwehelyth ;
    Hir hoedl, boed hwyr dy ail byth !

[1] The bridge destroyed appears to have been near the church.

[2] The precise meaning of these lines, following close upon an imperfect one, is not apparent.

[3] The vagueness of the title shows that it was devised at a late period, by a person who was unable to comprehend with certainty what persons were referred to in the poem, or what was its subject.

2.

" Byth bro Curig at ragor—hil llon
        Howel Lloyd a Threfor ;[1]
    Byrdde i'th barth, beirdd a 'th[2] borthor,
    I 'w byrdde 'stent[3] beirdd a 'u stor.

3.

" Mae 'n feirdd fel dy gael gelwyr—dawn
        Duw 'n dy ran, gobeithir ;
    Dan dy adael, doniau d'wedir,
    Siancin, wyr Siancin,[4] wers hir.

4.

" Ffurf gryf Siancin tyst ti wyd—i 'th [rhan]
        Iach Danwr a Rhys Llwyd ;[5]
    Ffriw 'n ganllaw hoff raen gwynll [wyd],
    Ffurf gwr a' i faint ffyrf gryf wyd.

5.

" Carw Morus[6] ffurf gryf cydgyfiawn—dy wg
        Dithau 'n gadarn coffhawn ;
    Ceri fyth gwaith cryf y 'th cawn,
    Carai[7] ffyniant ceirw cyff Einiawn.

6.

" Gwalch Einiawn gloewddawn glewddwys—cadarn
        Da genym dy gynwys ;
    Byw mal y 'ch cawn, bach, ddawn[ys],
    Yn ddigamwedd[8] oedd gymwys.

7.

" Dyn[9] lle rhof y 'ch caf i 'ch cyfan— .   .
        Catrin[10] hael Merch Morgan ;
    .   da iwch iach Fort[11] lydan,
    .   .   .   . Duw 'n eich rhan.

[1] See vol. ii, pp. 215, 271.   [2] Breyddeath in Ll. C.
[3] This word would seem to be a corruption of the Latin " ex-
tentus."   [4] See vol. ii, p. 274.
[5] Rhys Lloyd of Creuddyn.
[6] The father of the " Four Brothers," vol. ii, p. 274.
[7] Care, Ll. Cen.   [8] Digainwedd, Ll. Cen.
[9] The non-repetition of a word from the last line of the preceding
stanza shows an hiatus here.
[10] This Siencyn married Catherine, daughter of Morgan ab Rhys
ab Howel. In the Clochfaen pedigree, in the *Wynnstay MSS.*, it is
stated that this lady's mother was Catherine, daughter of Bedo ab
Rhys ab Llewelyn ad Dafydd Chwith of Cynwyl Gaio in Caermar-

[11] Fort, *i. e.*, bord.

8.

" . . . gwin . gwenllys—y Clochfan
. . . . . moethus ;
. llu mawr glân llew Morus
. adolym yn dy lys.

9.

" . i'th nod amod yma—yw lladd y bai ;
Lladd y byd y mae traha ;
Nid aeth yn[1] dy waith yna,
Yn dy oes dim onid sy dda.

10.

" Byw 'n dda draw i endiaw i gytundeb—Duw
Ydyw dull cyfiawndeb ;
Byw 'n ddrwg yw trin trawsineb ;
Byw y wneist heb gynwys bai neb.

11.

" Apla' n fyw d' wythryw o dreth wyd—y gwg
Pen fu 'r gwaith diarswyd ;
Apla' gwaed palfog ydwyd,
Apla' grym palfau gwr wyd.

12.

" Dyn draw, wyd canllaw da i ei caid—egni sad
Gynwys help gwirioniaid ;
Da 'n gynwys hyd wyn gweiniaid,
Dyn heb un plyg, da 'n ben plaid.

13.

" Ni phlygest, onest, union,—gyfiawn swydd
Ni byw o 'r bolchwydd neb o 'r beilchion ;
Ni roddest, ddurfrest ddewrfron,
I ddinas er torddynion.

thenshire, descended from Selyf (Solomon), King of Dyfed (Dime-
tia), son of Sawl Hir Felyn, Lord of Hwlffordd, King of Dyfed, ab
Tegwas of Abergweyn ab Gwyn ab Alan ab Alsar ab Idwal or
Tudwal, Prince of Dyfed, fourth son of Rhodri (Roderic) Mawr,
King of Wales. The armorial bearings of this family, as also of
the Williamses of Llwynrhyddod, in the parish of Llangurig, were,
quarterly, 1st and 4th *sable*, a wolf *argent*, his head and claws (Gwynedd) *gules*, for Meurig Goch, Lord of Cil y Cwm ; 2nd and 3rd
ermine, a chevron *or*, on a chief *argent*, a lion passant *gules*, for Cadifor ab Selyf, Lord of Cil y Cwm. For a further account of this
family, see *supra*, " History of Llangurig," vol. iii, p. 243.

[1] Ond, Ll. Cen.

X

14.

" . rydd gynydd i gweinion—neb[1] awr
A llawr dy weddillion ;
. . . . tan tylodion,
Gael weddus Llys Gelyddon.

There is here a considerable hiatus in the MS.
Some stanzas probably are wanting.

15.

" Chwerw 'stad fres wiad nid . . . .
. Ar helw Harri Wyth ;
Y rhain oedd oll o 'r un llwyth,
Caent rediad cyn troi adwyth.

16.

" Cirig adwyth y daethom—moes
—Moes, Wynn, gyrru 'n halon :
Bod, ar dyrfa, haeldra hon,
O dref Idlos draw, fodlon.

17.

" Boed brig plwyf Cirig o 'i cyd—hyna [fiaeth][2]
Yn odiaeth ar heidyd :
Da 'n Hafren ydyn' hefyd'
Glewon a gwyr glân i gyd.

The following ten lines must have belonged to two or more
different stanzas.

18.

" Glewder llid i 'w casau, glewder llewod . .
Wyr a glewder milwyr ar glod yr amaelant,
Glew iawn rym difeiaidd, glew [on ynt] er modd[iant]
Glew a neb o feddwl, glew i 'n byw a fyddant,

19.

" Glewon, myn Mair, y ceir, carant Idlos[3] beunydd,
Glân eu[4] deuau gynydd, glewon er digonant,
Tylodion gofal câs erioed nis dygasant,
Cirig a 'i râs lluddiodd, Cirig a roes [llwyddiant],
Gair i 'w coflywenyd . . Cirig foliant,
Cirig a 'i râd iddyn', Cirig anrhydeddant.

[1] Heb, Ll. Cen.
[2] This reading seems required by the rhyming word " odiaeth"
in the next line.
[3] Idis, Ll. Cen.   [4] Ei, Ll. Cen.

20.

" Gwyr a geir, [my]n Mair, a mynant—wrth ei alw
Cwyr, ag yna' i ddelw, Cirig Wyn addolant,
Am Cirig a' i ddelw yma . . 'r ymgroesant,[1]
Cirig a 'i groeso,[2] pawb Cirig a garant,
Cirig Ior ei hunan accw'r gwr a . .
Cirig hoiew Dduw Iesu, Cirig [a] wed[diant].

21.

An hiatus of four lines.

" [Cirig . . wyr iw 'r bryd i gyd a gadwant,
[I 'r Nef]ag un negeswr Cirig Wyn a [ânt].

22.

" .   .   .   .
.   .   .   .
.   .   .   . gwmpaniant,
.   .   .   . waed reiol gytun iawn a t'rawant,
.   .   . yniol wiwddysg, gytun 'r ymladdant,
.   .   . howaidd welion, gytun 'r heddychant.

23.

" [Nid y]dynt ffwl, nis dull na dall chwant—na dwl
Caid hwn un feddwl, cytun iawn a fyddant;
Cytun eu caid Eleirch, cytun a[3] cwerylant,
Cytun yw 'r hoiew garwyr, cytun a rhagorant,
Cytun hap ar fywyd, cytun eu pyrfeiant,
Cytun eu gwiw hoiewddysg, cytun eu gwahoddant.

24.

" Cytun bod dau 'r gwyliau y galwant—ger bron
Cytun y caid haelion, cytun y cyd-talant,
Pen difai waed oeddyn', pendefo[d] a wyddant,
Pen aig ydyn', ie, ymadrodd penna' i gyd a medrant,
Penna' llu trwy olud, penna' oll eu treblant,
Penna' n y bwlch anfeddwl, pen beilchion a fyddant.

25.

" Pennaf y caid Meistraid Mwstreant—hyd ym Mynyw ;
Penna' ffelof[4] heddyw, penna' fydd eu llwyddiant,
Pen gwraidd wiw gamp, pen y gair a ddygant,
Pen eu gwlad 'n hollawl, pen y glod ynnillant,
Pa le fwy lân hoiewlin, aplaf a gynhaliant,
Pa le fwy gwres a phenaeth,[5] plwyf â gras a ffyniant.

---

[1] Mgroesmaent, Ll. Cen.   [2] Gros, Ll. Cen.   [3] Ei, Ll. Cen.
[4] This word is unintelligible as it stands. The poet may have
written " Pennaf helynt," or " Penna 'n hollawl."
[5] Peneath, Ll. Cen.

ODE TO JENKYN AB MORYS OF CLOCHFAEN AND ANOTHER OF THE FOUR BROTHERS.

1.

" Long and lasting be thy health and life, thou upright man !
    the privilege
Of the strong-taloned bird from its sheltered nest is thine !
Thou art the tallest, the most generous gentleman of thy
    race !
Thine be it long to live, and late may thy son succeed thee !

2.

" May scions of the line of Howel Lloyd and Trevor,
In the land of Curig be ever on the increase !
Tables hast thou—thy porter ushers in bards—
For bards are the tables outspread with cheer.

3.

" They who are invited are bards, to the end that thou mayest
As it is hoped, a gift from God in thy portion ;   [obtain,
At parting with thee are recited the virtues
Of Jenkyn, grandson of Jenkyn, a long narration.

4.

" To Jenkyn's powerful frame art thou witness, to thy portion
Thou hast the pedigree of the Fire-bearer,[1] and of Rhys
    Lloyd :[2]
Thy mien bespeaks his character, amiable and holy ;
The hero's form and stature reappear in thy powerful frame.

[1] Madog Danwr.
[2] Rhys Lloyd of Creuddyn. His pedigree is given in *Mont. Coll.*,
vol. iii, p. 237. In vol. iv, p. 62, in a poem addressed to Ieuan ab
Gruffydd ab Howel Lloyd of Clochfaen, another Rhys Lloyd is mentioned, likewise of Creuddyn. This, in all probability, was Rhys
Lloyd of Llanfihangel y Creuddyn, son of Ieuan ab Rhys ab Iorwerth ab Cadifor ab Gwaethfoed, Lord of Cardigan, who bore *or*, a
lion rampant regardant, *sable*. He married Gwladys, daughter of
Ieuan ab Madog ap Gwenwys of Cawres or Cause, in the parish of
Worthyn, by whom he had two daughters, coheiresses, one named
Gwladys, who married Rhys Goch ab Ieuan ab Rhys Ddû, and had
the estate of Aberpylli in Llanfihangel for her portion, where her
descendants were living A.D. 1583 (Lewis Dwnn, vol. i, p. 48). The
other, in all probability, was married to Gruffydd ab Howel Lloyd of
Clochfaen, the grandfather of Jenkyn Goch of Clochfaen, who is
expressly stated in the poem to have been possessed of lands in
Creuddyn by the gift of Rhys Lloyd.

5.

" A Stag of Morys' powerful frame, and as just ; vividly
Shall we recall thy stern aspect :
Thou lovest toil, we find thee strong ;
The Stags of Einion's[1] stock love success.

6.

" Brave progeny of Einion, bright is thy genius, sturdy thy
      courage ; in thy strength
We are joyful to possess thee :
It befits us that we live to enjoy thee,
The gifted one we love, who hast no guile.

7.

" A man whom, when I give him away, I will have him all
      back again . .
Catharine, the generous daughter of Morgan,
  . good for you is a solid broad table,
  . . . . God in your portion.

8.

" . . . wine . the bright mansion of the Clochfaen,
 . . . . . luxurious ;
The great host of the noble lion, Morys,[2]
 . we worship in thy mansion.[3]

9.

" The note of thy covenant here is the destruction of evil ;
Arrogance is destroying the world :
In the work of thy life there has been done
Nought save that which is good.

10.

" Rectitude of life will lead to union at last : God
Is the Exemplar of justice :
To live wickedly is to encourage iniquity ;
Thy life has been such as to uphold vice in none.

[1] Who this Einion was is an obscure point. He is frequently referred to as a patriarch in the family.

[2] Morys ab Jenkyn Goch of Clochfaen.

[3] This seems to refer to a time when the monks of Strata Florida, who had the cure of souls in the parish of Llangurig (see *supra*, vol. ii, p. 255), having been ejected from their monastery, the offices of religion had to be secretly solemnised in the house of Clochfaen, the " mansion of Jenkyn," son of the " noble Lion Morys." Tanner informs us from the *Benet MS.* that " the prior and seven religious had pensions, A.D. 1553." The monastery therefore had been surrendered some years prior to that date (see *Arch. Camb.*, vol. iii, p. 126).

11.

"Of thine eight generations thine estate is the greatest; in
    aspect
Thou art fearless when there is work to be done:
Of a talented race thou art the ablest;
The ablest of men in the strength of thy hands.

12.

"O man, to him who finds it thou art an excellent prop; thy
    firm energy
Undertakes the aid of the innocent:
Well dost thou maintain the cause of the guiltless and weak,
Thou man that swervest not, well dost thou head thy
    followers!

13.

"Honest and true, thou hast not swerved; just in thine office,
The proud ones shall not live by their arrogance;
Thy dauntless breast, thine heart of steel hast thou not given
To a city, for all its men of high stomach.

14.

". . will give increase to the weak; at no time
Does the floor receive thy remnants:
  . . . . that the poor should obtain
Fire is befitting to Llys Gelyddon.[1]

An hiatus of several stanzas.

15.

"A bitter condition . . . . . .
  . for the gain of Harry the Eighth;
These were all of the same tribe;
Ere our affliction can be reversed, they must run their
    course.

16.

"Curig! we have come to affliction—give,
Give us, Blessed One! to drive away our foes;
Such beneficence will greatly rejoice
The populace in yonder town of Idloes.

[1] This is clearly the same place as that named in the eleventh
stanza of the elegy on Llewelyn ab Morys (*supra*, p. 67). At present no trace of any such place is to be found. The last word,
"Gelyddon," would seem to be identical with "Celyddon, in Coed
Celyddon," the forest refuge of the bard Merddin Wyllt (Merlin)
after the battle of Ardderyd in the sixth century. Can it be that
some exile from North Britain so named it in association with the
land of his childhood, on the same principle that one is reminded,
for instance, of Shakspeare by a river and town called Avon and
Stratford-on-Avon in the midst of the "bush" in Australia?

17.

" May the uplands of Curig's parish, of its ancient people
Be superabundant in population ;
On Severn also are they good
Brave and pure men all.

18.

" Men are they animated with the bravery of wrath against
their enemies—the bravery of lions ;
With the bravery of soldiers do they grasp at glory ;
Very brave is their blameless strength, brave are they to my
heart's content,
Braver than thought can reach, brave will they be during
life.
Brave men, by Mary, are they found, daily do they love
Idloes ;
Pure is the increase of both for the satisfying of brave men ;
Never have they deemed distasteful the care of the poor.
The favour of Curig hath prevented it, Curig hath brought
prosperity ;
A word to the memory, . . praise of Curig,
Curig do they honour—Curig for his favour towards them.

19.

" Men, by Mary, are they, who, in invoking him,
With wax tapers worship Blessed Curig in his image ;
For Curig and his image here . . . they sign themselves
with the Cross,
Curig do they welcome, they all love Curig.
The Lord Himself . . . . the man Curig yonder,
They earnestly pray to Curig, the energetic [servant] of
Jesus our God.

20.

An hiatus of four lines.

" . . . all men bear Curig in remembrance,
One—the Blessed Curig—is their conductor to Heaven.

21.

An hiatus of two lines and a half.

" . . . . they accompany,
. . . . of royal blood they strike very harmoniously
together
. . . concordantly with surpassing vigour and skill do
they fight,
. . . . . . concordantly do they make peace.

22.

" They are not irrational, they follow blindly no phantom of
passion or judgment ;
If one have a thought, they agree well together :
Like swans are they in harmony, concordantly do they
quarrel,
Concordantly are they ardent lovers, concordantly they excel ;
Concordant are their chances in life, concordant their pur-
veyance,
Concordant are their energy and skill, concordant their in-
vitations.

23.

" Concordantly do they both[1] invite to festivals, in public
Concordantly are they generous, concordantly do they pay :
Of a blameless race are they the head, they have learnt the
best manners,
They are the heads of society, yea, as to speech they are the
best informed of all ;
By their wealth they are heads of the host, at the head of all
is their shout,
Heading the ambush in the pass, of proud ones are they
the head.

24.

" Chief masters are they of musters—even so far as St.
David's ;
Chiefest in their career to-day, theirs is the chiefest pros-
perity :
The chief roots of noble achievements, they bear the chiefest
fame ;
The chief of all their country, they gain the chiefest praise ;
The purer and livelier the blood, the abler the upholders of
their line ;
Proportionate to the fervour of their rulers is the favour and
fortune of the people.

[1] Viz., the two surviving brothers.

WELSH POETRY, ILLUSTRATIVE OF THE HISTORY OF LLANGURIG.

By HOWEL W. LLOYD.

PART III.

In the last poem we have seen that, while the virtues of two of the four brothers of Llangurig are commemorated, those of Jenkyn are the most fully and prominently dwelt upon. It appears from the genealogies that William, the fourth brother, died unmarried, and that the second brother Owen, though married, is not known to have left any surviving issue. Thomas, the eldest son of Ieuan of Clochfaen, having been provided with an inheritance at Crugnant, Owen would naturally have been succeeded at Clochfaen by Jenkyn, the third brother. Which of the three, together with Jenkyn, survived the other two, does not appear, as his name is not found in any extant portion of the poem. If an inference may be drawn from the fact that the one was unmarried, and the other left no heirs, that they died early in life, Ieuan must have been the other survivor. It has been already remarked, how deeply to be regretted is the fact, that a poem so interesting from its political and social allusions should have come down to us in so very dilapidated and fragmentary a state.

This is to be lamented the more, because, more than any other of the poems, it furnishes contemporaneous evidence not only of the high estimation in which the Clochfaen family and its kindred branches were held at that time in their own immediate neighbourhood, and far and wide beyond it; but also of the causes which occasioned their being regarded by the classes below them, as in a peculiar and special manner their patrons

Y

and defenders. The devotion and affection rendered
them did not spring from mere feelings of clanship, nor
were these wholly the fruit of the ordinary service paid
in those days by inferiors to their superiors in education
and worldly position. This is shown especially in stanzas
8 to 16, wherein not only are the virtues ascribed to
Jenkyn particularised in a way that differs pointedly
from the common-place generalities of Welsh encomiastic poetry ; but facts and events are referred to
as having become special occasions for their exercise.
Paraphrased in plain prose, these stanzas are very sig-
nificant, and may, without much risk of error, be
referred to the year 1549, when the celebration of the
Mass was abolished throughout the kingdom by Act of
Parliament. By a slight amplification of the text he
seems to say, "In thy mansion—the bright mansion of
the Clochfaen—O Jenkyn, son of Morys, by thy favour,
and under the protection of thy men-at-arms, are we
driven to solemnise in the privacy of thy mansion the
holy rites of our ancient faith, deprived as we are of
our parish church. To thee do we look to put down
the evil that has come upon us. Thus will the rectitude of thy life be eventually rewarded by God, and
the wickedness of the evil-doers be brought to nought.
In thy talent, energy, constancy and goodness lies,
under God, our strength. Thou hast not oppressed
us, like others, in the pride and arrogance of their
hearts, nor abandoned thy faith in the hour of trial and
danger at the beck of the proud nobles of Edward's
court. The poor, who suffer elsewhere from the
plunder of the religious houses, and the enclosure of
the abbey lands, on which every poor family had been
privileged to graze its cow, are fed daily from thy
table. To a bitter condition, in sooth, has the country
been reduced for the mere gain of Henry VIII and his
profligate and unprincipled courtiers. Still we have no
hope that this wretched state of things will be reversed
till their madness has run its course. And thou, too,
Cyricus, holy martyr, and patron of our district, who

reignest with Christ in heaven, bestow on us thy blessing, and aid us with thy powerful prayers! So shall we be strengthened to endure with fortitude the assaults upon our holy religion with which it has pleased God to try our faith, in patience waiting for the time when this tyranny shall be overpast, and the consolation we shall obtain by the restoration of our rites and altars."

The Clochfaen and Llangurig families were content to dwell in comparative obscurity among their own people, at the head of whom they held themselves in readiness to place themselves at the call of duty. Driven from their parish church, their mansion became, as it were, a church in the catacombs among the mountains of Plinlimmon, for all those who loved the ancient ways and walked in the old paths.[1]

In the poem now to follow Jenkyn alone is commemorated, whether because he was at the time the sole survivor does not appear from any of the lines now extant. The poem is unhappily fragmentary, and the text frequently doubtful; still sufficient remains from which to obtain, in this nineteenth century of ours, a curious and interesting glimpse of the social customs of our forefathers in the fifteenth and commencement of the sixteenth, which might otherwise have escaped notice. The occasion for its composition would seem to have been the annual "wake," or feast of St. Curig, the patron saint of the village, which was kept on the 16th of June, and continued, perhaps for some days, during the whole or part of the octave. It would seem that Jenkyn, as

---

[1] Strype significantly relates that the Protector's friend, Sir William Paget, advised him, among other things, "To appoint the Lord Ferrers and Sir William Herbert to bring as many *horsemen* out of Wales *as they dared trust*."—*Eccles. Mem.*, Edward VI, 1549, edit. Oxford, 1822, vol. ii, book 1, part 1, p. 265. But we learn from Holinshed that the 1000 Welshmen, who had been landed at Bristol, "came too late to the fraie, yet soon enough to the plaie." For the city of Exeter, having been already taken by siege, "the whole countrie was then put to the spoile, and euerie soldier fought for his best profit; a just plague," as our chronicler naively adds, "upon rebels and disloiall persons."—*Chron.*, vol. iii, p. 10:5, edit. 1587.

head of the chief family of the place, unless it were in a magisterial or other official capacity, presided at the fair, and considered it his prerogative at least, if not his duty, to arbitrate at the games, to prevent or extinguish brawls, and punish disorderly conduct of the kind which subsequently, for want of such a check, brought into discredit the pastimes which were otherwise calculated to provide the peasantry with harmless recreation, and led to their discontinuance. His also was the place at the head of the festive board, to which, as well as to the drinking-bout after the banquet, all contributed their quota, called the "gild." On the occasion in question a dispute would seem to have arisen with regard to a second contribution, and the discretion of Jenkyn in promoting its peaceable settlement, apparently by assuming the responsibility of the whole of the payment, is made a special subject of encomium. Obscure as is the passage, a ray of light is thrown upon it by a usage which is said still to subsist at Llangurig. On every rent-day it is customary for the landlord to allow as much liquor as he may deem proper for the consumption of the guests at the tenants' dinner. If more than this allowance be required, the additional expense is defrayed by the subscription of all the guests.

We learn from the genealogies that Jenkyn was married to Catherine, daughter of Morgan ab Rhys ab Howel of Llangurig, ab Davydd ab Howel Vychan of Gilvachwen, co. Cardigan, Esq., descended from Cadivor ab Dyfnwal, Lord of Castel Howel, Gilfachwen, and Pant Streimon. It is this lady, with "mind on hospitable thoughts intent," who is commemorated in the poem. In the manuscript the latter is entitled vaguely, like most of the others, *A Poem to the Family of Clochfaen in Llangurig*. From the fact that there are no titles prefixed to the poems in Huw Arwystli's autograph in the quarto volume at Peniarth,[1] it may be inferred that those in the *Llyfr Ceniarth* were not

---

[1] *Peniarth Catalogue*, No. 250.

copied by the transcriber from the originals before him, but supplied from his own resources, an hypothesis which accounts sufficiently for their general looseness and inaccuracy.

CYWYDD I GENEDL Y CLOCHFAEN YN LLANGURIG.

Gwr â maint a grym yntaw,
Y'th menter[1] wrth y maint draw,
.   .   .   tan y fron
.   llwyd winau 'n[2] lle dynion,
.   .   ystryw[3] yw dy wraidd,
Siancyn wyr Siancyn[4] iraidd;
Breuddewr wyd, o bai ryw ddig,
Breugyw eryr Bro Gurig;
Mur ranwydd mawr yr hen weilch,
Mawr yw 'r balf am warrau beilch;
Llin edn[5] Howel, llawn odiaeth,
Llwyd, trwy waed Ieirll, draw y daeth;
O daw rhywiau[6] da i 'r hëol,
Edn i edn Tanwr wyt—aent ar ol.
Duw a 'i rhodd, Ffwg[7] dewriad ffon,
Doraeth[8] hynod wrth Einion.
O Gerri dau[9] gwraidd wyd,
Craig yn ol carw gwineulwyd.[10]
Dewr o ddyrnod oedd arnynt
D' aros, llid gweilch Rhys Llwyd gynt.
.   .   o' th wobrwyaeth[11] briawd,
I ddai Rent,[12] les iddyn', tylawd.
Cathrin lân cydranai wledd
I' th fyw, Eryr, a' th fawredd.
Porthiant ŷd i 'th parth hwnt oedd,
A mawr, sad, o 'r Mars ydoedd.
.   bob peth i 'r wyneb wych

.   .   .   .   .   .

[1] "Menter" is not found in the dictionaries. An ancient Welsh melody, still in use, bears the title of *Mentre Gwen.* It would seem to be a corruption of the English word "venture," itself perhaps corrupted from the Welsh "antur;" *pace* Dr. Johnson, who deduces it from the French "avanture." But whence comes this last, unless from the Celtic? [2] 'r, L. C. [3] ystriw, L. C.
[4] *i. e.*, Jenkyn Goch. [5] eow, L. C. [6] rhiwiau, L. C.
[7] fwg, L. C. [8] doreth, L. C.; ynod, L. C. [9] dai, L. C.
[10] gwinelwyd, L. C. [11] obrwayth, L. C.
[12] For "y deuai Rhent."

z

.   .   .   .   .   .

Ni roed, eurner wyd arnyn',
Win, fedd, er anfodd un.
Triniwr[1] beilch dy ran o 'r bri,
I was gwaedwyllt nis gadewi ;
Ni fagech law fwg awch[lym]
Yn y ffair, on 'd pherid[grym] ;[2]
Gwr [h]ynod a gyrr wenwyn,
Cadwed yr ael gydâ i drwyn.
Ni thynwyd arf o' th wain di,
Heb roi bâr obry i 'w beri.
O rhoed hwynt fâr, rhaid hwyn' fu,
Erchi 'r enaid, a chrynu.
Ni thrwsiwyd, o' th nawfed ach
Un a chalon uchelach.
I' th dai odiaeth diodydd,
A bwyd i bawb, o daw bydd.
Braidd[3] a' u nych, a 'r breuddyn chwyn[4]
Etto i yfed i 'r terfyn.
Troi gwirod traw ag agos,
Yn rhawiau [w]naen 'r hyd y nos ;
Ai da hyn, wedi hynny,
Roi i gytild[5] gwraig y ty ?
Talwyd un gild,[5] dyled yw 'n gwaith,
I gael talu gild[5] eilwaith ?
Da genyd ei digoni,
Dalu dy hun ei dyled hi,
Ni chawdd[6] gair, iechyd gwerin
I 'w addoli ar dy ddeulin[7]
Gwr ni ddwg graen weddw wych

.   .   .   .   .   .
.   .   .   .   odiaeth
.   .   .   ar warr dy waith
.   .   .   os dymunwn
.   .   .   .   aur ar dwn.

Huw Arwystli ai cânt, Mehefin 15ed., 1600.[8]

[1] Triniwr, L. C.
[2] The last two syllables are supplied from conjecture.
[3] Beirdd, L. C. ; ai, L. C.
[4] chwyrn, L. C. The sense of this couplet is obscure.
[5] tild, L. C., and "gilt" in next line.
[6] hi chawd, L. C.   [7] dai lin, L. C.
[8] This date is clearly apocryphal. David Lloyd of Clochfaen,
Jenkyn's son, was Mayor of Llanidloes, Escheater, and Justice of
the Peace in 1574. See *supra*, vol. ii, p. 194.

ODE TO JENKYN AB MORYS OF CLOCHFAEN IN LLANGURIG.

Man of stature, and of strength,
Thy daring is proportionate to thy size,
Three imperfect lines.
Jenkyn, thou grandson of Jenkyn the Sturdy,
Thou art ready and resolute, if there be any provocation,
Thou spirited fledgling of the Eagle of Curig's Land.
Thou huge rampart of the domain of the ancient Falcons.
Mighty is thy talon's clutch of the necks of proud ones.
Wondrously perfect is the line of Howel
Lloyd, that hath come down from afar, through the blood of
    Earls.[1]
If families of high birth enter the street
Thou art a pullet of the Fire-bearer's[2] pullet—let them give
    place.
Thy staff hath the stoutness of Fulk's[3]—it is God's gift.
Distinguished on Einion's side is thy race.
From Kerry thou possessest two roots,
Who art a rock in the path of a tawny stag.
Stout, if a blow from thy fist fell upon them,
Would be those who await thee, whose wrath is that of Rhys
    Lloyd's falcons of old
  .   .   by thy special donation
Has rent come to the poor for their benefit.
The fair Catharine[4] hath distributed the banquet,
For thy support, O Eagle, and for thy greatness.
There was provision of corn for thy party yonder,
And great and powerful was it over the March.
  .   everything fair to the view,
An hiatus of two lines.
There hath not been given—so bountiful a lord art thou over
    them—
Wine or mead to the discontent of any one.
A marshaller of proud ones, thou wilt not leave

[1] Tudor Trefor, Lluddoccaf, and Caradog, who were successively
Earls of Hereford and Gloucester.

[2] Madog Danwr.

[3] Sir Fulke Fitz Warren, a Lord Marcher, son and heir of Sir
Warren de Weaux, a nobleman of Lorraine. He attacked, defeated,
and slew Sir Meurig Llwyd, Knt., Lord of Whittington, and took
possession of his castle and lordship, which were confirmed to him
by Henry III.

[4] For the pedigree of Catharine, wife of Jenkyn Goch, see vol.
ii, p. 271.

Thy meed of honour to a hot-tempered servant.
Thou wouldst not support a hand as sharp as smoke
In the fair, wert thou not compelled to it:
A man of mark will dispel mischief;
Let such a one use his nose to guard his eyebrow.
Never hath weapon been drawn by thee from its sheath,
Save when necessitated by offence given from below.
If they have given thee offence, of necessity they must
Tremble, and beg for their lives.
Never was equipped, since thy ninth ancestor,
One of higher mettle than thou art.
At thy mansion is the very best of drink,
And of meat, for all who enter it.
Scarcely will it pain them, when the gallant gentleman urges it,
Again to drink on to the end.
They would toss off the liquor, far and near,
In shovelsfull, all the night long.
Is it a decent thing that, after this,
All should pay their quota to the goodwife?
One contribution[1] has been paid; is it a duty on our part
To have to pay a contribution a second time?
Thou wert pleased to satisfy her,
By paying her due thyself.
There is no offence in a word—the weal of the populace
Is to be worshipped on both thy knees.
A man who will not bear a smart widow's temper

*The poem concludes with one blank, and three imperfect, and
(in their present state) unintelligible lines.*

The next poem appears in the *Llyfr Ceniarth* in the
shape of two disjointed fragments, the latter of which
is found tacked on to that printed above,[2] commencing

" Da fu Duw, a difai dyn,"

and relating to Ieuan of Clochfaen, the eldest of the
"four brothers." Its concluding lines prove it to be
part of an elegy on Owain, the second brother. The
other fragment, which terminates abruptly in an *hiatus*,
is as plainly the commencement of an elegy on the
same Owain. Taken together, the two fragments be-

[1] " Gildio, *compotationum expensas persolvere.*—Davies's *Dict.*"
[2] P. 76.

come intelligible, and form a tolerably harmonious whole. Gwenllian, the wife of Ieuan, appears as Owain's sister, and swoons away with grief for her brother-in-law. The fragments which may have originally formed but one elegy, or may be separate portions of two by different authors, are here thrown together under the title of one of them, viz. :—

CYWYDD MARWNAD OWAIN [AB MORYS][1] AB SIANCYN GOCH O LLANGURIG.

Gwae ninnau, Duw gwyn! o'n dig,
Gae 'r bryn cwyr ger bron Curig.
Du oedd wyneb dydd Ionawr
I gwyno mab Gwinai mawr.
Doe fu torri daear a phren,
Rhoi daear ar iad Owen:
Yn ol y corph wylo y caid,
Dydd angladd deuddeng wlad;
Oerodd y wlad ar ddwy lys,
Heddyw i farw hydd Forys;
E fai três ar[2] fôr trosoch,
Wers gan gwymp wyr Siancyn Goch:
Oeriai 'stîl[3] grêf Arwystl gron
O frig Ceri i fro Caron.[4]
Gwae 'r Creyddyn! garw ceryddwyd!
Gwae drasau llin gwaed Rhys Llwyd!
Pan edrychwyd paun drechach?
Pa un oedd well pan yn iach?
Mentrai wyneb y trinoedd,
Mwy na deg mewn adwy oedd.
Ni ddoe Arthur oddiwrthaw,
Ban fai drin heb anaf draw,
Nid ae gawr ond a gurwyd,
Dan hawl law edn Howel Llwyd.
Cyn o' i farw cae neu fûr oedd,
Adwy fry wedi ei farw ydoedd.
.   .   chladdiad wych luddwr
.   well ag arf yn lle gwr.

[1] The bracketed words are omitted in L. C.
[2] Tressai, L. C.   [3] Anglicè, "steel."
[4] i. e., from Kerry in Montgomeryshire to Tregaron in Cardiganshire.

Bydd waeth-waeth[1] oes byth weithian,
Gladdu glaif[2] neu gleddau glân,
.   .   lwyddiant y flwyddyn,
.   .   leinw hap ymlaen hyn.
.   fod gwlaw Ebrill tawel,
.   aid â' i ffrwd cyd y ddêl
E ddaw rad oedd sôr hoywdeg,
O flaen twrf oleuni teg;
Anian 'r heulwen, yn rhylew,
Aiaf garw hwnt a fag rew;
Cynnydd ai, cyn ei ddiwedd,
Ar Owain wyrch yr un wedd:
Y dyn oedd a dawn iddaw,
A' i olud tros y wlad draw,
Ar hoel ddoe 'r haul oedd wen,
A niwl yno[3] 'n ol Owen.
Galw ar ei fedd gwelir fi,
Ynte Owen yn tewi.
Gwae 'r tir isod, gwae 'r trasoedd,
Gwae wlad gwalch goludog oedd,
Gwae dri brawd a geidw 'r brodir,
Gwae 'r tir o hyd agor tir;
Gwae ninnau 'n llwyr gynne 'n llas
Gwae erioed gweled gwr dulas;
Mawr weled [y] mor-filwr
Mwy bo 'n gael meibion y gwr,

.   .   .   .   .
Mor oer [i 'n] ucho, Mair wen!
    Here a leaf is torn out of the MS.
Oer oedd unllef roe ddoe [wan]
Yn ei llewig Wenllian.
Câr gwiw hael, carw Gwehelyth,
Tra[4] chwaer oedd fyw, ni chwardd fyth.
Merched hyd nef yn llefain:
Mae 'r ia neu[5] rew ymronnau rhain.
Och! heb wleddoedd chweblwydd[yn]
Och! brydded, och! briddo dyn;
Och! oferedd, och! farwn;
Roi ar Dduw[6] Saint air dros hwn;
Och! drymed ucho dramwy;
Och! mwy nag ym min[7] Gwy.

Och! yngan; och! a gwynwn,
A mwy fyth am y fath hwn!
Och Dduw 'n glain wych duai glew nerth!
Och, drom am na chaid ei werth!
O 'r llif pa well, er lles pen,
Na chrio oni cheir Owen?
Aed—bu ewyllys Duw bellach—
Owen i nef wen yn iach.

Huw Arwystli a' i câut, Ionawr 8ed., 1500.

The following is an attempt at a metrical paraphrase, rather than a translation of the foregoing poem. Care, however, has been taken to adhere to the substance of the original by avoiding, as far as possible, the introduction of new ideas. It may serve, by comparison with the prose translations, to convey a notion to the English reader of the extent to which the genius of our bards has been cramped by the strictness of their metrical rules.

ELEGY ON OWAIN AB MORYS AB JENKYN GOCH OF LLANGURIG.

Woe to us, blessed God! because of thine anger towards us,
Bearing is all the hill-side sad tapers of wax before Curig.
Lo! the January day hath dight its visage in blackness—
Mourns the day itself for the son of Gwinai the mighty![1]
Yesterday hath there been cutting of earth and of wood for the laying
Over the temples of Owen the earth, as he lay in his coffin.
Full twelve lands made wailing that day, as they followed his body.
In cold sorrow is steeped the country for two of its mansions,[2]
—Sorrow that death hath snatch'd the noble scion of Morys.
Now should the ocean chant a funeral dirge for Owen,
"Fall'n is the grandson of Jenkyn the Red" should be its burden.
Cold is the heart of steel that beat high for the round Arwystli,
From the heights of Ceri as far as the region of Caron.[3]
Woe is Creiddyn now! chastised hath she been severely!

---

[1] This may be the name of an ancestor; or it may mean "the excellent auburn-haired youth," if the word be read as "gwinau."
[2] Clochfaen, namely, and possibly, Llys Gelyddon.
[3] Literally, "hart."

Woe is the line of Rhys Lloyd's blood, and all of his kindred!
When hath there ever been seen upon earth a more powerful
　　gallant?
What man better than he, when whilom in health and in
　　vigour,
Boldly the hero would face the foe when arrayed for battle?
Not ten men in a pass, if they met, could overmatch him;
If King Arthur himself had fought him in single combat,
Not King Arthur himself had ridden scatheless after.
Surely a giant were worsted, if giant had dared to attack him,
Under the process[1] made by the hand of Howel Lloyd's pullet.
Like to a fortress or rampart was Owen before his departure;
Now is the rampart a breach, for Owen lives no longer!

Two imperfect lines.

Worse shall the world wax now, for the bright blade of Owen
　　is buried!

Four imperfect lines.

Then shall that which was gloom be changed into lively en-
　　joyment,
Just as the light serene oft-times is foreshadowed by tempest;
'Tis the bright sun's nature, by anticipation, to nurture
With its pervading force, the frost of the rugged winter;
So, overcasting the time, in similar manner, hath increase
Haply befallen Owen for a season before his departure,
Owen gifted with talents, of wealth far and wide the possessor.
Yesternoon on the street the sun with its rays fell brightly;
Owen is gone, and to-day it is buried in gloom for Owen!
Lo, I am here, on his grave, and calling—but Owen is silent.
Woe to the earth beneath, woe, woe to his kindred above it!
Woe to the country around, that rejoiced in the wealth of the
　　rich man!
Woe to the Brothers Three, the defenders now of the district!
Woe to the earth itself, for the earth it is constantly opened!
Woe to us all beside, for we all have been slain with sorrow!
Woe that we e'er should have gazed on the livid corpse of the
　　hero!
Great have we seen the soldier by sea, may his sons be yet
　　greater!

Hiatus of one, or three lines.

Mary, blest Virgin Mother! how grievous it is to bewail him!

Here follows an *hiatus* of several lines, and a leaf

---

[1] The word "hawl" seems to be here a figurative expression derived from a process of law.

has been torn from the MS. The last line has certainly the appearance of being a closing one, and if so, the above lines must have formed a separate elegy, and the following fragment have been part of another. In that case, probably, each was composed by a different author.

Faintly Gwenllian hath uttered a cry, ere she swooned in her
    sorrow,
Cold on our hearts hath it struck,—that cry of sorrow for Owen!
Owen, the pride of his race, her noble and generous brother ;
Ne'er will his sister smile, while she bides in the land of the
    living.
Up to the Heaven above hath ascended the wailing of
    maidens,—
Frozen with grief are[1] their bosoms ! six years are we left
    without banquets.
Woe for the burial! Woe the world's vanity! Woe is the
    Baron !
May the Saints offer their prayers for the peace and repose of
    his spirit !
Woe for the greatest on Wye that we heavily make lamenta-
    tion !
Woe for the tidings abroad ! and the grief that it daily grows
    greater !
Woe to us, God ! that the lustre which shone in our jewel is
    darkened.
Woe to us ! heavy the grief that its worth is departed for
    ever.
What, for the loss of our Owen, save rivers of tears can con-
    sole us ?
And—to the Will divine sith nought now is left save submis-
    sion,
Speed him to Heaven with prayers that God may receive him
    to glory.

The statement appended to this poem that it was composed by Huw Arwystli on the 8th January, A.D. 1500, would seem to be possibly entitled to greater respect than others of a similar character. It is scarcely conceivable that so circumstantial a date should have

---

[1] This, perhaps, may refer to the eldest of Owen's sons, who may at this time have wanted six years of his majority, and not have lived to attain it.

been the deliberate invention of the transcriber : hence
it is reasonable to infer that he found it in the original
manuscript from which he copied. But it is by no
means equally probable that the author's name likewise
was subscribed there; it does not therefore follow that
Huw Arwystli wrote it, and it is almost inconceivable
that he should have done so at a date so exceedingly
early. It is reasonable, then, to conclude from this
date that Owen died at an early age; a fact which is
supported by the internal evidence of the poem, since
it is stated broadly that his three brothers survived
him. It is clear, however, from the context that he
had attained to the vigour of manhood, and had even
achieved some exploits by land, and also by sea, if as
much may be inferred from the strange epithet " sea-
soldier" (môr-filwr) which is applied to him. This he
would probably have done in the service of Henry VII,
before and during the expedition which led to the victory on Bosworth Field, and the expression would
seem to point to his having been engaged confidentially
in the service of that monarch when an exile on the
Continent, and aided him perhaps secretly to visit from
time to time, as he is known to have done, his adhe-
rents in the Principality. The wish expressed with
regard to Owen's sons seems at variance with the genealogies, which represent him as dying without issue.
They may, however, have lived for some years, yet
have failed to attain their majority, as seems to be implied in the words: " Six years are we left without
banquets!" Again, Owen must have survived his wife,
of whose name all mention is omitted, while that of his
sister-in-law Gwenllian is introduced. The vast wealth
of Owen and his brothers, so frequently referred to in
the poems, may be partly accounted for by the fact that
they all held the Clochfaen property in common, instead
of sharing it between them agreeably to the old Welsh
custom of gavelkind. It would be interesting to know
whether this arrangement was the effect of their father's
will, or of the spontaneous abandonment by each of
their distinctive rights.

Of the remaining poems in the Ceniarth manuscript relating to Llangurig, three only, two of which are mere fragments, contain any direct reference to the families of the resident gentry. The others were written in honour of Saint Cyricus, its patron saint, and, containing as they do some curious information calculated to throw considerable light on the vexed question of the origin of the ancient devotion to that martyr and his mother Julitta in the principality, which extended to a far greater portion of it than the mere confines of Plinlimmon, they may appropriately form the subject of a separate article. Of the three former poems, the only complete one, subscribed by Huw Arwystli, contains eighty-six lines, and bears the title of "A poem (*Cywydd*) addressed to the families...in Curig's Parish." But, as in the midst of these occur more than one *hiatus*, and the latter part, commencing from the forty-first line, is encomiastic of a parson of Darowen, Sir Lewis by name, with the view to obtain of him the gift of a horse, it is probable that they are no more than the "*disjecta membra*" of two separate compositions. The poem commences thus :—

"Apla' yw lle cerdd plwy' [Curig.]"
"The parish of Curig is the seat of most skilful song."

The only important lines which it contains germane to our subject are the following :—

"Ni adawodd Duw un dydd dig
 Wahanu 'r ceirw yn nhir Curig.
 Glana' gwaed lle 'r glân gwawdyr,
 Ceirw 'n gad yn crynhoi gwyr.
 Llu 'n glwyd gref yn llanw gwlad gron,
 Llewod unoed Llwyd[1] union;
 Gwyr oll yn bwrw gair well-well,
 Gwyr, mi wn, da, ni goreuwell."
"God hath not suffered a single day of wrangling
 To disunite the stags of Curig's land.
 Purest is the blood where the panegyrists are pure;

___
[1] Or "grisly lions."

Stags [are they] who array their men in battle.
A host like a strong round shield, filling the land,
Lions in even line are the Lloyds, equal in age,
Men all growing ever in public esteem,
Men so good, that none I know are better."

Of the two more fragmentary poems one breaks off in the middle, consequently the author's name is missing. It bears the title of "An Ode to the Families of Clochfaen." As much of its contents differ little in substance from those already given, an extract or two from it will suffice. In the first will be found an allusion, which it could be wished were less obscure as to its time and object, to an aid in men given to "the Saxon" by the family of Morys, *i. e.* probably the Four Brothers. It begins, in its present shape, thus :—

" Un agwedd, wrth fynegi,
A Mursen feinwen wyf fi ;
Chwer[th]in, a thro[i] mîn i 'r medd
Wylo blin y 'r ail blynedd.
E ŵyr Duw y roed Ieuan
Ymwrw 'n oed dydd ym mron tân ;
O lawer swydd hen ffordd yw lys,
Gair mawr a gai dir Morys,
Am ei roi i Sais mawr les wyr
　.　　Ieuan werth tri o wyr."

" I bear a likeness, if the truth be told,
To a fair coquettish dame,
Who laughs, and puts her lips to the mead,
Yet weeps wearily in the second year.[1]
Ieuan, God knows, was given
To place himself, as the day waned, before the fire ;
To many an office[2] is his mansion the ancient road,
The land of Morys hath gained a high repute
For its gift to the Saxon of a large aid in men.
　.　　.　　Ieuan the worth of three men."

The next extract appears to relate to the choir of the Church of Llangurig, for which it was perhaps in-

---

[1] As this seems to have reference to a preceding passage, these lines can scarcely be the true commencement of the poem.
[2] Or, "from many a shire."

debted to the monks of Strata Florida, of which it was a vicarage. From the allusion to its wealth and liberality it may be inferred that the date of the poem is prior to the commencement of the Reformation troubles:

" Côr gloew Nef cwrr glan afon,
  Gardd i holl gerddwyr yw hon.
  Aml yw 'n gwîn am lân ganiad,
  Aml un gael aur ymlaen gwlad.
  . le trym i dylawd dramwy,
  . teg yw i mi deutu Gwy."
" A resplendent choir of Heaven is in a nook of the river's
    bank,
  A garden for all minstrels is this.
  Abundant is our wine for the sacred song,
  Many a one obtains gold in sight of all the land.
  . a spot delightful for a poor man to traverse,
  . fair to me are both sides of the Wye."

The following extract is from a poem which is interesting for more reasons than one, It furnishes the solitary instance of a poem by Huw Arwystli, addressed to a member of the Clochfaen family, which has been found elsewhere than in the Ceniarth MS., being taken from No. 250 of the Collection of W. W. E. Wynne, Esq., of Peniarth, to whom the writer is indebted for the kindness of copying it. And it furnishes a contemporaneous proof of the correctness of the pedigree (published in the *Archæologia Cambrensis*, vol. for 1867, 3rd series, p. 27,) of the person to whom it is addressed, viz. Rhys ab Morys ab Llywelyn of Llangurig, who was the younger brother of Jenkyn Goch of Clochfaen, and therefore great uncle of the Four Brothers " of that ilk." Morys, the son of Llywelyn, and father of Rhys, seems to have been the first of the family to settle in Mowddwy, having married Mahallt, daughter and possibly heiress of Howel Mowddwy, Esq. The object of the poem is to solicit the gift of a horse, which it would seem, though the passage is somewhat obscure, was to be ridden by the poet to Arwystli, where he proposed to apply it in some way, which is not made apparent, to the payment of his debts. Of the animal no more need be said than that, to judge from the qualities of shape, speed, mettle, and trotting and leaping powers ascribed to him by the bard, he might have shamed all competitors in the hunting-field, if he could now be brought out for a day with the Cheshire, or with Sir Watkin. Surely the bards must have deemed themselves seised of some poetical copyhold, entitling them to claim as a heriot for their verse the very pride of the stable.

CYWYDD I RYS AP MORYS AP LLEWELYN O 'R CLOCHFAEN YM MRO CURIG, I OFYN MARCH.

Y llew îr braf oll o 'r brig,
Brau a gerir bro Girig.
Braich a chledd, amgeledd gwlad,
Rhys, aer Forys, îr fyriad.
Wyr Llywelyn, dir yn rhodd,
Penaeth gwŷr, pwy ni 'th garodd?
Gwr yn ara', od aeth grym, ydwyd,
Glân fettel llew Howel Llwyd.
O 'r âch Benwyn wych benaeth,
Natur îr ynot yr aeth;
Llwythau 'r gwydd pob lleithigaur,
Gwaed Trefawr yn goed hen aur;
Gwaed Philip iwrsib aeth
Fychan, tarian anturiaeth.
O Gydewen gwiw dywys
Llwyth Blaenau trasau it', Rhys;
Tref a gwlad marchnad am Wy,
Aig meddiant Howel Mawddwy.
Dy briod eigyr obrwyawl,
Ammhech,[1] a gyd ffydd a mawl;
Lloer Siancyn, tryff i 'n at ras,
Nid o wr a hardder ei hurddas;
Wyr Rhys Llwyd hardd i fardd fydd,
O' i law wîn a llawenyd.

TRANSLATION.

Thou lion, brave and vigorous, for thy activity
Art thou beloved by all on the upland.

[1] This word is doubtful. As copied from the original it is "awmech."

Thine arm and thy sword are thy country's protection,
Rhys, heir of Morys, thou hast a powerful arm.

* * * * *

Grandson of Llewelyn, unwearied in bounty,
Chieftain of men, by whom art thou not beloved ?

* * * * *

A man of deliberation, when force hath assailed thee,
A lion of Howel Lloyd's pure metal.
A noble chieftain from the race of Benwyn.
An energetic nature hath entered into thee ;
A tribe whose every scion hath a golden seat,
Of the blood of Trevor, a forest of ancient gold.
Of the blood of Philip . . .
Fychan, a very shield in daring.
Thy descent, Rhys, is nobly deduced
From the tribe of Blaenau of Cydewen,
From the town and land of merchandise on the Wye,
Is the fount of the possession of Howel of Mowddwy.

* * * * *

Thy bride was a maiden who requited thee,
Faultless in virtue and fidelity,
As from the moon is her favour turned towards us,
Her dignity is not enhanced by that of Jenkyn her father.[1]
The grandson of Rhys Lloyd will be liberal to the bard,
From his hand come wine and gladness.

The next and last extract is from the last part of a long poem, in which is related the Legend of S. Curig, to which it does not seem properly to belong. The state in fact of the whole of these poems is suggestive of fire, mice, moth, everything in short that could have rendered the work of the copyist one of extreme labour and difficulty. The lines are so genuine an outburst of love and affection for the spot that, independently of the other evidence already adduced for the fact that the birthplace of our bard was in its immediate neighbourhood, the language is so far removed from the dry conventionalism ordinarily characteristic of Welsh encomiastic verse, as to have left no room for doubt, if any had previously existed :—

[1] " Rhys was married to Margaret, daughter of Jenkyn ap Rhys Lloyd of Llangurig,"—*Arch. Camb.*, 1867, p. 27.

" P'le well un plwy' ni ellir,
  Plwy' Cirig nid tebyg tir ;
          Hiatus of a line and a half.
  Fy nhir eisoes, fy nhrysor,
  A 'm maes ŷd gynt, a'm 'stôr,
  Fy lluniaeth, a 'm llawenydd,
  Fy lles erioed, fy llys rydd,
  Fy aml wîn, fy melynaur,
  Fry yn mhwrs fy arian a 'm aur ;
  Fy llun, fy mhob peth, fy lles,
  Fy holl iechyd, fy lloches.
  *   *   *   *
  Llaw Dduw, a 'i barch llwyddo y bydd
  Llu ein genedl yn llawn gwinwydd ;
  Ni aned neb ond unwr
          o waed Himp y Tanwr.
  Canwaith, fel y cae weiniaid,
  Yr aeth fry i help wrth fy rhaid.
  Fy helpu 'n rhydd, rhag dydd dig,
  Y ceir carwyr côr Curig :
  Na ddont i lawr, ydynt lân,
  Y gair da a gai rodd Ieuan."

" Nowhere can there be a better parish,
  There is no land like the parish of Curig.
  Long since my own land—my treasure,
  My cornfield, and my storehouse in time past,
  My maintenance and my joy,
  My gain since time began, my free mansion,
  My abundance of wine, my yellow gold,
  My silver and gold laid up in my purse,
  My picture, my profit, my all,
  My whole safety, and my retreat.
  *   *   *   *
  The hand of God, because we revere Him, will prosper
  The host of our race, as prolific as the vine ;
  Yet not a man, save one, hath been born
  A true graft on the blood of the Fire-bearer !
  A hundred times, when he knew us to be poor,
  Has he come to help me in my need.
  My generous helpers, against the day of wrath,
  Are the lovers of the choir of Curig.
  Let them not be brought low, for they are pure,
  'Tis Ieuan's gifts that bring him good repute."

A few remarks may be added in conclusion on the

frequent occurrence in these, and most others of the
Welsh poems of the same period, of the blemish in
poetical composition known as confusion of metaphor.
From a comparison of the heroes of the poetry with
oaks or vines, we are stunned by the suddenness and
rapidity with which they appear again as stags, falcons,
eagles, swans, or lions, and this occasionally in the
midst of actions grotesquely incongruous with the representative qualities of the birds, trees, or quadrupeds
with whose nomenclature they happen to be associated.
In such cases a covert allusion might be suspected to
the science of heraldry, and to the armorial bearings of
the respective families, but this when it happens to
occur is by way of rare exception rather than the rule.
Yet from the high repute attained by the authors of
these apparent monstrosities it would seem that the
literary palate of the contemporary Welsh "public"
was rather tickled than offended by them. The explanation would seem to lie in the fact that the sensi-
tiveness of both reciter and recipient became deadened
by constant repetition. The discordant epithets thus
in process of time came to be regarded as synonyms, a
certain number of which appeared necessary to the per-
fection of every panegyric ; and the ideas which would
be naturally appropriate to each figure of speech,
though lost in the outward framework of the words,
were found to be sufficiently suggested to the mind by
a species of mental reservation. As a necessary but
lamentable consequence it was forgotten, in process of
time, that metre and alliteration are but secondary
adornments of poetry, admissible only in strict subor-
dination to originality of conception clothed in appropriate imagery. Hence, by a not unnatural transition,
the former in too many instances have been found
gradually to usurp the place of the latter, and at length
to supersede them altogether, while skill in alliterative
consonancy came to be pursued as the end rather than
as a means for the conveyance of poetical force and
beauty. Thus the original play of fancy and imagina-

A A

tion, for which the Cymric mind had abundantly shown its capacity in the works of the earlier bards, became cramped and exhausted, until the very existence of the art became imperilled by its ultimate reduction to the mere study of alliterative surprises and a paltry playing upon words.

———————

HISTORY OF LLANGURIG.

PART II.—APPENDIX, 1873.

SINCE the History of Llangurig by Mr. Edward Hamer was published, the following additional information has been obtained by the Chevalier Lloyd of Clochfaen, K.S.G.

The CLOCHFAEN PEDIGREE, according to the *Golden Grove MS.* in the Record Office.

MADOG ab Gruffyd ab David ap Cynwrig ab Rhiwallawn ∓

Meredydd ∓

Ieuan ∓

Einion. He bore *Argent* three boar's paws couped and erected *sable* armed *gules*.

Ieuan or John ∓

Madog Danwr. *Ermine*, a lion rampt. *sable*, in a bordure *gules*, mulletée, others say bezantée, and others cinquefoilé¹ ∓

Meredydd, Budr ei Hossnau ∓ ....daughter of Howel ab Trahaiarn.

Philip ∓

Iorwerth ∓

Philip Fychan ∓

Ieuan ∓ Myfanwy, d. of David Fychan ab David ab Iorwerth of Manafon.

Madog ∓

Lucy ux. Adda ab Howel

Howel Lloyd ∓

Meredydd ∓ Efa, d. of Howel ab Iorwerth ab Trahaiarn ab Iorwerth of Garthmil, ab Einion ab Rhys
a

Lucy Bach ux. Ednyfed ab Gruffyd of Sonlli.

¹ The *Harl. MS.* 1977, p. 64, states that Madog Danwr had Llangurig and many other lands given to him for his services, and that he bore *ermine*, a lion rampant *sable*, in a bordure *gules*, charged with eight lions rampant or.

B B

a
Goch ab Llewelyn Fychan ab Llewelyn Eur
Dorchog. *Argent*, three lions passant gard. *Gules* for Trahaiarn ab Iorwerth.

Ieun ∓ Catherine, d. of Ieuan ab Madog ab Einion ab Gruffydd Fychan.

Ieuan Bwl, ancestor of the Lloyds of Berth Lloyd.

Howel-Lloyd ∓

Gruffydd ∓

Ieuan ∓

Rhys ∓ Margaret, d. and coheiress of Ieuan ab Rhys Gethin of Creuddyn, ab Ieuan ab Rhys ab Llawdden
ab Iorwerth ab Uchdryd ab Edwyn ab Goronwy. *Gules*, a griffin segreant *or*, for Llawdden.

Thomas ∓

Margaret ux. Ieuan Gwynn.

Jenkyn Goch ∓ Catherine, d. of Maurice Fychan.

Tangwystl ux. Llewelyn Lloyd.

Ieuan ∓

John ∓

John Vaughan.

CEFN YR HAFODAU.[1]

Llewelyn, ab Iorwerth ab Gruffydd ab Meredydd ab Madog Danwr ab Madog ∓ Ieuan ab
Meredydd ab Madog ab Gruffydd ab David ab Cynwrig ab Rhiwallon.

Philip ∓ .... d. of Gruffydd Llwyd ab Gruffydd Fraslwyd ab Gruffydd ab Meilir ab Selyf
ab Brochwel ab Aeddan of Llanerch Brochwel.

.... ux Ieuan ab Gwilym ab Goronwy Gethin.

Llewelyn ∓ ....d. of Rhys Gethin ab Llewelyn ab Gwalter.

Rhys ab Llewelyn ab David Clwith of Cynwyl Gaio in Caermarthenshire. ∓ Angharod, heiress of ∓ Llewelyn ab Howel ab Rhys ab
ab Rhys ab Iorwerth ab Gruffydd Fychan ab Gruffydd ab David   Cefn yr Hafodau.   David of Gilfachwen.
Fychan ab David Fongam ab David ab Meurig Coch, Lord of Cil y
Cwm. Quarterly 1st and 4th *sable*, a wolf passant *argent*, its head and nails *gules* for Meurig Goch, 2nd and 3rd Cadifor ab Selyf.

[1] *Lewys Dwnn*, vol. i, p. 309.   *Harl. MSS.* 1969, 4181.

GLANDULAS.

LLEWELYN ab Ieuan ab Meredydd ab Madog Goch, of Arwystli, ab Madog Fychan ⨯
ab Madog ab Ieuan ab Meredydd ab Madog Danwr.[1]

Matthew ⨯ Arddun, d. of Llewelyn ab Gruffydd, of Bettws, descended from Tudor Trefor.

Richard ⨯ Elen, d. of Rhys ab Ieuan ab David ab Rhys.   Gwenhwyfar ux. Ienkyn ab Ieuan ab Philip, of Berthlloyd.

Ieuan ⨯

David ⨯ Elen, d. of Rhys ab Maurice ab Llewelyn of Llangurig, ab Ieuan ab Gruffydd ab Howel Lloyd, of Clochfaen.

Edward.   John.   Llewelyn.   Catherine.   Elizabeth.   Margaret.

[1] Wynnstay MSS. Madog Danwr was the son of Ieuan ab Meredydd ab Madog ap Gruffydd ab David ab Cynwrig ab David ab Rhiwalon. Lewys Dwnn, i, p. 311.

CLOCHFAEN AND CRUGNANT,

According to John Salusbury of Erbistog, Esq. (Rhyl MSS.)

GRUFFYDD ab Howel Lloyd, of Llangurig, ab Philip ab Meredydd ab Madog Danwr (Ignifer), who served the Lord of ⨯
Powys, and for his services was rewarded with all Llangurig for himself and his heirs, and a grant of a plain border
gules, charged with eight mullets or, round his arms, which were ermine, a lion ramp. sable.

Ieuan ⨯ Gwenllian, d. of Ieuan ab Gruffydd Goch ab Ieuan ap Philip ab Meredydd ab Madog Danwr.

Ienkyn Goch ⨯ Catherine, daughter and heiress of Maurice Fychan ab Maurice of Ceri.

Maurice ⨯ Margaret, d. of Llewelyn ab Rhys Lloyd ab Iorwerth ab Llewelyn ab Rhys.

Ieuan ⨯ Margaret, d. of Rhys Lloyd ab Llewelyn, to Cadifor ab Gwaethfoed.   Ienkyn of Clochfaen.

a

Thomas of Crugnant.=Elen, daughter of Thomas ab Rhys ab Thomas Lloyd ab Meredydd ab Morgan.   The mother of Thomas
living A.D. 1583. | ab Rhys was Jane, d. of William Herbert ab Sir Richard Herbert, knight.

| a

Rhys of Crugnant=Elizabeth, d. and coheir of David ab Rhys ab Maurice ab Llewelyn ab Ieuan of Llangurig. Her mother was
| Jane, d. of Meredydd ab John ab Meredydd of Ceri, ab Rhys ab David Lloyd of Newtown Hall.

Ieuan of=Jane, d. of Rhys ab Thomas ab y Bedo ab Stephen of Cwm   Margaret, ux. Rhys ab Ieuan   Florence, ux. David
Crugnant. Deuddwr.¹   Her mother was Deilu, d. of Jenkyn ab Llewelyn   ab Rhys of Llangammarch in   ab Ieuan ab David
ab David ab Ieuan Ddu of Esgair Graig in Llangurig pariah.   Buallt.¹   of Llangurig.¹

¹ *Wynnstay MS.*

LLANGURIG AND CREUDDYN.

Harl. MSS. 2288, p. 68.   *Lewys Dwnn,* vol. i, p. 15-26.

Gwaethfoed ab Clodien ab Gwrydir Hir, Lord of Cardigan.∓Mortydd, d. and coheiress of Ynyr, King of Gwent. Party
Or, a lion rampant regard. *sable.* | per pale *azure* and *sable* three fleurs-de-lys *or.*

Cadifor, Lord of Cardigan∓Jane, d. of Elystan Glodrudd, Prince of Fferlis.

Iorwerth∓Agnes, d. of Robert ab Llywarch ab Trahaiarn, Lord of Cydewain. *Sable* three fleurs-de-lys *argent.*   Ifor.

Gruffydd∓Elen, d. of Meredydd ab Cadwgan Fantach ab Cadwgan ab Llewelyn ab Gruffydd
| ab Meredydd ab Edelfrych ab Peredur Peiswyn.

Rhys of Llanuwch Aeron∓

Llewelyn∓   Iorwerth of∓Gwladys; d. of Rhys ab Llewelyn Fychan, of Creuddyn, ab Llewelyn ab Gruffyd ab
             Creuddyn | Einion ab Collwynn ab Tangno, Lord of Effionydd. *Sable* a chev. inter three
                      | fleurs-de-lys *argent.*

Gruffydd of∓
Creuddyn

| a | b

| b

Rhys Lloyd of Creuddyn ⊤ Gwladys, d. of Ieuan ab Madog ab Gwenwys. *Sable*, three horse's
  coheiress. | heads erased *argent*.

Gwladys ux. Rhys Goch ab Ieuan ab Rhys ab Llewelyn ab Cadwgan Goch of Carrog.

Ienkyn of Llangurig ⊤ ....d. and heir of Rhys ab Llewelyn Goch.

Rhys of Llangurig ⊤

David of Llangurig ⊤

Ienkyn of Llangurig ⊤

Ienkyn of Llangurig, living 1543.

Margaret ux. Rhys ab Maurice ab Llewelyn, 2nd son of Ieuan ab Gruffydd of Clochfaen.

Golenbryd ux. David ux. Cemaes ab Llewelyn ab Ieuan Blainey ab Philip ab Ieuan Fychan ab Ieuan ab Rhys ab Llawdden, Lord of Uwch Aeron.

Florence ux. Llewelyn Fychan (living A.D. 1588) ab Llewelyn ab David ab Ieuan Ddu ab Ieuan Dwn ab Philip ab Ieuan ab Gruffydd ab Meredydd ab Madog Danwr.

| a

Rhys of Creuddyn ⊤
  coheiress.

Llewelyn of Creuddyn ⊤

Ieuan or Iorwerth of Creuddyn ⊤

Rhys Lloyd of Creuddyn ⊤

Llewelyn of ⊤ Elen, d. of Gruffyd ab Creuddyn | Llewelyn ab Rhys of Creuddyn, Esq., ab Llewelyn ab Rhys ab Iorwerth ab Rhys ab Gruffydd ab Einion ab Collwyn ab Tangno, Lord of Eifionydd

Margaret ux. Maurice ab Ienkyn Goch of Clochfaen. *Harl. MS.* 1973, page 4.

The pedigree of MALLT, wife of Jenkyn Lloyd of Clochfaen.

(*Harl. MS.* 1969, 2299.)

UCHDRYD ab Edwyn, Lord of Cyfeiliog. *Argent* a cross flory engrailed, *sable* inter ⊤ Agnes, d. of Llewelyn Eur Dorchog, Lord of
four Cornish choughs ppr. Together with the sons of Cadwgan ab Bleddyn, he | Ial. *Azure*, a lion statant gardant, his tail
defeated the Normans in Cerodigion and Dyfed in A.D. 1095. | between his legs and reflexed over his back *or*.

Philip of Cyfeiliog ⊤ Janet, d. of Rhys ab Howel ab Trahaiarn.

| a

a

Meredydd of Cyfeiliog. He was one of the witnesses to a charter of Gwenwynwyn, Prince of Upper Powys to the Abbey of Strata Marcella in A.D. 1199.

Gruffydd of Cyfeiliog, one of the twenty hostages given by Prince Gwenwynwyn to King John in A.D. 1204 (*Arch. Camb.*, July 1867, p. 119).

Llewelyn of Cyfeiliog

Madog=Elizabeth, d. of Owain ab Neuadd Wen in Llanerfyl.

Meredydd ab David of Llanerfyl. Quarterly *gules*, and *argent*, four lions passant gard. counterchanged

Cadwgan, ancestor of the family of Wenalt.

Howel

Eva ux. Ieuan ab Meilir of Rhiwsaeson in Llanbrynmair.

David Bwl=Tangwystl, d. of Llewelyn Gogof, Esq., second son of Ieuan Llwyd ab Llewelyn ab Tudor of Mathafarn, Esq. *Argent*, a lion passant *sable*, into three fleurs-de-lys *gules*.

Gruffydd=Jane, d. of Ieuan ab Madog ab Llewelyn ab Gruffyd.

David Gethin=Angharad, d. of Ieuan Llwyd ab Dio ab Einion ab Adda ab Ieuan ab y Moelglas of Cawg in Llanbrynmair.

Llewelyn=Mabli, d. of Ieuan Fychan ab Ieuan ab Cadwgan ab Llewelyn ab Gruffydd ab Meredydd ab Philip ab Uchdryd.

Howel=Mabli, d. of Ieuan Fychan.

Gwilyn of Llanbrynmair=Gwen, d. of Ieuan ab David ab Llewelyn of Wenalt ab Cadwgan ab Llewelyn ab Gruffydd of Cyfeiliog.

Ieuan.   Gwilyn.

Rhys ab Gwilym of Llanbrynmair=

Llewelyn of Llanbrynmair=Catherine, d. and coheiress of Morgan ab David of Llanbrynmair ab Howel ab Owain ab Gruffydd ab Ieuan ab Meilir of Rhiwsaeson.

Ieuan=Goch.

Ieuan=Llwyd of Llanbrynmair.

Owain   Elen

Owain. Meredydd. Ieuan. Mary. Gwenllian. Rhydderch. Ieuan. Richard.

Ieuan of Llanbrynmair
a

David of Llanbrynmair
b

Morgan of Llanbrynmair
a   b

c

d

a		b		c		d
Mallt ux. Ienkyn Lloyd of Cochfaen.		Richard =Sarah, d. Morgan of John of Caelan Jones of in Llan- Llan- brynmair. brynmair.		Owain of Llan- =Mallt, d. of Thomas ab Ieuan ab David Goch of Carno ab Ieuan brynmair. ab David Lloyd ab Meredydd ab Llewelyn Fychan, descended from Gwen, one of the twenty hostages given by Gwenwynwyn to King John in A.D. 1209,[1] and son of Goronwy ab Einion ab Seisyllt, Lord of Mathafarn.		Elen.

Bridget, sole heiress ux. Morgan Lloyd, second son of Ienkyn Lloyd of Clochfaen, and Mallt his wife,
d. of Morgan ab David of Llanbrynmair.

[1] *Archæologia Camb.*, July 1867, p. 119.

LLANLLODDIAN. (*Harl. MSS.* 1973. *Lewys Dunn*, vol. i, xxvii.)

IEUAN ab John ab David Fychan ab David Lloyd ab Gwellin ab Gwilym ab Einion ab Ieuan ab Einion ab Llewelyn ab Meilior Grûg=
ab Gruffydd ab Iorwerth ab Owain ab Roderic ab Howel ab Gwaeddan, Lord of Tregynon and Westbury, ab Brochwel
ab Aeddan, Lord of Cegidfa, Broniarth, and Deuddwr. *Sable*, three horse's heads erased *argent*.

John =Dorothy, d. of Rhys ab Hugh, younger son of Owain ab Ieuan Blaney of Aberbechan.
Sable, three horse's heads erased *argent*.

Thomas of Belan Deg, in the parish of Manafon=Margaret, d. of Richard Lloyd.

John Thomas of Llanlloddian=......d. and heiress of John Owen of Llanlloddian.

Evan Jones of Llanlloddian and *jure uxoris* of Llan- =......d. and heiress of ...... Cupper of Llandysilio		Mary ux. Rhys	
dyssilio Hall, High Sheriff for Montgomeryshire, 1712. Hall, in the Lordship of Iâl or Yale.		Lloyd of Clochfaen.	

CREUDDYN. (*Harl. MSS.* 1969-1973, p. 96).

UCHDRYD ab Edwyn ab Goronwy. *Argent*, a cross flory engrailed,=Agnes, d. of Llewelyn Eur Dorchog,
sable inter four Cornish choughs ppr. Lord of Iâl

Iorwerth ∓ Elen, d. of Hêdd Moelwynog, Lord of Uwch Aled. *Sable, a hart argent, attired or.*

Llowdden, Lord of Uwch Aeron. *Gules, a griffon segreant or.* ∓

Rhys ∓ Eva, d. of Gruffydd ab Llewelyn ab Gruffydd ab Rhys ab Iorwerth.

Rhys Fongam.

Ieuan ∓ Gwenllian, d. of Sir Elidur Ddu, Knight of the Holy Sepulchre.

Llowdden ∓ ......d. of Llewelyn ab Gruffydd ab Ieuan Llwyd of Mathafarn.

Jane, ux. Llewelyn Goch ab Llewelyn Caplan, ancestor of the Powells of Nanteos.

Rhys Gethin ∓ of Creuddyn.

Ieuan Fychan, ancestor of John Lloyd of Cefn Melgoed, Esq., and David ab Llewelyn ab Ieuan Blaeney of Cemaes.

Ieuan ∓

Meredydd of Creuddyn ∓

Gruffydd ∓

Margaret, coheiress, ux. Rhys Dda of Pont y Rhydgaled.

Mabli, coheiress.

Gruffydd of Creuddyn ∓

Dio ∓

Gutto of Creuddyn ∓

Ieuan ∓ Janet, d. of Ieuan Goch ab Meredydd ab Rhys ab Gruffydd ab David of Gwanwis.

Ieuan of Creuddyn ∓

Morgan ∓ Annie, d. of Ienkyn Goch of Clochfaen.

David of ∓ Creuddyn.

David ∓ Jane, d. of Rhys Benllwyd ab Rhys ab Howel ab David ab Meredydd ab David Fychan ab David Fongan of Cynwyl Gaio. *Sable, a wolf passant argent, its head and nails gules.*

Ieuan of Creuddyn = Tangwystl, d. of Ieuan Wynn of Dolbachog in Arwystli, Esq., and Gwenllian, his wife, d. of Thomas ab Rhys Ddu of Pont y Rhydgaled.

Morgan = Margaret, ux. 1st Lewys ab David ab Ieuan Gwynn ab Ienkyn of Cefn yr Hafodau; 2nd. Ienkyn ab Llewelyn ab David of Esgair Graig.

John Wynn = Gollenbryd, d. of Richard ab of Creuddyn, 1588. Maurice Vaughan of Trawscoed co. Cardigan.[1]

Catherine, ux. David Lloyd ab Ienkyn ab Maurice of Clochfaen.

Margaret, ux. Llewelyn ab Ieuan ab Rhys Ddu ab Gruffydd ab Einion ab Iorwerth ab Mérddydd ab Madog Danwr.

[1] *Lewys Dwnn*, vol. i, art. Trawscoed, p. 50.

HUGHES OF PENNANT Y BELAN

In the parish of Rhiwfabon in Maelor Gymraeg.

Cae Cyriog MSS.

BLEDDYN, the eldest son of Tudor ab Rhys Sais,[1] Lord of Chirk, Nanheudwy, and Maelor Saesneg (refer to the account of Plâs Madog), married Agnes, daughter of Llewelyn ab Idnerth, Lord of Buallt, son of Meredydd Hên ab Howel ab Seisyllt, Lord of Buallt, son of Cadwgan ab Elystan Glodrudd, Prince of Fferlis, by whom he had issue Owain, Lord of Chirk, Nanheudwy, and Maelor Saesneg, who married Eva, relict of Iorwerth ab Owain Brogyntyn, Lord of Edeyrnion, and daughter and heiress of Madog Goch, Lord of Mawddwy and Caer Einion, an illegitimate son of Gwenwynwyn, Prince of Upper Powys, by whom he had issue five sons: 1. Iorwerth Hên, his successor; 2. Owain Fychan, ancestor of the Dymokes of Penley Hall in Maelor Saesneg; 3. Thomas, ancestor of the Pennants

---

[1] Rhys Sais died A.D. 1070.

C C

of Downing and Penrhyn Castle; 4. Cynwrig Sais; and, 5. Rhirid, and a daughter named Elen.

Iorwerth Hên, the eldest son of Owain, was Lord of Chirk, Nanheudwy, and Maelor Saesneg, and married Angharad, eldest daughter and coheiress of Gruffydd,[1] third son of Meilir Eyton, Lord of Eyton Erlisham and Borasham (*ermine*, a lion rampant *azure*), by whom he had issue an elder son,

Iorwerth Fychan, Lord of Chirk, Nanheudwy and Maelor Saesneg. He married Catherine, relict of Meredydd of Rhiwfabon, second son of Madog ab Gruffydd Maelor, Prince of Powys Fadog, and daughter of Gruffydd ab Llewelyn ab Iorwerth, Prince of North Wales, who bore quarterly *gules* and *or*, four lions rampant countercharged, by whom he had a son and heir,

Iorwerth Foel (Llwyth Nanheudwy), Lord of Chirk, Nanheudwy and Maelor Saesneg. Roger Mortimer, Lord Paramount of Chirkland or the Swydd y Waun, granted lands in the townships of Gwern Osbern and Pen-y-Clawdd to Iorwerth Foel on payment of twenty pounds sterling per annum. The witnesses to the grant were, Ieuaf ab Adda,[2] Llewelyn his son,[2] Owain,

---

[1] Gruffydd married Angharad, daughter and heiress of Llewelyn ab Meurig ab Caradog ab Iestyn ab Gurgant, Prince of Glamorgan, who bore *gules*, three chevronels *argent*.

[2] Ieuaf ab Adda ab Awr of Trefor. He married Myfanwy, daughter of Madog ab Cynwrig Fychan ab Cynwrig ab Hoedliw of Christionydd Cynwrig, fifth son of Cynwrig ab Rhiwallón, by whom he had issue five sons: 1. David. 2. Howel, ancestor of the Trefors of Trefor Hall, Joneses of Frondeg, Lloyds of Trefor, and Llangollen, Joneses of Garthgynan in Llanfair Dyffryn Clwyd, and Roberts of Eglwyseg, Lloyds of Pentre Cuhelyn, and Lloyds of Berth and Rhagad. 3. Llewelyn, who witnessed the charter. He married Susanna, daughter and coheiress of Llewelyn ab Madog ab Einion ab Rhirid ab Iorwerth of Iâl, son of Meredydd ab Uchdryd ab Edwyn, Prince of Tegeingl, by whom he had issue four sons: 1. Madog, for whose descendants see page 11; 2. Ieuan or Iohn Trefor 1: S.T.B. Bishop of St. Asaph, who built Llangollen Bridge, and died in A.D. 1352; 3. Adda; and 4. David, ancestor of the Lloyds of Plâs Ieuaf in Trefor. Ieuaf ab Adda, and his wife, Myfanwy, are both buried in the church of Valle Crucis, where their

son of Gruffydd Foel, and the Lord Hwfa, his brother; Llewelyn ab Cynwrig ab Osbern; and Madog, son of Cynwrig Foel; and attached to the deed was the seal of Roger Mortimer, with his coat of arms, and around it the inscription "Sigillum Mortuo Mare." Roger Mortimer got possession of the lordship of Chirk by grant from Edward I, October 7th, A.D. 1282, and was imprisoned in the Tower of London in A.D. 1332, where he died in A.D. 1336.

Iorwerth Foel married Gwladys, daughter and co-heiress of Iorwerth ab Gruffydd ab Heilin of Frongoch, now called Celynog in Mochnant, Esq., ab Meurig ab Ieuan ab Adda Goch of Mochnant ab Cynwrig ab Pasgen, Lord of Cegidfa and Deuddwr. Iorwerth ab Gruffydd of Frongoch, bore (1) *sable*, three horses' heads erased *argent*; and (2) *argent*, a chev. inter three rooks with *ermine* in their beaks *sable*; and married Alice, daughter of Hwfa ab Iorwerth ab Gruffydd ab Ieuaf ab Niniof ab Cynwrig ab Rhiwallon. *Gules* two lions passant *argent*, for Iorwerth ab Gruffydd. By his wife Gwladys, Iorwerth Foel had issue, five sons.

1. Madog Lloyd of Bryncunallt, who bore the arms of Tudor Trefor in a bordure *gules*. He married Margaret, daughter of Llewelyn ab Ieuaf ab Adda ab Awr of Trefor, by whom he was ancestor of John Wynn[1] ab John of Bryncunallt, who married Catherine, daughter of Richard ab Rhydderch ab David of Myvyrion, descended from Iarddur, Lord of Llechwedd Isaf and Creuddyn, by whom he had two daughters coheirs, the

tombs are still to be seen; their fourth son, Ieuaf Llwyd, died without issue; their fifth son, Adda Goch of Trefor, bore the arms of Tudor Trefor in a border gobonated *argent*, and *gules* pellatty, and married Angharad, daughter of David ab Adda ab Meurig ab Ieuan ab Adda Goch ab Cynwrig of Mochnant, ab Gwyn ab Gruffydd, Lord of Cegidfa. Llewelyn ab Cynwrig ab Osbern Fitz Gerald, was of Corsygedol in Merionydd.

[1] John Wynn of Bryncunallt, was the son of John ab Thomas ab John Lloyd ab Madog ab Gruffydd ab Rhys ab Gruffydd ab Madog Lloyd of Bryncunallt, eldest son of Iorwerth Foel.

eldest of whom married ...... Wynn of Tower; and the second, who married Richard Lloyd of Whittington, died without issue.   John Wynn ab John of Bryncunaullt sold that estate to Sir Edward Trevor, Knight, High Sheriff for Denbighshire, in A.D. 1622.   The Wynns of Eyarth and the Lloyds of Seaton Knolls descend also from Madog Lloyd.

2. Gruffydd of Maelor Saesneg, ancestor of the Lloyds of Tal y Wern and the Lloyds of the Bryn in the parish of Hanmer.

3. Morgan of Maelor Saesneg, ancestor of the Yonges of Bryn Iorcyn, now represented by the Conways of Bodrhyddan and Bryn Iorcyn, and the Yonges of Croxton.

4. Ednyfed Gam, of whom presently ; and,

5. Ieuan of Llanfechain.

Ednyfed Gam, the fourth son of Iorwerth Foel, had Pengwern, in the parish of Llangollen, in the comot of Nanheudwy, for his share of the territories of his ancestors; he married Gwladys, daughter and coheiress of Llewelyn ab Madog ab Einion ab Rhirid of Iâl, son of Iorwerth ab Meredydd ab Uchdryd ab Edwyn ab Goronwy, Prince of Tegeingl, *argent* a cross flory inter four Cornish choughs ppr. ; by whom he had issue six sons, and a daughter Margaret, the wife of Gwilym ab Madog Lloyd.

1. Iorwerth Ddu, the eldest son of Ednyfed Gam, of whose line we shall treat presently.

2. David, who married, first, Gwenllian, daughter of Adda Goch[1] ab Ieuaf ab Adda ab Awr of Trefor in Nanheudwy, by whom he had a son named Edward or Iorwerth, of whom presently ; and, secondly, David married ....., daughter of Gruffydd Fychan ab Gruffydd of Rhuddallt, and sister of Owain Glyndwr, by whom he had a daughter Margaret, who married, first, Robert Lloyd ab Gruffydd ab Goronwy ; and, secondly, Howel ab Llewelyn of Llwn On, in the parish of Wrexham,

---

[1] Adda Goch of Trefor, bore the arms of Tudor Trefor, in a border gobonated *argent*, and *gules* pellaty, counterchanged.

ancestor of the Jones-Parrys of Madryn and Llwyn On. Edward, the son of David ab Ednyfed Gam, married Angharad, daughter of Robert Puleston of Emerall, and Lowry his wife, sister of Owain Glyndwr, by whom he had issue three sons: 1. Robert Trefor, Steward of Denbighshire, Sheriff of Flintshire, Justice and Chamberlain of North Wales, who died unmarried in A.D. 1492, leaving an illegitimate son, Sir William Trefor, Chaplain to John ab Richard, Abbot of Valle Crucis, predecessor of David ab John ab Iorwerth ab Ieuan Baladr[1]; 2. John Trefor Hên; and 3. Richard Trefor, who married Agnes, daughter of Meredydd Lloyd, by whom he had a son Edward Trefor, Constable of Oswestry Castle, who married Jane, daughter and heir of Richard Westbury.

John Trefor Hên, who died A.D. 1493, married Agnes, daughter and coheir of Sir Piers Cambray or Cambres of Trallwng, knight, by whom he had four sons: 1. Robert Trefor of Plâs Têg, who died in the lifetime of his father in A.D. 1487, and was buried in Valle Crucis Abbey. He married Catherine, daughter and heiress of Llewelyn ab Ithel of Plâs Têg in Yr Hôb, by whom he had a son John Trefor, ancestor of the Trefors of Plâs Têg. 2. Edward Trefor, Constable of Whittington Castle, who died in A.D. 1537. He married Anne, daughter of Geoffrey Cyffyn Hên, Constable of Oswestry Castle, by whom he had two sons, John Trefor Goch of Wignant, who was ancestor of the Trefors of Bryncunallt; and Thomas Trefor, ancestor of the Trefors of Treflech, near Oswestry. 3. Roger Trefor of Pentre Cynwrig, who married Gwenllian, daughter of Rhys Lloyd of Gydros, son of Gwilym ab Einion, by whom he had Roger Trefor of Pentre Cynwrig, who, by Angharad his wife, daughter of David Lloyd ab John ab Edward of Plâs Is y Clawdd, had a son, John Trefor of Pentre Cynwrig, ancestor of the Trevors of Bodynfol and Trawscoed. 4. Richard,

---

[1] *Harl. MS.* 4181.

who married Mallt, daughter and heiress of Ienkyn[1] ab David ab Gruffydd of Trefalûn, by whom he had a son, John Trefor of Trefalûn, ancestor of the Trefors of that place.

3. Ieuan ab Ednyfed Gam, ancestor of the Joneses of Weston Rhyn, in St. Martin's.

4. Meredydd ab Ednyfed Gam, fourth in descent from whom was William ab Reignallt ab David of Carreg Hwfa, whose daughter and heir, Margaret, married Robert Lloyd of Bryngwyn.

5. Gruffyd ab Ednyfed Gam, who was ancestor of the Pughs of Ty Cerrig in Llanymyneich.

6. Llewelyn of Halchdyn in Maelor Saesneg, who the *Harl. MS.*, 4181, states to be the eldest son of Ednyfed Gam. He married Anne, daughter of Sir Roger Puleston of Emerall, knight, by whom he had a son, Madog of Halchdyn, ancestor of the Lloyds of Halchdyn.

Iorwerth Ddû of Pengwern, the eldest son of Ednyfed Gam, according to the *Cae Cyriog* and other manuscripts, married Angharad, daughter of Adda Goch ab Ieuaf ab Adda ab Awr of Trefor, by whom he had issue four sons: 1. Adda; 2. Goronwy; 3. Tudor; 4. Ieuan, who was a bishop; and three daughters: 1. Margaret, who married Madog ab Ieuan ab Madog, Lord of Eyton, in Maelor Gymraeg; 2. Myfanwy, who married Goronwy ab Tudor ab Goronwy of Penllyn, ab Gruffyd ab Madog ab Rhirid Flaidd; and, 3. Eva, a maiden lady, who lived with her sister Margaret at Eyton, and built Overton Bridge.

Adda of Pengwern, the eldest son of Iorwerth Ddû, married Isabel, sister of Owain Glyndwr, and daughter of Gruffydd Fychan ab Gruffyd of Rhuddallt, fifth

---

[1] Ienkyn ab David ab Gruffydd ab David ab Llewelyn ab David ab Goronwy ab Iorwerth ab Howel ab Moreiddig ab Sanddef Hardd, Lord of Morton in Gresford. *Vert*, semy of broom slips, a lion rampant *or*. Ienkyu married Angharad, d. and heiress of Ieuan ab Einion ab Iolyn ab Iorwerth ab Llewelyn ab Gruffydd ab Cadwgan ab Meilir Eyton, Lord of Eyton. *Ermine*, a lion rampant *azure*.

Baron of Glyndyfrdwy, by whom he had issue three sons: Ieuan, Rhys, and Meredydd.

Ieuan of Pengwern, the eldest son, married Angharad, daughter and heiress of Ednyfed ab Tudor ab Gruffyd, Lord of Tre Castell in Môn, son of Tudor Hên ab Goronwy ab Ednyfed Fychan, Lord of Brynffanigl, by whom he had three sons: (1) Ieuan Fychan, (2) ......, and (3) Iorwerth or Edward, of whom presently. One of his daughters, named Isabel, married Gruffydd ab Ieuan ab Einion, son of Gruffydd ab Llewelyn of Corsygedol.

Ieuan Fychan of Pengwern and Tre Castell, married Angharad, daughter and heiress of Howel ab Tudor of Mostyn in Tegeingl, son of Ithel Fychan of Mostyn and Ewlo Castle, who bore *azure*, a lion passant *argent*, and did homage for his estates in A.D. 1300. Ithel Fychan was the son of Ithel Llwyd ab Ithel Gam of Mostyn, ab Meredydd ab Uchdryd ab Edwyn ab Gronwy, Prince of Tegeingl, by whom he had a son, Howel of Mostyn Pengwern and Tre Castell, the ancestor of the Lord Mostyn of Mostyn, Sir Pyers Mostyn of Talacre, Bart.; Mostyn, Lord Vaux of Harrowden; and the Mostyns of Llewesog and Segroed.

Iorwerth or Edward, the third son of Ieuan ab Adda of Pengwern and Tre Castell, had Plâs Newydd, in the Lordship of Chirk, for his share of the property. He received the name of Yn Iawn, or the Iust, and married Catherine, daughter and sole heir of Llewelyn ab Madog ab Llewelyn of Trefor, third son of Ieuaf ab Adda ab Awr of Trefor,[1] and relict of David Trefor ab

---

[1] Llewelyn, the third son of Ieuaf ab Adda ab Awr, married Susannah, daughter and coheiress of Llewelyn ab Madog ab Einion ab Rhirid of Iâl, son of Iorwerth ab Meredydd ab Uchdryd ab Edwyn ab Goronwy, Prince of Tegeingl, by whom he had issue, besides a daughter, Margaret, wife of Madog Lloyd of Bryncunallt, four sons: (1) Madog, who married Catherine, daughter of Hwfa ab Ieuaf ab Hwfa ab Madog yr Athro of Plâs Madog in Bodylltyn, by whom he was father of Llewelyn, who married Lucy, daughter of Sir David Whitmore of Cilcen, ab David ab Ithel Fychan ab Cynwrig of Ysgeifiog and Llaneurgain; (2) Ieuan or Iohn Trefor,

Iorwerth ab Ieuaf ab Adda Goch of Trefor, by whom
he had issue two sons, John ab Edward, and Ednyfed
ab Edward, and a daughter, Angharad, wife of Ienkyn
Deccaf.

Iohn Edwards Hên of Plâs Newydd, the eldest son,
was Receiver of Chirkland from 2 July, 13 Henry
VIII, to 22 Henry VIII, and died in A.D. 1498. He
married Gwenllian, daughter of Elis Eyton of Watstay
in Rhiwfabon, by whom (who died in A.D. 1520) he
had issue three sons: 1. William Edwards of Plas
Newydd,[1] Constable of Chirk Castle, Keeper of
Black Park, and one of the body-guard to King Henry
VIII, who granted him permission to have the vizor of
the helmet over his coat of arms up, so that the face
could be seen, and also gave him permission to bear
the motto "A fynno Duw derfydd." He died in A.D.
1532, having married Catherine, daughter and sole
heiress of John Hookes of Aberconwy, Esq. (*argent*,
achev. inter three owls *azure*), by whom (who died in
A.D. 1532); he was ancestor of the Edwardses of Plâs
Newydd and Cefn y Wern. 2. John Wynn of Llanddyn
in Nanheudwy, who, by Elizabeth his wife, daughter of
Hugh Lewys of Anglesey, had issue two daughters,
coheiresses: (1) Catherine, who married John Lloyd ab
Madog of Bryncunallt; and (2) Margaret, the wife of
Thomas Lacon ab John ab Thomas ab Sir Richard
Lacon of Brogyntyn, knight. 3. David Lloyd of Plâs
Is y Clawdd, of whom presently. Besides these three
sons, John Edwards Hên had three daughters: (1) Cathe-
rine, who married, first, Tudor Lloyd of Bodidris in
Iâl, and, secondly, Robert Powel of Whittington Park,
ab Howel ab Gruffydd of Abertanat, ab Ieuan Fychan
ab Ieuan Gethin ab Madog Cyffyn; (2) Jane, the wife

Bishop of St. Asaph, who built Llangollen Bridge, and died
A.D. 1357; (3) Adda; and (4) David, ancestor of the Lloyds of
Plâs Ieuaf in Trefor.

[1] His eldest son, John Edwards of Plâs Newydd, was High Sheriff
for Flintshire in A.D. 1546, and for Denbighshire in A.D. 1547, and
married Jane, daughter of Sir George Calverley of the Lee in
Cheshire, knight.

of Llewelyn ab Ieuan ab Howel ab Ieuan Fychan of
Moeliwrch, fourth son of Ieuan Gethin ab Madog
Cyffyn of Lloran ; and (3) Márgaret, Arglwyddes y
Fantell a Fodrwy (Lady of the Mantle and Ring), who
married, first, Richard Lloyd of Llwyn y Maen, and,
secondly, Thomas Salter.

David Lloyd of Plas Is y Clawdd, in the parish of
Chirk, the third son of John Edwards Hên of Plâs
Newydd, Esq., married Gwenllian, daughter (by Margaret his wife, daughter of Harri Goch Salusbury of
Llewesog, Esq.) of Robert ab Gruffydd ab Rhys of
Maesmor in Llangwm in Dinmael, by whom he had
issue two sons, Robert and Roger, and five daughters :
(1) Angharad, wife of Roger Trefor of Pentre Cynwrig ;
(2) Maude, wife of John Wynn ab Meredydd ab Howel
ab Gruffydd Fychan ; (3) Gwenllian, wife of Thomas ab
Richard of Trewern ; (4) Gwenhwyfar ux. Thomas
Hanmer of Pentrepant,[1] near Oswestry ; and (5) Jane,
ux. Howel ab Adda.

Robert Lloyd of Plâs Is y Clawdd, the eldest son of
David Lloyd, married Catherine, daughter of Edward
Pryse of Eglwyseg, Esq., ab Rhys ab David ab Gwilym
ab Iorwerth ab Ieuaf ab Allo ab Rhiwallon Fychan of
Trefnant in Caer Einion, by whom he had issue two
sons : (1) Edward Lloyd of Plas Is y Clawdd, who
married Grace, daughter of Owain ab John Wynn ab
Ieuan ab Rhys of Bryn Cynwrig, by whom he was
ancestor of the Lloyds of Plas Is y Clawdd ; and
(2) Ieuan Lloyd. ·

Ieuan Lloyd, the second son of Robert Lloyd of Plâs
Is y Clawdd, was of Glyn Ceiriog.   He married Gwen-

---

[1] Thomas Hanmer of Pentrepant, was the son (by Catherine, his
wife, daughter of John Hanmer of Lee, ab Ienkyn Hanmer) of
Richard ab David ab Howel Goch ab Meredydd ab Madog Heddwch
ab Meilir ab Tangwel ab Tudor ab Dolphyn ab Llewelyn Eur
Dorchog, Lord of Iâl. His eldest son, David Hanmer of Pentrepant, married Elizabeth, daughter of Roger Kynaston of Mortyn,
son of Humphrey Kynaston, by whom he had issue three sons :
Thomas, who died S.P.; John Hanmer, D.D., Bishop of St. Asaph,
who died S.P.; and Richard Hanmer of Pentrepant.

D D

hwyfar, daughter of David ab Meredydd, by whom he
had two sons, John Lloyd and Edward of Glyn.

Edward of Glyn, the second son of Ieuan Lloyd, was
the father of Hugh of Glyn, who had two sons : (1) Edward ab Hugh of Glyn ; and (2) John ab Hugh of
Rhiwfabon. Edward ab Hugh of Glyn had a son,
Hugh Edwards of Glynn, whose only daughter and
heiress, Jane, married Richard Wynn, of Aber Cynllaith,
descended from Idnerth Benfras ; both Richard
Wynn and Jane were living in 1697.

John ab Hugh of Rhiwfabon married Elizabeth,
daughter and heiress of John ab Ieuan ab Howel of
Pen y Nant y Belan, in the parish of Rhiwfabon, by
whom he had two sons, (1) Thomas Hughes and
(2) Gruffyd Hughes, who, by his will dated A.D. 1706,
left to the poor of Rhiwfabon lands adjoining Pentre
Isa farm, the annual rent of which, in 1828, was £21.

Thomas Hughes of Pennant y Pelan, Receiver of the
King's Rents in the greatest part of Maelor and other
places, A.D. 1697. He married Sarah, fourth daughter
and coheiress of Edward ab Rondle of Rhuddallt in the
parish of Rhiwfabon, son of John ab John ab Madog ab
Ieuan ab Madog ab Ieuaf ab Madog ab Cadwgan Ddû
ab Cadwgan Goch ab Y Gwion ab Hwfa ab Ithel
Felyn, the eldest son of Llewelyn Aurdorchog, Lord of
Iâl, and Prime Minister of Gruffydd ab Llewelyn ab
Seisyllt, King of Wales. By this lady, Thomas Hughes
had issue three daughters, coheirs :—

1. Mary, who married William Platt of Rhydonen,
in the parish of Llanynys in Dyffryn Clwyd, son and
heir of Richard Platt of Pantglas, near Ruthin, and
Mary, his wife, daughter and sole heiress of John
Edwards of Rhydonen. By his wife, Mary, William
Platt had issue an only daughter and heiress, Sarah,
who married at Llanynys on the 20th December, 1723,
Rhys Lloyd of Clochfaen, in the parish of Llangurig,
High Sheriff for the county of Montgomery in A.D. 1743.
Mrs. Sarah Lloyd died at the age of 85, and was buried
at Llangurig, January 10th, A.D. 1781. Her only son,

Ienkyn Lloyd of Clochfaen, Esq., High Sheriff for Montgomeryshire in 1755, married at Erbistog, April 30th, A.D. 1743, Elizabeth, eldest daughter and heiress of Edward Lloyd of Plâs Madog, in the parish of Rhiwfabon, Esq. Elizabeth Lloyd, the heiress of Plâs Madog, was born April 10th, and baptised at Rhiwfabon, May 10th, A.D. 1718, and died at Christionydd, aged 40, and was buried at Rhiwfabon, December 12th, A.D. 1758. By her said husband, she had one only daughter, Sarah, the heiress of Clochfaen, Plâs Madog, and Rhydonen, who was born February 19th, and baptised March 2nd, A.D. 1746. The account of her marriage and her descendants have been given in the former part of this History.

2. Phœbe, the second daughter and coheir, married David Lloyd of Llangollen, second son of Edward Lloyd of Llangollen, who died in the lifetime of his father, and was the son and heir of John Lloyd of Trefor, who died in A.D. 1686, son of Edward Lloyd ab Edward Lloyd ab John ab Madog ab Edward of Trefor, second son of Howel ab Ieuaf ab Adda ab Awr of Trefor.

3. Rebecca, the third daughter and coheiress of Thomas Hughes, married John Griffith, eldest son and heir of John Griffith of Cae Cyriog, Esq., the author of the folio volume of *Heraldry and Genealogy*, from which this account is taken. John Griffith, junr., of Cae Cyriog, in right of his wife, Rebecca, became possessed of Pennant y Belan, and took up his residence there. He was the ancestor of the present Thomas Taylor Griffiths of Wrexham, Cae Cyriog, and Pennant y Belan, Esq., F.R.C.S., of whose descent an account will be given in a future page.

Thomas Hughes of Pennant y Belan, by his will dated A.D. 1715, left £15 to the poor of the parish of Rhiwfabon.

RHUDDALLT, IN THE PARISH OF RHIWFABON.

Cae Cyriog MS.

LLEWELYN Eurdorchog, Lord of Iâl and Ystrad Alun, in the principality of Powys Fadog, the Prime Minister of Gruffydd ab Llewelyn ab Seisyllt, King of Wales, was lineally descended from Sanddef Bryd Angel, the son of Llywarch Hên, Prince of the Strath Clyde Britons in the sixth century.[1] He bore *azure*, a lion passant gardant, his tail between his legs and reflected over his back *or*; and married Eva, sister of Bleddyn ab Cynfyn, Prince of Powys, by whom he had issue six sons who were legitimate: (1) Ithel Felyn, of whom presently; (2) Iorwerth; (3) Idris, who was the ancestor of the Owens of Scrwgan and the Hanmers of Pentrepant in the Lordship of Oswestry, and the Lloyds of Llangollen Fechan, and the Owens of Tref Geiriog in Nanheudwy; (4) Dolphyn;[2] and (5) Ednowain,

---

[1] Llewelyn Eurdorchog was the son of Coel ab Gweryd ab Cynddelw Gam ab Elgud ab Gwrisnadd ab Dwywg Llythyraur ab Tegawg ab Dyforfrath ab Madog Madogion ab Sanddef Bryd Angel ab Llywarch Hên. *Lewys Dwnn*, ii, p. 242.

[2] Dolphyn or Dolphwyn had a son, Llewelyn, whose only daughter and heiress, Eleanor, married Eunydd, Lord of Dyffryn Clwd and Trefalun. *Harl. MS.* 1972.

the ancestor of Ednowain ab Peradwen or Bradwen,
Lord of Dolgellan, who bore *gules*, three snakes
ennowed in triangle *argent*. And Llwyelyn Fychan,
who was the ancestor of Trahaiarn ab Iorwerth, Lord
of Garthmul, who bore *argent*, three lions passant in
pale *gules*, armed and langued *azure*, the ancestor of
Madog y Twppa of Plâs y Twppa in Bettws Cydewain,
and of the Lloyds of Berthlloyd in the parish of
Llanidloes. Llewelyn Eurdorchog had two other sons,
Ithel Goch and Iorwerth Fychan, who were illegitimate.

Ithel Felyn, the eldest son of Llewelyn Eurdorchog,
was Lord of Iâl and Ystrad Alûn. His possessions
were the townships of Llys y Cil, Allt y Gymbyd,
Bodanwydog and Coedrwg in Iâl; the townships of
Llwyn Egryn and Gwernaffyllt, and Y Cil Rhydin, in
the township of Hendre Biffa in Ystrad Alun; the
townships of Caerfallwch and Hendre Fygillt; Pentre-
hyfaid, and Castell Meirchion, in Tegeingl; Nantclwyd
and Garth y Neuadd in Dyffryn Clwyd; Traian in the
Lordship of Whittington; Arnan Mab in the Lordship
of Oswestry; a great part of Glyndwfrdwy, and some
lands in Cynllaith and Maelor Gymraeg. He bore
sable, on a chev. inter three goat's heads erased *or*,
three trefoils of the field; and married Lucy, daughter
and heiress of Howel ab Brochwel ab Bledrws, who
bore *sable*, three roses *argent*,[1] by whom he had issue
three sons, Hwfa, Llewelyn, and Ystwg.

Hwfa, the eldest son of Ithel Felyn, Lord of Iâl and
Ystrad Alun, married Elen or Alswn, daughter of
Gruffydd ab Cynan, king of Gwynedd, by whom he had
issue six sons: 1. Y Gwion, of whom presently. 2. Caswallon of Llys y Cil, whose son Iorwerth of Llys y Cil,
was one of the witnesses to a Charter of Prince Madog
ab Gruffydd Maelor, confirming a grant of lands to the
monastery of Valle Crucis in A.D. 1202, and was father
of Cynwrig of Llys y Cil and Y Fanechtyd in Dyffryn
Clwyd, who married Janet, daughter of Henry de Laci,
Earl of Lincoln and Lord of Denbigh, by Joanna his

[1] *Harl. MS.* 1972.

wife, daughter of William Martin, Baron of Cemeis in South Wales.[1] By this lady, Cynwrig had issue a son named Goronwy of Y Fanechtyd, who had issue one daughter Annesta, wife of Ieuaf ab Hwfa ab Madog yr Athro of Plâs Madog in Bodylltyn, and two sons: (1) Madog, ancestor of Tudor ab Ieuan ab Tudor of Iâl, and of John Wynn of Y Fanechtyd, Esq., who was living in A.D. 1598; and (2) Goronwy Gethin ab Goronwy, who was ancestor of Richard Davies, Bishop of St. David's A.D. 1567; 3. Ionas ab Hwfa ab Ithel Felyn; 4. Goronwy ab Hwfa; 5. Howel Foel ab Hwfa, who had Castell Meirchion, and was father of Einion of Maes y Groes, father of Madog, father of Dai, father of Ieuan of Maes y Groes, whose son, Gruffydd of Maes y Groes, sold Castell Meirchion to Tudor Mûl Hên of Ruthin, who had married his sister Margaret;[2] and, 6. Ieuaf ab Hwfa, who was ancestor of several families in Cymmo and Bryn Eglwys and of David Powel, D.D., Vicar of Rhiwfabon, the Historian.

Y Gwion, the eldest son of Hwfa ab Ithel Felyn, married the daughter (and heiress)[3] of Meredydd ab Cadwgan of Nannau, by whom he had issue Cadwgan Goch, who married Dyddgu, daughter of Ithel ab Howel ab Moreiddig ab Sanddef Hardd, Lord of Morton in Gresford, by whom he had issue two sons: 1. Cadwgan Ddû, of whom presently; and (2) Cadwgan Frych, who had Y Gaerddin, in the parish of Rhiwfabon, and was generally called Y Brych of Gaerddin.[4] His descendant, John Thomas of Gaerddin, who was living in A.D. 1680, was the son of Thomas ab John ab

---

[1] *Harl. MS.* 1972.   [2] *Golden Grove MS.*   [3] *Ibid.*

[4] Cadwgan Frych of Y Gaerddin had a son Madog of Y Gaerddin, whose line ended in an heiress named Gwerfyl, the daughter of Howel ab Ieuan ab Howel ab Cynwrig of Y Gaerddin, son of the before-named Madog ab Cadwgan. This lady married Meredydd ab Deicws ab Madog ab Adda Llwyd of Ystrad Alun. *Ermine* a lion rampant *azure*, by whom she had an only daughter and heiress, Angharad, who married John ab Ieuan Goch ab David Goch ab Y Bady of Rhuddallt, by whom she had a son named Roger, father of John Rogers who was living at Rhuddallt in A.D. 1620.

Edward ab Ieuan ab David Goch. This John Thomas sold his lands of Gaerddin to Eubule Lloyd of Eglwyseg, brother of Ellis Lloyd of Penylan, Esq., who built a new hall there.

Cadwgan Ddu, the eldest son of Cadwgan Goch, married Mallt, daughter of Sir Gruffydd Lloyd,[1] by whom he had issue three sons : (1) Iorwerth, ancestor of the Bithels of Llwyn Egryn, the Evanses of Llwyn Egryn, Griffiths of Hendre Biffa, and several others in Ystrad Alun and Iâl ; 2. Madog of Rhuddallt, of whom presently ; and (3) Einion, the father of Einion Fychan, the father of Bleddyn, who married Angharad, daughter of David ab David ab Ieuan ab Iorwerth ab Goronwy, by whom he had two sons : (1) Madog of Coed y Llai in Ystrad Alun, whose daughter and heiress, Mali, married Llewelyn ab David ab Goronwy of Gwysanau, Esq.; and (2) Gruffydd ab Bleddyn, who married Gwerfyl, daughter of Howel ab Tudor ab Goronwy ab Gruffydd ab Madog ab Rhirid Flaidd, Lord of Penllyn, by whom he had a son, Reinallt ab Gruffydd ab Bleddyn of the Tower, in the township of Broncoed in Ystrad Alun, A.D. 1465, and a daughter Alice, wife of David Lloyd of Iscoed ab Madog Lloyd ab Gruffydd of Maelor Saesneg, second son of Iorwerth Foel. Madog of Rhuddallt, the second son of Cadwgan Ddu, married Margaret, daughter of Iorwerth ab David Hên ab Goronwy Hên of Llai, in the parish of Gresford, son of Iorwerth ab Howel ab Moreiddig ab Sanddef Hardd, Lord of Mortyn in Gresford parish, by whom he had issue a son and heir, Ieuan ab Madog of Rhuddallt, who married Angharad, daughter (by Gwerfyl his wife, daughter and sole heir of Roger Fychan ab Sir Roger de Powys, knight, Lord of Whittington) of Philip Kynaston of Stoke, near Ellesmere, ab Gruffydd Kynaston of Stoke and Cae Howel, and of Gaer y Dinlle, Esq., by whom he had issue one son, Madog, of whom presently, and two daughters : (1) Angharad, wife of Deio ab Madog Lloyd of Bodylltyn, ab Gruffydd

[1] *Golden Grove MS.*

of Maelor Saesneg, second son of Iorwerth Foel, Lord of Chirk and Nanheudwy; and (2) Margaret, wife of Ieuan Bach ab Ieuan ab Einion Gethin of Christionydd ab Einion ab Ieuan ab Gruffydd ab Cynwrig Efell, Lord of Eglwyseg.

Madog of Rhuddallt, the son of Ieuan ab Madog, married Angharad, daughter of Madog, third son of Llewelyn ab Ednyfed Lloyd of Plas Madog, by whom he had a son and heir.

John ab Madog ab Ieuan of Rhuddallt, married, first, the daughter (by Agnes his wife, daughter of Tudor ab Howel ab Ieuan, third son of Ednyfed Gam of Pengwern) of Robert Tegin of Fron Deg, ab David Tegin ab Tegin ab Madog ab Iorwerth Goch ab Madog ab Ieuaf ab Niniaf ab Cynwrig ab Rhiwallon, by whom he had two daughters: (1) Margaret, wife of Gruffydd ab Ieuan ab John of Blaen Iâl; and (2) Catherine, wife of Roger ab John ab Ieuan Goch ab David Goch ab Y Badi of Rhuddallt, ab Madog ab Iorwerth Goch, fourth son of Madog ab Llewelyn, Lord of Eyton. John ab Madog ab Ieuan married, secondly, Margaret, daughter of Howel Puleston ab Edward Puleston of Plâs Isaf in Christionydd, second son of Madog Puleston of Bers, who bore *argent*, on a bend *sable*, three mullets of the field, by whom he had issue three sons: (1) John; (2) Gruffydd; and (3) Madog, who died without issue, and three daughters, Catherine, Gwenhwyfar, and Margaret.

John ab John ab Madog of Rhuddallt, married Catherine, daughter (by Anne, his wife, daughter of Edward Puleston of Trefechan in Christionydd, third son of Howel ab Edward Puleston of Plâs Isaf in Christionydd, second son of Madog Puleston of Bers) of John ab Howel of Cefn y Bedw in Christionydd Cymwrig ab Edward ab Y Bady Llwyd ab Iorwerth ab Ieuan ab Einion Gethin of Christionydd in the manor of Esclusham, and in the parish of Rhiwfabon, son of Einion ab Ieuan ab Gruffydd ab Cynwrig Efell, Lord of Eglwysegl, who bore *gules*, on a bend *argent*, a lion passant *sable*. John ab John ab Madog died A.D. 1599, having had issue by his wife Catherine two sons: (1) Rondle ab John; and (2) John ab John.

Rondle ab John of Rhuddallt married Margaret, relict of John Bynner, and second daughter (by Jane his wife, daughter of John Edwards of Plâs Newydd in the parish of Chirk, High Sheriff for Denbighshire in A.D. 1547) of John Ellis of Alrhey, third son, but eventual heir, of Elis ab Richard of Alrhey, Standard Bearer to Owain Glyndwr in A.D. 1404. *Ermine* a lion statant gardant *gules*, for Ednyfed, Lord of Broughton, second son of Cynwrig ab Rhiwallon. Rondle ab John died in A.D. 1599, in the same year as his father, leaving issue a son and heir,

Edward ab Rondle of Rhuddallt. He married Anne; daughter (by Catherine his wife, sister of John Roger Broughton of Dinynlle Isaf, in the parish of Rhiwfabon, and daughter of Roger Broughton of that place) of John ab John of Dinynlle Isaf, a native of Chirk parish, by whom he had issue four daughters, coheirs.

1. Catherine. She purchased her other sisters' portions of their father's estate, and married, first, David ab Edward of Trefor, by whom she had two children, Hannah, who died young, and one son, Richard Davies of Rhuddallt and Trefor, living 1697, who married Anne, daughter of John Barnes of Warrington in Lancashire, by whom he had issue Edward Davies and John Davies.

2. Mary, who married Edward Williams of Morton, in the parish of Gresford.

3. Elizabeth, the wife of David Jones of Llansilin, son of John ab David of Glyn.

4. Sarah Edwards, who married Thomas Hughes of Pennant y Belan.

RHIWFABON.

THE manor of Rhiwfabon is one of the seventeen
seignorial manors of the Lordship of Maelor Gymraeg,
and is divided into the three seignorial townships of
Rhiwfabon, Marchwiail, and Tref y Rûg or Rhwytyn.
The parish of Rhiwfabon is divided into twelve townships, viz., Hafod, Bodylltyn, Rhuddallt, Belan, Coed
Christionydd and Christionydd Cynwrig, both of which
lie in the seignorial township of Christionydd Cynwrig,
in the manor of Esclusham, Mortyn Uwch y Clawdd,
alias Mortyn Wallicorum, which lies in the manor
of Eglwyseg, Mortyn Is y Clawdd, *alias* Mortyn Angli-
corum, which is in the manor of Fabrorum, Dinhinlle
Uchaf and Dinhinlle Isaf, both of which are in the
manor of Dinhinlle, and Tre Robert Lloyd.

The greatest part, if not all, of the townships of
Hafod, Bodylltyn, Rhuddallt and Belan, which form the

seignorial township of Rhiwfabon, appears to have belonged to the princes of Powys Fadog, and were given by Madog ab Gruffydd Maelor, Prince of Powys Fadog, the Founder of the Monastery of Valle Crucis, who died in A.D. 1236, to his second son, Meredydd, who was styled Meredydd of Rhiwfabon from that circumstance. Meredydd took up his residence at Watstay, now called Wynnstay, and married the Princess Catherine, daughter of Gruffydd ab Llewelyn ab Iorwerth, Prince of Wales, who bore quarterly *gules* and *or*, four lions rampant counterchanged. By this lady, Meredydd had issue one only daughter and heiress, named Angharad, who had her father's landed estate, part of which was the ancient camp called Caer-Ddin, and vulgarly Gardden, and a farm called Cae Cuwppa adjoining it, which remained in the Eyton family till the late Mr. Eyton Evans of Watstay exchanged them with his father in law, Sir Gerard Eyton of Eyton, for some other compensation. Angharad married Llewelyn ab Gruffydd ab Cadwgan, Lord of Eyton, Erlisham, and Boresham, and who thus, in right of his wife, became possessed of the Watstay Estate, and of whose family it will be requisite to give a short account.

Elidur, Lord of Eyton, Erlisham and Borasham, the second son of Rhys Sais, Lord of Chirk, Nanheudwy, Maelor Saesneg, and Whittington, who died in A.D. 1070. He married Annesta, daughter of Lles ab Idnerth Benfras, Lord of Maesbrwg, in the Lordship of Oswestry, by whom he had issue eight sons: (1) Madog Warwyn; (2) Meilir Eyton, of whom presently; (3) Morgan; (4) Iorwerth; (5) Cynwrig; (6) Madog Sutton, Lord of Sutton[1] and Gwersyllt, who was ancestor of the Suttons and Lewises of Gwersyllt;[2] the estate of Gwersyllt Isaf remained in the Sutton family till

---

[1] The manor of Iscoed in Maelor Cymraeg contains the townships of Sutton, Dutton Difaeth, Dutton y Brain, Caecaedutton, Borasham Hwfa, Borasham Ruffri (Gruffydd), Gwrtyn, Beeston and Erlisham.

[2] The manor of Burton in Maelor Cymraeg, contains the townships of Trefalun or Alynton, Gwersyllt, and Gresford.

A.D. 1660, when it was sold by Captain Sutton, an old cavalier, who was ruined in the royal cause, to Colonel (afterwards Sir Geoffrey) Shakerley of Shakerley in Lancashire; (7) Sanddef, who bore *ermine*, a lion rampant in a bordure *azure*; he had lands in Erlisham and Marchwiail, and was ancestor of the Lloyds of Crewe, Erlisham of Erlisham, John Wynn Kenrick of Marchwiail, Lewys of Galchog in Tegeingl, and Humphries of Cilystryn; and (8) Matthew Rhwytyn, who had the township of Rhwyton, in the parish of Bangor Is y Coed, but in the manor of Rhiwfabon, the township of Seswick in the manor of Pickill, and the township of Bedwal in the manor of Fabrorum. He was ancestor of the Deccafs of Rhwytyn, Tyfod, Parcau, Rhydybenni, and Erbistog.[1]

Meilir Eyton, the second son of Elidir ab Rhys Sais, was Lord of Eyton, Erlisham, and Borasham, and from him Pentre Meilir takes its name. He married, and had issue five sons: (1) Cadwgan, of whom presently; (2) Ednyfed, the father of Iorwerth, who married Angharad, daughter of Ieuaf Fychan ab Ieuaf ab Niniaf ab Cynwrig ab Rhiwallon, by whom he had an only daughter, Tanegwystl, wife of Adda ab Awr of Trefor; (3) Gruffydd, who married Angharad, daughter and heiress of Llewelyn ab Meurig ab Caradog ab Iestyn ab Gwrgant, Prince of Glamorgan, who bore *gules*, three chevronells *argent*, by whom he had issue four daughters coheirs: (1) Angharad, wife of Iorwerth Hên ab Owain ab Bleddyn, Lord of Chirk, etc.; (2) Gwladys, who married, first, Howel ab Moreiddig ab Sanddef Hardd, Lord of Mortyn, in the manor of Burton, and, secondly, she married Cynwrig, Lord of Christionydd Cynwrig,[2] the son of Hoedliw ab Cynwrig ab Rhiwallon; (3) Angharad Fechan, who married Cadwgan y Saetheth of Mochnant, Lord of Henfachau, who bore *argent* a chev. *gules*, inter three pheons pointed to the centre

---

[1] The manor of Abenbury in Maelor Gymraeg, contains the townships of Abenbury, Eyton, Erbistog, and Sonlli.

[2] The manor of Esclusham in Maelor Gymraeg contains the townships of Esclusham, Bersham Brymbo and Christionydd Cynwrig.

sable ; and (4) Gwenllian. The fourth son of Meilir Eyton was Madog ; and (5) Iorwerth, who had two sons : (1) Ednyfed ab Iorwerth, who had two daughters coheirs—first, Myfanwy, wife of Madog Ddu ab Gruffydd ab Cynwrig Efell, Lord of Eglwysegl,[1] in Maelor Gymraeg, who bore *gules*, on a bend *argent*, a lion passant *sable*, and, second, Margaret, wife of Iorwerth ab Awr ab Ieuaf ab Niniaf, ancestor of the Lloyds of Plâs Madog in Bodylltyn ; and (2) Gruffydd ab Iorwerth, who had a daughter and heiress, Efa, who married Ithel ab Eunydd, Lord of Trefalun and Gresford in the manor of Burton—1, *azure*, a lion salient *or* ; 2, *azure*, a fess *or*, inter three horses' heads erased *argent*, for Rhys ab Marchan, Lord of Dyffryn Clwyd.

Cadwgan, the eldest son of Meilir Eyton, was Lord of Eyton, Erlisham, and Borasham ; he married Myfanwy, daughter and coheir of Ednydd ab Llywarch ab Brân, Lord of Cwmmwd Menai, who bore *argent* a chev. *sable,* inter three rooks ppr., with an ermine spot in their bills, by whom he had a daughter Clementia, wife of Ithel ab Howel ab Moreiddig ab Sanddef Hardd, or the Handsome, Lord of Mortyn, *vert*, semé of broomslips a lion rampant *or*, and a son and heir.

Gruffydd ab Cadwgan, Lord of Eyton, Erlisham, and Borasham ; from him the township of Borasham Ruffri takes its name. He married Janet, daughter of Sir Fulke Fitz Warren, knight, Lord of Whittington, son and heir of Sir Warren de Weaux, a nobleman of Lorraine, quarterly and per fess indented *gules* and *argent*, in the dexter chief a canton chequey *or* and *azure*, by whom he had issue one son, Llewelyn, his successor, and three daughters : (1) Margaret, who married Gruffydd Fychan, "Y Barwn Gwyn", Lord of Glyndyfrdwy, Iâl, and half of Cynllaith, third son of Gruffydd ab Madog, Lord of Castell Dinas Bran, and Prince of Powys Fadog, palii of eight *argent* and *gules*, a lion rampant salient ; (2) Agnes, wife of Iorwerth ab Hwfa Llwyd ab Gruffydd

---

[1] The manor of Eglwysegl contains the townships of Trefechan, Broughton, Stansti Villa, Acton, Morton Uwch y Clawdd, *alias* Morton Wallicorum, and Erddig.

Goch ab David ab Tegwared of Traian in the Lordship of Whittington—*sable*, a chev. inter three spears' heads *argent*, imbrued *gule* ; and (3) Elen, wife of Llewelyn ab Gruffydd ab Iorwerth of Llansantffraid and Drewen.

Llewelyn ab Cadwgan, Lord of Eyton, Erlisham, and Borasham, married, first, Angharad, daughter and sole heiress of Meredydd of Rhiwfabon, second son of Madog ab Gruffydd Maelor, Prince of Powys Fadog ; palii of eight *argent* and *gules*, a lion salient *sable*, by whom, according to the *Cae Cyriog MS.*, he had four sons : (1) Madog, his successor ; (2) Iorwerth, who had lands in Bwras or Borasham and Rhuddallt, and was ancestor of William Bwras of Bwras and others ; (3) Gruffydd, who had lands in Bodylltyn ; and (4) Howel Grach, who had lands in Bodylltyn, and four daughters : (1) Lucy, wife of David ab Iorwerth, Baron of Hendwr, ab Madog ab Gruffydd ab Owain Brogyntyn, Lord of Edeyrnion, *argent* a lion rampant *sable*, debruised by a baton sinister *gules*, by whom she was mother of Madog, Baron of Hendwr, who bore *argent*, on a chev. *gules*, three fleurs-de-lys *or* ; (2) Margaret, wife of Madog ab Ednyfed Goch of Bers or Bersham, ab Cynwrig ab Gruffydd Fychan, descended from Ednyfed, Lord of Broughton, who bore *ermine*, a lion statant *gules*, the second son of Cynwrig ab Rhiwallon ; (3) Angharad, wife of Gruffydd ab Ieuaf ab Iorwerth, descended from Eunydd ab Gwernwy, Lord of Trefalun, *azure*, a lion salient *or*.

Other authorities, however, state that Llewelyn, Lord of Eyton, married a second wife, Gwenllian, daughter of Owain ab Trahaiarn ab Ithel ab Eunydd, Lord of Trefalun and Gresford ; and that Howel Grach and Iorwerth were her sons ; but as Howel Grach had his share of lands in Bodylltyn, which did not belong to the Lords of Eyton, but belonged to the estate of Angharad, the first wife of Llewelyn, it is not probable that if he had been the son of Llewelyn by his second wife, that he could have had any of the lands belonging to his first wife. Owain ab Trahaiarn was one of the

witnesses to the charter of Prince Madog ab Gruffydd
Maelor to the Abbey of Valle Crucis in A.D. 1202.

1. Madog, the eldest son of Llewelyn ab Gruffydd,
had Eyton Watstay, Erlisham or Erlys, *alias* Eurlys,
and Borasham or Bwras. He married Angharad,
daughter of David Hên ab Goronwy Hên ab Iorwerth
ab Howel ab Moreiddig ab Sanddef Hardd, Lord of
Morton; and dying in A.D. 1331, was buried, on the
Feast of St. Matthias, in the north aisle of Gresford
Church, leaving issue four sons and five daughters:
(1) Ieuan, who had Eyton and Watstay, who was ancestor
of the Eytons of Eyton, Watstay, and Pentre Madog
in Dudleston; (2) David Lloyd of Hafod y Bwch had
lands in Borasham, which were forfeited by his grandson,
Howel ab Ieuan ab David Lloyd, to the King of England, for joining Owain Glyndwr.   These lands, and the
old house of Borasham, were purchased from the Lord of
Bromfield, on the attainder of Howel ab Ieuan ab
David Lloyd, by Thomas de Weild or Wylde of Holt,
son of Jenkyn de Weild, ab Richard de Weild ab
David de Weild ab Richard de Weild ab John de
Weild or de Wylde of Holt in Maelor Gymraeg. *Argent*,
a chev. *sable*, on a chief of the second three martlets of
the field.   Catherine, the eldest daughter and coheir of
Thomas de Weild, married William Brereton, second
son of Sir Randle Brereton of Malpas, in Cheshire,
knight, who thus, *jure uxoris*, became possessed of
Borasham. (3) Howel ab Madog ab Llewelyn. (4) Iorwerth Goch, who had lands in Rhuddallt.   He married
Lucy, daughter of Goronwy ab Tudor ab Goronwy ab
Ednyfed Fychan, Lord of Tref-Castell in Môn, by
whom he had a son named Madog, who was the
ancestor of John Rogers of Rhuddallt, who was in possession of his lands there in A.D. 1620;[1] and of Roger
Gruffydd of Rhuddallt, who had also possession of his
lands there in 1620; but, in 1697, his lands passed into
the possession of Cynwrig Eyton of Eyton, Esq.

The daughters of Madog ab Llewelyn, Lord of Eyton

---

[1] Norden's *Survey of Bromfield and Iâl.*

and Watstay, were : (1) Erddylad or Erminallt, the
wife of Tudor ab Ithel Fychan, Lord of Mostyn and
Ewlo Castle, who bore *azure*, a lion passant *argent*, by
whom she had a son and heir named Howel, Lord of
Mostyn and Ewlo Castle, whose only daughter and
heiress Angharad, married Ieuan Fychan ab Ieuan ab
Adda ab Iorwerth Ddû of Pengwern in Nanheudwy,
the ancestor of the Mostyns of Mostyn, Talacre, and
Llewesog; (2) Gwenhwyfar, wife of Gruffydd ab Iorwerth ab Einion of Soulli, ancestor of the Sontleys of
Sonlli—*ermine*, a lion rampant *sable*; (3) Angharad,
wife of Llewelyn ab Gruffydd ab Meredydd; (4) Lucy,
wife of Llewelyn ab Madog Foel of Marchwiail—
ermine, a lion rampant in a bordure *azure*; and (5) Margaret, the wife of Iorwerth Fychan ab Iorwerth ab
Awr, by whom she had a son, Ednyfed Lloyd, the
father of Llewelyn, the father of David, who was living
A.D. 1467 (7 Edw. IV),[1] and who married Margaret,
daughter and heiress of Dio ab Hwfa ab Madog yr
Athro of Plâs Madog in Bodylltyn, by whom he had a
son named John, the ancestor of the Lloyds of Plâs
Madog.

2. Gruffydd of Bodylltyn, the second son of Llewelyn
ab Gruffydd, Lord of Eyton, was the father of Ednyfed
of Bodylltyn, whose only daughter and heiress, Lucy,
was the second wife of Madog Lloyd of Iscoed, the
eldest son of Gruffydd of Maelor Saesneg, the second
son of Iorwerth Foel, Lord of Chirk, by whom she had
a son, Deio of Bodylltyn, whose line ended in an heiress,
Gwenllian, who married Roger Eyton, a younger son
of John ab Elis Eyton of Watstay, Esq., ancestor of the
Eytons of Bodylltyn.

3. Iorwerth, the third son of Llewelyn ab Gruffydd,
had lands in Borasham and Rhuddallt. He married
Margaret, daughter of Iorwerth ab David ab Goronwy
ab Iorwerth ab Howel ab Moreiddig ab Sanddef Hardd,

---

[1] Proceedings before the Commissioners appointed by the Lords
of Bromfield and Yale, at the great court of those lordships held at
Holt Castle 7 Edward IV, A.D. 1467.

Lord of Mortyn, by whom he had a son, Iolyn of Bwras or Borasham, the father of Einion, the father of John, the father of William Borasham, the father of William Bwras or Borasham of Borasham, who had an only daughter and heiress, Angharad, who married Lewys Sutton of Sutton, Esq., ab Robert Sutton.

4. Howel Grach of Bodylltyn, the fourth and youngest son of Llewelyn ab Gruffydd, Lord of Eyton, married Margaret, eldest daughter and coheiress of David, Lord of Pentyrch, Celli Caswallon, Penarch, and Rhiwarch in Caer Einion, the fifth son of Gruffydd ab Gwenwynwyn, Prince of Upper Powys, who died in A.D. 1289, and was buried in the church of the Franciscan Monastery, or Grey Friars, in Shrewsbury. Her mother was Elen, daughter and heiress of Howel, third son of Madog ab Gruffydd Maelor, Prince of Powys Fadog.[1] Quarterly first and fourth *or*, a lion ramp. *gules*, for Gruffydd ab Gwenwynwyn; second and third *or*, a lion's gamb erased *gules*, for Gwenwynwyn.[2] By this lady, Howel Grach had issue an only daughter and heiress, Angharad, who married Madog yr Athro, who, according to the *Harl. MS.* 4181, and Mr. Joseph Morris of Shrewsbury, was the son of Hwfa ab Iorwerth of Hafod y Wern. *Sable*, three lions passant in pale *argent*; but according to the *Cae Cyriog* and the *Harl. MSS.* 2299, as also the *Add. MS.* 9864-5, he was the son of Hwfa ab Iorwerth ab Gruffydd ab Ieuaf ab Niniaf ab Cynwrig ab Rhiwallon. *Gules*, two lions passant *argent*, for Iorwerth ab Gruffydd. By his wife Angharad, Madog yr Athro became possessed of the lands in Bodylltyn which formed the Plas Madog estate, where he built the house now called Plâs Madog. Lewys Dwnn, however, in his account of the Lloyds of Plâs Madog, calls this place Plâs Madog Warwyn,[3] from Madog Warwyn, the eldest son of Elidir ab Rhys Sais, Lord of Eyton; so Madog yr Athro may have only rebuilt it. By his wife Angharad,

---

[1] *Golden Grove MSS.*   [2] *Harl. MSS.* 1973, p. 4.
[3] *Cae Cyriog MS.*

F F

Madog yr Athro had issue a son, Hwfa of Plâs Madog, who married Agnes, daughter of Madog Goch of Lloran Uchaf in Cynllaith, the son of Ieuaf ab Cuhelyn ab Rhyn ab Einion Efell, Lord of Cynllaith, who bore party per fess *sable* and *argent*, a lion rampant counter-charged, by whom he had issue two sons: (1) Hwfa; and (2) Dio or David, who must have had Plas Madog, and not David ab Hwfa ab Ieuaf ab Hwfa ab Madog yr Athro, as the following pedigree will clearly prove.

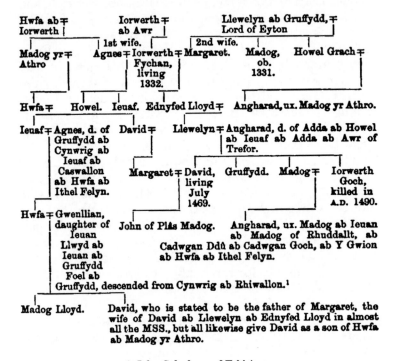

David, who is stated to be the father of Margaret, the wife of David ab Llewelyn ab Ednyfed Lloyd in almost all the MSS., but all likewise give David as a son of Hwfa ab Madog yr Athro.

[1] John Salusbury of Erbistog.

The Pedigree of MADOG YR ATHRO and the BERSHAMS of BERSHAM,

According to the *Cae Cyriog MS.; Harl. MSS.* 1972, 2294, 4181; *Add. MSS.* 9864-5.

Ieuaf ab Niniaf ab Cynwrig ab Rhiwallon. = Ermine a lion rampant *sable*, armed and langued *gules*.

Eva, daughter of Einion ab Howel ab Ieuaf, Lord of Arwystli. *Gules*, a lion rampant *argent*, crowned *or*.

2nd son.
Gruffydd of Bersham. = Eva, daughter and coheiress of Bledrws ab Ednowain Bendew, Chief of one of the Noble Tribes of Gwynedd. *Argent* a chev. *gules*, inter three boar's heads couped *sable*, for Bledrws. Ednowain Bendew lived at Llys Coed y Mynydd, in the parish of Bodfari in Tegeingl, and bore *argent*, a chev. inter three boar's heads couped *sable*.

Iorwerth ab Gruffydd of Bersham. = Margaret, daughter of Cynwrig Fychan ab Cynwrig ab Hoedliw of Christionydd Cynwrig, fifth son of Cynwrig ab Rhiwallon. *Gules*, two lions passant in pale *argent*.

Hwfa ab Iorwerth = Janet, daughter of Ithel Dalfrith ab Trahaiarn Goch of Lleyn in Gwynedd, son of Madog ab Rhys Gloff of Bersham. ab Rhys Fychan ab Gruffydd ab Rhys ab Tudor Mawr, Prince of South Wales. *Azure*, three dolphins naiant embowed *argent*, for Trahaiarn Goch.

Madog yr Athro. Harl. MS. 2299. = Gruffydd yr Athro, after his wife's death he became a Priest, and was Parson of Llangedwyn, where he died, and is buried.

Howel = of Bersham.

Agnes, 1st wife of Iorwerth Fychan ab Iorwerth ab Awr ab Ieuaf ab Niniaf ab Cynwrig ab Rhiwallon.

Margaret, ux. Ithel Llwyd ab Ithel Gam of Mostyn.

Cicilia, ux. Sir Roger de Powys, Knight of Rhodes and Lord of Whittington.

Alice, ux. Iorwerth ab Gruffydd ab Heilyn of Fron Goch in Mochnant, ab Meurig ab Ieuan ab Adda Goch of Mochnant, ab Cynwrig ab Pasgen ab Gwyn, Lord of Cegidfa and Deuddur.

Ieuaf Ddû of Bersham =

Gruffydd.

Gruffydd of Bersham =

a

Howel of Bersham ⊤

William of ⊤ Bersham.

Madog Goch of Frondeg ⊤   John.

Catherine, ux. John ab Ieuan ab Deicws of Llanerchrugog. *Ermine. a lion rampant sable.*

Roger.

William of ⊤ Lowry, d. of John Wynn ab David ab
Frondeg in | Gruffyd of Caerddinog, in Llanfair
the parish of | Dyffryn Clwyd, and relict of Ienkyn
Wrexham. | ab Elis. *Lewys Dwnn,* vol. ii, 349.

John Wynn, the friend of Richard White, *alias* Gwyn of Llanidloes, who was burnt at a stake at Wrexham for not abjuring the Catholic Faith, October 15, A.D. 1584.

Roger of Frondeg.

John of Frondeg.

...... ux. Lancelot ab David Goch ab David of Escluaham ab Robert ab Gruffydd of Croes Foel.

John of ⊤ Angharad, daughter of Matthew, younger son of David ab Gruffydd ab David ab Madog, *alias* y Bady ab David Goch
Bersham. | of Hafod y Bwch, in the parish of Wrexham, ab Gruffydd ab Iorwerth Fychan ab Iorwerth ab Ieuaf ab Niniaf ab
| Cynwrig ab Rhiwallon.

Elizabeth, ux. Owain Hughes ab Hugh ab John ab Ieuan ab Deicws of Llanerchrugog.

John Bersham of Bersham ⊤ Gwen, daughter of Elis.

John Bersham.

Robert Bersham.

Richard Bersham.

Gruffydd Bersham.

LLOYD OF THE BRYN, in the parish of Hanmer in Maelor Saesneg.

GRUFFYD of Maelor Saesneg, ⊤ Gwerfyl, daughter and coheiress of Madog ab Meredydd ab Llewelyn Fychan ab Llewelyn ab Owain
second son of Iorwerth Foel, | Fychan ab Owain, Lord of Mechain Is Coed, second son of Madog ab Meredydd, Prince of Powys
Lord of Chirk and Nan- | Fadog. *Argent,* a lion rampant *sable,* in a bordure indented *gules. Harl. MS.* 2299, f. 42. The *Cae*
heudwy (refer to Hughes of | *Cyriog MS.* state that Gwerfyl was the daughter of Meredydd ab Llewelyn Fychan ab Madog ab
Pennant y Belan). | Owain Fychan, Lord of Mechain, son of Madog ab Meredydd.

a		b	c	d	e	f	g
Madog Lloyd of Iscoed.		Llewelyn Ddu of Abertanat.	David.	Madog Ddu.	Iorwerth Foel.	Morgan Goch.	Goronwy Ddu of Abertanat.

∓ Catherine, daughter of Owain Barton of Cheshire.

2nd wife.
∓ Lucy, daughter of Iorwerth Fychan ab Iorwerth ab Awr ab Ieuaf ab Niniaf.

3rd wife.
∓ Gwerfyl, daughter and heiress of Ed-nyfed ab Gruffyd of Bodylltyn, third son of Llewelyn ab Gruffydd, Lord of Eyton.

Deio of ∓ Angharad, daughter of Ieuan ab Madog ab Cadwgan Ddu ab Cadwgan
Bodylltyn. | Goch of Rhuddallt, descended from Ithel Felyn, Lord of Iâl.

Madog of ∓ Gwenllian, daughter and heiress of Madog Lloyd of Bodylltyn ab Hwfa
Bodylltyn. | ab Ieuaf ab Hwfa ab Madog yr Athro.

Edward of ∓ Alice, daughter and heiress of Madog ab Einion ab David ab David ab
Bodylltyn. | Iorwerth of Hoslli, ab David ab Goronwy ab Iorwerth ab Howel ab
Moreiddig ab Sanddef Hardd.

Gwenhwyfar, heiress of Bodyllton, wife of Roger Eyton, an illegitimate son of John ab Ellis Eyton of Watstay, by Efa,
daughter and heiress of Richard ab David ab Sidan. Roger Eyton died in A.D. 1581, and was ancestor of the Eytons of
Bodylltyn.

David of ∓ Gwenllian, sister of Reignallt of the Tower, near Mold, and daughter of Bleddyn ab Einion Fychan ab Einion ab
Iscoed. | Cadwgan Ddu ab Cadwgan Goch, ab Y Gwion ab Hwfa ab Ithel Felyn, Lord of Iâl.

Ienkyn of Willington ∓ ...... daughter of | Madog, Lloyd ∓ Maude, daughter and heiress of Gruffydd ab Morgan Goch
in the parish of | Maurice Young ab | of Willington. | ab Gruffydd of Maelor Saesneg, second son of Iorwerth
Hanmer. | Ienkyn Young. | Foel.

David Lloyd of ∓ Gwen, daughter and heiress of John Lloyd | Gruffydd Lloyd, ancestor of the Lloyds of Tal y Wern.
Willington. | of Oswestry ab Tomlyn Lloyd of Oswestry,
| second son of Madog Lloyd of Llwyn y Maen.

Ieuan of ∓ Margaret, d. of
Rhuddallt. | Madog ab Iorwerth
ab Madog.

Gwenllian, heiress, ux. Ienkyn
ab Llewelyn ab Ithel Goch ab
Llewelyn ab Madog ab Einion
ab Madog ab Bleddyn ab Cynwrig ab Rhiwallon.

Argent, an eagle displayed with two necks *sable*.

a

b

a
John Lloyd of Bryn Halchdyn ⊤ Alice, daughter of Randle
in the parish of Hanmer. | Lloyd of Talywern.

b
Robert Lloyd of Willington, ances- ⊤ Catherine, daughter of William
tor of the Lloyds of Willington. | Willascote of Willascote.

Robert Lloyd of the Bryn, one of the ⊤ Elen, daughter of David Lloyd ab Elissan of Plâs yn Iâl.
Body Guard of Queen Elizabeth. | *Ermine*, a saltire *gules*, a crescent *or*, for difference.

Dorothy, ux. Thomas Lloyd of Plâs Uwch y Clawdd in the parish of Rhiwabon,
Esq., descended from Rhys Grûg. *Argent*, a lion rampant *sable* armed langued
and crowned *gules*.

Robert Lloyd ⊤ Margaret, daughter and
of the Bryn. | heiress of Robert Sefton
of Mollington in Cheshire.

Eubule Lloyd ⊤ Catherine, daughter of Thomas Whitley of Aston, in the parish of Hawarden, and Dorothy, his wife, daughter of
of the Bryn. | Thomas Ravenscroft of Bretton, co. Flint.   *Argent*, on a chief *gules*, three garbs *or*.

Luke Lloyd ⊤ Esther, daughter of James Betton, D.D., of Shrewsbury, which lady (having eventually survived her two brothers
of the Bryn. | and all her sisters, with her nephew, James Betton, and his sisters, the children of her eldest brother James) became
| the sole heir of this branch of the Betton family. *Argent*, two pales *sable*, each charged with three crosslets fitchy *or*.

Catherine, heiress ⊤ Thomas Kenyon of Peel Hall, co. Lan-
of the Bryn. | caster, ancestor of the Lords Kenyon.

Sarah Lloyd, buried at Rhiw- ⊤ Samuel Lloyd of
fabon, June 7th, A.D. 1699.   Plâs Madog.

RHIWABON REGISTERS.

Piers, son of Edward Lloyd, was baptised Jan. 5, A.D. 1601.

Edward Lloyd of Plâs Madog, Esq., was buried Jan. 1, 1637.

Anne, wife of Edward Lloyd of Plâs Madog, was buried August 22, 1636.

Elizabeth, wife of Edward Lloyd of Plâs Madog (daughter and heiress of Owain Lloyd), was buried Oct. 28, 1676.

Mrs. Anne Lloyd, wife of William Lloyd of Plâs Benion, was buried March 21, A.D. 1700.

Samuel, son of Edward Lloyd of Plâs Madog, Esq. (and Elizabeth, his wife), was baptised June 1, 1633.

Mrs. Sarah Lloyd, wife of Samuel Lloyd of Plâs Madog, was buried June 7, A.D. 1699.

Samuel Lloyd of Plâs Madog, Esq., was buried May 2, A.D. 1701, aged 63.

Edward, son of Samuel Lloyd, gentleman, was baptised Dec. A.D. 1686.

John, son of Samuel Lloyd of Plâs Madog, Esq., was buried Dec. 28, 1694.

William, son of Ditto, was buried Dec. 1, 1698.

Charles, son of Ditto, was buried Dec. 16, 1698.

Samuel Lloyd of Plâs Madog was buried Sept. 2, 1723.

Mrs. Anne Lloyd, wife of Edward Lloyd of Plâs Madog, Esq., was buried Sept. 26, 1745.

Elizabeth, daughter of Edward Lloyd of Plâs Madog, Esq., was baptised May 10, A.D. 1718.

Elizabeth Lloyd de Christionydd Cynwrig (wife of Ienkyn Lloyd of Clochfaen) was buried Dec. 12, A.D. 1758, aged 40.

Edward Lloyd of Plâs Madog, Esq., was buried Aug. 11, A.D. 1760, aged 74.

Madog infans de Plâs Madog (son of Ienkyn Lloyd and Elizabeth his wife) was buried Jan. 22, A.D. 1774.

Sarah, daughter of Ienkyn Lloyd and Elizabeth, his wife, was baptised March 2, A.D. 1746.

Ienkyn Lloyd of Plâs Madog, Esq., was buried February 5, A.D. 1766, aged 42.

Edward Lloyd of Plâs Madog, Esq., by his will dated A.D. 1757, left to the poor of the parish of Rhiwabon £150, to be distributed in coals, schooling for three boys and two girls, from the Township of Christionydd and Coed Christionydd, secured by a rent charge on lands in Westyn Rhyn in the Parish of St. Martin's, co. Salop. These lands were purchased from the Lloyd family by Mr. Kenyon of Penylan.

Anne Lloyd of Plâs Madog, by will, date unknown, charged a small farm called Caer Llwyn, in the parish of Gwytherin, with the yearly payment of £1. This money is to be distributed on St. Thomas's Day. The proprietor of Caer Llwyn is now Mr. Fitzhugh of Plâs Power, near Wrexham. *Report of the Charity Commissioners.*

Colonel Charles Thomas Edward Hinde became Major-General in Feb. 1870, and died on the 15th May in the same year.

Mr. I. Y. Wm. Lloyd of Clochfaen was created a Knight of the Order of St. Gregory the Great, in September 1870, by His Holiness Pope Pius IX.

FROM THE MISCELLANEA HISTORICA.

By the Rev. W. V. LLOYD, M.A., F.R.G.S.

Grand Jury.

4 James I, 1606.

Evanus David de Clochfaen, gen.
Ienkinus Mores ab R's de Llanywored,[1] gen.
Hoellus ap Stephen de Llangerick, gen.
Ienkinus Mores ap Ieun Lloyd de Glynhaveren, gen.
David ab Rhys ab Ienkyn de Glynbrochan, gen.

9 James I, 1611.

Ienkinus David de Llangerick, gen.[2]

20 James I, 1622.

Evanus David de Llangirrick, gen.[3]

1 Charles I, 1625.

Evanus David de Llangerig, gen. (on the list, but not on the Grand Jury.)
Morgan Evans de Llangerig, gen. (on the list, but not on the Grand Jury.)

---

[1] Ienkyn ab Maurice ab Rhys ab Maurice ab Llewelyn of Llanywared, second son of Ieuan ab Gruffydd ab Howel Lloyd of Clochfaen. He married Elen, daughter of David Lloyd ab Ienkyn ab Maurice of Clochfaen.

[2] Ienkyn, second son of David Lloyd ab Ienkyn ab Maurice ab Ienkyn Goch of Clochfaen and brother of Evan ab David of Clochfaen. He married Elizabeth, daughter of Owain Blayney of Ystymgwyn, ab Howel ab Owain ab Howel ab Ieuan Blayney of Grûgynog.

[3] Evan David of Clochfaen.

10 Charles I, 1634.

Morganus Evans de Glinbrochan, gen.

Evanus ab Ienkin ab Rees de Llanywared, gen.[1]

11 Charles I, 1635.

Ed'r'us Evans de Clochvaine issa, gen.[2]

14 Charles I, April 29, 1638.

Ed'r'us Evans de Clochvaine issa, gen.

2 Charles II (2nd of Commonwealth, 1650).

David Lewis ab Ienn Lloyd, gen., Maior de Llanidloes.

Riceus Lloyd de Llanywored,[3] gen., on Grand Jury List for
   Llanidloes Hundred, but not selected for Grand Jury.

David Ienkin Mores de Glynhafren, gen., on same.

Under presentments.

12 Charles II, 7th Oct., 1661.

The presentments of Arthur Ierman, one of the Chief Con-
stables of the hundred of Llanidloes, the seventh day of
October, 1661. I doe p'sent Evan Lloyd of Llangirrick[4] in the
sd. countie, gen., for absenteing himself from his p'ishe Church
of Llangerrick afores'd ev'y Sunday from the 21 day of July in
the yeare afors'd. I doe p'sent Edd. Lloyd, gen., of the same
for the like." xx. The m'ke of Arthur + Ierman.

13 Charles II, 26 July, 1662.

David Ienkyn Morris de Llangericke, gen.,[5] on Llanidloes
Hundred of Grand Jury List, but not selected.

14 Charles II, 16 Oct., 1663.

Ienkinus Lloyd de Llaniwared, gen.,[6] and Edwardus Lloyd

---

[1] Evan ab Ienkyn ab Rhys ab Maurice ab Llewelyn ab Ieuan ab
Gruffydd ab Howel Llwyd. He married Margaret, daughter of
Thomas ab John ab Howel.

[2] Edward Evans of Clochfaen Isaf, was the son of Evan of Clochfaen Isaf, second son of Ienkyn ab Maurice ab Ienkyn Goch of
Clochfaen.

[3] Rhys Lloyd of Clochfaen, in the Township of Llanywared. He
married, A.D. 1626, Margaret, daughter of Ienkyn Lloyd of Rerth-
lloyd.

[4] Evan Lloyd of Bwlch y Gareg, third son of Rhys Lloyd of
Clochfaen.

[5] David ab Ienkyn ab Maurice ab Rhys ab Maurice ab Llewelyn
ab Ieuan ab Gruffydd ab Howel Lloyd.

[6] Ienkyn Lloyd of Llanywared was the second son of Rhys Lloyd
of Clochfaen, and Margaret his wife. He succeeded to the Clochfaen Estate in consequence of his eldest brother, Edward Lloyd,
having no issue.

de Glyngynwyd,[1] gen., on Grand Jury list of Llanidloes Hundred. Edward Lloyd was not, however, for the following sufficient reasons (as a recusant) selected.

Presentments before the Grand Jury.

" Item, the said Jurors upon their oaths present that Evan Lloyd of Bwlch y Garreg, in the p'ish of Llyngerick in the said county, gent.,[2] and Mary his wife, for not frequenting their p'ish Church of the said p'ish or elsewhere ; contrary to the statute.

" Item, Edd. Lloyd, gen., of the same parish, and Margaret his wife for the like."

15 Charles II, 16 April, 1664.

Apud Dom. mansional Ricei Beamond de Trefegloes in com Mont., gen., Coram Maurico Lloyd, gen., uno Coronator, etc., bailed David Ienkyn Mores, gen., et Evan Lloyd de Glynhavran in die Com. gener de morte comis Ricei ab Richard de Glynhavren. At the same time, " Mores Bowen de Glynhavran, gen.," bailed " Evanus Lloyd nup' de Glynhavran Uwchcoed in com pred, gen."

15 Charles II, 7 Oct., 1664.

" Edrus Evans de Llangirick, gen.," on the Grand Jury list of Llanidloes Hundred, for the Assizes held at Llanfyllin, but not selected.[3]

---

[1] Edward Lloyd of Glyngynwydd must have been the eldest son of Rhys Lloyd of Clochfaen, as we have no knowledge of any other person bearing that name in Llangurig parish at this time.

[2] Evan Lloyd of Bwlch y Garreg must also have been one of the sons of Rhys Lloyd of Clochfaen, as Bwlch y Garreg Uchaf is mentioned as one of the farms belonging to the Clochfaen Estate, in the marriage settlements of Rhys Lloyd and Margaret, daughter of Ienkyn Lloyd of Berthlloyd in A.D. 1626.

[3] Edward Evans of Clochfaen Issa.

The descendants of JOHN BRERETON of Esclusham, Esq.

Harl. MS. 1971-1972.

1st wife.

| Elizabeth, only daughter of John Salusbury of Lleweni, Esq., Chamberlain of Denbighshire, and M.P. for Denbigh in 1554. and Catherine, his wife, daughter and heiress of Tudor ab Robert Fychan of Berain, Esq. *Gules*, a lion rampant *argent*, ducally crowned *or*, inter three crescents of the second. | Owin Brereton of Borasham, Esq., High Sheriff for Denbighshire 1581, and 1588. | Catherine, daughter of Harri Goch Salusbury of Llewesog in Llanrhaiadr Duffryn Clwyd, Esq., and relict of John Lloyd of Bodidris in Iâl, Esq., High Sheriff for Denbighshire in 1551. |

| 2nd son. | | 1st son. | | |
| John Brereton of Esclusham, Esq., ob. Jan. 24, A.D. 1622. Buried at Wrexham. | Margaret, daughter of Hugh Wynn of Wigfair in Meriadog. and relict of Robert Empson of London. *Vert* three eagles displayed in fess *or*. | Edward Brereton of Borasham, Esq., held an Eisteddfod in A.D. 1597. High Sheriff for Denbighshire in A.D. 1598, in which year he died. | Anne, daughter of John Lloyd of Bodidris, in Iâl, High Sheriff for Denbighshire in 1551. | Catherine Brereton. | William Lloyd of Plâs Madog in Bodylltyn. |

Edward Lloyd of Plâs Madog Esq. Buried at Rhiwfabon, Jan. 1, A.D. 1637.   Owain Lloyd.

| 1st coheir. | | 2 coheir. | | 3 | 4 |
| Elizabeth Brereton, ob. Feb. 26, A.D. 1656. | Thomas Bulkeley of Coedan in Anglesey, Esq. | John Ffachnallt of Ffachnallt, co. Flint, Esq. *Argent* a chev. inter three boar's heads couped *argent*. | Jane Brereton. S. P. | Owain Lloyd, second son of William Lloyd of Plâs Madog and Catherine Brereton, his wife. | Dorothy. | Elen. |

| Thomas Lloyd, a Merchant, died at Hamburg. S. P. | Edward Lloyd of Plâs Madog, ob. A.D. 1692. | Elizabeth Lloyd, only daughter and heiress. Buried at Rhiwfabon, August 28th, A.D. 1676. |

Besides the Lloyds of Plâs Madog there were several other families of the House of Cynwrig ab Rhiwallon who had estates in the parish of Rhiwfabon, the chief of whom were the Hugheses of Llanerchrugog, the Griffiths of Cae Cyriog, and the Badys of Plâs yn y Delf, of whom a short account will now be given.

LLANERCHRUGOG, IN THE PARISH OF RHIWFABON.

Cae Cyriog MS.

CYNWRIG ab Rhiwallon, who was slain in battle in A.D. 1073, married Judith, daughter of Ifor Hen, Lord of Rhôs, by whom he had issue nine sons : (1) Niniaf, of whom presently ; (2) Ednyfed, ancestor of the Broughtons of Broughton and Marchwiail, and the Ellises and Powels of Alrhey ; (3) Gruffydd ; (4) Bleddyn, ancestor of Hugh Jones of Bersham,[1] John Roberts of Ty Cerig, in the parish of Rhiwfabon,[2] Edward John Tudor of Bersham, now Mr. Power's house in Bersham ;[3] (5) Hoedlin of Christionydd Cynwrig, ancestor of Gruffydd ab David of Christionydd Cynwrig, whose daughter and heiress, Margaret, married, first, John

---

[1] Hugh Jones was the son of John Jones, who was living in A.D. 1620, ab John ab Edward ab David ab Ieuan ab Ienkyn ab Llewelyn ab Ithel Goch ab Llewelyn ab Madog ab Einion ab Madog ab Bleddyn ab Cynwrig ab Rhiwallon.

[2] John Roberts of Ty Ceryg, A.D. 1632, ab Robert ab Ieuan ab Thomas, of the parish of Rhiwfabon, ab Ieuan (or John) ab Ienkyn ab Llewelyn ab Ithel Goch, etc.

[3] Edward Tudor of Ty Belots and of Bettws y Mhers, in Bers or Bersham, was the son of John ab Tudor ab Ieuan (or John) ab Ienkyn ab Llewelyn ab Ithel Goch ; he was living in 1600, and married Mary, daughter of John Gwilym. Ty Belots is now called Plâs Power, from the Power family ; it now belongs to Mr. Fitzhugh.

Thomas of Caernarfon, and, secondly, William Price, gent.; (6) Bledrws; (7) Einion, ancestor of David Bird of Eastwick, in the parish of Ellesmere; (8) Llewelyn; and (9) David, ancestor of Howel Lloyd of Llangurig; and a daughter, Gwenllian, the wife of Rhirid Flaidd, Lord of Penllyn.

Niniaf or Niniau, the eldest son of Cynwrig ab Rhiwallon, married, and had issue a son,

Ieuaf ab Niniaf, who had Llwyn On, Sonlli, Eyton Uchaf, Frondeg, Erddig, Esclys or Esclusham, Hafod y Bwch, Hafod y Wern, Llwyn y Cnotiau and Abenbury, and part of Rhiwalo. He married Eva, daughter of Einion ab Howel ab Ieuaf, Lord of Arwystli. *Argent*, a lion rampant *sable*, crowned *or*, by whom he had issue nine sons: (1) Iorwerth, of whom presently; (2) Gruffydd, ancestor of Madog yr Athro, and the Bershams of Bersham; (3) Einion, who had Sonlli and Eyton Uchaf, ancestor of the Sontleys of Sonlli and the Eytons of Eyton Uchaf; (4) Ieuaf Fychan; (5) Awr, ancestor of the Jeffries of Acton, Lloyds of Plâs Madog, and Robert ab William of Trefynant; (6) Llywarch; (7) Howel, ancestor of Ienkyn ab Ieuan ab David Lloyd; (8) Ednowain; and (9) Madog, ancestor of Richard Tegin, Sergeant at Arms,[1] Owain Badi of Delf, near Llanerchrugog, and Jones of Frondeg.[2]

[1] Richard Tegin, Sergeant-at-Arms, was the son of Robert Tegin of Frondeg, son of David ab Tegin ab Madog ab Iorwerth Goch, ab Madog Goch ab Ieuaf ab Niniaf ab Cynwrig ab Rhiwallon.

[2] Edward Jones of Frondeg was the eldest son (by Gwenllian, his wife, daughter of David ab Llewelyn ab Ednyfed Llwyd of Plâs Madog) of John ab Ieuaf ab Iolyn of Frondeg ab David ab Deicws ab Ieuaf ab Iolyn Foel ab Madog Goch ab Madog ab Ieuaf ab Niniaf, etc., by whom he had a son, Edward Jones of Frondeg, who married Janet, second daughter of Roger Deccaf ab David Deccaf of Rhwytyn, in the parish of Bangor Is y Coed, descended from Elidir, Lord of Eyton, by whom he had an only daughter and heiress, Janet, who married John Edwards of Stahsti, Esq., descended from Edwyn ab Goronwy. Of this family were also John Roberts of Esclusham, A.D. 1600, and his brother, Richard Roberts of Dinhinlle Uchaf in Christionydd, who were the sons of Robert ab Richard ab David ab Richard ab Iolyn ab Ieuan Foel ab Madog Goch ab Madog ab Ieuaf ab Niniaf. *Harl. MSS.* 1972, 2299.

Iorwerth ab Ieuaf, the eldest son, had Llwyn On, and much land in Wrexham, Gresford, Marchwiail, Holt, Erbistog, and Bangor Is y Coed. He married Margaret, daughter of Cynwrig Fychan ab Cynwrig ab Hoedliw of Christionydd Cynwrig, *ermine* a lion rampant *sable*, by whom he had issue three sons: (1) Gruffydd of Llwyn On, had much lands in Marchwiail, Bangor and Erbistog; he married Margaret, daughter of Rhys Fychan ab Iorwerth ab Rhys Grug, son of the Lord Rhys, Prince of South Wales, by whom he had a son and heir, Iorwerth of Llwyn On, the ancestor of the Jones Parrys of Madryn and Llwn On; (2) Iorwerth Fychan, of whom presently; and (3) Hwfa ab Iorwerth of Hafod y Wern,[1] and a daughter, Gwenllian, wife of Owain Wan, Lord of Caerlleon.

Iorwerth Fychan, the second son of Iorwerth ab Ieuaf of Llwyn On, had lands in Erddig, Esclusham, Hafod y Bwch and Cadwgan. He married, and had issue, a son and heir,

Gruffydd, who had his father's lands. He married Lucy, daughter of Ieuaf ab Llewelyn ab Cynwrig Efell, Lord of Eglwysegl—*gules*, on a bend *argent*, a lion passant *sable*—by whom he had issue four sons: (1) Madog Ddu; (2) David Goch, of whom presently; (3) Howel of Croes Foel, who married Dwgws, daughter of Madog Lloyd of Iscoed, eldest son of Gruffydd ab Iorwerth Foel, Lord of Chirk, by whom he had a son, Gruffydd of Croes Foel, who was the ancestor of the Joneses of Croes Foel and the Joneses of Plâs Cadwgan; and (4) Llewelyn, who was the ancestor of the Erddigs of Erddig, and the Traffords of Treffordd in Esclusham.

David Goch, the second son of Gruffydd ab Iorwerth Fychan, had Hafod y Bwch; he was the father of Madog, *alias* Y Badi of Hafod y Bwch, who had two sons: (1) David; and (2) Iorwerth, who married

---

[1] Hwfa ab Iorwerth of Hafod y Wern, bore *sable*, three lions passant in pale *argent*. His family is now represented through heirs female, by Philip Davies Cooke of Hafod y Wern and Owston, Esq.

Annesta, daughter of Ieuaf ab Hwfa ab Madog yr Athro of Plas Madog.

David, the eldest son of Madog ab David Goch, had Hafod y Bwch; he married, and had issue two sons: (1) Gruffydd of Hafod y Bwch; and (2) Dio of Llanerchrugog.

1. Gruffydd of Hafod y Bwch, married Margaret, daughter and coheir of Ieuan Fychan ab Ieuan ab Howel y Gader of Cader Benllyn, son of Gruffydd ab Madog ab Rhirid Flaidd, Lord of Penllyn—*vert*, a chev. inter three wolf's heads erased *argent*, langued *gules* —by whom he had issue a son and heir, Robert of Hafod y Bwch, who married Margaret, daughter and heiress (by Janet his wife, daughter of Richard Young ab Maurice ab Jenkyn Young of Bryniorcyn in Yr Hôb) of Howel ab Ieuan, third son of Robert ab Gruffydd ab Howel ab Gruffydd ab Howel of Croes Foel, by whom he had a son, John Wynn Roberts of Hafod y Bwch, Sergeant at Arms, ancestor of the Robertses of Hafod y Bwch.

2. Dio of Llanerchrugog, the second son of David ab Madog ab David Goch, married Angharad, daughter of Meredydd ab Llewelyn Ddû ab Gruffydd ab Iorwerth Foel ab Iorwerth Fychan, second son of Iorwerth ab Ieuaf of Llwyn On, by whom he had issue a son,

Deicws ab Dio of Llanerchrugog, who married Lucy, daughter of Tegin ab Madog ab Iorwerth Goch[1] of Frondeg ab Ednyfed Foel ab Ieuaf Fychan ab Ieuaf ab Niniaf, by whom he had issue three sons: (1) Ieuan; (2) Madog; and (3) David of Cae Cyriog, in the parish of Rhiwabon.

Ieuan of Llanerchrugog, the eldest son, married Gwenhwyfar, daughter of Ieuan ab Llewelyn ab Gruffydd, second son (by Lucy his wife, daughter and coheiress of Ieuan[2] ab Philip ab Meredydd ab Gruffydd

---

[1] The *Harl. MSS.* 1972 and 2299 state that Iorwerth Goch was the son of Madog ab Ieuaf ab Niniaf.

[2] Ieuan ab Philip married Myfanwy, daughter and coheiress of David Fychan of Manafon ab David ab Iorwerth ab Einion ab Cynfelyn. Her mother was Margaret, d. of David ab Elissau ab Iorwerth ab Owain Brogyntyn.

ab Madog Danwr of Llangurig) of Ednyfed ab Gruffydd ab Iorwerth ab Einion Goch ab Einion, Lord of Sonlli and Eyton Uchaf, son of Ieuaf ab Niniaf ab Cynwrig ab Rhiwallon, by whom he had issue a son and heir,

John ab Ieuan of Llanerchrugog, who married Catherine, daughter of Howel ab Gruffydd ab Ieuan Ddu of Bersham, ab Howel ab Hwfa ab Iorwerth ab Gruffydd of Bersham, second son of Ieuaf ab Niniaf ab Cynwrig ab Rhiwallon—*gules*, two lions passant in pale *or*, for Iorwerth ab Gruffydd of Bersham—by whom he had issue a son and heir, Hugh, and four daughters: (1) Elizabeth, wife of William Lloyd of Plâs Uwch y Clawdd,[1] in the parish of Rhiwfabon, descended from Rhys Grûg, Lord of Llandovery, who bore *argent*, a lion rampant *sable*, armed langued and crowned *gules*; (2) Angharad, wife of Randle ab John ab David ab Llewelyn of Plâs Madog; (3) Marsli, wife of John ab John ab Robert ab Gruffydd ab Howel of Croes Foel, by whom she had a son, Hugh Jones of Croes Foel, father of Richard Jones of Croes Foel, in the parish of Wrexham; and (4) Alice, wife of Edward ab Howel of Trefechan in Christionydd, second son of Edward ab Madog Puleston of Christionydd; *argent*, on a bend *sable*, three mullets of the field for Madog Puleston.

Hugh of Llanerchrugog, the son and heir of John ab Ieuan, married Catherine, daughter of John Eyton of Watstay, Esq., ab John ab Elis Eyton, by whom he

---

[1] William Lloyd of Plâs Uwch y Clawdd was the twin brother of John Lloyd of Plâs y Badda in Mortyn Is y Clawdd, and son of David Lloyd of Plâs Uwch y Clawdd and Plâs y Badda, ab Deicws ab Madog ab Ithel ab Ednyfed ab Gruffydd ab David ab Rhys Fychan ab Rhys Grûg, Lord of Ystrad Tywi, who bore *argent*, a lion rampant *sable*, armed langued and crowned *gules*. John Lloyd of Plâs y Badda was father of John Wynn Lloyd, the father of Robert Lloyd, who was living in A.D. 1600, and sold Plâs y Badda to Sir Thomas Middleton Hên of Chirk Castle, who built a new house there, now called Plâs Newydd or New Hall. William Lloyd of Plâs Uwch y Clawdd, was father of John Lloyd, the father of Thomas Lloyd, whose four daughters, eventual heirs of their brother John Lloyd, sold Plâs Uwch y Clawdd to Sir Thomas Middleton Hên of Chirk Castle.

had issue (1) John, of whom presently ; (2) Roger ab Hugh, who married Myfanwy, daughter of John, second son of Edward ab Meredydd of Christionydd and of Frondeg, in the parish of Wrexham, son of Gruffydd ab Adda ab Howel of Trefor, by whom he had issue, David, Charles, Alice, Elen, and Catherine ; (3) Owain[1] ab Hugh, who married Elizabeth, daughter of John Bersham of Bersham ab William ab Howel ab Gruffydd ab Ieuan Ddu of Bersham—*gules*, two lions passant in pale *argent* ; and (4) Richard ab Hugh, who married, first, Elizabeth, daughter of John ab Edward, by whom he had issue John and Gwen ; he married, secondly, Alice, daughter of Rondle ab David, by whom he had issue three sons, Edward, Thomas, and George, who were all living in A.D. 1607, and six daughters, of whom Margaret, the eldest, married Lancelot Lloyd of Gorsedd Goch. Hugh ab John ab Ieuan of Llanerch- rugog, had likewise two daughters, Catherine, wife of Edward Erddig ab John Erddig of Erddig, and ......, wife of Hugh Wynn of Bryn Owen, son of John ab William of Bryn Owen, third son of David Eyton of Eyton Uchaf, ab Llewelyn ab Ednyfed ab Gruffydd, Lord of Sonlli and Eyton Uchaf or Trefwy.

John ab Hugh of Llanerchrugog, the eldest son, married Gwenhwyfar or Gwenllian, daughter of John Erddig of Erddig, ab David Goch ab Howel ab Ieuan ab Llewelyn ab Gruffydd ab Iorwerth Fychan ab Ior- werth ab Ieuaf ab Niniaf, by whom he had issue one son, Richard Hughes, and four daughters : (1) Cathe- rine, wife of Randle Davies ; (2) Elen, wife of Walter Panton, Vicar of Tirveccan in Ireland ; (3) Mary, who married, first, John ab Edward, and, secondly, Gruffydd ab Edward ; and (4) Jane, wife of Richard Lloyd, third son of William Lloyd of Plâs Madog.

Richard Hughes of Llanerchrugog, the eldest son,

---

[1] Owain had a daughter and heiress, Marslli, who married John Sonlli ab John Sonlli of Frondeg, fourth son of Robert Wynn Sonlli of Sonlli ab Morgan Sonlli of Sonlli, Esq., by whom she had one son, Robert Sonlli.

H H

married Jane, daughter (by Jane, his third wife, daughter of Meredydd ab Goronwy ab Gruffydd of Dyffryn Aled) of David ab Matthew Wynn ab David of Trefor, ancestor of the Trefors of Trefor Hall, by whom he had two daughters, Elizabeth, and Margaret, who married Lancelot Hughes of Gorsedd Goch in Maelor, and a son and heir,

Edward Hughes of Llanerchrugog, who married his cousin Jane, daughter of Richard Hughes of Cadwgan Fechan, by whom he had issue two sons, Roger Hughes, who died *s. p.*, and Richard Hughes, who went to Virginia, and, on his return, married Maig, daughter of Lancelot Lloyd of Gorsedd Goch,[1] and relict of John Rathbone of Chester, by whom he had no issue, and one daughter, Parnel Hughes, the heiress of her brothers Roger and Richard Hughes. She married John Payne of Morton in Flintshire, Attorney-at-Law, and, dying in A.D. 1696, left an only son and heir, John Payne of Llanerchrugog, who married a lady in London, but whether they had any issue is unknown.

The Llanerchrugog estate now belongs to a family of the name of Jones, but by what title is unknown.

CAE CYRIOG, IN THE PARISH OF RHIWFABON.

JOHN of Cae Cyriog, son and heir of David of Cae Cyriog, who was living in A.D. 1560, son of Ieuan of Cae Cyriog, who was living in A.D. 1500, son of Llewelyn of Cae Cyriog, who was living in A.D. 1480, the son of David of Cae Cyriog, the third son of Deicws ab

---

[1] Lancelot Lloyd of Gorsedd Goch in Maelor, living in A.D. 1604, was the son (by Margaret his wife, daughter of Lancelot Bostock ab Robert Bostock of Churton in Cheshire) of Thomas Lloyd of Gorsedd Goch, ab Lancelot Lloyd ab William Lloyd ab Gruffydd ab Iolyn Lloyd ab David ab Ieuaf Lloyd ab Howel Fychan ab Howel Wyddel ab Iorwerth ab Einion ab Ithel ab Eunydd ab Gwernwy, Lord of Trefalun and Gresford. *Azure*, a lion salient *or*.

Dio of Llanerchrugog, married, first, Elizabeth, daughter and coheiress of Robert ab John ab Robert of Synder, by whom he had issue three sons, the youngest of whom was Gruffydd, of whom presently. John ab David married, secondly, Jane, daughter of Geoffrey Bromfield[1] of Bryn y Wiwer, in the parish of Rhiwfabon, Esq., and relict of John Lloyd ab Randle ab John of Plâs Madog, by whom he had issue two sons, William, who died in London *s. p.*, and Gruffydd, and a daughter, Ermine, who married Edward Fowler of Bryn-y-fallen. John ab David of Cae Cyriog died, and was buried at Rhiwfabon, Feb. 20, 1619, and was succeeded by his third and only surviving son,

Gruffydd of Cae Cyriog. He married, first, Jane, Brochtyn (Broughton), daughter of John Brochtyn ab David Brochtyn of Rhiwfabon, ab John Brochtyn, *alias* John ab John ab Tudor. This Jane was sister of Edward Broughton or Brochtyn, whose son William sold his ancient patrimony, and died without issue in Ireland. By this lady, Gruffydd had issue three sons: John Griffith, of whom presently; Roger and Edward; and two daughters, Margaret and Mary, at whose birth the mother died. Gruffydd married, secondly, Gwen, daughter of David ab David of Llan y Cafn, in the parish of Overton Madog, by whom he had David Gruffydd and Catherine; and, thirdly, he married the widow of Gruffydd Goch of Cefn.

John Griffith of Cae Cyriog, son and heir of Gruffydd ab John ab David, married, first, Elizabeth, daughter (by Joice, his wife, daughter of John Eyton of Bodylltyn, ab Edward ab Roger Eyton of Bodylltyn) of William Eyton, second son of Cynwrig Eyton of Eyton,

---

[1] Geoffrey Bromfield, who was descended from Idnerth Benfras, Lord of Maesbrwg, was one of the valets of the King's Bedchamber, and was appointed Ranger for life of the Little Park near the Camp, in the Lordship of Chirk, 30 Henry VIII (A.D. 1539), Patent Rolls, part 7, m. 2 (30). He married Margaret, daughter of Thomas ab Ieuan ab Ienkyn of Rhiwfabon ab Llewelyn ab Ithel Goch ab Llewelyn Sais ab Madog ab Einion ab Madog ab Bleddyn, fourth son of Cynwrig ab Rhiwallon.

Esq., and Elizabeth, his wife, daughter of Sir Richard Brooke of Morton in Cheshire, knight. John Griffith married, secondly, Alice, daughter of Thomas ab David of Rhiwfabon; she died A.D. 1675; and, thirdly, he married Jane, relict of Robert Wynn, jun., of Trefechan in Christionydd, and daughter of Owain Lloyd of Plâs y Drain,[1] in the Township of Mortyn Uwch y Clawdd, in the parish of Rhiwfabon, son of David Lloyd of Pentre Clawdd, the son of John ab Robert ab David ab John, descended from Ithel Felyn, Lord of Iâl. This David Lloyd sold Pentre Clawdd to Cynwrig Edisbury of Stryt yr Hwch. The above John Griffith died May 26, A.D. 1688, leaving issue by his first wife Elizabeth, three sons, John, Roger, and Peter.

John Griffith of Cae Cyriog, the eldest son and heir of John ab Gruffydd ab John, was the author of a folio volume of Heraldry and Genealogy, from which this account is taken. He had a large and excellent library, which contained, among other valuable works, the *Black Book of Basingwerk Abbey*, by Guttyn Owain, which is still in the possession of his great great grandson, the present Thomas Taylor Griffith, Esq., of Wrexham and Pennant y Belan. He married Catherine, daughter (by Margaret, his wife, daughter of ... Venables of Ysgeifiog) of Hugh Piers[2] of Penbedw, son of Piers

[1] Owain Lloyd of Plâs y Drain, now called Llwyn Owain, married Barbara, daughter of Henry Williams ab William Williams ab William ab William of Cwchwillan, co. Caernarfon, Esq. This Henry Williams sold Cwchwillan to the Earl of Pembroke. He married Jane, daughter and heiress of Thomas Salusbury, third son of Sir John Salusbury of Llyweni, and his mother was Barbara, daughter of George Lumley, and sister and heir of John, Lord Lumley, and relict of Humphrey Lloyd. *Harl. MSS.* 1969, 4181. *Wynnstay MS.* Owain Lloyd was buried at Rhiwfabon, July 19, A.D. 1671. His mother was Catherine, daughter of Howel ab Edward ab Badi Lloyd ab Iorwerth ab Ieuaf ab Einion Gethin of Christionydd ab Einion ab Ieuan ab Gruffydd ab Cynwrig Efell, Lord of Eglwyseg.

[2] The mother of Hugh Piers of Penbedw was Catherine, sister of William Dolben, Esq., High Sheriff for Denbighshire in A.D. 1632, and daughter of Robert Wynn Dolben of Denbigh, Esq., and Jane, his wife, daughter of Owain ab Reignallt of Llynllugwy, Esq. For an account of the family of Hugh Piers, v. *Lewys Dwnn*, vol. ii, art. Diserth in Tegeingl.

ab Hugh ab Piers ab William of Diserth in Flintshire, Esq., by whom he had issue one son, John Griffith, and one daughter, Margaret. He died Oct. 31, A.D. 1698, aged 44, and was succeeded by his only son,

John Griffith of Cae Cyriog, who was born in February 1678, and married, Jan. 13, A.D. 1701, Rebecca, daughter and coheiress of Thomas Hughes of Pennant y Belan, Esq., by which marriage he became possessed of Pennant y Belan, which he made his residence. By Rebecca his wife, who died in A.D. 1724, he had issue two sons, John and Thomas, and, dying in September 1763, was succeeded by his eldest son,

John Griffith of Pennant y Belan and Cae Cyriog. He was born in A.D. 1702, and subsequently went to Jesus College, Oxford, and became Vicar of Nannerch. He married Miss Jones of Park Side, and, dying without issue, was succeeded by his brother,

Thomas Griffiths of Pennant y Belan and Cae Cyriog, who was born March 25, A.D. 1711. He married Mary, relict of Mr. Williams of Ellesmere, and, dying in April, A.D. 1808, aged 97, was succeeded by his eldest son,

Thomas Griffith of Wrexham, Pennant y Belan, and Cae Cyriog, baptised August 28, 1753, married Mary, daughter and coheiress of William Tandy of South Littleton House, near Evesham, Esq., the eldest son of John Tandy, Esq., and Elizabeth his wife, eldest daughter and coheiress of Francis Taylor of South Littleton, son and heir of the Rev. William Taylor, or, as it is written in the *Register*, Taylour, who married Judith Chaslett, daughter of John Chaslett of Cropthorne, co. Worcester, D.D., Prebendary of Worcester Cathedral in 1607. Thomas Griffith died in September, A.D. 1847, aged 93, and was succeeded by his second son, who survived him, the present

Thomas Taylor Griffith, Esq., F.R.C.S., of Wrexham, Pennant y Belan, Cae Cyriog, and South Littleton. He married Mary, eldest daughter of Captain Robertson of Keavel in Fifeshire, descended from Robertson of Stuean, by whom he had issue : (1) Thomas Llywelyn

Griffith, Rector of Deal, born Feb. 1828, married
Mary Moncrief, daughter of Captain Whitmore, R.E.,
eldest son of General Sir George Whitmore, R.E., by
whom he has issue Thomas Llywelyn G. Griffiths;
(2) James Drummond Griffith, born July 22, 1829, of
Baliol College, Oxford, Barrister-at-Law; and one
daughter, Elizabeth, born July 24th, 1832, who died
September, A.D. 1839.

PLAS YN Y DELF AND STANSTI.

Harl. MSS. 1972, 2292.   *Cae Cyriog MS.*

JOHN ab David ab Ieuan ab Bady ab Ieuan Foel ab Madog Goch ab ∓
Madog, eighth son of Ieuaf ab Ninaf ab Cynwrig ab Rhiwallon.

Robert Bady ∓ Margaret, daughter of Roger Deccaf ab David Deccaf of
of Stansti. | Rhwytyn in Bangor Is y Coed, Esq. *Ermine a lion rampant
              | asure.*

Roger Bady of Stansti ∓ Jane, daughter of Edward Brereton of Borasham,
and Plâs yn y Delf in | Esq., High Sheriff for Denbighshire in A.D. 1598.
Rhiwfabon, 1600. | *Argent, two bars sable.*

Owain Bady of Rhiwfabon, A.D. 1630. ∓ Jane, daughter of Edward Lloyd of
He sold Plâs yn y Delf to Sir | Plâs Madog, Esq., and Anne, his
Thomas Middletyn Hên of Chirk | wife, daughter of John Eyton of
Castle, knight. | Leeswood, Esq.

Robert Bady of ∓ ......, daughter of John Edwards of Plâs Newydd in Chirk,
Chirk, 1697. | Esq., and Catherine, his wife, daughter of Rondle Brough-
               | ton of Broughton, Esq.

Timothy Bady.   Edward Bady.   John Bady.

PENTRE CUHELYN IN NANHEUDWY,
AND Y BERTH IN LLANBEDR.

Cae Cyriog MS. Harl. MS. 2299.

GRUFFYDD, second son of Adda ⊤ Angharad Fechan, daughter of Llewelyn
ab Howel ab Ieuaf ab Adda | ab Owain ab Gruffydd ab Owain ab Bled-
ab Awr of Trefor. | dyn ab Owain Brogyntyn, Lord of Dinmael
| and Edeyrnion.

| 3rd son.
Robert of Pentre ⊤ Jane, daughter | Meredydd, ancestor of | 2 4
Cuhelyn. He, to- | of David ab | the Joneses of Fron- | Iorwerth,
gether with his | Meredydd ab | deg in Christionydd. | ancestor of
brother Edward, | Llewelyn | | Y Badi of
went and settled | Chwith, | | Iâl.
in Llanfair Dyff- | descended from | 2
ryn Clwyd. | Edwyn ab | Edward, ancestor of the Lloyds of Trefor,
| Goronwy, | the Joneses of Garthgynan in Llanfair
| Prince of | Dyffryn Clwyd, which last family bore,
| Tegeingl. | *gules,* a cross of Calvary mounted on
| | three steps *or,* and the Matthews of
| | Coedladd in Rhiwfabon parish.

Gruffydd of Pentre Cuhelyn ⊤ Catherine, daughter of William | Tudor ⊤
| ab Gruffydd ab Ienkyn ab |
Ieuan Lloyd of ⊤ Simon ⊤ | Rhys ab Tudor. | Thomas ⊤
Pentre Cuhelyn. | Lloyd. |
| | David Lloyd of Llanbedr, ⊤
Hugh Lloyd of ⊤ Ieuan | buried July 7, A.D. 1620. |
Pentre Cuhelyn. | Lloyd. |
| Thomas Lloyd of Y Berth in Llanbedr, ⊤
Lowry, heiress of Pentre | buried Feb. 2, 1648. |
Cuhelyn, married John |
Matthews, who in her right | John Lloyd of Berth ⊤
became possessed of Pentre |
Cuhelyn, and was living in | Edward Lloyd of Berth, ⊤
A.D. 1667, by whom she had | living in A.D. 1682.[1]
a son, John Matthews of
Pentre Cuhelyn.

[1] He was ancestor of the late Judge Lloyd of Berth, who bought the
Rhagad Estate in Edeyrnion, the father of the late Edward Lloyd of Rhagad,
Esq., of whose family an account has been given in a previous chapter.
Howel William Lloyd, Esq., the youngest son of Edward Lloyd of Rhagad,
Esq., is the accomplished translator of the Welsh Poems illustrative of the
History of Llangurig, which had been most kindly sent him by Nicholas
Bennett of Glanyrafon, near Llanidloes, Esq.

COED Y LLAI IN GRESFORD.

Harl. MSS. 4181.

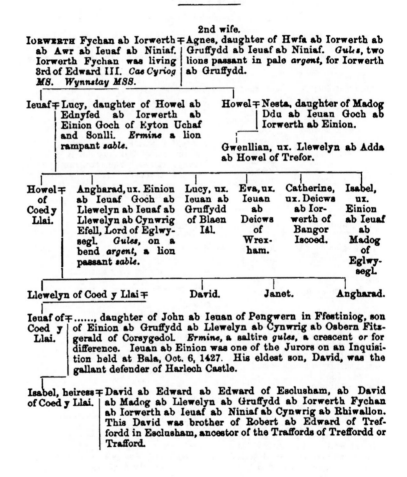

2nd wife.

IORWERTH Fychan ab Iorwerth ⊤ Agnes, daughter of Hwfa ab Iorwerth ab
ab Awr ab Ieuaf ab Niniaf. | Gruffydd ab Ieuaf ab Niniaf. *Gules*, two
Iorwerth Fychan was living | lions passant in pale *argent*, for Iorwerth
3rd of Edward III. *Cae Cyriog* | ab Gruffydd.
MS. Wynnstay MSS.

Ieuaf ⊤ Lucy, daughter of Howel ab   Howel ⊤ Nesta, daughter of Madog
| Ednyfed ab Iorwerth ab | Ddu ab Ieuan Goch ab
| Einion Goch of Eyton Uchaf | Iorwerth ab Einion.
| and Sonlli. *Ermine* a lion
| rampant *sable*.   Gwenllian, ux. Llewelyn ab Adda
                                      ab Howel of Trefor.

Howel ⊤	Angharad, ux. Einion	Lucy, ux.	Eva, ux.	Catherine,	Isabel,
of	ab Ieuaf Goch ab	Ieuan ab	Ieuan	ux. Deicws	ux.
Coed y	Llewelyn ab Ieuaf ab	Gruffydd	ab	ab Ior-	Einion
Llai.	Llewelyn ab Cynwrig	of Blaen	Deicws	werth of	ab Ieuaf
	Efell, Lord of Eglwy-	Iâl.	of	Bangor	ab
	segl. *Gules*, on a		Wrex-	Iscoed.	Madog
	bend *argent*, a lion		ham.		of
	passant *sable*.				Eglwy-
					segl.

Llewelyn of Coed y Llai ⊤   David.   Janet.   Angharad.

Ieuaf of ⊤ ......, daughter of John ab Ieuan of Pengwern in Ffestiniog, son
Coed y | of Einion ab Gruffydd ab Llewelyn ab Cynwrig ab Osbern Fitz-
Llai. | gerald of Corsygedol. *Ermine*, a saltire *gules*, a crescent or for
| difference. Ieuan ab Einion was one of the Jurors on an Inquisi-
| tion held at Bala, Oct. 6, 1427. His eldest son, David, was the
| gallant defender of Harlech Castle.

Isabel, heiress ⊤ David ab Edward ab Edward of Esclusham, ab David
of Coed y Llai. | ab Madog ab Llewelyn ab Gruffydd ab Iorwerth Fychan
| ab Iorwerth ab Ieuaf ab Niniaf ab Cynwrig ab Rhiwallon.
| This David was brother of Robert ab Edward of Tref-
| fordd in Esclusham, ancestor of the Traffords of Treffordd or
| Trafford.

Arms of Edward Lloyd of Plâs Madog, Esq., 1667, according to John Salusbury of Erbistog, Esq., and the *Cae Cyriog MS.*

1. *Ermine,* a lion rampant, *sable,* armed and langued, *gules.*
2. *Vert,* semy of broomslips, a lion rampant, *or.*
3. *Or,* a lion rampant, *azure.*
4. *Vert,* three eagles displayed in fess, *or.*
5. Party ber bend sinister, *ermine,* and, *ermine,* a lion rampant, *or.*[1]
6. *Azure,* a lion rampant party per fess, *or,* and, *argent,* in a border of the third charged with eight annulets, *sable.*
7. *Argent,* a chev., *gules,* inter three boar's heads couped, *sable.*[2]
8. *Ermine,* a lion rampant, *azure.*
9. *Or,* a lion rampant, *gules.*
Crest.—A demi lion rampant, *sable,* in a ducal coronet, *or.*

Arms of Owain Brereton of Borasham, Esq., as they appeared in the Hall at Plâs Madog, A.D. 1689.

1. *Argent,* two bars, *sable,* for Brereton.
2. *Argent,* a chev. inter three crescents, *gules.* Ipstans of Ipstans.
3. *Or,* two ravens ppr., Corbet of Wattlesborough.
4. *Argent,* a chev., *sable,* on a chief of the second three martlets of the field. De Weild of Borasham.
5. *Ermine,* a lion rampant in a bordure, *azure,* for David Lloyd of Crewe.[3]
6. *Argent,* a chev. inter three boar's heads couped, *sable.*[4]

---

[1] This coat is for Madog yr Athro.

[2] This coat is for Eva, daughter and coheiress of Blettrws ab Ednowain Bendrew, v, page 24, for the pedigree of Madog yr Athro, and also page 265.

[3] David Lloyd of Crewe was the son of David Lloyd ab Thomas ab Rhys ab Hwfa Grûg ab Hwfa ab Sanddef ab Elidir ab Rhys Sais. Lucy, the daughter and heiress of David Lloyd of Crewe, married Jenkyn de Weild.

[4] This coat is for Margaret Wen, wife of John Brereton of Borasham, and daughter and heiress (by Jane, his wife, daughter and heiress of William Glegg of Gayton, in Cheshire, Esq.) of Richard ab Ieuan of Llaneurgain ab David ab Ithel Fychan of Llaneurgain ab Cynwrig ab Rotpert ab Iorwerth ab Rhirid ab Iorwerth ab Madog ab Ednowain Bendew of Llys Coed y Mynydd, in the parish of Bodfari, in Tegeingl, and Chief of one of the Noble Tribes of Gwynedd.

I I

7. *Vert*, three eagles displayed in fess, *or*.[1]
8. *Vert*, a stag tripp. regard., *argent*, attired, *or*, for Cynwrig Fychan of Wepra.[2]
9. Party per pale, *or* and *gules*, two lions rampant addorsed counterchanged, between them a hymmock or phi, *'argent*, for Ithel Anwyl of Northope.[3]
10. *Argent*, a cross flory engrailed, *sable*, inter four Cornish choughs ppr.
11. *Sable*, two lions counterpassant, *argent*, collared, *gules*. Glegg of Gayton.
12. *Ermine*, a lion rampant in a bordure, *azure*, Madog Foel of Marchwiail,[4] in the Lordship of Rhiwfabon.[5]

---

[1] For Angharad, wife of Ithel Fychan of Llaneurgain or Northope, and daughter and heiress of Robert ab David of Holt, Esq., son of Howel ab David ab Gruffydd of Ystymcedig.

[2] For Angharad, wife of David ab Ithel Fychan of Northope Hall, and daughter and sole heiress of Cynwrig Fychan of Wepra, ab Cynwrig ab Madog ab Iorwerth ab David ab Cadwgan Llwyd of Wepra, ab Gwgan ab Cynan ab Ithel Llwyd ab Cadwgan ab Llywarch Fychan ab Llywarch Goch ab Llywarch Holbwrch, Lord of Rhos and Rhufoniog, who bore *vert*, a stag trippant, *argent*, attired and unguled *or*.

[3] For Gwladys, wife of Cynwrig Fychan of Wepra, and daughter and heiress of Ithel ab Cynwrig of Monachlog Rhedyn in Llaneurgain, ab Bleddyn ab Ithel Anwyl of Ewlo Castle, and one of the Captains of Tegeingl, son of Bleddyn, a younger son of Ithel Llwyd ab Ithel Gam, Lord of Mostyn, son of Meredydd ab Uchdryd ab Edwyn, Prince of Tegeingl.

[4] For Margaret, wife of William Glegg, Esq., and daughter and heiress of William ab Madog ab Llewelyn ab Madog Foel of Marchwiail, son of Iorwerth ab Hwfa Fychan ab Hwfa Grûg ab Hwfa ab Sanddef ab Elidir, Lord of Eyton.

[5] The Lordship of Rhiwfabon is divided into three manors, viz., Rhiwfabon, Tref y Rug, and Marchwiail. The parish church of Rhiwfabon, which was at first a chapel of ease to the mother church of Llangollen, and dedicated to St. Collen, and the festival kept on May 21, is in the manor of Rhiwfabon. "Kappel Kolhen a galwant gae lle mae Kroes ymbwy Rhiwabon: Ei gwyl mabsant a gadwant dhydh gwyl Golhen dair wythnos o har".—E. Lhuyd. *History of the Diocese of St. Asaph*, by the Rev. D. R. Thomas, M.A. The church is now dedicated to the Blessed Virgin Mary; and the festival is kept on August 15, the feast of her Assumption. The change of the dedication may probably have been made in A.D. 1238, when Hugh, Bishop of St. Asaph, made "Concessio totius Ecclesie de Llangollen domui de Valle Crucis,—reservata institutione vicarii."

Folkestone, Nov. 4, 1873.

MY DEAR HAMER,

I have written the Appendix to your *History of Llangurig*, as it gives some facts that were obtained after the history was published, and also that I might be able to correct some erroneous statements that I sent you, relative to the Clochfaen pedigree. The first was relative to the pedigree of Mallt, the wife of Ienkyn Lloyd of Clochfaen, and daughter of Morgan ab David of Llanbrynmair. The pedigree that I sent you of this lady, and which you have published, was taken from the pedigree of Jones of Esgair Evan, in Sir Bernard Burke's *County Families.* I now give another pedigree of Morgan David, taken from the *Harl. MSS.* 1969 and 2299, which you will find at page 4, and which differs very much from the one previously sent. The second mistake I made was relative to the arms that I have assigned to the family of Pritchard of Ceniarth. I was led into this mistake by finding in Lewys Dwnn, vol. i, the pedigree of a family descended from Meredydd ab Cynan, who bore quarterly, *gules*, and, *argent*, four lions passant counterchanged, headed *Ceniarth*, whereas it ought to have been *Heniarth*, and I did not discover the mistake till too late to correct it. A third wrong statement I made was, that the arms of Thomas Hughes of Pennant y Belan in the parish of Rhiwfabon were, *or*, a griffon segreant, *gules*, which are the arms of Robin ab Gruffydd Goch, Lord of Rhôs and Rhufoniog. My reason for making that statement was that Mr. Hughes signed all the Deeds and Documents that I have seen of his, and sealed them with a seal bearing *or*, a griffin segreant, *gules*, which led me to suppose that he was of the family of the Hugheses of Cefn y Garlleg, who descended from Gruffydd Goch ; and it was not until Mr. Thomas Taylor Griffith of Pennant y Belan most kindly lent me his valuable *Book of Pedigrees* that I discovered who he really was and to what house he belonged. I have to make you a thousand apologies for causing you to publish these mistakes, but you will now perceive how it was that I gave you wrong information. The late Mr. Jones, Curate of Barmouth, who was a son of Mr. Jones of Esgair Evan, shewed me the Esgair Evan pedigree in manuscript, previous to its being sent to Sir Bernard Burke ; and, to the best of my recollection, he told me that it had been drawn up by the late Rev. Walter Davies of Mechain, and probably from some MSS. in his possession, together with what information the family could give him. Hoping that the Appendix may contain no erroneous statements,

I remain, my dear Hamer, yours very sincerely,

J. Y. WM. LLOYD, K.S.G.

To Edward Hamer, Esq.

LLOYD OF THE BRYN, IN THE PARISH OF HANMER.[1]

IORWERTH FOEL, Lord ⊤ Gwladys,[2] dau. and coheiress of Iorwerth ab Gruf-
of Chirk, Nanheudwy,   fydd ab Heilin of Fron Goch in Mochnant, ab
and Maelor Saesneg,   Meurig ab Ieuan ab Adda ab Cynwrig ab Pasgen,
called by Reynolds   Lord of Cegidfa and Deuddwr. 1. *Sable*, three
"Baro de Halchdyn."   horses' heads erased, *argent*. 2. *Argent*, a chevron *sable*, inter three Cornish choughs, each with
a spot of *ermine* in their bills, ppr.

Gruffydd of Maelor ⊤ Gwerfyl, dau. and coheiress of Madog ap Meredydd ab
Saesneg.   Llewelyn Fychan ab Llewelyn ab Owain Fychan ab
Owain, Lord of Mechain Is y Coed, second son of
Madog ab Meredydd, Prince of Powys Fadog. *Ar-*
gent, a lion rampant *sable*, in a border indented *gules*.
Gwerfyl was heiress of Aber Tanad and Treflodwel.
Her elegy was composed by Gutto 'r Glyn.

Madog Lloyd of ⊤ Catherine, dau. of Owain Barton of Cheshire, first wife.
Is y Coed.[3]

David Lloyd of ⊤ Alice, dau. of Bleddyn ab Einion Fychan ab Einion ab
Is y Coed.   Llewelyn of Ystrad Alun, ab Cadwgan Ddu ab Cadwgan
Goch ab Y Gwion ab Ithel Felyn, Lord of Ial
and Ystrad Alun. *Sable*, on a chev, inter three goats
heads erased *or*, three trefoils of the field.

a

---

[1] The parish of Hanmer contains six townships, Hanmer, Bettisfield,
Bronington, Ty Broughton, Willington, and Halchdyn.

[2] Gwladys was buried in Hanmer church, where her tomb yet remains
with this inscription:—HIC JACET WLADYS VXOR IERWERTH VOYL. ORATE,
P. EA.," round the verge of the coffin lid. Within the inscription is a very
fine floriated cross, almost identical with that described by Camden, i, 12,
as being at St. Buriens in Cornwall (Rev. M. H. Lee, vicar of Hanmer).

[3] Is y Coed is a manor partly in Maelor Gymraeg and partly in Maelor
Saesneg in the parish of Malpas.

a

Ienkyn Lloyd of ⊤ . . . . , dau. of Maurice Yonge of Bryn Iorcyn in the
Is y Coed. | parish of Llanestyn in Yr Hob, ab Ienkyn Yonge ab
| Morgan Yonge ab Iorwerth ab Morgan of Maelor
| Saesneg, third son of Iorwerth Foel, Lord of Chirk.

David Lloyd of ⊤ Gwen, dau. and heiress of John Lloyd ab Tomlin Lloyd of
Is y Coed. | Oswestry, second son of Madog Lloyd of Llwyn y Maen,
| lineally descended from Meurig Lloyd, who became pos-
| sessed of Llwyn y Maen and Llanfordaf by his marriage
| with Agnes, dau. and coheiress of Ieuaf Fychan of Llwyn
| y Maen and Llanfordaf, Constable of Knockyn Castle,
| son of Ieuaf ab Cuhelyn ab Rhun ab Einion Efell, Lord of
| Cynllaith. *Argent*, an eagle displayed with two necks,
| *sable*, for Meurig Llwyd.

John Lloyd of ⊤ Alice, dau. of Randle Lloyd ab Gruffydd Lloyd of Tal y
the Bryn in | Wern, ab Madog Lloyd of Willington, ab David Lloyd of
Halchdyn. | Is y Coed, ab Madog Lloyd ab Gruffydd ab Iorwerth Foel.

Robert Lloyd of the ⊤ Elen, dau. of David Lloyd of Plas yn Ial, seventh son
Bryn, one of the | of Elissau, second son of Gruffydd ab Einion ab
guard to Queen | Gruffydd ab Llewelyn ab Cynwrig ab Osbern Wyd-
Elizabeth, *ob.* A D. | del of Cors y Gedol. *Ermine*, a salier *gules*, a cres-
1589. Buried at | cent *or* for difference. The mother of Elen was
Hanmer, March | Gwenhwyfar, dau. of Richard Lloyd ab Robert
11th, 1589. | Lloyd of Llwyn y Maen.

Robert Lloyd of ⊤ Margaret, dau. and heiress   Dorothy, *ux.* Thomas Lloyd
the Bryn. | of Robert Sefton of Mol-   of Plas Uwch y Clawdd in
| lington, co. Chester.   the parish of Rhiwfabon.

Luke Lloyd of ⊤ Catherine. dau. of Thomas Whitley of Aston, in the parish
the Bryn, | of Hawarden in Merffordd, *argent*, on a chief *gules*, three
bapt. Oct. | garbs *or*, and Dorothy, his wife, dau. of Thomas Ravens-
22, A.D. 1608; | croft of Bretton in the same parish, ab George Ravens-
ob. Mar. 31, | croft, son and heir (by Catherine his wife, third dau. of
A.D. 1695, | Richard Grosvenor of Eaton, co. Chester). of Thomas
aged 86. | Ravenscroft ab George Ravenscroft ab Ralph Ravenscroft
| ab Harri Ravenscroft, and . . . . his wife, dau. and sole
| heir of Ralph Holland of Bretton and Rose his wife, dau.
| and heiress of John Skeffington of Bretton.

Luke Lloyd ⊤ Esther, dau. of James Betton of Shrewsbury, D.D., which lady
of the | (having eventually survived her two brothers and all her
Bryn. | sisters, with her nephew, James Betton and his sister, the
| children of her eldest brother, James) became the sole heir
| of this branch of the Betton family. *Argent*, two pales
| *sable*, each charged with three crosslets, fitchee *or*.

| 1st coheir. | 2nd coheir.
Catherine Lloyd, heiress of   Sarah Lloyd, married to Samuel Lloyd of
the Bryn, married Thos.   Plâs Madog, Esq., ancestor of the Che-
Kenyon of Peel Hall, co.   valier Lloyd of Clochfaen and Plâs Mad-
Lancaster, Esq., ances-   og, Knight of the Order of St. Gregory
tor of the Lords Kenyon.   the Great. Mrs. Lloyd died at Plâs
   Madog, and was buried at Rhiwfabon,
   June 7, A.D. 1699.

Philip Henry thus alludes to the death of Luke Lloyd the elder :—

"Luke Lloyd, Esq., of the Bryn, in Hanmer parish, my aged and worthy friend, finished his course with joy, March 31, 1695, being Lord's Day. He was in the 87th year of his age, and had been married almost 69 years to his pious wife (a daughter of Mr. Whitley of Aston), of the same age, who still survives him. He was the glory of the little congregation, the top branch in all respects of our small vine, and my friend indeed. When he made his will, under the subscription of his name he wrote, Job xxx, 25, 26, 27.

"Luke Lloyd had been in his youth a staunch Cromwellite, and had served with some distinction in the Revolutionary war.[1] His sword is kept at Gredington. The carved oak pulpit in Hanmer church is noticed by the Duke of Beaufort in 1684, bearing these inscriptions in gold letters, 'X^{tus} est Agnus Dei qui tollit peccata mundi.' 'Be swifte to heare.' 'Take heed how ye heare,' and the name 'IESUS,' with the date of its being given, 1627. The story told about it is that Luke Lloyd forbad the clergyman of that day praying for the king, and when he persisted, threatened him with his stick. As compensation for this brawling in church he offered, and gave the pulpit.[2]

"A.D. 1666, Aug. 15. Mr. Luke Lloyd, jun., indited at the assizes at Flint for disturbing Mr. H(ylton), vicar of Hanmer, in the time of the administration of ye Lord's Supper. Witnesse sworn deposed that Mr. H(ylton) refusing to give him the sacrament in his pew, as he had been used to do, after the blessing was pronounced, and the people dismissed and gone, he came up to him to know the reason, but that Mr. H. and some few of his friends were then at the table, eating and drinking what was left of the consecrated elements; which (being appointed reverently to be done by the rubrick) the judge declared to be part of the sacrament, though the clerk deposed that Mr. H. was talking with R. E. when Mr. Lloyd came up to him. The jury brought him in not guilty, but were sent out again by the judge, and the second time brought him in guilty, and he was fined."[3]

In Sir John Hanmer's *Memorials of Hanmer Parish*, p. 57, there is a letter from Sir Thomas Hanmer to Sir Job (Judge) Charleton on the subject, March 12, 1665.

---

[1] *Life of Lord Kenyon*, by G. K.
[2] Rev. H. M. Lee, Vicar of Hanmer.
[3] Philip Henry's MSS.

The following is the inscription on the tomb of Luke Lloyd :—

"Here lyeth the body of Luke Lloyd of the Bryn, gent., and Katherine his wife, who lived in the marriage state together 68 years. He died the thirty-first day of March, 1695, being 86. She died January 12, 1701, aged 91."

This branch of the Lloyd family were settled in Is y Coed before they came to the Bryn, and Philip Henry bought from them Eastwick's tenement, now belonging to Jos. H. Lee, Esq.[1]

The following inscription is likewise in Hanmer Church :—

"Here lies in peace Mary, the wife of Roger Kenyon of Cefn, daughter and heiress of Edward Lloyd of Pen y lan, Esq., by Mary, daughter and coheiress of Edward Lloyd of Plas Madoc, Esq. She was great niece of Ellis Lloyd of Pen y lan, Esq., and to William Lloyd, Lord Bishop of Norwich, one of those prelates who, having sworn fidelity to King James II, refused taking the oath to his successor, choosing rather to be deprived of his bishopric than let go his integrity.

"Filial piety, connubial affection, parental tenderness, a steady attachment to her friends and benevolence to all, were eminently united in her character. She died in childbed, leaving her disconsolate husband, three sons, and two daughters, Feb. 4, A.D. 1781, aged 30."

---

[1] Rev. Matthew Henry Lee.

Y BERTH.   See page 285.

———

DAVID LLOYD, of Berth, was son of Thomas, son of
Tudor, second son of Robert of Pentre Cuhelyn in
Llanfair Dyffryn Clwyd, whither he and his brother
Edward had migrated (temp. Henry VII.) from Pentre
Cuhelyn in Llangollen, in the lordship of Chirk,[1] where
their ancestor, Cuhelyn, third son of Tudor-ab-Rhys
Sais, fourth in descent from Tudor Trevor, through his
second son, Lluddoccaf, had inherited lands from his
father.[2] The last-named Pentre Cuhelyn is said to
have been recently a farm, the ruins of which are still
extant, on the Pengwern estate in the parish of
Llangollen.[3] Tudor, the grandfather of David, had an
elder brother, Gruffydd of Pentre Cuhelyn, who married Catherine, daughter of William ab Gruffydd ab
Rhys ab Tudor, by whom he had two sons, Ieuan of
Pentre Cuhelyn, in Llanfair Dyffryn Clwyd, and Simon,
and a daughter named Angharad or Gwenllian, who
married Lewis, son of Sir Evan Lloyd, Kt. of Bodidris

---

[1] *Cae Cyriog MS.*
[2] *Harl. MS.*, 2299 ; *Add. MS.*, 9864-5.
[3] " Byegones ", in *Oswestry Advertiser*, August 1873.

in Iâl.[1] Simon had a son named Ieuan, of whom no further mention is made. Ieuan of Pentre Cuhelyn married Margaret, daughter of Rowland ab John ab Ithel,[2] by whom he had a son, Hugh Lloyd of Pentre Cuhelyn in Llanfair Dyffryn Clwyd, who left an only daughter, Lowry, the heiress of that place.[3] On whom this lady bestowed her hand and fortune the pedigree does not say, but ends abruptly with the name of her son, John Matthews, living 1667. This Pentre Cuhelyn is now a farm on the Berth estate, but it does not appear when or how it became so.

Among the family deeds is one " made between David Lloyd ap Thomas, of the Parish of Llanbedr in the county of Denbigh, gentleman, and Edward ap Harry of Garthkynan, in the said county, gentleman, of the one part, and Edward ap John ab David of Lloyneth (Llwynedd) and Riscoke (Rhyscog) in the said county of Denbigh, gentleman, and Edward ap John Lloyd of Llanrudd in the said county, gentleman, of the other part covenanting for a recovery to be suffered " before John Thelwall, Esquier, Steward of the said Lordshippe or Manor of Lloyneth and Ryscocke or his Deputie," for the conveyance of a messuage or tenement, then inhabited by Edward ap John to David Lloyd ap Thomas and Edward ap Harri for the use of the said Edward ap John. The deed bears the date of 20th December, 1609, 6th James I.

According to Harleian MS. No. 2299, David Lloyd was married to Elizabeth, daughter of Thomas Lloyd of Llangwyfan, Denbighshire. But in the pedigree of the Lloyds of Llangwyfan, in Add. MSS., 9864, fol. 4, she was the fourth daughter of Edward Lloyd of Llangwyfan and his wife Mary, daughter of Ieuan Wyn ab Cadwalader of Voelas. In Llangwyfan Churchyard is a raised monument of this family in freestone, bear-

---

[1] Robert Vaughan's (of Hengwrt) *Book of Pedigrees*, in Peniarth Library.

[2] Gruffydd Hiraethog's do in do.

[3] *Cae Cyriog MS.*, in possession of Dr. Griffiths.

ing the following inscriptions :—1. "Anno Domini, 1615. Ego Thomas Lloyd in domo dormivi XXVII Decemb : ao : supra sculpt : cujus corpus supter (sic) hunc lapidem a. h. sepultum ao ejus ætatis [illegible."]

2. "Hic etiam reponuntur reliqua Edward Lloyd de Llangwyfan Gener : qui extremum confecit diem Martii quinto Anno Domini 1660. Ætatis suæ 43 (or 48)."

3. "Here lyeth the Body of Edward Lloyd, son and heir apparant of Thomas Lloyd, of Llangwyfan, gent., who married Elizabeth, daughter of John Madockes, gent., by Jane his wife, heiresse of Vron Iw, who dyed without issue at Ty Gwyn in Llanhychon ous (sic for house) and rens (sic) Anno Domini, 1630, Ætatis suæ 24."

After the erection of the new church at Llanbedr, some inscribed tombstones of the Berth family in the old church were discovered by the removal of the stone steps in front of the Communion Table. On the oldest of these (of freestone) is this inscription :— "Here lieth the Bodi of David Lloyd, Gent. Buried the seaventh (sic) Day of July, Anno Dom. 1620."

David Lloyd was succeeded by his son, THOMAS LLOYD, of Berth, of whose marriage nothing is recorded in the pedigrees. He had a daughter named Anne, who, some years previous to 1639, became the wife of Thomas Edwards, Esq., of Brynpolin, in the parish of St. Asaph, descended from Rhodri Mawr, and from Hedd Molwynog, chief of one of the fifteen noble tribes of North Wales. Her husband died on the 17th December, 1663, at Llandaff, and is buried in the Cathedral there. Her son, Richard Edwards, became possessed of the estate of Old Court, in the county of Wicklow, in right of his wife, Elizabeth Kynaston, daughter and heiress of Colonel John Kynaston, who had served against the king in an expedition for the reduction of North Wales to the obedience of the Parliament, and captured Rhyddlau Castle, of which he became Governor. On the 7th June, 1647, he landed in Ireland from Chester, with his Welsh Regiment of Foot, "after four days' plying at sea," accompanying the Commissioners from the Parliament, who had come to treat with the Marquis of Ormond, the Lord Lieutenant, for the surrender of Dublin. After his death in 1649, a grant of land, of which Old Court formed a portion, was made to his widow by Oliver Cromwell.[1] In the Churchyard of Llanbedr is a tomb with the following inscription :—" Underneath lie the remains of John Brabazon, second son of John Edward Edwardes, of Old Court, county Wicklow, Kingdom of Ireland, Esq., of a family originating from this Vale. He died 23rd September, 1793, aged eleven years." Thomas Lloyd was buried at Llanbedr in February, 1648, as appears from a second inscription on his father's tombstone, cut so as to face the first : " —Here lieth the body of Thomas Lloyd, Gent. Buried the second day of February, Anne Dom., 1648. He left also a son."

JOHN LLOYD of Berth, of whose marriage also no record has been found. From extracts made from the parish registers, it appears that he died about three years before his father, on the 17th April, 1645. He had a family of five daughters, viz., Elizabeth, born 1628, died 1656, married to John Conway, by whom she had a daughter, Lucy, born 1655; Anna, born 1633; Katherine, born 1634, died 1641. Maria, born 1639; Jane, born and died 1642, and a second Jane, born 1644; and five sons, viz., Thomas, born and died 1642; Edward, born 1631; Trevor, born 1635, died 1641; Simon, born 1637, died 1653; John, born 1640. He was succeeded by his eldest surviving son,

EDWARD LLOYD, of Berth, who would seem from the mention made of the name in his son's marriage settlement, to have married a lady named Margaret ——, living a widow in 1680. His family consisted of four daughters, Maria, born 1654, died 1664, buried January 25th, at Llannefydd; Elizabeth and Magdalene

---

[1] Burke's *Landed Gentry*, ed. 1863.

(twins), born and died 1658 ; Martha, born 1661 ; and
three sons, viz., John, born 1655 ; Trevor, born 1657 ;
David, born 1659.   The date of his death does not
appear from the register, but he must have been living
in 1660.   His eldest son, JOHN LLOYD, of Berth,
married (in 1680) Elizabeth, daughter of —— and Alice
Mostyn, of Hendrefegillt, county Flint, as appears
from a deed in which a capital messuage called " Y
Berth " is settled upon her.   She died in 1689.   2ndly,
Elizabeth ——, died in 1700.   He had six daughters,
three of whom, Alice, born 1685, died 1694 ; Elizabeth,
born and died 1700 ; and Lettice, born 1687, died in
infancy ; Jane, her twin sister, born 1687 ; Catherine,
born 1684 ; and Sidney, born 1689 ; and two sons,
Robert, the younger, born 1686, and the elder, baptized January 1681, his successor, viz., EDWARD LLOYD,
of Berth, married to Anne, eldest daughter of Maurice
Lewis, Esq., of Trysglwyn (or Treslwyn) in Anglesey, as
inscribed in her tombstone, in the old Church of
Llanbedr :—" Here lyes interred Anne Lloyd, of Berth,
widow and relict of Edward Lloyd, Esq., who dyed on
the 17th January, 1746, aged 58.   She was," &c., as
above.   Below the inscription is a coat of arms, apparently *ermine*, a lion rampant *arg.* crest, a unicorn's
head within a coronet, over a helmet.   Their family
consisted of two daughters, Susanna (if not of a previous generation, her baptism not being registered) died
7th November, 1706 ; and Elizabeth, born 1709, living
in 1741, and five sons.   Edward, the eldest son, died
a few months after his father, and was buried in the
same grave with him in the aisle.   Their tombstone is
inscribed :—" Here lyes (*sic*) interred the bodyes of
of Edward Lloyd, the father, and Edward Lloyd, the
sone, Both of Berth, who dyed the one on the 2nd day
of January, 1721, aged 44, and the other on the 7th day
of October, 1722, aged 14."   David, the third son, born
1711, is described in a deed, dated 20th September,

1 This place is mentioned in the Record of Carnarvon, *temp.*
Edward I.

1770, as of Llany Myneich, county Montgomery, clerk, and one of the Trustees named in his brother Hugh Lloyd's will; Trevor, born and died 1713; Maurice, born 1714; Robert, born 1716. He was succeeded by his eldest surviving son

HUGH LLOYD, of Berth and of Furnival's Inn, married to Ursula, second daughter of Howel Lloyd, Esq., of Wigfair, county Flint, by his wife Phoebe, second daughter of Hedd Lloyd, Esq., of Havod Unos, by whom he had six sons :—1, John, born 1743, died 1744, buried in Chester Cathedral; 2, Edward, born 1744, died 1744; 3, John, of whom presently; 4, Thomas, born 1746, living in 1766, went to sea; 5, Howel, born 1747, went to sea in 1761, living in 1768; 6, Hedd, born 1749, settled in Chester; and two daughters, 1, Ursula, born 1751, died 1751; 2, Phoebe, born 1754, married in 1790 to the Hon. John Campbell, Lord Stonefield, in Argyleshire, one of H.M.'s Justices of the Court of Session in Scotland. Hugh Lloyd was buried in the old Church of Llanbedr, where, on a stone in the aisle is inscribed :—" Here also lyes the body of Hugh Lloyd, gent., who became the eldest son of the above Edward and Anne Lloyd, and dyed in September, 1756, leaving John Lloyd, his eldest son, and other children." On the tombstone of Anne Lloyd is also inscribed :—" Here lie the remains of Yrsula Lloyd, of Berth, Esq. She died the 28th September, 1795, aged 75." That she was a handsome old lady appears from a picture of her at Rhagatt, bearing a strong family likeness to some of her descendants. Was succeeded by his eldest surviving son

JOHN LLOYD, of Berth, of Gray's Inn and the Middle Temple, a King's Counsel, and Chief Justice of the Caermarthenshire Circuit, of whom a short account is given in Williams' ' Eminent Welshmen.' He married Margeret, youngest daughter of Josiah Morrall, Esq., of Plas Iolyn, county Salop, by Margaret, his wife, daughter of John Lloyd, Esq., of Pontriffith. In her marriage settlement she is described as Margaret

Morrall, of Pengwern, Spinster, niece of Edward Lloyd of Pengwern, who would seem to have been also her guardian, as her fortune of £3,500 was paid by him. Judge Lloyd was educated at Ruthin School, and was distinguished as well by the strength of his memory as by the soundness of his judgment. His extensive practice enabled him to add considerably to the family property by the purchase of the Iâl,[1] Rhagatt and Llanynys estates. He was also an excellent sportsman, and a tree is still shown in which a hare was once seen to take refuge from the pursuit of his harriers. When another was observed to be sinking after a long chase, he is said to have exclaimed—" Nothing can save her now but a Cardiganshire jury !" The issue of his marriage was two daughters, Margaret, died at Cheltenham, unmarried, A.D. 1841, and is buried there at the Parish Church. She was possessed of great mental capacity, and a sparkling humour which never failed her, despite a distressing asthma, from which she suffered during the greater part of her life. She also delighted in fly-fishing, and was an excellent horsewoman, often traversing the Berwyn Hills from Bodvach in Montgomeryshire, where in her early days she resided, to visit her brother's family at Rhagatt ; 2, Francis, married to Richard Watkin Price, Esq., of Rhiwlas, co. Merioneth ; and two sons, John, the younger, a captain in the Royal Navy, was lost at sea 1814. Judge Lloyd died on the 9th September, 1806, and was succeeded by his elder son,

EDWARD LLOYD, of Berth, county Denbigh, and Rhagatt, county Merioneth, born 1778, was educated at Westminster School, and at Brazenose College, Oxford. He was called to the Bar, and was for fifty years Chairman of Quarter Sessions for the latter county. His portrait, by Eddis, R.A., purchased by

[1] Among the farms purchased in Iâl was Hafod yr Abad, in the township of Maes yr Ychain, in the parish of Llandysilio. This place is situate at the foot of the western slope of Rhiwfelyn, on the brook called Nant Morwynion. The whole township of Maes yr Ychain belonged to the monastery of Valle Crucis.

public subscription, in recognition of his services, is in
the County Hall of Dolgelly.   Mr. Lloyd was possessed
of considerable literary acquirements, and was distinguished by his wit and humour in society.   He was
also an excellent sportsman, and possessed of a breed
of greyhounds highly prized by coursers for their excellence and fleetness.   He married Francis, daughter
(by Frances, daughter of Sir Richard Perryn, Knight,
Baron of the Exchequer) of John Edward Madocks, of
Vron Iw, Esq., descended from Sir Robert Pounderling,
Knight, Constable of Dyserth Castle, county Flint,
temp. Edward II, whose monument is in Tremeirchion
Church, and from Edward I, King of England, through
Emma (or Ermin) daughter of Thomas Puleston, of
Picill, Esq. (Pickhill) married to David Madocks, Esq.,
of Vron Iw, living in 1676, son of John Madocks, of
Bodffari, Esq., married to Jane Williams, heiress of
Vron Iw, descended from Marchweithian, chief of one of
the fifteen noble tribes of North Wales.   Seventeen
children were the issue of this marriage, of whom
eleven were daughters, viz. :—Francis Margaret, born
Oct. 20, 1810, died 1857, married to Sir Rober Wil-
liames Vaughan, of Nannau, county Merioneth, Bart.,
who died without issue in 1858 ; 2, Margaret Charlotte,
born 1813, died 1815 ; 3, Charlotte Ursula, born May
30, 1815, died Dec. 18, 1815 ; 4. Mary Charlotte,
born January 23, 1819, unmarried ; 5, Charlotte, born
February 20, 1820, married to Richard John Price, of
Rhiwlas, county Merioneth, Esq., who died 1842 ; 6,
Harriet, born 1821, died 1825 ; 7, Jane Margaret, born
August 30, 1822, married to the Ven. Henry P.
Ffoulkes, Archdeacon of Montgomery ; 8, Eliza Black-
burn, born January 6th, 1824, married to Meredith
Vibart, Esq., late Captain, E. I. C. S., and Adjutant of
Edinburgh Volunteer Artillery ; 9, Harriet, born July
25, 1826; 10, Ursula, born Oct. 18, 1827, died February
2, 1828 ; 11, Julia Anne, born 1831, died 1841 ; and six
sons—1, John, born Sept. 25, 1811, of whom presently ;
2, Edward (married to M., daughter of John Madocks,

of Glan y Wern and Vron Iw, Esq., M.P. for the Denbigh
Boroughs) born Oct. 26, 1812, died 1864, leaving a
daughter, Sophia, and a son, Edward, of whom presently ; 3, Howel William, born Aug. 27th, 1816, married to Eliza Anne, daughter of George Wilson, of
Nutley and Brighton, county Sussex, Esq., by his wife,
Elizabeth Smallpiece, decended from Robert Smallpiece,
of Hockering, in Norfolk, to whom arms were granted
by patent of Queen Elizabeth, in 1574 (*sable*, a chevron
engrailed *argent* between three rosettes of the 2nd,
crest, an eagle with wings erect ppr. (Add MSS. 14297—
179 B.) ; 4, Charles Wynn, born Nov. 30, 1817, died
April 17, 1818 ; 5, Owen, born June 6th, 1825, died
Aug. 20, 1825 ; 6, Charles Owen, born December 23,
1828, fell in action before Moultan, in the East Indies,
Sept. 12th, 1848.   Mr. Lloyd, died Oct. 14th, 1859,
and was succeeded by his eldest son,

JOHN LLOYD, of Berth and Rhagatt, educated at
Westminster, and Christ Church, was an excellent
amateur painter, and also possessed considerable skill in
photography.   He wrote, also, some humorous poetical
pieces.   He married Gertrude Jane Mary, daughter of
Philip Godsal, Esq., of Iscoed, co. Flint, and grand-
daughter of the first Lord Wyndham.   He died without issue, May 22nd, 1865, and is to be succeeded (after
his widow) by his nephew, on his attaining his majority.

Edward Lloyd, a minor, educated at Eton, &c.

On a piece of family plate is a coat of arms, the history of which is unknown, in which the arms of Tudor
Trevor are impaled *argent* a cross flory *gules* between
four Cornish choughs ppr.   On dexter chief a canton
azure.

On a seal belonging to the family are the arms of
Tudor Trevor impaling *gules* a lion rampant reguardent
argent.   Crest, a unicorn's head within a coronet *argent*.
The history of this seal is also unknown.

On another family seal are engraved the arms of Tudor
Trevor only, with a crest, a unicorn's head erased.   Its
history is likewise unknown.

LLANGURIG. (*Wynnstay MS.*)

LLEWELYN, second son of Ieuan ab Gruffydd ab Howel Lloyd of Clochfaen. See p. 49. ⊤ Gwenllian, d. of Ieuan Llwyd ab Howel.

Maurice ⊤ Mallt, d. of Howel Mawddwy ab Gruffydd ab David Goch.[1] Her mother was Janet, d. of Gwilym ab Gruffydd Derwas of Cemmaes.

Rhys ⊤ Margaret, d. of Jenkyn ab Rhys Lloyd of Llangurig, by a daughter and coheir of Rhys ab Llewelyn Goch. See page 235.

Margaret, ux. Lewys ab Ieuan ab Rhys ab Y Bedo of Gwnws.

Maurice ⊤ Elen, d. of Lewys ab Maurice ab Ieuan Fychan of Rhiw Ardden, Llanbadarn.

Gwerfyl Gwyn, d. of David Lloyd ab Thomas ab Owain ab Philip ab Rhydderch, to Gwaethfoed.

Jenkyn ⊤ Tangwystl, d. of Richard ab Maurice Fychan of Trawscoed, co. Cardigan.

Lewys. Margaret. Eliza. Catherine. Jane. Lucy.

Thomas Maurice.

Rhys Maurice.

Jane, ux. Ieuan ab Howel ab Meredydd.

Ieuan Gwynn of Llan y Wared, 1599: on Grand Jury 10 Charles I, 1634. See page 271.

Margaret, d. of Thomas ab John ab Howel.

Jenkyn Maurice, one of Grand Jury, 4 James I, 1606. See page 270.

Elen, d. of David Lloyd ab Jenkyn of Clochfaen.

David, on Grand Jury List, Llanidloes Hundred, 13 Charles II, 1662, but not selected. See page 271.

L L

	a	b	c	d	e	f

[1] See *Cwm yr On*, p. 84.

3 | a	4 | b	5 | c		d	e	f
Thomas, see p. 90.	David, see p. 96.	John, on the Grand Jury, 1505. Sion Ceri addressed an ode to him.	=Honor, d. of Richard Lloyd, Esq, ab Humphrey Lloyd.[1] 37 Elizabeth,	Goleubryd, ux. (1) Gruffyd ab Ieuan, (2) Rhys ab Iohn ab David Goch of Glasgwm.	Tangwystl, ux. Ieuan ab Richard ab Howel ab Richard of Rhaiadr Gwy.	Elen, ux. David ab Ieuan ab Richard ab Matthew ab Gwilym ab Meredydd ab Madog Goch, of Llanidloes. See Glandulas.

Edward.   Thomas.   Mary.   Jane.   Eliza.

GLYN HAFREN IN LLANGURIG.[2]

MAURICE ab Ieuan Lloyd ab David ab Maurice ab Lewys∓Margaret, d. of Ieuan ab David ab Howel ab William.

Ienkyn, on Grand Jury ∔ James I, ∓Mallt, d. of Lewys ab Rhys. 1606. See page 270.   David∓Awdrey, d. of David ab Maurice ab Owain.   Morgan∓Mallt, d. of Cadwaladr ab Thomas ab Llewelyn ab Bedo. See pp. 271-2.

David Ienkin Maurice de Glyn Hafren, on Grand Jury 2nd Charles II, 1650.

[1] Humphrey Lloyd of the Great Haim in Fforden. He married two wives; by the first, who was a daughter of Rhys ab Maurice ab Owain of Aberbechan, he had a son Richard Lloyd. *Lewys Dwnn*, vol. i, page 289; note 6.

[2] *Lewys Dwnn*, vol. i, p. 309.

CYWYDD MARWNAD MR. MORGAN LLOYD[1]
O'R CLOCHFAEN, LLANGURIG.

Och fy awen, oer fy achwyn,
Beth a geni, beth o gŵyn?
Och! weithian Caelan ceula,
Digrif wyf, dwfr ag iâ:
Gwn y bydd glenydd â gwlaw,
A diliw rhwng ei dwy law;
Gwag yw'r plwyf, mwy am y mawl,
Unig iawn, anigonawl;
Adwy a ddaeth, wedi dydd,
Adwy lydan, hyd wledydd,
Adwy am wr oedd dymerus,
Ym mhob llan, ag ymhob llys.
Duw a ddel, a da ddylai
Ebwch hir, a'i fab uwch ai,
Gydâ ei lwydd, i gadw ei le,
O fawl antur, fel ynte.
Torri cyf[2] wna o'r cyfion,
Twrw oer torri gau ffon,
Twrw mawr gwynt,[3] torri 'n un gant,
Torri pen teuau'r Pennant;
Torri angel ymgeledd,
Torri nod glain, torri enaid gwledd.
Poen dorri pan darawyd,
Mawr egin llon, Morgan Lloyd.
Ni thorir aneth[4] arail,

---

[1] The following pedigree illustrates the elegy:—

Richard Morgan of Caelan ⊤ Sarah, d. of John Jones of
in Llanbrynmair.　　　|　Cawg in Llanbrynmair.

Morgan Lloyd, second son of Jenkyn ⊤ Bridget, heiress of Caelan.
Lloyd of Clochfaen,

Rev. Littleton Lloyd, *ob. s. p.*　　Sarah ⊤ Edward Pritchard of Ceniarth.

Rowland Pritchard of Caelan.

For earlier portion see p. 54.
[2] For "cyff", *metri gratiâ.*
[3] So I read for "mam gwedd" in the MS., but the line is corrupt, having a syllable in excess.
[4] Aneth, for "annedd", *metri gratiâ.*

Is derm ei oes dro mo'i ail;
Hydd araf, call rhoi ced,
Llew gwrol, llaw agored;
Lluniwr hedd, yn llenwi rhad,
Llawen cywrain, llawn cariad,
Ei fonedd hafaidd hyfryd,
Os da barch, er ys dyddiau byd;
Trefor had, trwy fawrhydi,
Iarll Henfordd, briffordd ei bri;
O hil Fadog friw, enwog fraith,
Danwr hael, yn dwyn rheolaith,
Hên ben haeddol boneddig,
A'i brig ar Gurig i gyd.
Yna'r hen dad dyladwy,
Bodd plaid, a bioedd y plwyf;
Imp o rinwedd yw'r anian
Enwog Llwyd,[1] or Berth-lwyd lân.
Hen anrhydedd yn rhedeg
O fonedd wlad Wynedd deg.
Llin Hywel at rhyfel tref,
Gwych a mwythus, goch a Mathef.
Mwyna' rhyw, yn mynnu' r'hol,
Da, diddig, a dedwyddol.
Ochi i'w lys boenus beunydd,
Fod heno rô ar ei rudd,
Ai roddi yn wr iraidd oed
Y'nghul arch, y'nghanol oed;
Pa alar, hap, o heli,
O gŵyn fawr a ganafi,
I gysuro ei gû seren,
Rywiog, wych, ei gwraig wen?
Daw un a'i dwyn i anerch
I'w guaf fab, ag i'w ferch,
A'r ifangc, un wyr o fun,
. . .   ei dad yma .[2]

. . . .
Mae'r cerain', mawr eu cariad,
Yn rhoi llef, yn'r holl wlad;
Noeth yw'r plwyf ei weniaith plaid,
Pan dynai Duw ei enaid.
Da fyddai mewn defosiwn,
Pa ddygai Dduw heddyw hwn?
Dwyn gweiniaid, trueiniaid, tro,

---

[1] Engioed in MS.   [2] Probably, ymofyn.

Yn gafod gydag efo.
Trwm weled llymed pob llys
Amdano, wyneb daionus.
Hael a fu yn ei dy da,
Ag o'i fîr, ag o'i fara;
Trugarog, arlwyog lys,
A chu erioed, a chariadus.
Duw a godo, llê ei grodwyd,
Etto yn llwyr Littleton Llwyd,
A Sarah, hyd yn des hir ach,
Hir oes bery Rees Lloyd bach.
O ran cyweirio, 'r un cariad,
I'r ail lô, ar ôl y tad,
Amynedd am ei enaid,
Ym mhob plwyf, ag ym mhob plaid,
Ei geraint, a braint ei brig,
O Gorwen i Langurig;
A hir oes heb loes, heb ludd,
A llu wyn a llawenydd,
A gras Duw yn eirias don,
I'w plant hwy, ac i'w hwyrion.
Mil seithgant, dwesant,[1] a dwy,
Brudd oedd a barodd adwy:
Rhoi pen mwyn mewn pwn meini,
Oni fo lais nefol lu:
"Cod, fwyn wr, cwyd i fyny!"

DAFYDD MANUEL, 1702.

---

[1] For "dywedant".

ELEGY ON MR. MORGAN LLOYD OF THE CLOCHFAEN, LLANGURIG.

By David Manuel, 1702.

Alas, my Muse! woeful is my wail,
What sorrowful song shalt thou sing?
Curdled, alas, is Ceulan's water
With ice, and yet I am merry!
Assuredly her banks will be hereafter
In flood between their two sides.
Empty is the parish, henceforth, of praise,
All desolate, and not to be comforted;
From that day forth a gap is made,
A wide gap, o'er all the land;
A gap made by a man of perfect temper,
In every village, and in every mansion.
May God bring,—well would it requite
Our long groaning—his son to mount into
And keep his place, with his prosperity,
With a reputation like his for boldness.
Sadly is it felt that the staff of the just
Should be broken in twain like a bent stick;
There is a stir as of a strong wind
For in one are cut off a hundred;
Cut off is the head of the house of Pennant,
Cut off is its Guardian Angel,
Cut off is its primest jewel, cut off is the soul of
 the banquet.
Painful was the blow, when struck down
Was Morgan Lloyd, the strong yet gentle sapling!
The support of the dwelling, who succeeds him,
Shall not be cut off ere his course be run;
A gentle Hart is he, who well knows how to
 give gifts,
A Lion brave and open-handed,
An ensuer of peace, one who freely fills,

Merry, ingenious, full of affection,
In nobleness cheerful, like summer,
Worthy of respect, if any such ever has been.
A scion of the majestic line of Trevor,
Earl of Hereford, chiefest in honour;
Of the race of Madog Danwr of varied fame,
Liberal, and bearing rule,
As the ancient head of a noble stock,
With his descendants, over all Curig's Land.
Then the ancient meritorious sire,
By service done to his cause, acquired the parish.
By nature ever a virtuous graft upon these
Are the Lloyds of fair Berth Lwyd.
Their ancient honour flows
From the stock of the land of fair Gwynedd,[1]
Of the line of Howel, a warlike house,
Fair and delicate, red as Mathew,
A most courteous race, willing to be questioned,
Good, without anger, and cheerful.
The mansion will mourn with daily pain,
That the gravel this night is on his cheek.
That he, a man of vigorous age,
In the prime of life, is laid in the narrow chest;
What lament—haply with salt tears—
What loud plaint shall I sing,
To console the gentle star,
His fair wife, kindly and noble?
One shall come, and bring her to salute
Her dearest son, and his daughter,
And her young and only grandson,
. . .   his father.
. . . .

The relatives, deep is their affection,
Are uttering a cry in all the land;
The parish was bereft of his winning speech,
When his soul was taken by God.
Passing devout was he,

---

[1] The Lloyds of Berth Lwyd were descended in the male line through Trahaiarn, Lord of Garthmael, from Llewelyn Eurdorchog, Lord of Iâl and Ystrad Alun, which were anciently in Powys Fadôg; but in the reign of Henry VIII they were added to the counties of Denbigh and Flint, which were in Gwynedd. This family descended by heirs female from Madog Danwr, and assumed his arms.

Why did God take him to-day ?
Many a time would he take in a shower
The weak and the wretched with him.[1]
'Tis heavy to behold how mournful is every
    mansion
For him, with his kindly countenance.
Liberal has he been, in his good house,
Of his beer as well as his bread ;
A charitable, well-provided mansion,
And one ever liberal and compassionate.
May God still, on the spot where he was interred,
Highly honour Littleton Lloyd,
And Sarah, proportionately to their long descent.
And long be the life of the little Rees Lloyd,
And may he cultivate the same affection ·
To the second generation, after his father.
For his soul let there be patience
In every parish, and in every society
Of his relatives, and those he exalted,
From Corwen even to Llangurig.
And long be their life, without hurt or hindrance,
And a host be it blest with gladness ;
And may the grace of God, in waves of fire,
Descend on his children and grandchildren.
One thousand seven hundred and two, they say,
Was the sorrowful year that made the gap,
When 'neath a pile of stones was placed his
    gentle head, to remain
Till the voice of the heavenly host shall come :—
" Arise, thou gentle man, and mount aloft !"

---

[1] *I.e.*, Would give them a lift in his carriage.

THE LEGEND OF ST. CURIG.

At a period of great antiquity, not later than, and possibly anterior to, the seventh century, a person of foreign appearance, and habited in the garb of a pilgrim, disembarked from a ship that had brought him to a spot near to that on which stands the modern town of Aberystwyth. He tarried not at the point of landing, in the vale of the Ystwyth river,—then, doubtless, a tangled wild of marsh and thicket to the water's edge,—but straightway bent his steps up the steep and pathless ascent towards the heights of Plinlimmon. Reaching at length the summit, and weary with his walk, he sat on a rock, and scanning the surrounding prospect, he espied on the bank of the Wye a spot which he deemed eligible for his future resting-place. There, the work doubtless of his own hands, uprose first a humble hermitage and chapel, and afterwards a church, which, though not of spacious dimensions, became celebrated for the beauty of its architecture and the elegant carving and design of its massive oaken roof. The rock whereon the pilgrim sat bears to this day the name of "Eisteddfa Gurig", or Curig's Seat. The church on Plinlimmon, adjacent to the highest point of the macadamised mail-road from Aberystwyth to Hereford, still bears testimony to its founder by its name of "Llangurig," the Church of St. Curig. Moreover, a crozier or pastoral staff, stated by Giraldus to have belonged to him, and to have been endowed with a supernatural healing power, was for centuries preserved with a loving veneration for his memory in the church of St. Harmon's on the Radnorshire border : a proof that he became a bishop (perhaps of Llanbadarn Fawr, hard by the scene of his landing), or else the abbot of a religious community, which in that case must have been founded by himself.

Such is the legend of Curig Lwyd, which has led to

M M

the hypothesis adopted by Professor Rees, that he was not only the original founder of the church of Llangurig, but also its patron saint,—an hypothesis to which a certain additional colour would be given by the traditional appellation of "Curig Lwyd", or "the Blessed", by which he was popularly known. A wider investigation, however, of the subject will lead unavoidably to the inference that the Professor, critically accurate and cautious as he usually is in his surmises, was somewhat premature in thus determining the question ; and this is the more surprising inasmuch as he has himself furnished us with a list of churches in Wales, the dedicatory titles of which alone might have led him to doubt the soundness of such a conclusion. In his *Essay on the Welsh Saints*[1] he tells us that the churches of *Llanilid a Churig*, Glamorganshire, and *Capel Curig*, Caernarvonshire, are dedicated to Juliet and Curig together ; and that Juliet is also the saint of Llanilid Chapel, under Defynog, Brecknockshire. There are also two other churches, those, namely, of Porth Curig, Glamorganshire, and Eglwys Fair a Churig, Carmarthenshire, of which the Professor states that it is uncertain to whom they are dedicated. The festival of Juliet and Cyrique, he adds, is June 16th. If these churches were dedicated to the martyr St. Cyricus or Quiricus, whether jointly or otherwise with his mother Juliet, the probability would lie, *primâ facie*, in favour of the hypothesis that Llangurig was so too. Nor is there anything, in fact, to oppose to it, save the existence of the legend, and the analogy of other churches in Wales believed to have derived their names from those who respectively founded them, and who, from that act alone, were afterwards, in the popular estimation, honoured with the title of Saints. In such a case, moreover, it would appear not a little remarkable that one bearing the name of the infant martyr should have landed on our island, and have devoted the remainder of his life in it to the special service of religion in so wild and remote

[1] Page 307, and note, p. 82.

a region therein, unless, indeed, a positive connection existed between the peculiar devotion introduced by him and the saint whose name he bore, and under whose patronage he may have held himself to be in virtue of that name: an early instance, perhaps, of a practice which gradually became general in the Church. That this was really the case will appear highly probable from a comparison of the history of the saint and of his martyrdom with such notices as have come down to us of the *cultus* actually rendered to him in Wales during subsequent centuries; and if we add to this the narrative of the migration, so to speak, of that *cultus* from the eastern to the western churches, the probability will be changed into certainty.

It is stated by Ruinart[1] and by the Bollandists that various "acts" of these saints had been published in ancient times, one of which, included in the list of apocryphal works of Pope Gelasius, is printed by the New Bollandists[2] in Greek and Latin. Another account, believed by them to be genuine, is also to be found there, together with a statement as to its origin, from which it appears that Pope Zosimus (A.D. 417), who had seen an edition of their acts which appeared to him to be spurious, wrote to a bishop of Iconium named Theodorus, requesting to be furnished with such genuine particulars of the martyrdom of SS. Cyricus and Julitta as could then be obtained on the spot where it took place, during the tenth persecution of the Christians under Diocletian, somewhat more than a century before. In the course of his inquiries, Theodorus was referred to an old man who claimed kinship with these saints, and wrote a letter to the Pope addressed "Domino Fratri et Co-episcopo Zosimo", containing a narrative written in a very sober and matter-of-fact style, and free from the numerous extravagances which disfigure the spurious acts. The narrative of the martyrs' sufferings given by the Rev. Alban Butler (*Lives of the Saints*, June 16th) is abridged from the bishop's letter, which is printed in

---

[1] Ed. Ratisbon, 1869.   [2] Ed. Paris, 1867.

full by Ruinart and the Bollandists, and is in substance as follows :—" In the year A.D. 305, Julitta, a lady of rank and property, left her native city of Iconium in Asia Minor, with her son Cyricus and two maids, to escape the persecution then raging in that city under Diocletian the Roman emperor. She went first to Seleucia, but on finding that Alexander, the governor of that city, was a persecutor, she felt it unsafe to remain there, and proceeded to Tarsus. Here, however, Alexander happened to be at the very time of her arrival ; she had no sooner reached the place, therefore, than she was apprehended and brought before him, together with her infant. Her maids forsook her and fled, while she, to all the governor's queries, made no answer than this :—' I am a Christian.' The governor ordered her to be cruelly scourged with thongs, but, struck with the noble appearance of her child, he resolved to save him, and took him on his knee, endeavouring to soothe him with kisses. The child, however, stretching out his arms towards his mother, cried out after her in the same words, 'I am a Christian,' and, in struggling to be free that he might run to her, scratched the governor's face. The latter, enraged, threw him to the ground from the tribunal, and dashed out his brains against the edge of the steps, so that the whole place was bespattered with his blood. His mother, far from lamenting his death, made thanksgiving to God, as for a happy martyrdom. Then they proceeded to lacerate her sides with hooks, and on her feet they poured scalding pitch. When called upon to sacrifice to the gods, she persisted in answering, ' I do not sacrifice to devils, or to deaf and dumb statues, but I worship Christ, the only-begotten son of God, by whom the Father hath made all things.' Thereupon, the governor ordered that her head should be struck off, and that the body of her child should be thrown into the place where the bodies of malefactors were cast. The remains of both mother and son were afterwards buried secretly, by the two maids, in a field near the city. Subsequently, when peace had been restored to the Church under Constantine the Great, the spot was made known by one of them. Their tombs were visited by a great concourse of the faithful, who vied with each other, as it is related, in striving to secure, each one for himself, a portion of their sacred relics "for a protection and safeguard".

From this time forward the devotion to these holy martyrs spread widely over the East. A panegyric is still extant in their honour, written by Metaphrastes, or more probably by Nicetas the rhetorician, as is supposed, in the ninth century, the facts in which were furnished by Bishop Theodore's letter. Offices in their honour were sanctioned by St. Germanus and Anatolius, Patriarchs of Constantinople, A.D. 449-58, while others are known to have existed at Byzantium and Mauroleum. A complete office, with canon, by Josephus the hymnographer, A.D. 883, contains some verses commencing thus :

Κηρίκον ὑμνῶ σὺν τεκούσῃ προφρόνως Ἰωσὴφ.

St. Joseph speaks of their tomb as being bedewed with the grace of the Holy Spirit, and of cures being wrought there; but is silent as to its locality. The reason for this, as we shall shortly see, was in all probability the circumstance that the bodies themselves had, at a much earlier period, been conveyed away, and treasured up as precious relics in certain churches of the West. The story of their removal is thus given in an ancient MS. discovered at Rome,[1] as related by Henschenius the Bollandist, in his commentary for the 1st May, on the *Life of St. Amator*, a Bishop of Auxerre, who lived from A.D. 344 to 418, and was consecrated A.D. 388. This *Life* is said to have been written A.D. 580.

"After the lapse of many years from their gaining the crown of martyrdom, St. Amator, Bishop of Antissiodorum, accompanied by the most illustrious Savinus,

---

[1] The MS. commences thus : "Incipiunt miracula SS. Quirici et Julittæ, quæ Teterius Sophista, eorum servus, edidit, de corporibus eorum à S. Amatore Antiochiæ repertis."

travelling through the territory of Antioch, by the grace of Christ found their most holy bodies, and on his return brought them, with great devotion, to Gaul. On reaching the city of Autrice (Chartres) he so far yielded to the entreaties of Savinus as to bestow on him one of the boy's arms, which appears to have been deposited in the church at Nevers. The other remains he caused to be entombed a second time in the very house 'where the Bishop, powerful by the glory of his merits, is yet venerated by the faithful'. Whether the city of Antioch visited by St. Amator was that in Pisidia or in Syria, or more probably another of that name, near Tarsus, the scene of the martyrdom, is not stated. From the Nevernais the arm of St. Cyricus was removed by Abbot Hucbald to his monastery of Elno '*in Hannonia*'." [1] In the *Gallican Martyrology*, by Saussaye, it is stated that considerable portions of the relics were distributed among different churches in Gaul, "whereby a great devotion was stirred up everywhere towards the martyrs themselves, so that many churches, monasteries, and other 'trophies' (as they were then called), were erected in their honour. Among them Toulouse, Arles, Carnot, and Auvergne, are specially named. The devotion also extended itself to Spain, where, at Burgos, an office with nine lections is known to have been recited in their honour. In France, Cyricus became known indifferently by the names of St. Cyr and St. Cyrique; and the name of 'Cir Ferthyr', once attached to the site of a ruined chapel in Lleyn, Carnarvonshire, may possibly be a translation of the former." [2]

From the foregoing account it will not be difficult to explain how, in early times, a Gaul inspired with the prevalent devotion to these martyrs may have been called by the name of one of them; may have landed on the coast of Wales, bringing with him, mayhap, a small but treasured portion of the relics in his own

[1] Perhaps St. Amand's in Flanders, of which Hainault is a province.

[2] Rees' *Welsh Saints*, p. 332; *Arch. Camb.*, 4th Ser., v, p. 87.

country esteemed so precious ; may have built in honour of this, his patron saint, a humble chapel, enlarged subsequently into a church, with its monastic establishment adjacent ; and taken precautions for the preservation, after his death, of the memory of the acts and sufferings of one whom he himself held in such tender veneration, by translating some narrative of them in his own possession into the language of the people to whom he had been the means of introducing the knowledge and *cultus*, as saints, of himself and his martyred mother.

That such was actually the fact is not obscurely intimated in several scattered notices which are to be found in the manuscript works of Welsh bards and elsewhere. In a fragmentary poem on St. Curig in the *Llyfr Ceniarth MS.*, a *Book of his Life* is referred to as extant in the author's time. Other fragments of poems in the same MS., by Sion Ceri and by Huw Arwystli, relate also certain circumstances of the martyrdom, in all probability derived from this traditionary biography. And lastly, some curious "*emynau*", or hymns, in the Welsh language, are found in the volume of *Lives of Cambro-British Saints*, published by the Welsh MSS. Society, comprising a "Lectio" evidently intended for the instruction of the people on the annual festival, together with some collects, which leave no doubt as to the identity of the saints whose actions are referred to with those whose acts were recorded by Bishop Theodore for the information of Pope Zosimus.

With these fragmentary notices is connected another question of no little interest relative to the genuineness and authenticity of the acts of these martyrs traditional in the Principality. Was the narrative contained in them substantially identical with that furnished by the Bishop of Iconium to the Pope ? Or did it rather savour of inspiration drawn from the spurious writings referred to in the Bishop's letter as "containing over-boastful and inconsistent sayings, and trivialities foreign to our Christian hope", and which are ascribed by him to the "machinations of Manichees and other heretics who make a mock of, and endeavour to create a contempt for, the great mystery of godliness"? It would be natural to suppose that from the time of the publication of the authentic Acts, the spurious ones would have speedily ceased to obtain currency, and have fallen into oblivion. So far, however, from this being the case, we find them incurring the condemnation of Pope Gelasius (A.D. 492-6), "having been brought, together with their relics, from the East". We are left to infer, therefore, that Bishop Theodore's account, when forwarded to Rome, was either not at all, or but partially, circulated in Asia: hence St. Amator, when carrying away with him the bodies of the martyred mother and son, must have taken with him also the apocryphal account of their death. And this inference is confirmed by the fact that these apocryphal Acts were edited by Hucbald, who, as we have seen, was presented with the arm of St. Cyricus at Nevers, and who died in the year 930. And again, A.D. 1180, they were edited by Philip, an abbot of the Premonstratensian Abbey of Bona Spes, for John, the abbot of the church of St. Amandus at Elno. John, it would appear, furnished Philip, in the first instance, with a copy of the apocryphal Acts, together with Hucbald's work, for we find him stating in a letter to John that he had made in them considerable corrections, and had omitted much that appeared to him profane, irrelevant, or absurd.

If these were the *Acts* brought by St. Amator into Gaul, it would follow almost of course that they alone would have been known to Curig Lwyd, and by him disseminated in Wales. The Welsh fragmentary notices will be found amply confirmatory of this view; and as they and the foregoing account are reciprocally illustrative of one another, we propose now to allow them to speak for themselves. The first of these notices is that in the *Emynau Curig* (Hymns of St. Curig), as the devotions printed in the *Lives of the Cambro-British Saints* already mentioned are strangely called. The third of these is as follows: "The holy martyr Curig was discreet from his childhood. He suffered martyrdom, and was very wise, and a teacher of heavenly things, and opposed the cruel commandment of Alexander the king, and rejected a lordly life, from a pure heart and the wisdom of a perfect man. He desired not the vain things of this world, but that he might obtain the joys of Paradise; and suffered for the triune God and one Lord severe persecution from men, and for love to Christ the King he endured the torments of fire on his body and on his arms; and through faith in the Trinity he persevered in faith and in prayer to God, so that the faithful might escape the pains of Hell, and obtain the joys of the heavenly kingdom, by the words of the Catholic faith, and become no less perfect in Christ than that martyr. Therefore we piously call on the undefiled Curig, our helper in Heaven, that by his prayers we may obtain and deserve the very glorious reward which he is said to enjoy with the hosts of angels for ever and ever. Amen."[1]

This *Emyn*, or lesson, furnishes a remarkable coincidence with the apocryphal life published in the *Acta Sanctorum* of the Bollandists. It represents the martyr as speaking and acting as an adult, whereas the latter describes Cyricus, though an infant, as speaking with the words of a full-grown man, and as reproving Alexander for his idolatry and cruelty, and even challenging him to inflict on him strange and unheard of tortures of his own devising, through which he passes in succession unhurt, by the power of God. With these the allusions, obscurely thrown out in the following fragments of Welsh poems, mainly agree. The first is attached in the MS. to a portion of Huw Cae Llwyd's poem on the Four Brothers, of Llangurig, who was born, and probably passed his life, in the neighbourhood of that place, but need not, therefore, be his.[2]

[1] *Lives of the Cambro-British Saints*, pp. 276 and 610.
[2] The language of Huw Cae Llwyd proves that he was a South Wallian writer; but Llangurig is on the borders. The poems in the text, at least in the state in which they are here presented, cannot, we think, be the production of that accurate prosodian and mellifluous poet.—ED. *Arch. Camb.*

N N

THE FIRST FRAGMENT.

Llurig fendigedig wyd,
Ceidwad [in'] a'r Ffrainc ydwyd,
Mae i'th wlad, fel y wnaeth [wedd]
Dy achau, a llyfr dy fuche[dd]
Mae'n rhan, o bedwar ban byd,
Dy wyrthiau, rhaid yw wrthyd !
Da fyd fu ar dy feudwy,
A'i leian gynt ar lan Gwy.
   Mael gad, pan geisiodd Maelgwn
Lunio hud i leian hwn,
Ei feirch, a'i gewyll efo,
A arwe[i] niodd wr yno ;
Trigo'r llaw wrth y cawell,
Ynglyn, ni wnai Angel well ;
A'i wyr aeth ar ei ol
A lynant bawb olynol ;
Hwynthwy oedd[ynt] arnat ti
Yn dy guddigl di 'n gweddi ;
Drwy dy nerth, Gurig Ferthyr,
Y rhoddai yn rhydd ei wyr ;
A'i gwyrthiau, 'n ael gorthir,
A wnaeth Duw o fewn i'th dir ;
Delwau o gwyr, rhwng dwylaw Gwen,
A lunioedd leian lanwen ;
Y rhith, ac nid aurheithwyd,
Dinbych [Llan] Elidan Lwyd :
A'i delw, nid o hudoliaeth,
Rhoi llef ar Dduw Nef a wnaeth ;
A'i gradd, fel y gweryddon,
Gydâ Sant a gedwais hon.
Maelgwn aeth, mal y gwn i,
Ei delwaith i addoli ;
Hwn a roddais, yn bresent,
Glasdir at glos, da ei rent,
Hysbys yw bod llys a llan,
A theml i chwithau y man.
Ni bu rwydd rhag Arglwyddi
Daro dyn wrth dy wyr di ;
Chwithau a fu'n dadleu 'n deg,
Ar Ustus gynt ar osteg :
Ar fraich deg oedd faich dy fam
Silits a roes hwyl . am
Holl feddiand Alexander
A fu megis gattiau gêr.
Pob cwestiwn gan hwn o hyd
Wrth ddadl di a gwrthodyd.

THE SECOND FRAGMENT.

Plwyf hardd sydd, brif ffordd a bryn,
Lle rhed Gwy 'r hyd dwfr a glyn;
Plwy' heddyw aplaf hoywddyn,
Pa le ceir gwell, plwyf Curig Wyn?
Curig, fab gwar, llafar, llen,
Yw'n tad, a'n porthiant, a'n pen.
Caru hwn, creda' i, cai radoedd mawlgerdd,
Y trwbl a ddug, teirblwydd oedd,
Bilain dordyn aeth i'w dwrdio,
Alexander oedd falch dro.
Silit ddinam, ei fam fo,
Wen a welad yn wylo;
Ofer gwelad! Na âd Gurig
Wr garw o'i ferth 'rolddig;
Dewai 'n fyw, dyna alaeth,
Dewai 'n gnawd gwyn, ag nid gwaeth;
Ni thyfodd, fe garodd gwr,
Ar ei dir erioed oerwr.
Nerthwr 'n yw 'r gwr a garwyd,
Gwych iawn, ac a chwyr addolwyd;
Yma a thraw a wellhawyd
I garwr glân Gurig Lwyd.
Duw Lwyd cynhenwyd gwenwynig—i'w trais
Tros fy anwylyd foneddig.
Chwerw i doe chwarae dig
Dichwerwedd Duw a Churig.
  Tra dewr o natur ydwyd,
Trig ar y gair, trugarog wyd;
Treni'r dewr walch trymai;
Taer, dewr wyt, Duw, ar dy rai.

THE THIRD FRAGMENT.

Pwy a aned er poeni,
Pwy'n deirblwydd no'n Harglwydd ni?
Curig bob awr y carwn,
Goreu help oedd garu hwn.
Poen oedd i'w wedd pan oedd iau,
Pen Merthyr poen a wethiau.
Pob gweinied pawb a geiniw
Bonedd Ffrainc beunydd a'i ffriw.
Perlen a glain parch naw gwlad,
Plwy' Curig, pa le fwy cariad?
  I rwydd Saint a roddais i
Anrheg arnom rhag oerni.
  .   .   .   .   .

THE FOURTH FRAGMENT.

Ni bu wan yn byw ennyd
Nid ofnai 'i groen boen o'r byd.
Alexander oedd herwr
Ar Dduw, ac oedd oerddig wr.
Iddew o'r faingc oedd ar fai
Amborth oer a'i merthyrai.
Efo â llid, a'i fam lân,
I'r pair aeth, wr purlan ;
Ni ddarwena 'i ddwr annoer
Ar hwynthwy mwy na'r nant oer.
Teirblwydd a fu 'n arglwydd 'n hyn
Tri mis lai, Duw, a'i rwymyn';
Yn fab iach yn fyw y bu,
Ac â maen i'w gymynu.
Yn lludw ei ddaith a'n lludiodd,
Ac yna fab gwyn i'n f'oedd.
Ag oerddrwg y gwr drwg draw
E fu asiaeth i'w feisiaw ;
Troes Duw hwynthwy tros dyn teg
Trwy'r astell draw ar osteg ;
Torrai Iddew trwy wddwg
Ni'm dorwn draw am dyn drwg.
O'i esgidiau nadau a wnaed,
Yno fal anifeiliaid.
Crist yw'n rhan, croeso Duw'n rhodd,
Curig a'i fam a'i carodd.
Saith angel rhag bodd oedd,
Sel at y saith Silita oedd.
Mab a fu'n gwledychu'n gwlad,
A merch ir, mawr o'i chariad,
          ...... digariad gorynt
O lan Gwy, a'i leian gynt.
Ac arall, mab Rhyswallawn,
Feddwl oer, a fu ddwl iawn ;
Meddylio, cyn dyddio'n deg,
Am oludau, em loywdeg ;
A Churig [Wyn] ni charai,
Dwyllo neb un dull a wnai ;
Ei addoli ef ar ddau lin,
Ar war bryn a wna'r breniu ;
Cwympo yma, camp ammharch,
Colli o'i wyr a chylla ei farch ;
A Churig, fab gwych hoywrym,
A ddiddigiodd wrth rodd rym :
A diddan nid oedd anodd,
A glowson' roi glas yn rhodd.

Tyredig swmp a roid seth
Mal eurdrefn, aml ardreth ;
Tri thir, mal traeth euraid,
Tri yn un cylch, tri yn un caid.
Caer fy arglwydd, lle'i ceir fawrglod,
Cwmpas dy glai, er dy glod ;
Llangurig, pob lle'n gywraint,
Llawer hyd braff, lle rhad braint ;
Troell wen hardd, tri lliw'n hon,
Tir Curig at tair coron,
P'le well un plwy ni ellir,
Plwy Curig nid tebyg tir.

TRANSLATION.

A coat of mail art thou
To us, and to the French, too, a guardian.
Thy country possesses, as it made it, the form
Of thy descent and the Book of thy Life.
The portion of the four quarters of the world
Are thy miracles.   Great is our need of thee !
Happy has been the Hermitage,[1]
With its nun, of yore on the bank of the Wye.
   When Maelgwn, mailed for battle, sought
To practise a deception on the nun of this spot,
His coursers and his baggage
Were brought there by the man.
To a hamper his hand cleaved ;
It was held tight ; no angel could make it more so.
Also his men who followed him
Were held fast,—all, one after the other.
When these made earnest prayer
To thee in thy chapel,
By thy power, O martyr Cyricus,
He set his men free,
And God wrought, on the brow of the upland,
His wonders within thy territory.
The nun, pure and holy,
Fashioned figures of wax between her fair hands :
The likeness, and it was not disfigured,
Of blessed Elidan of the church of Denbigh ;[2]

---

[1] Curig Lwyd's Hermitage probably is meant, on the spot where the church was afterwards built. The nun would seem, from the context, to have occupied it after his death.

[2] Llanelidan, five miles from Ruthin.

And her image, by means of no deception,
Uttered a voice to the God of Heaven;
And, like the youths, she maintained
Her position with the saint.
Maelgwn went, as well I know,
To the figure thus made to worship,
And for an offering he gave
Pasture land of great price to the sacred enclosure.
Well known to fame are now
Your glebe house, churchyard, and temple.
Thy men are not free to strike a man
In presence (or for fear) of their lords.
Well hast thou pleaded also
Of yore, before a judge, in open court,
When a burden on the fair arm of thy mother
Julitta, who gave thee example;
In whose eyes the possessions of Alexander
Were all but as worthless things.
By thee was each question of his
Refuted in disputation.

The resemblance to the apocryphal Acts in these last lines is unquestionable. The preceding ones seem as clearly to contain the substance of a tradition referring the foundation of the church of Llangurig to Maelgwn Gwynedd, whose repeated injuries to religion, and subsequent reparation of them, as told by the contemporary Gildas, seem to have procured for him the privilege of being made the typical representative of such legends: at least he is found similarly figuring in the *Life of St. Brynach* and others. The adoption of the legend by the Welsh bard is valuable so far as it proves that the foundation of the church of Llangurig was referred, in or about the fifteenth century, to a period dating so far back as the sixth; and that it could not, therefore, have been built for the first time by the monks of Strata Florida, to whom it seems afterwards to have appertained as a vicarage. The next is a fragment of a poem by Sion Ceri, a bard certainly of the fifteenth century.

Beautiful is the parish, on highway and hill,
Where flows along the vale the stream of Wye,
The parish to-day of one energetic and powerful,
Than the parish of Blessed Curig, where will you find a better?
Curig, a youth gentle, eloquent, and learned,

Is our father, our head and our support,
My belief is that to love him brings down graces; the trouble
He endured, when three years old, ought to be praised in
    song.
The tyrant Alexander, proud of temperament,
And of a high stomach, proceeded to menace him.
His guileless mother, the blessed Julitta,
Was seen to weep.
A fine spectacle!   It had no power to restrain
The murderous wrath of the cruel wretch towards Curig.
While he lived he held his peace,—therein lies the sorrow.
In his holy flesh he was silent[1] and unconcerned,
The man of cold heart who loves him not
Ne'er hath prospered in his territory.
It is our beloved saint who strengthens us;
Highly exalted is he who is honoured with tapers of wax.[2]
Everywhere have favours been received
By pure lovers of the holy Curig:
On behalf of my beloved and exalted one
Was God aroused to wrath by violence stirred by venom.
Bitterness comes of bandying strife
With the loving-kindness of God and of Curig.
By nature thou art exceeding firm,
Dwell on the word—thou art merciful;
Fury will weigh down the steadfastness of the brave:
Thou, O God, art merciful to thine own.

Defects in the metre, as well as the sense, prove the corruptness of several of these lines.   The identity of its legend, however, with the apocryphal Acts is evinced by the epithet of "eloquent" ascribed to the martyr, when only three years old, whose deeds are magnified apparently at the expense of the mother, whose Christian heroism seems to be tacitly ignored. The remaining fragments are from the pen of Huw Arwystli, who is emphatically the poet of Llangurig, as shown by his recently published poems on the principal families of that place.[3]   In these, notwithstanding the vexatious mutilation of the text, some striking coincidences of

---

[1] This seems irreconcilable with the previous statement as to his eloquence.

[2] It is still a common custom on the Continent to burn a wax taper as an offering before the statue of any saint whose prayers are desired to obtain some special favour from Heaven.

[3] In *Montgomeryshire Collections*, vol. iv, p. 54.

the Welsh legend with the apocryphal Acts are plainly discernible.

> Who is it was born to suffer pain,
> Who but our patron, when three years old?
> Not a moment passes but we love Curig,
> There is no better help than to love him.
> Tortured was his frame in his infancy,
> To the person of a martyr pain was befitting.
> Illustrious is his merit, noble was his birth,
> Gentle his demeanour; let all daily serve him.
> Where does love exist, if not in the parish of Curig,
> The pearl and the gem revered by nine lands?
> To the beneficent saint have I given
> Gifts to secure us against cruelty.

The beginning of the next is wanting.

> Ne'er in the world for long hath lived a weak one,
> Who dreaded not pain of body.
> 　Alexander was a despoiler of God,
> When angered, a cruel man was he.
> In guilt a very Jew—from the seat of judgment
> With monstrous cruelty he martyred him.
> He, with his pure mother, indignantly
> Entered the cauldron—the pure and bright one.
> The water heated for him bubbled not
> More than would a cold stream.
> Three months short of three years old
> Was our patron when thus they bound him.
> When a child, and in perfect health,
> By a stone was he dashed to pieces.
> His passage through ashes hath angered us,
> To us, therefore, he is a blessed saint.
> Through that wicked and cruel man,
> A framework of boards was to be ventured upon;
> These were turned by God to the advantage of the saint,
> For, thro' the boards, in sight of all,
> The Jew[1] fell, and broke his neck.
> For that wicked man I feel no pity.
> On the spot, from his shoes, issued
> Yells, like those of brute beasts.
> Christ is our portion, may God receive graciously our gift,
> Curig and his mother loved Him,
> Seven angels were filled with delight,
> Julitta was a spectacle for the seven.
> 　A youth there was—one who ruled the land,
> And a young maiden, greatly beloved,

---

[1] Jew is used here as a term of opprobrium.

[*hiatus*] were without affection
For the Wye's bank, and its nun of old time,
And another, the son of Rhyswallon,[1]
Was cold of heart, and dull of understanding,
Before the day dawned his thoughts would run
Upon riches, and brilliant gems;
And he loved not holy Curig;
He would cozen any one in any way.
On both his knees is the king
Worshipping him on the slope of the hill;
Here a shameful mischance befals him,
He loses his attendants, his steed breaks away.
And Curig, a saint as generous as powerful,
Was appeased by virtue of an offering,
And was readily induced to console him.
We have heard that the gift of a close was given him,
An eminence, steep and towering, was bestowed,
Like a pile of gold, an ample tribute;
Three lands like a golden strand,
Three in one ring, three in one were obtained,
The enclosure, my patron, wherein thou art greatly honoured,
Of Llangurig, each spot exactly measured,
Encircles thy soil, for thine honour.
Many a good length is there, where there is free privilege,
A bright and beautiful circle,[2] wherein are three colours,
In the land of Curig, with a prospect of three crowns,
Better parish can there not anywhere be
Than the parish of Curig, no other land is like it.

There are three or four passages in these two fragments in striking conformity with the spurious Acts. Such are the incident of the caldron or *cacabus*, that of the shoes out of which issued horrible yells, the seven angels who descend from heaven, and the age of the child, exactly two years and nine months. There is some variation in the details. In the Acts the caldron is filled with burning pitch; in the poem, with boiling water. In the former, the shoes, on the Governor's demanding a sign, become alive; nay, more, eat and drink; and finally are transformed into a bull, out of whose neck springs a he-goat, instead of being left, as

---

[1] This may be a false reading for Caswallawn, the father of Maelgwn Gwynedd, who is the subject of the legend as told in the poem attached to that of Huw Cae Llwyd.

[2] Or "wheel". Can this mean a *corona* or chandelier?

in the nursery tale, after the dissolution of the Governor's body by fire; and the seven angels appear for the purpose of restoring to life a thousand persons, who embrace Christianity after being beheaded by the Governor's order. On the other hand, the martyr's death, by being dashed against a stone, would seem to have been derived from the genuine Acts; unless, indeed, the passage, which is certainly obscure, is rather to be referred to an incident in the spurious work, in which a space is scooped out of a large stone, capacious enough for the two martyrs to sit in, the sides of which are afterwards filled with molten lead. The whole, in fact, bears marks of an attempt to reduce the narrative of the spurious Acts within credible dimensions by the elimination of its absurdities; a theory borne out by the statement in the *Emynau*, that Cyricus was an adult who from his childhood had been distinguished for his piety and ability; and also by the statement that the *Life* published by Hucbald, and obtained, doubtless, by him from Nevers, underwent a similar process of castigation, first by himself, and a second time, subsequently, by his editor, Abbot Philip.

The most remarkable fact connected with the history of these Acts is, perhaps, this, that the genuine narrative furnished by Bishop Theodore to Pope Zosimus within a century after the event, never succeeded in superseding them in popular estimation. It affords a strange confirmation of the saying, which has almost passed into a proverb, "Give a falsehood a start of twenty-four hours, and the truth will never overtake it." Father Combefis, a Dominican, by whom Bishop Theodore's letter in the original Greek was exhumed from among the MSS. in the King's Library at Paris in 1660, expressed a hope that the public reading of the apocryphal Acts proscribed by Pope Gelasius, already suppressed at Nevers, might be put down by authority also at Ville Juif (a corruption of Villa Julittæ), a town six miles south of Paris, where they were read annually from a pulpit to a great concourse of people. And

Father Porée, a Premonstratensian, writing in 1644, states that the use of these, which had thus usurped the place of the genuine Acts, was in his time widely disseminated throughout France. So difficult is it to eradicate a popular usage, especially when calculated to gratify the love of the marvellous, so deeply rooted in our nature. It is instructive, moreover, to learn from Bishop Theodore's letter, that these, and similar extravagances in legendary saints' lives, do not necessarily owe their origin to motives of gain or self-interest on the part of those who may be made the unconscious means of handing them down to posterity, as has often been erroneously supposed. In this instance, we have seen that they were actually due to the malice of enemies of the Christian faith, on which it was sought to cast discredit by the substitution of false for true narratives of the deeds of those whose lives and death, if recorded simply and without such exaggeration, would have furnished the strongest testimony to the truth of their belief.

In conclusion, an anecdote may not be out of place which may possibly serve to illustrate the simple faith of the villagers of Llangurig in the power of their patron saint to obtain them favours from heaven. A traveller by the Shrewsbury and Aberystwyth mail, not many years back, while beguiling the tedium of the journey by careless gossip with the coachman, was informed by him, as an extraordinary fact, that the finest crops of wheat in the county of Montgomery were said to be grown in the parish of Llangurig, despite the apparently unsuitable nature of the land and climate for that object. Can this have been a remnant of the old belief long after the memory of the saint, and the popular devotion to him, had faded from the popular mind? The apocryphal Acts of Cyricus close with a prayer by him for those who should honour him hereafter, that they might obtain their petitions according to their necessities, one of which was that they might be blessed in their wine, oil, corn, and all their substance. Whether attributable or not to this passage in his legend, the published Welsh poems[1] in his honour teem with expressions of such a belief in the power of his prayers, and of belief also in the reception of tangible tokens without number of his protection and favour.

H. W. LLOYD.

[1] In *Montgomeryshire Collections,* vol. v, p. 49, and vol. vi, p. 224.

COWYDD I SION AB RHYS AB MAURICE.[1]

Mae o Einion ymwanwr,
Mynnu'r gamp mae'n oreu gwr,
Mae hwy arfau'r mab hirfawr,
Mae llun gwych fal Lleon Gawr.
Y mae grym y gwr yma,
O dywaid, hwn ei dad da.
Mae gwayw Sion mwy a'i gâd ef,
Mynn ei waithdrafn mewn wyth dref.
Mae cledd du yn gyrru'n gwaith,
Mentr teilwng mewn tair talaith.
Er ffo dewrion lle bon' byth,
Na chwilio gwych wehelyth.
Ni ffy Sion, hoff yw ei swydd,
Er gwarau gwr a gorwydd ;
Gwas dewrwych, a gais daraw,
A'i gweryl aeth gar ei law.
Gwr yw Sion a gurai saith,
Gwr dinam, garw, diweniaith,
Ni roi gefn er ei gyfarch,
Sein ar ŵr mai Sion yw 'r arth.
Gwr yw Sion gorau y sydd,
Argofion â 'r gwayw efydd ;
Llew glân o Elystan Llwyth,
Lle'i daliodd llû â'i dylwyth.
Lliw gwyn o Frochdyn a'i frig,
Lle mae arwydd llew Meurig.
Sarff yw gâs, Syr Ffŵg o ŵr,
Os am ynys ymwanwr ;
Dyged o *Gorbed* y gair,
Draw Farwn, byth drwy fawrair.
Y Mochdref mae ef am waed
At ais a gwrdd t'wysogwaed.[2]
Trig ar f'wng trwy Geri fawr

---

[1] From *Add. MSS.* 14,901, No. 12, in the British Museum.
[2] Mochdref, a parish adjoining Llandinam, and near Newtown.

Traws flin-walch teiroes flaenawr.
Nid enyll neb o'i dynion
Am droi swydd i'm daro, Sion :
Ni fyn Sion union anair,
E fyn â'r ffynn ofni'r Ffair ;
E fyn gael fo iawn i gyd ;
A fynodd, a fu enyd.
Ef yw'r bŵ i fawr a bach ;
Heb ochel ni bu weliach.
Dewr yw Sion, a dyrys ŷw,
Drwy gedyrn fel draig ydyw.
Oen diddig oni ddigier,
Obry'n mysg *brawn* a mêr.
Ei wraig a rydd rywiawg ran
O'r gorau aur ac arian.
Ei bwyd rhoes heb wâd yn rhydd
Odidawg, a'i diodydd.
Gwen, gu, lân, gan galenig,
Gwen bûr-ddoeth, gwn, heb awr ddig.
Lloer Siancyn gwreiddin graddol,
Llirddynt had, llwyddiant i'w hol.
[Gwraig] Sion gŵyrael Llangurig
Lloer i bro, lliw aur i brig,
I gŷd hefyd gâd, Dofydd,
Gwen a Sion dau cân' oes hydd,
A'i gwr êl o'i gwerylon,
Ag y sydd gorau, Sion.
Ni bu Rys wynebwr well
Yn eich hoedl oedd na Chadell,
Na Morys yn ei mawredd,
Nag Einion wych, gwn, un wedd,
Nag Elystan aig lwys dad,
Na deunaw gynt yn y gâd.
Y Nudd yw Sion oedd i'w serch,
Addaw[1] rhoddion ail Rhydderch,
Nerth Einion wrth ei ynys,
A fu 'm mhob braich Sion mab Rhys.
Nerth Dduw i Sion, wyrthiau'r Saint,
I'w dâl hynod êl henaint.

SION CERI A'I CÂNT.

---

[1] Adaw in MS.

AN ODE ADDRESSED TO IOHN AB RHYS AB MAURICE,[1] OF LLANGURIG.

By John, the Bard of Kerry.

A tilter comes of Einion's race,
None better loves the game,
A youth stout and tall—his arms are taller still,
Noble is his form, like that of Lleon Gawr.[2]
The strength of our hero
Is said to equal that of his doughty father.
Greater still hath the spear of John been proved,
In eight towns is the effect of its thrust desired.
·In battle he drives his black sword
With a worthy daring in the three principalities.[3]
From where they stand to the last, though brave men fly,
His noble tribe will never yield their ground.
Fly will not John, his duty is dear to him,
In the play of horse and horseman.[4]
A youth stout and mettlesome, who will strive to strike,
When his quarrel has come to his hand.
John is a hero who can beat seven,
A hero void of offence, rough, no flatterer,
Who, though he be courted, will not cringe,—
The bear is the sign that the man is John.
A hero is John, possessed of the best
Reminiscences, with the brazen spear.
A pure-bred lion of Elystan's tribe,[5]
Where with his people he avenged himself on a host.
Of the white hue of Broughton and its branch,[6]

---

[1] Maurice ab Madog ab Einion ab Howel of Mochdref, Esq., son of Tudor ab Einion Fychan, Lord of Cefn y Llys, descended from Elystan Glodrudd, Prince of Fferlis. He married Tangwystl, daughter and coheiress of Gruffydd ab Jenkyn, Lord of Broughton, who bore, *sable*, a chev. inter three owls, *argent*. By this lady, Maurice had issue six sons: (1) Ieuan Lloyd; (2) Rhys; (3) David; (4) Llewelyn; (5) Maurice Fychan, whose daughter and coheiress Catherine, married Jenkyn Goch of Clochfaen; and (6) Ieuan Gwyn.

[2] A king of Britain, according to the Bruts, who built Chester, called to this day Caer Lleon Gawr, the fortress of Lleon the Giant. Williams's *Eminent Welshmen*, p. 276.

[3] Of Gwynedd, Powys, and Dyfed.   [4] The tournament.

[5] Elystan Glodrydd.   [6] Perhaps an allusion to the family coat.

Where is the symbol of the lion of Meurig.
He is a hateful serpent, a Sir Fulke of a man,[1]
If called to combat for the Island.[2]
Derived from Corbet was the epithet,[3]—
The Baron yonder, for a perpetual fame.
To Mochdref does he owe his blood—
The blood impulsive in the breast of princes.
For three generations there dwells a chieftain
To trouble the perverse and vain throughout the extent
    of Kerry.
Not one of its men shall be free
To strike me, John, for exercising my calling.[4]
The upright John will not allow abuse :
He will have the Fair awed by the staves (of the officers).
He will have justice dealt to every one,
And what he wills at once has come to pass.
He is a terror to great and small ;
Beware him those who would keep a whole skin !
John is both stout and formidable,
He is a dragon amidst the strong ;
A gentle lamb, if he be not angered ;
Then he descends upon them with his brawn and marrow.
A goodly share will his wife bestow
Of the best of gold and silver.
Her provision she distributes without stint,
Which is excellent, as also her liquor.
She is fair, kindly, and pure, lavish in gifts,
Fair, and very wise, to my knowledge, and never angry.
Bright as the moon is she, sprung from the root of Jenkyn,
May her seed shoot forth, and may her posterity prosper.
The arched eyebrow of John's wife is to Llangurig
As the moon to the land, radiant as gold o'er the hill.
On John and his lady bestow then, O God,
To live together the hundred years of the Hart,

---

[1] Sir Fulke Fitzwarren.   [2] *I.e.*, of Great Britain.

[3] Madog ab Einion ab Howel of Mochdref, married Anne, daughter of Piers Corbet, Lord of Lee or Leigh, Juxta Caus, descended from Roger Corbet, Lord of Leigh, who bore, *or*, two ravens ppr., in a border engrailed, *gules*, second son of Robert Fitz Corbet, Baron of Caus ; *Harl. MS.* 1396 ; *Lewys Dwnn*, vol. i, p. 314. Einion married Nest, daughter and heiress of Adda ab Meurig ab Adda ab Madog ab Maelgwyn, Lord of Kerry and Maelienydd.

[4] *I.e.*, of a Clerwr, or Minstrel. They were sometimes subjected to legal measures in consequence of their erratic habits of life.

And may her husband John come forth
From his quarrels however is best;
Rhys was no better opponent,
In your lifetime, nor was Cadell,
Nor Maurice in his might,
Nor the noble Einion, I ween, in any way;
Nor Elystan, the father of the pure race,
Nor twice nine of any of those of yore.
A very Nudd is John to those he loves,
He promises gifts like a Rhydderch.[1]
To his country Einion's strength
Is John the son of Rhys in both his arms.
May John gain strength from God, and miracles wrought
    by the Saints,
To uphold him until he be old and full of renown.

---

[1] Rhydderch Hael, or the Generous.

DESCENT OF IOHN AB RHYS
AND OF CATHERINE,
OF

AB MAURICE OF LLANGURIG,
WIFE OF IENKYN GOCH
CLOCHFAEN.

Lewys Dwnn, vol. ii, p. 313.   *Add. MS.*, 9865.

CADOR or Cadifor Wynwyn, Lord of Buallt and Maes Yfed, ab Cadfan, ab Owain ab Idnerth ab Iorwerth Hirflawdd ⊨
ab Teyronwy ab Teon ab Gwynaf da ei Freuddwyd. etc.

Severus, Lord of Buallt and Maes Yfed (now called Radnorshire) ⊨ Lucy, d. of Morgan Hen ab Howel, King of Morganwg.
Azure, three open crowns in pale *or*.

Cecilia, ux. Dingad, Lord of Maelor Gymraeg, Yr Hôb, and Ystrad Alun, third son of Tudor Trevor.

Ifor, Lord of Buallt, Maes Yfed, Maelienydd, ⊨ Isabel, d. of Tryffin ab Merfyn, Prince of Powys, third son of Roderig Mawr. *Or*,
Ceri, Elfael, and Cedewain.   a lion's gamb, erased *gules*.

Cuhelyn, Lord of Buallt, Maes Yfed, Maelienydd, ⊨ Rhiengar, d. and sole heiress of Goronwy ab Tudor Trevor, King of Gloucester,
Ceri, Elfael, and Cedewain.   Earl of Hereford, and Lord of Erging and Ewias.

a

Elystan Glodrudd, King of Gloucester and Hereford, and by conquest King of Fferlix, = Gwladys, d. and sole heir of Rhun ab which is the territory between the Wye and the Severn. This district Elystan won from Cynan Feiniad, Lord of Tref Gar-Dryffin ab Hwgan, King of Brecknock, and thus acquired the surname of Glodrudd; i.e., ron, and son of Gwaethfoed, Lord of Ruddy fame. He was born in the Castle of Hereford A.D. 933, and was named after of Cardigan. Argent, three boar's the Saxon king, Athelstan, who was his godfather. He was living in A.D. 1010, but was heads, couped sable. killed in a civil broil at Cefn Digoll in Powys. He bore gules, a lion ramp. regardant or.

Cadwgan, Lord of Radnor or Maes Yfed, Buallt, Maelienydd, Ceri, Cedewaen, and Elfael. He founded = Eva, d. of Gwrgant ab the Cistercian Monastery of Cwm Hir, in the parish of Llanbistair, in the Comot of Uwch Mynydd in Ithel ab Owain, King Elfael, and built three churches, which he dedicated to St. Michael—one in Ceri, one at Cefn y Llys, of Morganwg or Gla-and another at Bryn Pab Ieuaf in Buallt. He was buried at Abbey Cwm Hir. William the Con-morgan, and sister of queror fought against him and took the counties of Hereford and Gloucester. Iestyn ab Gwrgant.

1	2	3	4	6	6
Idnerth, Lord of Radnor, Ceri, Maelienydd, and Elfael.	Iorwerth, Lord of Cedewain.	Cadderth.	Hoedliw Goch, ancestor of the Vaughans of Bugeildy, and Llynwent.[1]	Seysyllt, Lord of Buallt.	Elidur, of Buallt.

9	10	11	12
Iefa, Lord of Arwystli.	Sir Iestyn, Knt.	Gwrgeneu.	Madog.

1	3	4	5	6
Madog, Lord of Ceri, Mae-lienydd, and Elfael. See page 340.	Gruffydd.	Iorwerth.	Hoedliw.	Ednyfed, ancestor of the Owens of Rhiwsaeson and the Williamses of Pentref Cynddelw in Llanbryn Main.

1	2	7	8
Ifor, Lord of Radnor. He and = Morfydd, d. of his brother Gruffydd defeated Marchudd ab the Normans at Aber Llech Carwedd of in 1094, as they were return-Môn. ing from Gwent.	Idnerth, Lord = Gwenllian, d. of Aaron ab of Radnor, Y Paen Hên ab Io. ab Ceri, Meirchion. Maelienydd, and Elfael.	Elidir Fychan.	Llewelyn, Lord of Buallt.⁵

[1] Hoedliw Goch was the ancestor also of the Lloyds of Rhaiadr Gwy, Phillips of Llanddewi Ystrad Ennau, Powel of Cwm Deuddwr, Lloyd of Llananno, Powel of Cascob, Meils of Tre'r Delyn or Harpestone, and the families of Groes Gynon and Gardd Faelog in Llanbistair, A.D. 1597.

[2] He was the ancestor of the Lloyds of Rhôs Fferrig and of Sir Gruffydd ab Elidir, Knight of Rhodes, who bore argent, on a cross sable, five crescents or, in the dexter chief, a spear's head erect gules. Sir Gruffydd was the ancestor of Sir William Thomas of Aberglasney, Knight Banneret, High Sheriff for Co. Carmarthen in 1589, whose son, Rhys Thomas of Coed Helen, Co. Carnarvon, was High Sheriff for that county in 1574, and grandfather of Sir William Thomas of Coed Helen, Knight, High Sheriff for Co. Carnarvon, 1608, ancestor of the present Rice William Thomas of Coed Helen, and Trevor Hall, Esqr. The Earls Cadwgan, and the Morrises of the Hurst, descended likewise from Llewelyn, Lord of Buallt.

| a

Goronwy, Lord of Radnor. ⚭ Lucy, d. of Ifor ab Cadifor ab Gwaithfoed, Lord of Cardigan. Or, a lion ramp. regardant sable.

Ienaf, Lord of Cefn y Llys,¹ in the Camot of Is ⚭ Eva, d. of Meurig² ab Meredydd Mynydd, and Cantref of Elfael, which is now Gethin ab Cadwgan ab Id-called the Hundred of Cefn y Llys. nerth ab Llewelyn ab Rhys Grug, Lord of Llanymdyfri, son of the Lord Rhys ab Gruffydd, Prince of South Wales. Argent, a lion ramp. sable, armed langued and crowned gules, for Rhys Grug.

| b Ifor Fychan. | c Llewelyn. | d Iorwerth. | e Madog.

Howel. Madog. Rhun. Goronwy Fychan. | b

Goronwy. Meurig of Llanfihangl Helygen, in the Camot of Glyn Iethon, in the Cantref of Maelienydd, now called the Hundred of Rhaiadr Gwy.

Einion, Lord ⚭ Janet, d. and heir of Owain ab Meredydd ab Rotpert, Lord of Cefn y of Cedewasn, ab Llywarch ab Trahaiarn ab Caradog ab Gwyn Llys. ab Collwyn. Owain died in 1235. Argent, a lion salient crowned gules.

Einion Fychan, ⚭ Jane, d. of Llewelyn Moelwyn, Lord Lord of Cefn of Buallt, ab Meredydd Bengoch y Llys. ab Howel ab Seisyllt ab Llewelyn ab Cadwgan ab Elystan Glodrudd.

Ivor. Iorwerth. Tudor. | c

Gwerfyl, ux. Einion ab Seisyllt, Lord of Mathafarn.

Lleian, ux. Howel ab Madog of Trallwng.

Arddun, ux. Aaron ab Gruffydd ab Aaron of Môn.

Tudor, ⚭ Margaret, d. of Madog ab Gwrgenen Fychan of Croes Lord of Gynan ab Gwrgeneu ab Llewelyn ab Idnerth ab Cefn y Cadwgan ab Elystan. Llys.

Cadwgan. Howel. Einion Goch. Meredydd. Madog. | d

Annesta, ux. Gwyn ab Gruffydd ab Beli, Lord of Cegidfa, sable, three horses' heads erased argent.

Eva, ux. Meurig Fychan, Lord of Nannau. Or, a lion ramp. azure.

Arddun, ux. Rhys Fy-chan ab Rhys Ch-with.

Elen, ux. Llewelyn ab Llewelyn Goch of Môn. | e

| a | b | c | d | e

¹ In the parish of Cefn y Llys are the remains of a stupendous castle, situate on a very elevated and almost inaccessible spot of ground; three-fourths of which are surrounded by the river Ieithon. It is called Castell Glyn Ieithon, and is supposed to have been built by some of the Welsh princes, to prevent the incursions of the Normans. The Church of Cefn y Llys is dedicated to St. Michael.—Carliale's Dic. Top.

² Meurig had a son named Philip, who was the father of Llewelyn Crûg Eryr, Esqr., the ancestor of the Lewises of Harpstone Court, or Tre'r Delyn, co. Radnor; of John Dwn and his brother Lewys, Lords of Llynwenny, who were committed to ward by the Lord Rivers, temp. Edward IV—the one to the Castle of Uske, and the other to the Castle of Radnor, where they remained

Howel ab Tudor.=Angharad, d. and heiress of Madog, Lord of Cefn y Llys. Meredydd of Llanarmon. Meurig. Gwilym of Ceri. [a]
who first came Llewelyn ab Madog Ey-
to Mochdref. chan ab Madog ab Ramiph of Mochdref, and Janet his wife. *Sable*, three greyhounds courant in pale *argent*, in a border indented *or*.

Einion of=Nesta, d. and heir of Adda ab Meurig ab Madog of Graig. Tudor. Gwilym of Ceri. Meurig of Pen y Bettws. [b]
Mochdref. Adda, d. and heir of Madog,
Lord of Ceri or Kerry, who was one of the three hostages for Llewelyn ab Iorwerth, Prince of North Wales, who was put to death by King John in 1213. See p. 343.

David of Llanfair=Gwladys, d. of Me- in Cedewaen, now redydd ab Gwilym called Newtown. ab Madog Lloyd of Tref Gynon. *Sable*, three horse's heads erased *argent*. Rhys of Kerry. Morgan of Maelienydd. [c] [d] [e]

David Lloyd of Newtown, ancestor of the Baronet family of Pryce of Newtown Hall, and the Pryces of Glan Meheli, who are now represented by Lord Mostyn.

Madog=Anne, d. of Fiers Corbet, Lord Gruffydd of Mochdref.
of Kerry of Lee or Leigh, juxta Caus,
and Mo- co. Salop. *Or*, two ravens in
chdref. pale ppr. in a border engrailed *gules*.[1]

Meredydd of Mochdref.

Maurice of=Tangwystl, d. and coheir of Gruffydd ab Ienkyn, Einion. Ieuan. Gruffydd. Rhys. Janet. Arddun. Lucy.
Kerry and Lord of Broughton. *Sable*, three owls *argent*.
Mochdref.

Evan Lloyd of=Gwenhwyfar, d. Rhys of Mochdref.= David. Llewelyn. Maurice Fychan= Ieuan Jane, Alson,
Mochdref, ob. of Howel ab of Kerry. Gwyn. Gwenllian.
1469. 9, E. IV. Philip ab John of Llangurig.
Cadwgan.

Catharine, sole heiress, ux. Jenkyn Goch ab Ieuan of Clochfaen. *Harl MS.*, 1973, pp. 96d, 97d.

during life, for claiming the honour of Radnor by descent from Rhys Grûg. Llewelyn Crûg Eryr bore *sable* an eagle displayed *argent*. The celebrated Dr. John Dee or Ddû, the great mathematician in the reign of Queen Elizabeth, was likewise descended from Llewelyn Crûg Eryr.

[1] The ancient patrimony of Leigh or Legh juxta-Caus, remained in the Corbet family till it was sold by John Corbet of Sundorne Castle, and Albright Hussey, Esq., who died in 1759. The last heir male of this branch of the great Norman house of Corbet was the late Dryden Robert Corbet of Sundorne Castle, Esq., who died without issue in 1860, leaving his sister Annabella, wife of Sir Theodore Brinckman, Bart., the only remaining representative of the family.

THE LORDS OF MAELIENYDD AND CERI OR KERRY.

Harl. MS. 2,291.

MADOG, the eldest son of Idnerth ab Cadwgan ab Elystan Glodrudd, had the Lordships of Maelienydd, Ceri, and Elfael. In 1136 he took part with Owain and Cadwaladr, the sons of Gruffydd ab Cynan, King of North Wales, in their victorious attack upon the Normans in Cardiganshire, in which the latter were defeated with great slaughter, and their encroachments for the time successfully checked.[1] Madog married Rheinallt, daughter of Gruffydd ab Cynan, but, according to some authors, he married Jane, daughter of Drumbenog ab Maenyrch, Lord of Cantref Selyf. He died in 1141, leaving issue—1, Cadwallon, of whom presently ; 2, Einion Clyd, Lord of Elvael ; he lived at Aber Edw, in the Comot of Llêch Ddyfnog, in Elvael, where are still the remains of an ancient castle, near the confluence of the Edw with the Wye, and bore *gules*, a lion salient *argent* in a border of the second, charged with ogresses or pellets. He gave the lands now called Tir y Mynach, in the parish of Clyro, in Cantref y Clawdd, to the Abbey of Cwm Hir. Together with his brother Cadwallon, he joined his forces, with Owain Gwynedd and the other Welsh princes, against Henry II, at the battle of Crogen in 1165.[2] About the year 1177-8 Einion Clyd was treacherously slain by the Normans, who lay in ambush to kill him. His death was avenged by the Lord Rhys ab Gruffydd,

---

[1] *Mont. Coll.*, vol. i, pp. 236, 237.   [2] Brut y Tywysogion.

Prince of South Wales, who ravaged their lands in Maelienydd, and built the Castle of Rhaiadr Gwy. This castle was dismantled and totally demolished during the civil wars, and not a vestige now remains except the foss. Einion left issue, Walter Fychan, Lord of Elfael and Dunreven, who was living in 1215. Gervase and Meredydd, who were addressed by Prince Llewellyn ab Iorwerth, amongst other chieftains residing in the neighbourhood of Ceri, in a letter deprecating injury or violence to the Priory of Rattlinghope, which must have passed between the years 1199 and 1211.[1]

The other sons of Madog ab Idnerth were Meurig, Rhys, Howel, Meredydd, Cadwgan, David, and Gruffydd Foel, the ancestor of the Pryses of Mynachdy, in the parish of Bleddfa, in the comot of Is Mynydd, in Elfael. This family of Pryse bore *azure*, on a bend inter six lions rampant *or*, armed and langued *gules*, three cross crosslets of the third. Madog had also three daughters, Maud, ux. Llys ab Idnerth Benfras, Lord of Maesbrwg; Elen, ux. Adda ab Gruffydd ab Madog; and Dyddgu, who married first, Robert, Lord of Cedewain, and secondly, Collwyn ab Tangno, Lord of Efionydd and Ardudwy.

Cadwallon, the eldest son of Madog, succeeded his father as Lord of Maelienydd, which contains the co-mots of Ceri, Glyn Ieithon, Rhiw Abwallt, and Swydd Ygre.[2] He re-founded the Cistercian monastery of

---

[1] *Mont. Coll.*, vol. i, p. 239.

[2] In the parish of Llanddewi Ystrad Ennau is an ancient camp called *The Gaer*, which occupies the summit of a high hill impending over the Valley of the Ieithon, of an oval form, defended by two parallel entrenchments, and almost inaccessible on the Ieithon side. On a hill opposite is Bedd Ygre, or the Grave of Ygre, a large mound or tumulus of earth enclosed in a small moat, but evidently erected in commemoration of a British chief. Two miles hence, on a slight elevation, stood Castell Cymaron, of which not a fragment of the superstructure now remains; the site and moat are only visible. This is supposed to have been erected by the Normans, and destroyed soon after by the Welsh; but again rebuilt by Hugh, Earl of Chester, in 1142, when all Maelienydd be-

Cwm Hir, which he intended for sixty monks, in 1143. In 1165 he joined his forces with those of the princes of Gwynedd and Powys against Henry II at the battle of Crogen.[1] In 1175, he and his brother Einion Clyd, Lord of Elfael, and Einion ab Rhys, Lord of Gwrthreinion, in the Cantref of Arwystli, and other Welsh lords who had been in arms against the king, were taken by the Lord Rhys ab Gruffydd to the king's court at Gloucester, and received to the king's peace, after which they returned peaceably to their lands.[2] Cadwallon resided at Castell Dinbaeth, which is situate on an almost inaccessible rock, in a narrow defile, and overhanging the river Ieithron, in the parish of Llananno, in Elfael.

Cadwallon was waylaid and murdered on September 22nd, 1179, by the retainers of Roger, son of Hugh de Mortimer, in returning from the king's court, and while under the king's guarantee of safe conduct. Diceto tells us, says the Shropshire historian, of the hatred and fear which existed between Cadwallon and the English; also how his murderers were punished. Some who were proved guilty were put to the rack, and forfeited all their worldly possessions; others, who were suspected, were forced from the pale of society. But Diceto does not tell us who was the principal offender, namely, Roger de Mortimer, who suffered two years' imprisonment and forfeiture in consequence. During this period, probably on February 26, 1181, his father Hugh de Mortimer died; and in 1182 the sheriff of Herefordshire, balancing his account for the year 1181, is allowed a sum of money for the custody of the

came subject to him. It was often an object of contest between the Welsh and the Normans, and was afterwards possessed by the Mortimers in 1360, in whose posterity it continued for ages.—The Rev. M. Price, Vicar of Llanddewi. This parish is partly in the Comot of Is Mynydd (now called the Hundred of Cefn y Llys) and partly in the Comot of Uwch Mynydd (now called the Hundred of Knighton), in the Cantref of Elfael.—Carlisle's *Dic. Top.*

[1] Brut y Tywysogion.   [2] *Ibid.*

castle of Camerium (Cymaron), which was in the king's hands by reason of Mortimer's disgrace.[1] This castle had been built by Roger de Mortimer in the year 1143, after expelling the brothers from the territory. The said sheriff in 1179 charges two and a half merks for taking the prisoners, who were accused of the death of Cadewill (Cadwallawn), to the court at Windsor and to Worcester as the king had ordered.[2]

Cadwallawn married Eva, daughter of Philip ab Madog ab Adda, by whom he had issue: (1) Maelgwn, of whom presently, and (2) Howel, who was one of the hostages hanged by King John in 1213;[3] (3) Madog, and (4) Owain. Howel had issue: Morgan, Lord of Ceri, and Meredydd and Owain, who both did homage to Henry III, August 16, 1241; Cadwallawn had also four daughters, Joan, ux. Meredydd Bengoch ab Howel ab Seisyllt, Lord of Buallt; Eva, ux. Meredydd ab Gruffydd, Lord of Gwentlwg or Tredegar; Morfudd, ux. Idnerth ab Llewelyn Ddiried, son of Rhys Grug, Lord of Llanymddyfri; and Nesta, ux. Ifor ab Llewelyn, Lord of St. Clear's, descended from Bledri.

Maelgwn, the eldest son of Cadwallawn, succeeded his father as Lord of Maelienydd. He married Janet, daughter of Morgan ab Howel, Lord of ——, by whom he had issue: (1) Madog, of whom presently; (2) Meredydd, Lord of Ceri, in 1250.[4] He married Anne,

---

[1] This castle seems to have been built on lands belonging to the Abbey of Cwm Hir, for which other lands were given in exchange. "Concedimus etiam eis (monachis, scilicet) terras de Maysegragur, et Kayrweton, et Brennecroys, venditas pro Castro de Kaminarum." —*Cart.*, 16 Henry III, mem. 6, printed in Dugdale's *Monast.*, Lond., Bohn, 1846.

[2] *Mont. Coll.*, vol. i, p. 239.

[3] Howel is stated in the Charter already cited, to have given Foxton to the Abbey: "Terram de Foxton, quam habent de dono Howel, filii Cathwalan."—*Ibid.*

[4] This Meredydd appears also to be referred to in the above Charter as the donor of lands to Abbey Cwm Hir:—"Omnes terras quas habent de dono Mereduc filii Mailgun (here follows a list of twenty-three places) et communam pastuarum per totam Melemd" (Maelienydd).

daughter of Sir John Scudamore, Knight, by whom he had issue: (1) Madog, Lord of Ceri in 1278 (6 Edward I); (2) Llewelyn, whose son Howel was one of the Lords of Ceri in 1278; (3) Iorwerth, and (4) Adda Moel.

The third son of Maelgwn was Cadwallawn, Lord of Maelienydd, who died at Cwm Hir in 1234; the fourth son was Adda. Maelgwn, who died in 1197,[1] had likewise a daughter named Gwerfyl, who married Rhys Gloff, Lord of Cymyt Maen in Lleyn.

Madog, Lord of Ceri, the eldest son of Maelgwn. He was one of those to whom Llewelyn ab Iorwerth, Prince of North Wales, wrote on behalf of Ratlinghope Priory. It had been represented to the prince, who was at this period recognised as superior Lord of Ceri and Cedewaen, that Ratlinghope and Cotes, places consecrated to God and to pious uses, were so near to the land of Ceri as to be exposed to the occasional raids and forays which agitated the border. In the cause of religion he accordingly writes to the chieftains of North Wales and all others resident there, whether personally known to himself or not. He promises them the best of his aid and counsel in all their wants and just requests. He shows them that it is their interest not less than his own to foster and protect religion, its possessions and its shrines. He commands all whom his commands can bind, that as they love his person and his honour, they will protect and assist Walter Corbet (an Augustinian canon who has acquired these lands for pious uses) in his designs. He threatens, on the other hand, the loss of his friendship to any one who is disobedient to his wishes. Lastly, he addresses Madog, the son of Maelgwn in particular, reminds him how he had brought him up and promoted him. He conjures him not to return evil for good, but to protect the prince's honour, as he, the prince, would thereafter consult for and succour the said Madog.[2]

---

[1] *Brut y Saeson and Tywysogion*, Ed. Aberpergwm.
[2] *Mont. Coll.*, vol. i, p. 241.

Madog, Lord of Ceri, was one of the three hostages for the Prince Llewelyn ab Iorwerth, who were so cruelly put to death by John, King of England, in 1213. He married Rose, daughter of Sir Roger Mortimer, by whom he had issue, Adda of Ceri, who married Jane, daughter of Hugh ab Llewelyn ab Hugh of Payne (by Eleanor his wife, daughter of Robert Mortimer). By this lady Adda had several children, of whom Meurig of Ceri was the father of Adda of Ceri, whose only daughter and heiress, Nesta, married Einion ab Howel ab Tudor of Mochdref, as before stated.[1]

---

[1] According to *Hanes Cymru*, the true name of the kingdom of Elystan Glodrydd is Fferyllwg, or Fferllwg, of which those of Fferllys, Fferleg, Fferex, and Fferreg are corruptions. It was sometimes called also "*Y wlad rhwng Gwy a Hafren*", the country between Wye and Severn. The author adds that some persons regard the country now between those rivers as the original territory of Fferyllwg, together with a portion of Herefordshire. Mr. Price's own opinion was, that the nucleus of the kingdom of Fferyllwg was the district called by the Saxons "Dena", or the Forest of Dean, noted by Giraldus as "trans Vagam, citràque Sabrinam". The word "Fferyllwg", he says, expresses the distinctive character of the country, and, in his opinion, is derived from "Fferyll", a worker in metals, or rather in iron. Fferyllwg, then, is "the land of iron-work", which is to this day a speciality of the Forest of Dean. It was described by Giraldus as "ferro fertilem atque ferinâ". Again, Mr. Williams, in his *History of Radnorshire*, states that Fferllys was originally a part of the territory of the Silures (Essyllwg), and that this territory had continued to be governed by its own "reguli" during and since the Roman occupation up to the period of its conquest by Elystan Glodrydd; Hereford, the capital, being previously called Fferley. Of the body of Ethelbert, assassinated by Offa, it was written—

"Corpus tandem est delatum,
In Fferleiâ tumulatum".

If this be so, the origin of the names "Silures" and "Essyllwg" is easily accounted for. The inhabitants of Fferyllwg would have been called in Cymric "Fferyllwys", as those of Lloegr "Lloegrwys". These names the Romans corrupted into "Silures" and "Siluria", whence the Cymry again formed "Essyllwg". The name of Hereford may have been a Saxon or Norman corruption of Fferyllwg, originating in unsuccessful attempts at pronunciation of the word.

ELEGIES ON CADWALLAWN AND HOWEL,

SONS OF MADOC[1] AB IDNERTH AB CADWGAN AB ELYSTAN GLODRYDD.

By the Bards Cynddelw and Llygad Gwr.

Translated by HOWEL W. LLOYD, Esq.

THE petty kingdom of Fferllys, or Fferyllwg, preserved its integrity but for a brief period after its conquest by Elystan Glodrydd   The parts of it comprised within the counties of Hereford and Gloucester, including the Forest of Dean, were wrested by William the Conqueror from his son Cadwgan, whose son, Idnerth, appears as lord only of the lands forming his father's paternal inheritance.[2] Nor was he left in undisturbed possession of these; for William Rufus made a grant of them to Ralph de Mortimer, Lord of Wigmore, one of the Norman invaders of England, with power to conquer them for himself. For more than a century of warfare, however, the Mortimers do not appear to have succeeded in acquiring more of the territory from the descendants of Elystan than lay in the immediate neighbourhood of the castles which they erected in it, and garrisoned with their retainers. To this feud, and to the dissensions in the family itself, are to be traced the misfortunes of which there are incidental notices in the Chronicles, and which ended in the ultimate transfer to the Mortimers of the chief portion of the

[1] In *Myvyrian Archæology*, pp. 159 and 255, Ed., Denbigh.
[2] Mr. Jonathan Williams, in his *History of Radnorshire*, states that Radnor also, or Maesyfed, was seized by William I, who made it a royal demesne, whence it was called "the Honour of Radnor".

territory. Idnerth, the eldest son of Cadwgan, had twelve sons, of whom Madoc, the eldest, succeeded only to the Lordships of Maelienydd, Ceri, and Elvael. To his eldest son, Cadwallawn, he bequeathed the two former; and Elvael, the remaining Lordship, to his second son, Einion Clyd. In the year 1159, the brothers Cadwallawn and Einion Clyd were at variance; for we find that the former was made prisoner by the latter, and given up to Owain Gwynedd, who in turn delivered him into the hands of Henry II of England, by whom he was imprisoned at Worcester; whence, by the aid of his friends and foster brothers, he contrived to escape.[1] Another notice of Einion Clyd is in *Annales Cambriæ*:—"Annus MCLXX . . . Eynaun Clut vulneratus est a filiis Lewarchi filii Denawal (Dywal, C.) scilicet Meiler (Meilir, C.) et Ivor," p. 52. And in the Confirmation Charter of Henry III, already referred to, he is said to have been the donor to Abbey Cwm Hir of certain lands, "terram de Carnaff (Carno?) cum nemore quod vocatur Coedeirenis" (the Wood of Aeron).

The first elegy, of which the following is an attempt at a metrical version, is by the celebrated bard, Cynddelw. He was in high favour with most of the Welsh princes, his contemporaries, in the twelfth century, in whose praise several of his poetical compositions are still extant, and are printed in the original among those of the "Gogynfeirdd", in vol. i of the *Myvyrian Archæology of Wales.* Among them is this poem, interesting not only for its poetical power, but also for the relation it bears to a family remarkable for its singular accumulation of misfortunes. Its hero, Cadwallawn, was the eldest of several sons of Madoc, the son of Idnerth, and he and his brother Einion Clyd lost their lives in

---

[1] *Brut y Saeson*, p. 679; *Brut y Tywysogion*, Aberpergwm Edit.; p. 713 of *Myv. Arch.*, Edit., 1870. In *Annales Cambriæ*, the account of this event is reversed:—"A.D. 1161. Cadwalaun filius Madauc Eynaun Clyt fratrem suum tenuit, et Owino Grifini filio carcerandum tradidit: quem Owinus Fraucis dedit: sed per collectaneos et familiares suos de Wigorniâ liberatus, nocte evasit," p. 49.

the manner already related, the former by the stroke of a pole-axe, not without a desperate struggle with his assassins, so far as may be gathered from the elegy, in which a prudent discretion would appear to have been observed by the poet in his use of obscure and guarded language in reference to the event.

It is remarkable that the Welsh Bruts, *Annales Cambriæ* not excepted, are silent as to the manner of his death, though one of them, Brut y Tywysogion, states the simple fact that he was slain. "A.D. 1179. Ac yna y llas Kadwallawn". From this silence, and from the record of the death of his brother Einion Clyd, who had been similarly waylaid less than two years before, it might be supposed that the two events had been confounded, were it not that the French Chronicle of the Mortimers, allowed by Eyton to be authentic,[1] and the contemporaneous chronicler, Radulph de Diceto, who was Dean of London in 1181, actually mention "Cadwallon" by name as the person who was waylaid and murdered in returning from the king's court, and whilst under the king's guarantee of safe-conduct. As the latter appears to supply the fullest account extant, albeit hostile and prejudiced, of the event, and as the judgment exhibited therein of Cadwallawn's life and character contrasts strangely with that passed on him by his countrymen as displayed in the elegy, a translation of the whole passage is here subjoined:—

"A.D. 1179. Cadwallan, a person holding some Princedom in South Wales, often transgressed the limits defined of old time between the English and the Britons,[2] and by making violent inroads into the March, and panting open-mouthed for massacres of men, studied to pass the whole course of his life in frequent plunderings and maraudings. Dragged[3] at length before the King, and assailed by the cries of many persons,

---

[1] *Hist. of Shropsh.*, iv, pp. 205-6.

[2] "Fines inter Anglos et Britones limitatos antiquitus sæpe transgressus est." Offa's Dyke must be the boundary here referred to.

[3] "Tractus."

when, although then and there safe from the King under the conduct of the King himself, but always admonished in proportion to the enormity of his crimes, he had gone on his way back homeward, being casually intercepted by an ambuscade of the enemy, he was slain on the 22nd of September. Now, because this redounded greatly to the injury of the King's Majesty, Cadwallan, who so often before ought justly to have been awarded hanging for his deserts in accordance with public law, out of reverence for the King, from whose Court he was returning, ought, to the end that public law might not be outraged, to have had a safeguard from public law, until he should have betaken himself within the boundary predetermined for his full security by the indulgence of the Prince. Now, if any one be alarmed by the example of this unwonted event (although nothing like it has occurred in our own days, and although the King has not left this unpunished, though in avenging it the punishment exceeded due bounds[1]), if he should have been summoned[2] to the King's Court, let him approach it without fear. For the Welsh may mutually console each other that the death of one of their countrymen has received, in the deaths of many of the March-men, obsequies grievous to the English and odious to the Normans. Therefore, those privy to the murder, and become suspected from concurrent report, and proved liable by a public investigation, were involved in a heavy sentence, some being tortured on the rack,[3] and condemned in confiscation of goods, and others compelled to lead a wretched life in the hidden recesses of the woods."[4]

It never could have occurred to the worthy dean, although, from the permission accorded to Cadwallawn to return home with no worse treatment than a warning, it seems to have suggested itself to Henry II and his advisers, that the Welsh may have had some foundation of justice for their reprisals in the gratuitous grant of their hereditary territories to the Mortimers by the Red King, solely by the *paulo post futurum* title of their conquest of it by the sword; to say nothing of the previous assassination of no fewer than four of his brothers, Meredydd, Howel, Cadogan, and

---

[1] "Dum in ulciscendo pœnae modum excesserit."
[2] "Vocatus."   [3] "Patibulo."
[4] Diceto's *Ymagines Historiarum*, in Twysden's X Scriptores.

Einion, at the hands of these same enemies, the Mortimers. Cadwallawn could not have been "dragged"
against his will to the court, or he would have been
entitled to no safe-conduct. Nor could his conscience
have reproached him with any crime, the proof of
which, in the king's court, would have forfeited his
safe-conduct, and placed him in the power of those
who, he well knew, thirsted for his blood. Nor could
the king, without shame, have suffered the great ag-
gressors, the Mortimers, to escape scot-free after the
perpetration of so atrocious a deed. He must have
been aware that the real object of this, as of the
foregoing assassinations, was to establish that family
for ever in the possession of the remaining property
of those whom they had already violently ousted from
its largest and richest portion, and which they had
little prospect of securing for themselves, as long as
the brave and warlike princes lived, and had sons to
follow their footsteps, in defending it. The perpetration of such deeds was certainly far from atoned for by
mere deprivation and imprisonment for a year or two;
and this shadow of justice, which Diceto naïvely pro-
nounces excessive, would be one proof more, if such
were needed, of complicity in the judge.

The second elegy is one of the five extant compositions of Llygad Gwr, a bard who flourished in the
next generation to Cynddelw.

According to the "Llyfr Coch Hergest" edition of
the *Brut y Tywysogion*, Howel and his brother, sons
of Madoc ab Idnerth, were slain, how and wherefore
is not stated, nor the name of the second brother.
In the *Brut y Saeson*, the name of the second brother,
Cadwgan, is given, with the addition that they were
slain in a quarrel, "yn ymryson". In the Aberpergwm
edition of the *Brut y Tywysogion* these statements
are supplemented by the addition that there was a
quarrel between Howel and Cadwgan, sons of Madoc
ab Idnerth, and that they fratricidally killed each
other :—"Oed Crist 1140...y bu ymryson rwng Hy-

wel a Chadwgan meibion Madawc ab Idnerth, ac y
lladdasant y naill y llalL" This, however, appears to
have been copied from the *Annales Cambriæ*, under an
amusing misapprehension of the meaning of the words
" de se". " A.D. 1142. Howel et Kadwgaun filii Madauc
filii Ydnerth occiduntur, machinante Elya de se—" *i.e.*,
Howel and Cadwgan, sons of Madoc, son of Idnerth,
are slain by the contrivance of Elias de Say, whose
father, Hugh de Say, with Roger Mortimer, was
worsted by Rhys ab Gryffydd in an attempt to defend
Radnor in 1144. Elias was sixth in descent from Picot
de Say of Stokesay. He and his brother Robert died
without issue. His sister Margaret married Hugh de
Ferrers, and secondly Robert de Mortimer, by whom
she became mother of Hugh de Mortimer; by whom
Meredydd ab Madoc, another brother, was slain in 1146.[1]
Again, Meuric ab Madoc, the last brother, was slain by
his own men in the same year.[2] Thus, of nine royal
brothers, six at least died violent deaths—a sad and
striking illustration of the turbulence of the times!
Cadwallawn ab Maelgwn ab Cadwallawn, the last Welsh
lord of Maelienydd, died in 1234, at Abbey Cwm Hir,
where he had previously taken the religious habit.[3]
His brother Maelgwn built the Castle of Treffilan.[4]

ELEGY ON CADWALLAWN, SON OF MADOC.

By Cynddelw.

May God pour forth to me the gift assured
Of poesy, the varied lofty ode,
That I with honour meet may celebrate
A man, like ocean lashing up his ire,
That so I may compose, with language just,

---

[1] *Brut y Saeson.*

[2] "Meuric, filius Madauc, à suis dolo interfectus est."—*Ann. Cambr.* Ed. C.

[3] "Katwalan filius Mailgon sumpto religionis habitu apud Cumhyr obiit."—*Ann. Cambr.*, p. 80.

[4] "Maelgon filius Maelgon ædificavit castellum de Trefilan."—*Ib.*

R R

And studied force, Cadwallawn's elegy,
Like Einiawn's elegy by Morvran[1] framed.
What could I love, I, by my lord beloved,
Save honour, mead, and shaggy-coated steeds?
Stand not my tears in heaps, since he is dead,
Of chiefs my chiefest pleasure and delight!
Come suddenly upon me is the day
Of parting from the flesh that teemed with life,
Cadwallawn's fix'd, predestinated time.
The favours I declare of gracious lords
Dispensing happiness. An ardent flame
Of passion would I stir when I shall sing
The home of mournful, but erst comely bards.
Of one who brings us longing would I speak;
My tears are trickling for an eagle's might,
In sadness for the slaughter of my chief,
Now that the potent lord, the Cymry's prop,
First in the war-shout, of o'erbearing course,
Is gone. The fruitful earth is eloquent!
Who will maintain Cadwgan's generous seed,
A stalwart rampart raised around the fort,
Around the beverage they brew from corn?
Who will rush now where spears are thrust to slay?
From shafts now slackened, where the blue-edged wound?
Who on the war-path shall direct the fray?
What lion brave, with cruel blade, advance?
What courtly host, in wealthy palaces,
Shield, and imbue with force, the British bard?
Will alms be giv'n, when heaps are wasted all?
What harmony of worship will be tuned,
Now that the stranger hath cut off its life?
What warrior supreme shall warriors meet?
Who, as Cadwallawn erst, shall lavish gifts—
Cadwallawn, Rhodri's[2] gracious progeny?
To him th' affray was as a chord attuned,
And dreadful blows on Beli's lifted shield.[3]
His loss I know,—he show'red down splendid gifts;
Have I not lost a lord who freely gave?
His sons on me red silken robes bestow'd.
Within me do not stirring memories rise?
With wrathful indignation am I stirred;
To me his palm unclosed with gracious gifts;

---

[1] Morvran Ail Tegid, a bard of the sixth century.
[2] Rhodri Mawr, or Roderick the Great.
[3] *I.e.*, his shield was like that of Beli Mawr.

Unstinted, overflowing, undisguised.
I was an Ovate by his grace endow'd,
As all may know, so good a lord was he!
My golden tints and vessels have I seen
In mansions, where his love requited mine,
In tramp of hosts, in halls, mid songs at feasts,
In trodden courts, and gates, mid bardic lore,
What time I was beloved by Ceri's lord,
The love-compelling prince of lands renown'd.
His dinted target I must love perforce,
He loved my welfare, loved me in his house.
But since the prince of warriors is gone,
Who kept me well, but made nor heap nor store,
Silent am I.   Too long I hold my peace—
I will be mute no more,—'tis not my part.
For great Cadwallawn, manhood's glorious light,
A chain with bars the Southerners prepared.[1]
Cadwallawn's bounty it is mine to praise;
Whenever generosity was praised,
None were a third so generous as he.
His onset, as a flood o'erspreads the shore,
Forced its way foremost in the rush of war.
The glades of Powys did my chief revere
For qualities that gain a man respect;
Like Madoc, ever generous in will;
Stern to mow down his foes, yet kind withal.
Not Owain[2] brooded more o'er Britain's care,
Yet slaked his thirst of vengeance in the fight:
A man to fell men never fell'd before,
A man of manliest courage in distress,
A man who laid an ambuscade when pressed,
A mighty tow'r of strength, a noble king,
A man who made the Cymry seem disgraced,
A man who took their manliness away,
A man who caused St. David to withdraw
From them his patronage, tho' England's foe.[3]
A man who redden'd with a gushing stream
Of gore his blade, and Teivi's plain once fair,
And stain'd with mingled gore the azure sea.
Great is the day, to mark the love we bore
Our hero, for the joys he bless'd us with,
Against a host when valiant in the van.

---

[1] An allusion, probably, to his imprisonment at Worcester.   See
above, p. 346.   [2] Owen Cyveiliawg?
[3] By his prowess casting theirs into the shade.

Not vain our love ; his life of precious toil,
When fighting for our hearths, subdued our hearts.
His hewing steel he stain'd with crimson-red,
When, in the fiery conflict, death was rife,
By foes encompass'd in the combat's fray.
Lavish of alms, protector of the song,
His death that came of devastating war
Supremely hath afflicted me ; my smile
Perforce is stay'd : woe's me, my lord is lost !
Doth not earth's bosom hold him in the grave ?
Light of the battle's skirts, he yet was mild.
Slain is the king of bounty—grief is come !
As he hath seen me, would I saw him now !
Regret assails me, bitter is my pain !
Huge was his blade, and heavy with its tip
Of many-tinted brass ; the cavity
In his shield's centre waver'd not ; he took
Pride in his feats of valour, ere he fell.
Where'er he went his fame had gone before.
With twenty pounds he gifted me unask'd.
He never bade me from his sight depart ;
May God ne'er part him from the realms of bliss !
A king's encroachment is a tyranny ;
As he hath stood by me, so I by him.
What happ'd before will hap again ; all die !
Much, from the noble impulse of my soul,
The leader by my song will I extol,
Who loved to dare the venture of a wolf,
Who gifted bards with noble maintenance,
Himself their pattern of a perfect life,
Shelt'ring the winged tribe of flutt'ring birds,[1]
Slaying a foe who erst had left his side.
The crows' provider ne'er could bear reproach ;
The crows of Brynaich never wanted loads ;
Reproach was none that he could e'er deserve.
He was not one to store up heaps of grain,
Nor yet was he so far reduced in wealth,
But bards wayfaring would resort to him.
Whate'er he had to give was gain to all.
The soil was honour'd where he slew a foe.
Where'er he was, that spot was not disgraced.
He would not turn aside to do a wrong,
But, where he saw oppression, would oppress.

---

[1] *I. c.*, the bards who flitted like birds from place to place.

Too lofty-minded he to skulk from foes ;
Not one would dare so much as rouse him up.
As falcons are self-confident, so he,
Faultless, in pride of courage venturesome,
With brittle spear uplifted, batter'd shield ;
So was the mounted son of Madoc armed.
The glorious warrior, mead-fed, on the shore,
Freely as Mordaf[1] on me did bestow
Gifts lavish'd on me, ta'en from vagabonds ;
Ah ! scarce can I again pour forth my lay :
For so to nurture bards he used his wealth. ·
Around the Border he would Saxons fell,
His rage Gwynogion's[2] jurisdiction ruled,
And, let who would oppose, a hero he.
Who kings resist with force deserve not peace.
Angles he mangled,—and, when mangled, left.
The Lloegrians hear the fame of ravage still,
Though he be slain—the lion dire in fight,—
In wrath protecting all.   Exists to-day
No warrior now as heretofore.   To-day
No peace is left for me, but still the wound
Within my bosom doth distress me sore.
For my chief's crimson sword am I distress'd,
With deep affliction.   God deliver me !
Since fallen on me is this seeming shame.
To the sad measure of my mournful lot,
And to the measure of his bounty great,
Proportionate a poem have I framed
Of doughty struggles—various the lay.
My skill hath brought me importunity,—
Hath brought me wealth—falcons of plumage light,
Alike in colour, and in speed alike,
A gilded saddle, splendid, proudly gay,
From the majestic knight of coursers fleet.
Taken to-day—'tis this that maddens me !
For his distracting loss I smart with pain.
Defending Elfael, when, in autumn, he

---

[1] The third of the " Three Generous Ones" of the *Triads*.

[2] " Swydd Gwynogion", the original name of the second of the
three Comots of the Cantref of " Y Clawdd" in Maesyfed (Radnor),
corruptly spelled " Swyddinogion" in Parthau Cymry, *Myv. Arch.*,
p. 736, Denbigh Edition ; and Swydd Wynogion in Jon. Williams's
Hist. of Radnorshire, p. 69.   The term "Swydd" implied the office
of justice attached to the freeholder. " Glossary on Laws of Howel
Dda," *Myv. Arch.*, p. 1069.

Drench'd with his blood his country's gory soil,
None greeted me with deferential gift;
They came to meet me, but they spared me not;
Fell back each coward then, till he was slain,
Rush'd on each hero then, till he was felt;
From head to foot the tumbling helmets fell,[1]
While kin from kin sought succour ev'ry one.
Slain is the hero, fiery to behold,
Like a grim wolf, whose lair might lose its prey.
Gentle Cadwallawn's hand was open aye
To the world's pale ones' use, open his court,
Where strangers went for hospitality:
In life the bards were fostered in his breast.[2]
While lived the country's high-escorted king,
Of gain and wealth they found the daily use,
High-trotting steeds, tall-flank'd and grey were theirs.
A wolf was he, the root of manly strength,
In fight his valiant sword-strokes, wolf-like, fell,
Of Eithon's[3] fortress'd land the sov'reign chief,
Of Clyd[4] and Aeron[5] prince famed far and wide.
When tried in the discourse of speakers wise,
Cynddelw I,—my friends are never lost,—
Of speech harmonious ever, while I live,
My verse discussion gains in gentle speech.
In competition my encomium wins,
As scholars win, when grammar's in debate.
With vigour will I sing, as I know how,
As our disciples who have learning know.
After Cadwallawn, bounteous to bestow,
Munificently shining as the star
Seen in the dawn, a blessing to the poor,—
The suppliants of Britain,—and to bards,
No empty-handed one shall promise gifts.
His lance hath memories of mourning left,

---

[1] Or, "Head over heels the stumbling chieftains fell."

[2] Literally "folded", like sheep in a fold.

[3] Glyn Ieithon. The Comot was Swydd Glyn Ieithon or Swydd Ieithon. Parthau Cymry, *Myv. Arch.*, pp. 736 and 738.

[4] Clyd, then, reverted to him on the death of his brother Einion, A.D. 1177-8. Or Einion may have held Elvael under him.

[5] This cannot have been Aeron in Cardiganshire. Cwm Aeron, corruptly written Cymaron, where Roger Mortimer built a castle, must be meant. The river Aron, probably Aeron originally, runs through the "Cwm" or Glen. *Hist. of Radnorshire*, by Jon. Williams, p. 69. For "Coedeirenis" (Coed Aeron?), see p. 346.

And crimson gashes oozing out with gore.
The fiery prince hath left behind him sons,
Themselves would leave blood-tricklings in their foes.
Three[1] whelps of leaders bold to thrust the spear,
In fray of lances eager eagles three,
Privy to conflicts three, and sword-cuts dire,
Accordant three to minstrels, and to gifts,
Three diligent to aid at Saxons' gates,
Three bold, and fearless, mighty to avenge,
Three generously banded, close as one,
To bar dispersion, and the scare of throngs ;
Three native hawks, high-famed, of purest breed,
Stout youths, who wash their cheeks from stain of war.
Since now, by stroke of battle-axe cut down,
Our princely lion-monarch is laid low,
A chief supreme, from ancient sov'reigns sprung ;
Since our dispenser is in truth no more,
Lord God ! may he be guiltless in Thy sight.
Should wrath betide the friend of all the poor,
Pillar of Britons, and their shelt'ring shield,
Then, in the realms of light, Lord of the poor,
Let angels guard him to Heav'n's bright abode !

ELEGY ON HOWEL, SON OF MADOC.

By LLYGAD GWR.

Dreadful the loss ! my God, oh, woe is me,
Since none can save, that left me desolate,
Made many poor, laid Song and Music low,
When died my Lord, whose habitation lay
Mid peopled dwellings, on a golden plain.
The mighty hero's height is sunk to naught,
Who out-topp'd heroes with his haughty gait,
Of men the fearless pillar, when a path
He clear'd thro' foes encompassing a town.
Woe is the world without his lavish hand,
Sad that its gen'rous Guardian 's ta'en away !
I, too, must mourn, since now I clearly view
The course of things confused upon the earth.

---

[1] The names of four of Cadwallawn's sons are given in the pedigree (*supra*, p. 343), Maelgwn, Howel, Madoc, and Owain. One, therefore, could not have survived his father.

It is not good that Howel, Madoc's son,
A light that shone with glorious majesty,
Is laid within the bosom of the ground.
Eternity is long!   Long will the time
Appear without him now ; and trouble too
With consternation mingles our regrets.
Their trappings round him warlike throngs display'd,
And with his valour grew his nation's fame.
His wealth enrich'd the crowds who filled his court,
Draining the mead-horns in the banquet's cheer.
Fair token was it of the gifts to come,
When reckon'd were his hundred dignities.
The gate of Heaven open may he find ;
His lot be at the Son of God's right hand!
Unwise is he whose faith hath not been fix'd
Upon the Man, the best that e'er was born!
Our refuge He from Death when on the wing,
From all our tribulation, and our grief ;
Firm is our faith in Christ, made sad for us.
Woeful our wail for wrong—no hidden wrong,
That smote the Hero as a falcon brave :
To feel his loss hath made our blood run cold ;
No marvel is it if we groan aloud.
Does not reproachful memory arise,
For the loved Leader with his crimson'd sword,
Who knew no guile, was pure from all deceit ?
If I am low, then is not mine the loss ?
With fervour all sincere he praised his bards.
Is not the mourning dol'rous, is 't not dull,
To huge Hirddywel from far Berwyn's fells,
Because the fiery leader hath been ta'en,
With turmoil, like the herd's upon the hill,
Whose spear was blood-red, like a blast of blood ?
Oh, for the wounded warrior's gilded sword!
Oh, for the Flood to come—I care not when!
Oh, for his clarions that red harvests reap'd!
Oh, for his prowess, proof against the strong!
So brave in battle, oh that he is gone!
How long, alas! and he will ne'er return!
Oh, Mary! Michael! can then nought be done ?
O, God! that Howel's taken to Thyself,
Who ne'er drew back, hero of heroes he!
Of justice now be his the sure reward!
A lord revered, may he ascend on high,
Borne by the Prince of Angels up to Heav'n.

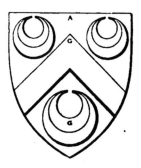

IPSTONE OF IPSTONE IN THE COUNTY PALATINE OF CHESTER.

Harl. MSS., 1396, 5529, fo. 31; 6128, fo. 60.
Lewys Dwnn, vol. ii, p. 353.

Sir John de ∓ Elizabeth, daughter and heiress of Thomas Corbet of Wat-
Ipstone, Lord | tlesborough, eldest son and heir of Sir Robert Corbet of
of Ipstone, | Morton Corbet and Wattlesborough, knight. Thomas
Ipstones, or | Corbet died A.D. 1375. He had two younger brothers,
Ipstans, *ob.* | Fulke, whose only daughter and heiress married John
A.D. 1394. | Lord of Mawddwy, son and heir of William Lord of
| Mawddwy, fourth son of Gruffydd ab Gwenwynwyn, Prince
| of Upper Powys; and Sir Roger Corbet of Morton Cor-
| bet, knight, ancestor of the Baronet family of Corbet of
| Morton Corbet.

William Ip- ∓ Maude, daughter and heir (by Elizabeth his wife, daughter
stone, Lord of | and heir of Sir Nicholas de Becke, knight) of Sir Robert
Ipstone, *ob.* | de Swinnerton, knight, son and heir of Sir Robert de
1, H. IV, A.D. | Swinnerton, in Com. Stafford, knight. Maude married
1399. | first, Sir John Savage of Cheshire, knight; secondly, Sir
| Piers Leigh; thirdly, William de Ipstones; and, fourthly,
| Richard Peshall.

William | Christian. | Alice, Lady ∓ Sir Ranulph or Randulphus Brereton
Ipstone | | of Ipstans | de Malpas, Knt., second son of Sir
died | | or Ipstones. | William Brereton de Brereton, Knt.,
issueless. | | | Lord of Brereton. *Argent*, two bars
| | | *sable.*

2nd son.
William Brereton ∓ Catherine, daughter and coheir of Thomas de Wylde of
of Borasham, | Borasham, Esq. *Argent*, a chev. *sable*, on a chief of
Esq., 1450. | the second, three martletts of the field.
| *a*

S S

a	1st wife.	2nd wife.

Edward Brereton of Borasham, Esq. ⚥ Elizabeth, d. of John Roydon of Pulford, Esq., and ... his wife, dau. of Thomas Hanmer of Llys Bedydd or Bettisfield, Esq. *Vert*, three roebuck's heads erased in bend *or*, in dexter chief a rose of the second. ⚥ Dorothy, d. of Richard Hanmer, and sister of Sir Thomas Hanmer, who was knighted at the taking of Terwin and Tourney.

Thomas Brereton, Rector of Northope, 1539; of Llandrinio, 1557; and of Gresford, 1566.	⚥ Margaret, d. of Ithel ab Gruffydd abBelyn.[1]	Elizabeth, ux. James Eyton of Eyton, Esq.	Joanna, ux. Cynwrig ab Richard of Penachlech.	Catherine, ux. Lancelot Lloyd of Tref Alun.

John Brereton of Borasham, Esq. ⚥ Margaret, d. and heiress of Richard ab Ieuan ab David ab Ithel Fychan of Llaneurgain, Esq.,[2] descended from Ednowain Bendew, chief of one of the noble tribes of Wales. *Argent*, a chev. inter three boar's heads couped *sable*.

	1st wife.	2nd wife.

Owain Brereton of Borasham, High Sheriff for co. Denbigh, 1580 and 1588. ⚥ Elizabeth, d. of John Salusbury, Esq., heir of Lleweni, M.P. for Denbigh 1554; and Catherine his wife, d. and heiress of Tudor ab Robert Fychan of Berain, Esq. ⚥ Catherine, d. of Harri Goch Salusbury of Llewesog, Esq., and relict of John Lloyd of Bodidris, Esq.

1	2
Edward Brereton of Borasham, High Sheriff for co. Denbigh 1598, in which year he died.	John Brereton of Esclusham. See page 273.

[1] Belyn settled at Nercwys, in Ystrad Alun, and was one of the sons of David ab Cynwrig ab Ieuan ab Gruffydd ab Madog Ddu of Copa'r Goleuni in Tegeingl, who bore Palii of six pieces, *argent* and *sable*. Madog was the son of Rhiryd ab Llewelyn ab Owain ab Edwin, Prince of Tegeingl.

[2] Ithel Fychan of Llancurgain, Esq., was the son of Cynwrig ab Rotpert ab Iorwerth ab Iorwerth ab Rhirid ab Madog ab Ednowain Bendew. He married Angharad, daughter and heiress of Robert ab David of Holt, Esq., son of Howel ab David ab Gruffydd of Ystym Cedig, Esq., descended from Owain Gwynedd (see pp. 287 and 288). The mother of Margaret, wife of John Brereton, was Jane, daughter and heiress of William Glegg of Gayton, in Cheshire, Esq. (see pp. 287 and 288).

APPENDIX.

THE following is a metrical version of three of the foregoing poems, by Mr. H. W. Lloyd, the originals of which, with literal prose translations, are on pages 156, 159, 162, 164, above.

ELEGY ON ELLEN, WIFE OF LLEWELYN OF LLANGURIG.

ASCRIBED TO HUW ARWYSTLI.

1.

Mary! the gloom of night hath us o'erspread,
  The bier's unwelcome work hath made us weary,
Ah, Mary! vengeance boots not for the dead;
  The hill-side crag for me were home less dreary.

2.

For Ellen, noble thro' her eight degrees,
  Cold is my heart, as blast upon the mountain:
By God's command alone the spirit flees—
  Ne'er hath her like been born of honour's fountain.

3.

A Lady's form hath vanished from the light,
  And Curig's Land is lifeless in its sorrow,
As when with blackening frost its face is dight;
  The joy of Howel's race hath found its morrow.

4.

With weak'ning vigils are our people worn,
  God on our land hath laid a long affliction;
Mute will our travail be until the morn,
  O God! that dawns upon our dereliction.

5.

A night of suffering hath befall'n the line
  Of Howel Lloyd and all its scions noble ;
Ah ! never, while we live, within a shrine
  Shall lie entomb'd a woman less ignoble.

6.

Fled from his land is Curig's purest blood,
  Of Creuddyn's best the grave hath gained possession,
And mourning on the house hath burst in flood,
  Its lord, Llewelyn, boots not intercession.

7.

The hearth is stricken—trunkless is the tree—
  To sick and poor alike their hope is blighted,
The land where chiefest would her children be,
  Is wounded sore by stroke on her that lighted.

8.

Her fair and gallant sons bear forth the shroud,
  Upon its oaken bier, with bitter wailing ;
Sound merrily no more or harp or crowd,[1]
  Naught save the sobs are heard of poor and ailing.

9.

Borne by the hands of all the country-side,
  Dim tapers these in slow procession follow ;
The name she leaves behind her will abide,
  Memorial in all hearts that is not hollow.

10.

Behind her Ellen's place of pain is left,
  Nor heat nor cold can reach her blissful mansion ;
The poor her smiles and bounty mourn bereft,
  Upon the path that knew their sweet expansion.

11.

In Llysgelyddon, whither throng'd the poor,
  Buried is she who gave of her provision ;
Woe is the sick despoiled of all her store !
  Mary ! how long her like shall fail our vision.

---

[1] The "Crwth", a musical instrument, the player on which was, by the English, called a Crowder, whence the name Crowdero in *Hudibras.*

THE FOUR BROTHERS OF LLANGURIG.

By Huw Cae Llwyd.

Who daily scatter weighty gold?
Whose veins the blood of Powys hold?
Whose soldiers are the best in fight?
The grandsons they of chiefs of might.
What brothers they—well known to fame,
Since every land hath heard their name?
Four comrades these, in force full strong,
To ban the boldest deeds of wrong.
In front, lo! Ieuan shields the rash,
Three thousand dare not wait his dash.
Braver than all—in either host—
Never will Owain quit his post;
The gentle Siancyn gives the wine;
William's the lion of his line;
Four sons of Morys, noble all,
These are Llangurig's ward, and wall.
In war their grandsire was renown'd,
Noble and valiant was he found,
Siancyn, who gave his men the wine,
(For lavish is grey Howel's line),
Madoc, the Fire-bearer's blood,
A man renown'd, of Einion's brood,
Kin to an earl; grey Rhys, of old—
All these the brothers' forbears bold.
A forest ever will they be,
Wide-spread is Rhys's progeny.
His grandsons' sons our island guard,
Their precious gifts are our reward.
How noble they—their hands, how free!
How mettlesome their chivalry!
How stately in their mien they stand,
Sharing alike their father's land!
A mighty oak, on every side,
Hath spread abroad its branches wide;
Those branches are their country's stay,
Its pillars loved and feared are they.
Together are they seen to grow,
Their love and wealth together go;

Saint Curig! shield them well from wrong,
Encased in mail, oh! make them strong.
Together they maintain the host,
Together feast, and share the cost,
Givers together in their time,
Together may they pass their prime.
The Cymry they together love,
The sick and poor their pity move.
On finest oats their steeds are fed,
By love their gallant men are led.
They guard their land, as did their sires,
With strength, like theirs, that nothing tires.
The men that true and loyal prove,
As squires shall reap the fruit of love.
Their stature to a rib is told,
Measured as mighty men of old.
As three vast rocks they stand secure,
The three bear all one portraiture.
The three have one consentient word,
They rule the fair with one accord.
Three lives, I ween, have all the three,
As four, then, may the fourth life be!

AN ODE ADDRESSED TO SION AB RHYS, THE SON OF MAURICE.

BY JOHN, THE BARD OF KERRY.

A Spearman comes of Einion's race,
   None better loves the game;
Of stature tall, with taller arms,
   As Lleon's, huge his frame.

In strength is John his father's peer,
   If true what old men say;
His lance is mightier in fight,
   Eight towns would crave its sway.

In north, and south, and Powys too,
   His sword drives o'er the field;
Tho' back brave combatants may fall,
   His clansmen never yield.

To John is honour ever dear,
   In horse and horseman's play;
He aims to strike, ne'er thinks to flee,
   When heated in the fray.

John, tho' but one, can beat full seven;
   Tho' rough, ne'er gives offence,
Yet scorns, when others cringe, to make,
   With flattery, defence.

The Bear[1] gives sign the man is John,
   By spear of brass he's known;
A lion of Elystan's line,
   His men will hold their own.

He blazons Broughton's argent coat,
   With Meurig's lion crest;
For country, as Sir Fulke, he holds
   His dragon-spear in rest.

From Corbet high descends his name,
   And Mochdref's Baron brood,
His prowess and his mettle prove
   He comes of royal blood.

A chief, thro' Ceri's wide extent,
   All troubling spirits fear,
John cows them all—not one may dare
   To strike me, far or near.

John's upright ways are fain to fill
   Each baser tongue with awe;
He will do right to one and all,
   And what he wills is law.

As the moon's gold, with crescent brow,
   So shines John's gentle wife,
God grant both, o'er Llangurig's heights,
   The hart's full length of life.

So may her lord, in every fight,
   The happy victor prove;
No doughtier combatant was Rhys,
   Nor Cadell, when they strove:

---

[1] John may have been a Lancastrian, and if so, may have borne the Bear and Ragged Staff, the Badge of Warwick.

Not noble Einion e'er, I ween,
　　Nor Morys in his might,
Not all Elystan's regal brood,
　　Stood stauncher in the fight.

A very Nudd, to all he loves,
　　Is John, his gifts abound
As Rhydderch's; in his country's cause,
　　His blows, like Einion's, sound.

May saintly aid obtain the strength
　　From God, for Rhys's son,
To end in age with fame the life
　　Thus in renown begun.

STANZAS[1]

Addressed by Cynddelw to Howel, son of Ieuaf, son of Owain, son of Cadwgan, son of Elystan Glodrydd, Prince of Fferlys. Howel was the last independent Lord of Arwystli, of the Royal House of Elystan Glodrydd.

> Rheiddin a'm rhoddes Hywel,
> Rheiddiawg, feiniawg, fanawg fil ;
> Cefais, gan dreth orddethawl,
> Tarw teg Talgarth yngwarthawl.

> Llef a glywaf gloew eilyrth,
> Llef eilon yn eilwydd ferth,
> Llef ban corn blaen cad ehorth,
> Llais garw, a llef tarw Talgarth.[2]

TRANSLATION.

1.

To me, with lavish lips hath Howel giv'n
A sleek and monstrous beast that tears the ground ;
A contribution choice have I received,
Talgarth's fair Bull, in bountiful exchange.

2.

I hear a startling sound of Music clear,
Of perfect and harmonious melody,
A horn loud sounding in the van of War,
A deep-toned sound, and that from Talgarth's Bull.[3]

---

[1] From the *Myvyrian Archæology of Wales.* The orthography is here modernised.

[2] Howel ab Ieuaf lived at Talgarth, in the parish of Tref Eglwys in Arwystli, a place which subsequently became the property of a family named Lloyd, descended from Brochwel Ysgythrog.

[3] From the abrupt termination of the last stanza it would seem that a part of this composition has been lost.

ADDITIONS AND CORRECTIONS.

CHAP. I.—*Inhabitants.* The census returns for 1871 gave the population of the parish as consisting of 897 males, and 804 females, making a total of 1,701 ; the number of inhabited houses was 302, uninhabited 10, and in building 3.

CHAP. III.—*List of Vicars.* In addition to those already mentioned as holding the living in the sixteenth century, should be added the name of *John Gwynn, M.A.*, son of Owen Gwynn, Esq., of Llanidloes, Sheriff of Cardiganshire in the year 1551, who, according to the MSS. of the late Joseph Morris, Esq., was "parson of Llangurig and Llanidloes".

Canon Ingram is stated to have died in 1711. In that year, however, he was collated to the rectory of Cemaes, his successor to that living being appointed in the year 1712.

Mr. Morris's MSS. furnish the name of another Vicar of Llangurig. Jane (born 1702), daughter of Jenkyn Lloyd of Clochfaen and Rachel Fowler, married "Richard Ingram, Vicar of Llangurig, son of Robert Ingram of Llanidloes, Esq." Richard Ingram was appointed rector of Cemaes in 1747.

CHAP. IX. The passing of the " Elementary Education Act of 1870", which led to the establishment of a School Board in the parish, has placed elementary education within the reach of all the children of the parish. In the formation of a Board, the expense of a contested election was wisely avoided, the following five members being chosen : Messrs. John Hughes, Henfaes (Chairman) ; J. B. Owen, Bryndulas (Vice-Chairman); Abraham Davies, Tynymaes (Treasurer) ; D. Davies, Penhyle ; and Richard Owen, Glyn-Brochan. They met for the first time April 27th, 1871 ; and, finding that they had to provide accommodation for about 400 children between the ages of 3 and 13, they at once entered into negotiations with the trustees of the school already in existence in the village. Some twenty months of the Board's existence was wasted in a fruitless attempt to come to some satisfactory arrangement regarding this school, or obtaining land upon which another might be erected. Ultimately, Mr. Watkins consented to sell a small close in the village for £105 ; and Mrs. Owen of Glansevern liberally presented to the Board a convenient site in the hamlet of Cwmbelan. A third site was selected in the upper part of the parish near Ty'n y Cwm, which cost the Board £16.

Schools, with teachers' residences, have been built at Llangurig and Cwmbelan, and were opened in the early part of 1874. When the three schools are in operation they are intended to accommodate the children of the whole parish, with the exception of those living in the valley of the Severn, where a school for the joint accommodation of the parishes of Llanidloes and Llangurig is being built near the Old Hall, the cost and management of which will be shared by the Boards of the two parishes. To enable it to carry out its scheme, it was necessary for the Llangurig School Board to borrow about £2,600 from the Public Works Loan Commissioners.

From a Parliamentary return made up to June 1874, we glean the following particulars regarding the Llangurig School Board: Cost of first election, £1 10s.; cost of election to fill vacancies, £4 2s.; cost of establishment, £27 14s. 2¼d.; cost of erection of schools, £1,507; cost of maintenance of schools, £15 5s. 2¼d.; other expenses, £68 9s. 4d.; total expenditure, £1,624 0s. 9d.; rateable value of the district, £6,360; gross amount for which precepts have been issued, £91 16s. 6d.; annual amount per £ in rateable value, 1·1d.

P. 76.—John Lloyd, eldest son of Edward Lloyd of Plâs Madog, who served in the Royal Army, was a captain in the regiment commanded by Col. Robert Ellis, of Y Groes Newydd, near Wrexham. In the engagement which took place at Middlewich, March 13th, 1643, Col. Ellis and Captain Lloyd were taken prisoners, the former continuing in custody until the following September (Phillips, *Civil War in Wales*, i, 142-5, ii, 62). Captain Lloyd subsequently took part in the attempt made by Lord Byron to relieve Beeston Castle, when six men of his company were taken prisoners January 18th, 1645, by the Parliamentarians under Sir William Brereton (*Ibid.*, ii, 227).

Col. Ellis was descended from Llewelyn ab Ynyr, lord of Gelli Gynan in Ial, and purchased the estate of Croes Newydd, which subsequently fell into the possession of F. R. Price of Bryn y Pys, Esq., by whom it was exchanged for some other property with Thomas Fitz Hugh of Plas Power, Esq.

P. 251.—Trahaiarn, lord of Garthmul, was the son of Iorwerth ab Einion ab Rhys Goch ab Llewelyn Fychan ab Llewelyn Eurdorchog (p. 250). For his bravery in battle, the Prince of Powys gave him the lordship of Garthmul and a new

coat of arms, viz., *argent*, three lions passant guardant, *gules*.
He married Agnes, daughter of Ieuan ab Madog ab Einion ab
Cynfelin, lord of Manafon, by whom he had issue four sons:
(1) Iorwerth, lord of Garthmul, who married Elen, daughter of
Madog Fychan, by whom he had issue Rhys, lord of Garthmul,
ancestor of the Walcots of Walcot, co. of Salop, Howel, and
Iorwerth Fychan, who was the father of Madog y Twppa of
Plas y Twppa in Bettws y Coed, ancestor of David ab Owain
of Llanwyddelan; (2) Ieuan, ancestor of the Lloyds of Berth-
lloyd; (3) Meredydd, ancestor of the Jones of Garthmul; and
(4) Gwion, according to some genealogists, the ancestor of the
Lloyds of Berthlloyd.

P. 251.—For Cynwrig of Llys y Cil and Y Fanechtyd, read
Cynwrig of Llys y Cil.

P. 252.—For Goronwy Y Fanechtyd, read Goronwy.

P. 277 (line 23).—For Meredydd ab Llewelyn Ddu ab Gruffydd ab Iorwerth Foel ab Iorwerth Fychan, second son of Iorwerth ab Ieuaf of Llwyn On, read Meredydd ab Llewelyn Ddu
of Aber Tanad and Blodwel ab Gruffydd of Maelor Saesneg,
second son of Iorwerth Foel, lord of Chirk, Nanheudwy, and
Maelor Saesneg.

T. RICHARDS, PRINTER, 37, GREAT QUEEN STREET.

LaVergne, TN USA
19 October 2009
161308LV00003B/76/A